Teaching Students with Mental Retardation

Teaching Students
with Mental Retardation

Providing Access to the General Curriculum

by

Michael L. Wehmeyer, Ph.D.
University of Kansas at Lawrence

with

Deanna J. Sands, Ed.D.
University of Colorado at Denver

H. Earle Knowlton, Ed.D.
University of Kansas at Lawrence

Elizabeth B. Kozleski, Ed.D.
University of Colorado at Denver

·P A U L·H·
BROOKES
PUBLISHING C⁰
Baltimore • London • Toronto • Sydney

Paul H. Brookes Publishing Co.
Post Office Box 10624
Baltimore, Maryland 21285-0624

www.brookespublishing.com

Typeset by Pro-Image Corporation, Techna-Type Division, York, Pennsylvania.
Manufactured in the United States of America by
Hamilton Printing Company, Rensselaer, New York.

Permission is gratefully acknowledged to reprint the cartoons appearing
in the chapter openers.

The cartoons appearing on pages 71, 107, 205, and 233 are reprinted by permission from *Ants in His Pants: Absurdities and Realities in Education,* cartoons by Michael F. Giangreco and illustrations by Kevin Ruelle, Minnetonka, MN: Peytral Publications. Copyright 1998 by Michael F. Giangreco. All rights reserved.

The cartoons on pages 17, 51, 141, and 177 are reprinted by permission from *Flying by the Seat of Your Pants: More Absurdities and Realities in Education,* cartoons by Michael F. Giangreco and illustrations by Kevin Ruelle, Minnetonka, MN: Peytral Publications. Copyright 1999 by Michael F. Giangreco. All rights reserved.

The cartoons on pages 3, 31, 95, 123, 161, 189, 219, 253, and 267 are reprinted by permission from *Teaching Old Logs New Tricks: More Absurdities and Realities in Education,* cartoons by Michael F. Giangreco and illustrations by Kevin Ruelle, Minnetonka, MN: Peytral Publications. Copyright 2000 by Michael F. Giangreco. All rights reserved.

Cover photograph by Mark E. Gibson. Copyright 1998 by Mark E. Gibson c/o Mira.

Excerpt (p. 13) from "Who We Are" in COUNT US IN: GROWING UP WITH DOWN SYNDROME, copyright © 1994 by Jason Kingsley and Mitchell Levitz; reprinted by permission of Harcourt, Inc.

Figure 1.1 (p. 8) and Figure 1.2 (p. 10) republished by permission of the American Association on Mental Retardation, from *Mental retardation: Definition, classification, and systems of supports* by R. Luckasson, D.L. Coulter, E.A. Polloway, S. Reiss, R.L. Schalock, M.E. Snell, D.M. Spitalnick, and J.A. Stark, copyright 1992. Permission conveyed through Copyright Clearance Center, Inc.

Table 10.1 (p. 170), Table 10.2 (p. 171), and Table 10.3 (p. 173) from FAMILIES, PROFESSIONALS, AND EXCEPTIONALITY: A SPECIAL PARTNERSHIP COLLABORATING FOR EMPOWERMENT (4th ed.) by Turnbull/Turnbull, © 2001. Reprinted by permission of Pearson Education, Inc., Upper Saddle River, NJ.

Library of Congress Cataloging-in-Publication Data

Teaching students with mental retardation : Providing access to the general curriculum /
    by Michael L. Wehmeyer ... [et al.].
        p.   cm.
    Includes bibliographical references and index.
    ISBN 1-55766-528-1
    1. Mentally handicapped children—Education—United States.   I. Wehmeyer,
Michael L.

    LC4631 .T43   2002
    371.92′8—dc21

                                                                          2001037585

British Library Cataloguing in Publication data are available from the British Library.

Contents

Personalized Educational Experiences for Students with
Mental Retardation
Future Directions: Implementing and Surviving Change
Summary
Additional Readings

About the Authors

Michael L. Wehmeyer, Ph.D., is Associate Professor in the Department of Special Education at the University of Kansas and Associate Director of the Beach Center on Disability, also at the University of Kansas. Prior to joining the university's faculty, Dr. Wehmeyer was Director of the Bill Sackter Center on Self-Determination at The Arc of the United States and Assistant Director in that association's Department of Research and Program Services. Dr. Wehmeyer taught adolescents with extensive and pervasive support needs in public and private schools for 7 years and also was a psychologist for the Texas Department of Mental Health and Mental Retardation for 1 year.

Dr. Wehmeyer's primary research is focused on promoting and enhancing self-determination and quality of life and developing high-quality educational supports for students with mental retardation, including a focus on providing access to and promoting progress in the general curriculum. Dr. Wehmeyer is the co-author or co-editor of numerous books, most recently *Teaching Self-Determination to Students with Disabilities: Basic Skills for Successful Transition* with Martin Agran and Carolyn Hughes (Paul H. Brookes Publishing Co., 1998), *Mental Retardation in the 21st Century* with James R. Patton (PRO-ED, 2000), and *Double Jeopardy: Promoting Gender Equity in Special Education* with Marilyn Rousso (State University of New York Press, 2001).

Deanna J. Sands, Ed.D., is Associate Professor in the Division of Technology and Special Services at the University of Colorado at Denver. Her professional experiences include teaching across infant, elementary, secondary and postsecondary settings with students who have extensive and pervasive support needs. Her research combines issues of quality of life, self-determination, curriculum, and voice for students with and without disabilities. She has directed numerous federally funded research and model development grants and currently coordinates a national partnership grant that combines teacher preparation programs in general and special education. Dr. Sands has served on state-level committees involved in standards-based education, performance assessments and transition services. She is the co-author of *Teaching Goal Setting and Decision Making to Students with Developmental Disabilities* with Beth Doll (American Association on Mental Retardation, 2000) and *Inclusive Education in the 21st Century* with Elizabeth B. Kozleski and Nancy K. French (Wadsworth/Thomson Learning, 1999). With Michael L. Wehmeyer, Dr. Sands co-edited *Self-Determination Across the Life Span: Independence and Choice for People with Disabilities* (Paul H. Brookes Publishing Co., 1996) and *Making it Happen: Student Involvement in Education Planning, Decision Making, and Instruction* (Paul H. Brookes Publishing Co., 1998).

H. Earle Knowlton, Ed.D., is Associate Professor of Special Education at the University of Kansas and has been a special educator for nearly 30 years. He began his career teaching students with learning disabilities and mental retardation in school, camping, and community settings. He was also a diagnostician and a parent trainer. For the past 23 years, he has been a faculty member in the Department of Special Education at the University of Kansas, and for the last 4 years, he has served as Associate Dean for Teacher Education and Undergraduate Studies in the School of Education. His research interests include lifestyle issues, curricular planning, and instructional methodology for students with mental retardation. Dr. Knowlton is also interested in personality and character attributes predictive of effective teachers in general education as well as special education.

Elizabeth B. Kozleski, Ed.D., is Associate Dean for the School of Education and a special education faculty member in the School of Education with an appointment to the Department of Pediatrics at the University of Colorado Health Sciences Center. Her bachelor's degree in early childhood education and her master's degree in special education were completed at George Mason University. She earned her doctorate in special education at the University of Northern Colorado in 1985. Dr. Kozleski is Institute Director for the National Institute for Urban School Improvement, a project funded by the U.S. Department of Education to facilitate the unification of current general and special education reform efforts as these are implemented in the nation's urban school districts. Her research focuses on building inclusive schools and communities, particularly within urban settings, and she is the co-author of *Inclusive Education in the 21st Century* with Deanna J. Sands and Nancy K. French (Wadsworth/Thomson Learning, 1999).

Foreword

If one were obliged to find four words to define this book, they would be grouped into two phrases: *mental retardation* and *providing access*. These four words and two phrases have protean meaning. Let's start with *mental retardation*. It is a term that has undergone several revolutions. The field no longer uses words such as *idiots, morons, imbeciles,* or *feeble-minded*. Indeed, it no longer uses *mental deficiency,* a term that the leading professional organization, American Association on Mental Retardation (AAMR), eschewed as one of us ended his presidency of that organization. Now, the trend is to abandon mental retardation and to find other phrases that meet three tests: they must be accurate, they must be less stigmatizing, and they must have power in policy-making circles.

That potential change of terms has significance beyond itself, as this book indicates. There is a sea-change occurring in the field of special education, and this book is centered on that change. One part of the change is providing access to the general curriculum for students with mental retardation (and for other students, too). So, quite properly, this book focuses primarily on how teachers can provide that kind of access. But providing access is connected to other changes; together, these changes constitute the sea-change. What are those changes and how does this book relate to them?

Here, the reader will encounter concepts and methods related to access, assessment, school reform, accountability, inclusion, places that provide arrays of services, and self-determination. These concepts and methods mirror state-of-the-art practices in special and general education. But they do more than that. They also express the core concepts in disability policy (Turnbull & Stowe, 2001).

For example, *access to the general curriculum* advances the core concepts of *inclusion* and *equal treatment*. To provide access to the academic, extracurricular, and other activities of a school is to integrate students with intellectual disabilities and (with reasonable accommodations to support them) to treat them as equal with students who have other disabilities and with students who have no disabilities.

Similarly, *assessment* reflects the core concept of accountability: students and schools must be accountable to each other and to taxpayers and families for the inputs that go into the students' education and for what those inputs yield in students' lives. School reform is all about the core concept of *professional and system capacity.* To advocate for and implement school reform requires professionals and systems to improve their capacities to provide integrated and accountable education. *Inclusion* is the school-based technique for overcoming segregation, and as IDEA reminds us, special education is not a place but a service (Section 1400[c](5)(A)). *Self-determination* manifests the core concept of *autonomy*—a person has choices about what happens to him or her.

When schools provide access and practice inclusion and when they engage in reform for all students, they put into place the concept of *anti-discrimination*— not singling out a particular student or group of students for less-than-favorable treatment simply because they have a certain trait (intellectual disabilities) but, instead, singling them out for favorable treatment (reasonable accommodations) so that they may attain plentiful participation in American life.

The point of all this is really quite basic: This book, the values that undergird it, and the techniques it espouses are inextricably linked to the evolving understanding of the meaning of the term *mental retardation* and its social significance and to the core concepts of disability policy.

Indeed, those concepts are the direct paths into lives that are characterized by full citizenship. Yes, it is important to have great expectations (as IDEA puts it, "high expectations"), but it is as important to know who can achieve them (students with intellectual disabilities), how they can achieve them (through state-of-the-art teaching techniques), and who can help them along that path (special and general educators alike). That's what this book is all about: evolving understandings of *mental retardation,* core concepts, state-of-the-art practices, and outcomes.

Read and profit. You cannot do the former without achieving the latter.

Rud and Ann Turnbull
Co-directors, Beach Center on Disability
Professors, Department of Special Education
University of Kansas at Lawrence

REFERENCES

Individuals with Disabilities Education Act (IDEA) of 1990, PL 101-476, 20 U.S.C. §§ 1400 *et seq.*
Turnbull, H.R., & Stowe, M. (2001). *A taxonomy for organizing the core concepts of disability policy affecting families who have children with disabilities according to their underlying principles.* Lawrence, KS: Beach Center on Families and Disability.

Preface

The Individuals with Disabilities Education Act (IDEA) Amendments of 1997 (PL 105-17) contain language that is prompting significant changes to the education programs of students with disabilities, including students with mental retardation. IDEA requires that students with disabilities must participate and progress in the general curriculum. These requirements, referred to as the "access to the general curriculum" mandates, were developed because of national policy makers' concern that students with disabilities were being left out of the accountability systems derived through school reform efforts. Once out of the accountability system, there is concern that students with disabilities will be ignored or further marginalized. Thus, policy objectives since the 1990s have focused on ensuring the involvement of students with disabilities in statewide assessment processes and involving special education in the broader school reform effort.

Regardless of how one feels about these changes, it is evident to anyone who spends any time in public schools that the nationwide emphasis on standards, testing, and accountability is changing the landscape in education. As discussed in the subsequent chapters, these efforts present some challenges to the education of students with mental retardation. However, this also presents a unique time in history to dramatically change the way that students with mental retardation are educated. The special education field can choose to struggle to retain its identity outside the sphere of influence of general education, or it can choose to work to make access to the general curriculum not just a buzzword but a vehicle by which students with mental retardation are held to high standards, are provided the supports they need to succeed, and are, perhaps most important of all, held to *high expectations*. Teachers across the country are struggling with how to provide access to and progress in the general curriculum for students with mental retardation. This text proposes a road map to achieve those outcomes.

Intended as a resource for upper-level undergraduate and graduate-level training for general and special education teachers of students with mental retardation and other students with more intensive support needs, *Teaching Students with Mental Retardation* is also intended for self-directed study by professionals currently in the field who interact with and teach students with mental retardation and intensive support needs. The book's foundation is a specific, unequivocal orientation that is *values-based, issues-oriented,* and *practice-oriented.* The text does not attempt to be introductory in nature and assumes that readers have some foundational knowledge about mental retardation.

VALUES-BASED FOUNDATION

This book is values-based in several ways. First, the text starts with the 1992 American Association on Mental Retardation (AAMR) definition of mental retardation (the most current definition) as a means to understand mental retardation. This value indicates that topics, issues, strategies, and so forth are not discussed in terms of a student's level of mental retardation (e.g., mild, moderate, severe, profound), as is still largely the case in the field, but discussed in terms of a student's instructional needs as a function of levels of supports, as suggested by the AAMR definitional framework. Chapter 1 defines mental retardation using a functional model, discusses levels of supports, and provides an overview of the implications of the 1992 definition for educators.

Second, this book advocates for students with mental retardation being educated with their peers in typical classrooms. The text does not argue for inclusive education; rather, it presumes inclusion as a necessary (but not sufficient) component of ensuring students' progress in the general curriculum. The topics and issues are predicated on an assumption that students with mental retardation are, and should be, educated with their peers. The emphasis in this text is less on the place where students with mental retardation receive their education than on what (i.e., the curriculum) and how (i.e., instruction) they are taught and how the educational process will ensure progress in the general curriculum and meet students' unique learning needs. It seems self-evident, however, that the place where students can have access to a challenging curriculum and receive high-quality instruction is, in fact, in the inclusive classroom.

A third value inherent in the book is the importance of self-determination for all students. It is the authors' strongly held belief that students with mental retardation need to have educational experiences that enable them to become more self-determined. The text embraces other values that are introduced within the context of separate chapters, including values about age-appropriate instruction and positive interventions for challenging behaviors.

ISSUES-ORIENTED FOUNDATION

While adopting the 1992 AAMR definition's emphasis on levels of supports instead of previous definitions' focus on level of mental retardation, the text addresses issues of supporting students with mental retardation with varying levels of needs. To determine what issues to address in the text, the lead author surveyed educators working with students with mental retardation and asked them to identify the top 10 issues they believed should be included in such a book. In addition, college and university professors were surveyed and asked to identify what types of topics should be included in such a text, and their recommendations were merged with teacher-identified topics. The chapter contents were derived from this survey process. As such, the issues addressed are those identified by teachers and teacher-trainers as most relevant and most important to their efforts.

PRACTICE-ORIENTED FOUNDATION

The intent of this text is to provide direction for action to achieve access to the general curriculum as well as to stimulate thought about and discussion of current issues (within a values-based context). It is not feasible to provide a comprehensive treatment of any given topic within this framework, and, frankly, to do so would be redundant to existing texts and materials. For example, one issue that appeared frequently in the survey was how to deal with problematic behavior of students with mental retardation, and Chapter 11 is devoted to positive behavioral supports. The intent of that chapter is to provide a discussion of behavioral supports, some essential information about implementing such supports, basic strategies, and what basic resources exist for further study and skills building. As such, readers are referred to current resources on behavioral supports, such as H. Lovett's *Learning to Listen: Positive Approaches and People with Difficult Behavior* (Paul H. Brookes Publishing Co., 1996), and *Positive Behavioral Support: Including People with Difficult Behavior in the Community* by L.K. Koegel, R.L. Koegel, and G. Dunlap (Paul H. Brookes Publishing Co., 1996). In other cases, such as discussions about designing educational supports, there are limited extant resources, and the text covers those topics in greater depth.

A practice-oriented text is one that, presumably, enables practitioners to function more effectively. In this case, that means that the text aims to help teachers—both in service and in training—to be better prepared and enabled to support students with mental retardation in gaining access to and progressing in the general curriculum. Lest one expects this text to provide detailed lesson plans or other unit components, it is important to note that the text's practicality lies in the emphasis within the text on teachers as educational decision-makers and as providers of educational supports. (Chapters 1–16 include *Chapter Objectives, Key Terms,* and *Additional Readings* sections.) However, it is the bias of the authors that if students with mental retardation are to gain access to the general curriculum and receive an excellent education, it will be because teachers are able to design supports that provide students with access to the general curriculum and make decisions about curricular and instructional activities on the basis of individual students' needs.

ORGANIZATION

The text is organized into four general sections. The first two chapters are introductory and focus on defining key concepts. Chapter 1 introduces a model for defining *mental retardation* that focuses on the relationship between the person's limitations and the social and environmental contexts in which that person functions, and it discusses implications for this way of thinking about mental retardation within the context of education. The second chapter provides an overview of what is meant by *curriculum design* and *curriculum decision making* and describes influences on curriculum design, including universal design. The next general section includes seven chapters that lay out the framework for achieving access for students with mental retardation. Chapter 3 provides an overview of what is meant by *access to the general curriculum*, describes a framework of curriculum modifications that provide access, and details a decision-making model that an IEP team can use to make decisions on the basis of the student's unique learning needs and the general curriculum. Subsequent chapters expand on the IEP team's role by discussing person-centered, student-directed planning and student program evaluation based on themes of empowerment. Chapters 7 through 9 describe how to create a learning community in which all students can progress, what classroom-level curriculum and instructional decisions can affect progress, and what teaching strategies work to enable students to progress in the general curriculum in inclusive settings.

Chapters 10 through 16 focus more specifically on those issues that teachers identified in the survey as areas of particular need or focus. Each of these chapters addresses topics or issues (e.g., achieving effective home–school partnerships, classroom management through positive behavioral supports, promoting self-determination, functional academics, community-based instruction, assistive technology) within the context of the model and process described in Chapters 3 through 9. The final chapter summarizes the process described in the previous chapters and provides a step-by-step discussion for implementing the processes.

REFERENCES

Individuals with Disabilities Education Act (IDEA) Amendments of 1997, PL 105-17, 20 U.S.C. §§ 1400 *et seq.*

Luckasson, R., Coulter, D.L., Polloway, E.A., Reiss, S., Schalock, R.L. Snell, M.E., Spitalnick, D.M., & Stark, J.A. (1992). *Mental retardation: Definition, classification, and systems of support.* Washington, DC: American Association on Mental Retardation.

Acknowledgments

The idea for this book emerged from conversations between the lead author and Acquisitions Editor Lisa Benson at Paul H. Brookes Publishing Co. Lisa's involvement throughout the writing of the text and her insight into directions for the text were critically important, and we acknowledge the important role that she played in shaping this book and bringing it to completion. Indeed, we would be negligent if we did not acknowledge the contributions of several of the Brookes staff, including Kimberly McColl, who served as Book Production Editor; Lisa Rapisarda, who is Editorial Manager; Kristine Dorman, who copyedited the manuscript; Maura Cooney, Lisa Yurwit, and Rebecca Torres, who were Acquisition Assistants through the writing process; and Erin Geoghegan, who designed the book cover and the interior. It is indeed a pleasure to work with the people at Paul H. Brookes Publishing Co., and we are grateful for their support and assistance.

We also acknowledge the important input to the flow and content of the text from Dr. Rachel Janney. Chapters in the book focusing on the intent of the federal "access to the general curriculum" mandates as well as the development of the model to address these issues for students with mental retardation emerged from grants funded by the U.S. Department of Education's Office of Special Education Programs (OSEP) to the Beach Center at the University of Kansas (PR Award #s H324D000025 and H324D990065), and we acknowledge that support while noting that the text does not necessarily reflect the opinion of the Department of Education. Drs. Anne Smith and Bonnie Jones of OSEP are the project officers for these grants, and we particularly acknowledge their direction and assistance. Finally, the colleagues who have influenced each of the authors' work are too numerous to name individually, so we will simply suggest that you know who you are and we thank you!

CHAPTER OBJECTIVES

1. Discuss the functional model of mental retardation.
2. Describe the role of sociocultural and environmental contexts in understanding mental retardation.
3. Define and describe a *supports model of service provision.*
4. Discuss the role of definition and categorization in education.
5. Identify how expectations and perceptions of mental retardation and disability affect education.

KEY TERMS

Mental retardation
Functional limitation
Disability
Intensities of needed supports
Constitutive definitions
Operational definitions

Understanding Mental Retardation

A Functional Model

GREAT MOMENTS IN SPECIAL
EDUCATION HISTORY:
THE 1970'S PROVIDE PROOF-POSITIVE
THAT DISABILITY IS
A SOCIAL CONSTRUCTION.

In the 1992 American Association on Mental Retardation (AAMR) handbook on the definition and classification of **mental retardation,** AAMR's ad hoc committee on terminology and classification introduced a definition and classification system that "reflects a changing paradigm [in the field of mental retardation], a more *functional* definition, and a focus on the interaction between the person, the environment, and the intensities and patterns of needed supports" (1992, p. viii; italics added). This system reflects AAMR's intent to link the classification of mental retardation to a system of supports and to move the diagnostic process away from its historic reliance on levels of impairment identified by performance on an IQ test. These definitional changes mirror the field of mental retardation's shift from an emphasis on providing *programs* for people with mental retardation to an emphasis on designing and delivering individualized *supports.*

DEFINING MENTAL RETARDATION

As discussed in the preface, this book presumes that readers have a foundational knowledge of mental retardation and, as such, does not engage in a prolonged discussion of the relative merits or deficits of AAMR's (1992) definition of mental retardation. (For comparison of the proposed benefits or disadvantages of this definition and classification system, please refer to the *Additional Readings* section at the end of this chapter.) Because the 1992 definition has not been adopted widely in educational environments, however, and is still relatively unfamiliar to many educators, it is worth reviewing the definition and the assumptions and implications of the classification system that accompany it:

> Mental retardation refers to substantial limitations in present functioning. It is characterized by significantly subaverage intellectual functioning, existing concurrently with related limitations in two or more of the following applicable adaptive skill areas: communication, self-care, home living, social skills, community use, self-direction, health and safety, functional academics, leisure, and work. Mental retardation manifests before age 18. (1992, p. 5)

Furthermore, the handbook states,

> The following four assumptions are essential to the application of the definition:
> 1. Valid assessment considers cultural and linguistic diversity as well as differences in communication and behavioral factors
> 2. The existence of limitations in adaptive skills occurs within the context of community environments typical of the individual's age peers and is indexed to the person's individualized needs for supports
> 3. Specific adaptive limitations can often coexist with strengths in other adaptive skills or other personal capabilities
> 4. With appropriate supports over a sustained period, the life functioning of the person with mental retardation will generally improve. (p. 5)

Readers familiar with previous AAMR definitions may note that the language in this version of the definition is not drastically different from that in earlier versions. In fact, some critics of the 1992 definition identified its relative similarity to previous definitions as its primary weakness (Greenspan, 1997). The definition and classification process does retain several features of previous definitions, including using intelligence testing as a component of the classification process, the requirement for emergence of mental retardation in an individual's developmental period (e.g., prior to age 18), and the need for a concurrent impairment in adaptive behavior. Unlike previous versions, however, the 1992 definition specifies the 10 adaptive skill areas in which limitations in adaptive behavior may occur.

Much of the discontent with AAMR's 1992 revisions relates to issues of diagnosis (MacMillan, Gresham, & Siperstein, 1993; Reiss, 1994), particularly the effect of changing the IQ score needed for diagnosis (Jacobson & Mulick, 1992; MacMillan et al., 1993). The IQ-score ceiling for classification of mental retardation, ranging from one standard deviation below the mean (approximately 85) in 1961 to two standard deviations (approximately 70) in 1973, has been the subject of much debate. Because the focus of this text is not on diagnostic implications of the definition but, rather, on educational and instructional implications, readers interested in further information about diagnostic issues should consult the resources listed in the *Additional Readings* section at the end of this chapter, particularly the eighth and ninth editions of the AAMR definition and classification handbook.

Given the obvious similarities between the 1992 AAMR definition of mental retardation and previous definitions, one wonders whether the statement made by Polloway, Smith, Chamberlain, Denning, and Smith that the "manual was a significant departure from the traditional classification system" (1999, p. 201) is warranted. After all, researchers, clinicians, and practitioners have argued for years about how to measure and quantify adaptive behavior and about the IQ score necessary for a diagnosis of mental retardation.

What does make the AAMR (1992) definition a significant departure from previous versions is that it takes the first step toward leading professionals to think differently about mental retardation and how they intervene in the lives of people with mental retardation. Polloway et al. asserted as much by commenting,

> The publication of the ninth manual on definition, classification, and terminology in mental retardation by the American Association on Mental Retardation formally asserted the importance of supports as a paradigm in the field of mental retardation. (1999, p. 201)

The challenge encountered by professionals in the field of special education is to operationalize this supports paradigm, and the first step in that process is to examine how the AAMR (1992) definition of mental retardation challenges professionals to think about mental retardation in relation to the design of such supports. The AAMR classification system proposes a functional definition of mental retardation in which mental retardation is not something that a person has or something that is a characteristic of the person but is instead a *state of functioning* in which limitations in functional capacity and adaptive skills must be considered *within the context* of environments and supports. AAMR proposed that "mental retardation is a *state* in which functioning is impaired in certain specific ways" (p. 10). A **functional limitation** is defined by AAMR as the "effect of specific impairments on the performance or performance capability of the person" whereas **disability** is described as the "expression of such a limitation in a social context" (p. 11). AAMR noted, accordingly, that "mental retardation is a disability *only* as a result of this interaction" (p. 10); that is, *only* as a result of the interaction between the functional limitation and the social context, in this case the environments and communities in which people with mental retardation live, learn, work, and play.

Yale University psychology professor emeritus Seymour Sarason once noted that "mental retardation is never a thing or a characteristic of an individual, but rather a social invention stemming from time-bound societal values and ideology that makes diagnosis and management seem both necessary and socially desirable" (1985, p. 233). The idea that mental retardation does not reside within the person as a disease and does not solely characterize a person is not new, yet it has not been emphasized among educators. The field of education's psychometric orientation has emphasized the idea that mental retardation *is* a characteristic of the person, but the AAMR (1992) definition moves the categorization process away from that perspective and more closely aligns it with the idea that mental retardation is a social construct that can only be defined within sociocultural and environmental contexts.

The reconceptualization of mental retardation proposed by AAMR (1992) places considerable emphasis on the "powerful role that social-ecological variables play in human functioning" (Schalock, 2001, p. 8). Quoting Ramey, Dossett, and Echols (1996), Schalock noted that social ecology's "primary axiom is that to understand one's behavior, the individual's environment must be taken into account" (p. 8). Why is this important for consideration by educators? By defining an individual's disability as a function of the reciprocal interaction between the environment and the person's functional limitations, the focus of the disability shifts from being an impairment within the student to being the relationship between the student's functioning and the environment and, subsequently, to the identification and design of supports to address the individual's functioning within that environment, with a primary focus on adaptations, accommodations, and modifications to the environment.

This represents a significant change in thinking about mental retardation. For most of the 20th century, the ways in which professionals oriented their roles in the lives of people with disabilities reflected the assumptions inherent in a deficits model of disability. People with disabilities were described as sick, aberrant, pathological, dysfunctional, or deficient. Educational labels reflected this deficit assumption as well, with terms such as *educable* or *trainable* reflecting beliefs about the person and the degree to which that person's impairment (that resided within the individual) affected his or her capacity to learn.

Changes in how disability is perceived can be seen in other areas as well. For example, the *Findings from Congress* section of the Rehabilitation Act Amendments of 1992 (PL 102-569) stated the following:

> Disability is a natural part of the human experience and in no way diminishes the rights of individuals to live independently, enjoy self-determination, make choices, contribute to society, pursue meaningful careers and enjoy full inclusion in the economic, political, social, cultural and educational mainstream of American society. (Sec. 2[a][3][A–F])

The language in the Rehabilitation Act Amendments of 1992 places the experience of disability on, not outside of, a continuum of typical human experiences. Among the anticipated outcomes of such a shift in perception is a change in the way that society views and perceives people with disabilities. Just as earlier perceptions of people with mental retardation as eternal children limited society's expectations for these individuals to live productive lives in the community, so too do current understandings of mental retardation as a disease or as a deficit residing within an individual influence society's expectations for people with cognitive disabilities. As suggested in the Rehabilitation Act Amendments of 1992, however, when people with disabilities are viewed as having the right to exercise self-determination, the right to live independently and pursue meaningful careers, and the right to contribute to and be fully included in society and when they are provided with the protections necessary to exercise these rights and participate fully in the community, the expectations about and for people with disabilities, including people with mental retardation, can change dramatically.

This change in perception has important implications for the field of education. Student outcomes are affected by teacher expectations of student performance capacity and by the stereotypes, beliefs, and biases formed on the basis of teachers' understanding of disability. Ryndak and Alper (1996) provided a compelling example of the effect of stereotypes on expectations for learning. They described a student named Maureen, labeled as having moderate mental retardation, who had received her education from the ages of 5 to 15 in self-contained classrooms for students with mental retardation. At the end of her final year in a segregated environment, Maureen's interdisciplinary team described Maureen as having functional levels consistent with moderate mental retardation. Her individualized education program (IEP) objectives from that year included improving phonics and comprehension skills to the second-grade level, reading and writing dollar amounts, and solving three- and four-digit addition and subtraction problems. Within the first year after Maureen entered an inclusive seventh-grade class at age 15, she was completing age-appropriate work with some adaptations, including excelling on age-appropriate math tasks involving the Pythagorean theorem and simple algebra. When Maureen graduated from high school with her peers 5 years later, she and her family made plans for her to be included in a college environment and live in the dormitory. Because Maureen continued to need accommodations and supports for a wide array of academic and other outcomes, this was not a case of her simply being mislabeled. Instead, Maureen's story illustrates the impact of viewing disability within a deficits perspective as well as the negative consequences of excluding students with mental retardation from the general curriculum.

Intensities of Supports

Viewing mental retardation as a *function* of the *interaction between capacity and environments or contexts* places greater emphasis on the need to provide supports and accommodations to enable individuals to, in fact, function within that environment. This is reflected in what may be the most obvious change in AAMR's 1992 definition and classification system from previous versions: the deletion of the "levels of mental retardation" classification scheme. Previous manuals had identified four levels of mental retardation (mild, moderate, severe, and profound), determined by performance on standardized intelligence tests. The 1992 classification system eliminated these levels and, instead, identified four **intensities of needed supports**. These intensities are categorized as follows:

Intermittent   Intermittent supports are required on an as-needed basis—for example, episodic or short-term supports during life-span transitions (e.g., job loss, an acute medical crisis). Supports may be high or low intensity when provided.

Limited   Limited supports are required continually but for a limited period of time. The limited intensity of support may require fewer staff members and cost less than more intense levels of support (e.g., time-limited employment training, during the transition from school to adulthood).

Extensive Extensive supports are required regularly. The extensive intensity of support is characterized by continuous involvement (e.g., daily) in at least some environments (e.g., work, home). It is usually long-term, not time-limited, support.

Pervasive Pervasive supports are required across environments. They are characterized by their constant, intense, potentially life-sustaining nature and typically involve more staff members and intrusiveness than do extensive or time-limited supports.

Defining Supports

Because the idea of supports—the process of providing supports and the categorization of levels of supports—is at the heart of the AAMR's (1992) definition, it is important to understand what is intended by the use of this term. The 1992 AAMR manual defines supports as

> Resources and strategies that promote the interests and causes of individuals with or without disabilities; that enable them to access resources, information and relationships inherent within integrated work and living environments; and that result in their enhanced interdependence, productivity, community integration, and satisfaction. (p. 101)

The manual introduces a model, depicted in Figure 1.1, to conceptualize the source of supports, their functions, intensities, and desired outcomes.

Luckasson and Spitalnik suggested that "supports refer to an array, not a continuum, of services, individuals, and environments that match the person's needs" (1994, p. 88). These authors refer to a "constellation" of supports needed by people with men-

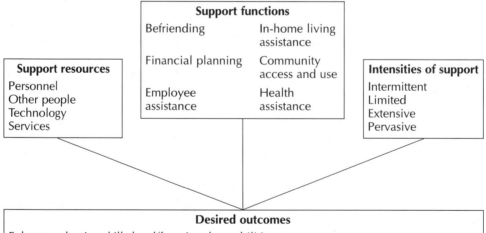

Figure 1.1. Supports-Outcomes Model from the American Association on Mental Retardation (AAMR; 1992) classification manual. (From Luckasson, R., Coulter, D.L., Polloway, E.A., Reiss, S., Schalock, R.L., Snell, M.E., Spitalnik, D.M., & Stark, J.A. [1992]. *Mental retardation: Definition, classification, and systems of supports* [p. 102]. Washington, DC: American Association on Mental Retardation; reprinted by permission.)

tal retardation in which, as illustrated in Figure 1.2, the person is in the center. This figure depicts different types of supports, radiating out from self-directed and self-mediated supports (e.g., the person, his or her family and friends) and nonpaid supports (e.g., co-workers, neighbors) to generic supports (e.g., dentist, doctor) and specialized supports (e.g., special education teacher, speech-language therapist).

When is a support not a support? Several characteristics of providing supports differentiate this intervention strategy from traditional models of service delivery. First, three key aspects of supports are identified in the AAMR manual: 1) they pertain to resources and strategies; 2) they enable individuals to gain access to other resources, information, and relationships within inclusive environments; and 3) their use results in increased integration and enhanced personal growth and development (AAMR, 1992). In other words, supports have the unambiguous intent to enhance community inclusion by enabling people to gain access to a wide array of resources, information, and relationships.

Second, supports are individually designed and determined with the active involvement of key stakeholders in the process, particularly the person benefiting from the support. Traditional service delivery models, whether education or adult services, were designed primarily in a top-down manner. Services were delivered in the form of programs that were designed, at least initially, to meet as many needs of the population of individuals with mental retardation as possible. Financial and other resource restraints typically resulted in eligibility standards that, in turn, often resulted in waiting lists to gain access to a given program. Such models typically became paradigm-bound and were driven as much by the needs of the provider as by the person attempting to gain access to those services.

Third, supports cannot be defined adequately by listing a limited set of resources, services, or strategies. As Figure 1.2 illustrates, traditional generic mental retardation services can be conceptualized as supports if they meet two criteria: 1) The individual with mental retardation and his or her family or allies must identify that particular service as a means of achieving self-determined goals pertaining to intervention, and 2) the unambiguous intent of the service must be to promote community inclusion and participation and enhance personal growth. Some current models of service delivery, including sheltered employment and congregate living facilities, simply do not meet that criteria and cannot be seen as viable support strategies.

The fourth and final factor differentiating supports from traditional models is that, as is emphasized throughout this chapter, a supports model requires an active and on-going evaluation of the ecological aspects of an individual's disability (because the disability can only be defined within the context of the functional limitation and the social context), and efforts to design supports must focus heavily on changing aspects of the individual's environments or social context or on providing the individual with additional skills or strategies to overcome barriers in those environments.

Moving to a supports framework within education is not without dissension. For example, Dever and Knapczyk stated the following:

> Unfortunately, the latest idea to come along is that we must provide people with mental retardation with "supports." This concept seems to encourage the toleration of dependency because it does not focus on teaching people to gain control over their own lives. To those of us who believe that we must teach, the idea that we should support people as they are is anathema because it allows us to tolerate the status quo. That is, by supporting people with mental retardation as they are, we perpetuate their isolation and dependency. Frankly,

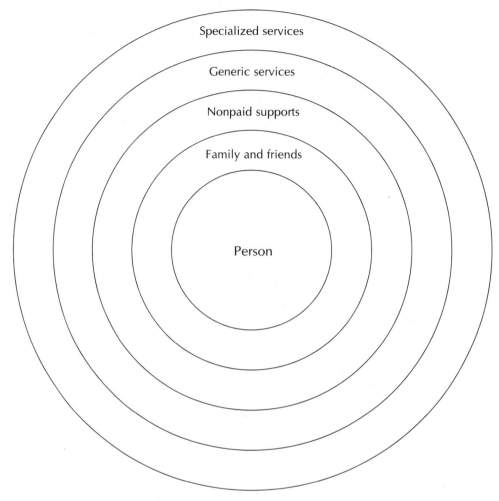

Figure 1.2. Constellation of supports. (From Luckasson, R., & Spitalnik, D.M. [1994]. Political and programmatic shifts of the 1992 AAMR definition of mental retardation. In V. J. Bradley, J.W. Ashbaugh, & B.C. Blaney [Eds.], *Creating individual supports for people with developmental disabilities: A mandate for change at many levels* [p. 88]. Baltimore: Paul H. Brookes Publishing Co.; reprinted by permission.)

we see little or no role for a teacher in the concept of supports. Our view is that we must try as hard as we can to teach people with mental retardation not to need us. Those whose vocation is teaching must help those who must learn, and our job is to help our learners develop the true dignity that comes from being contributing members of the community. (1997, p. 8)

Dever and Knapczyk's reaction to the supports construct clearly gives one pause to think and examine the degree to which a supports model does, if at all, perpetuate the status quo. Defenders of the supports model believe that the status quo is one of dependency and limited opportunities. The interpretation of the supports construct advocated in this text is broader than that implied by Dever and Knapczyk, who view the term *supports* only in the sense of something that props something else up. Indeed, making students with mental retardation dependent on someone else is not helpful. However, advocates of the supports model (AAMR, 1992; Luckasson & Spitalnik, 1994) repeatedly articulate that supports refer to a wide array of resources and strategies of which instruction and the educational process are clearly key components. These advocates also emphasize the individual as, in essence, the most natural support. Support sources range from the individual or his or her family members to generic and special services. The levels of intensities of supports clearly identify that they may be transient or intermittent and should only be provided on an as-needed basis. Finally, as mentioned previously, the focus on supports, as opposed to programs, frees us from the models of the past in which teachers, as experts, were responsible for helping students to learn—thus, "fixing" the students—and refocuses attention on the relationship between the functional capacity of the individual and his or her environment. Educators play a significant role in moving beyond stereotypes about people with mental retardation to working collaboratively with students to help them achieve greater self-sufficiency and enhanced capacity and to increase their level of self-determination.

Education's Need for and Use of Definitions

The field of special education has undergone a shift toward providing supports to enable students to achieve success and gain greater access to the general curriculum. Yet, too often, this philosophical shift has not resulted in changes to the educational services provided to students with mental retardation. Perhaps one reason that the 1992 AAMR definition has largely been ignored in the field of education is because it was developed as much with adult functioning and adult services in mind as it was developed for educational services. That may, in fact, account for interpretations such as that of Dever and Knapczyk's (1997), who perceived supports simply as means to provide for individuals or to keep them from falling, sinking, or failing. This adult services bias in the definition and classification system is also evident in Figure 1.1, particularly when examining the support functions and desired outcomes. It is admittedly difficult to discern the impact of this model of supports on the field of education and educational services. Although the AAMR definition and classification scheme has been used widely in educational environments, particularly in reference to the levels of mental retardation, it is by no means the sole definition of mental retardation available. Professionals in the medical disciplines, mainly psychiatrists, diagnose mental retardation on the basis of criteria listed in the *Diagnostic and Statistical Manual of Mental Disorders, Fourth Edition, Text Revision* (DSM-IV-TR; American Psychiatric Association, 2000). The American Psychological Association publishes its own *Manual of Diagnosis and Professional Practice in Mental Retardation* (Jacobson & Mulick, 1996). In fact, since the publication of the 1992 AAMR definition, there has been a discussion of the potential need for or benefit of an education definition of *mental retardation*—one that could address the unique needs of the educational process. To determine the best definitional framework to use within the context of the educational service system or, alternatively, to forge a new education-specific definition, it is necessary to consider the purpose of the definitional process.

One defines a construct for a variety of reasons, and definitions can be either operational or constitutive. **Constitutive definitions** tie or link a construct with other, typically related, constructs, whereas **operational definitions** assign meaning to a construct or variable by specifying the operations necessary to measure, observe, or promote it. Constitutive definitions are valuable for theory development, whereas operational definitions are necessary for designing interventions or making diagnostic decisions. The

AAMR definition has both constitutive and operational elements. Linking the construct of *mental retardation* with the constructs of *adaptive behavior, developmental period,* or *intelligence* is a way of constitutively defining the construct and places our understanding of the construct in relation to our understanding of these related constructs. Identifying the developmental period as birth through the age of 18 or a specific IQ score as the cutoff for a diagnosis of mental retardation are, alternatively, ways of operationally defining the construct.

As educators, we are charged with providing instruction that promotes learning and development. As such, we often have emphasized the operational over the constitutive aspects of the mental retardation definition. Thus, the definition and classification process was paramount in making diagnoses (largely the responsibility of the field of psychology, not education) and, subsequently, placement decisions. Typical special education services created programs for students with mild, moderate, or severe/profound mental retardation, and students were placed in those programs on the basis of their diagnosis. By and large, the definition and classification system had little effect on the ways in which teachers taught students with mental retardation, although one could argue that the placement decision in essence determined the instructional program (i.e., students with a specific level of mental retardation should receive this particular or specific instructional program).

The 1992 AAMR definition requires educators to pay more attention to constitutive aspects of the definition, with particular emphasis on the functional relationship between the environment or social context and an individual's functional limitations. Whereas the revisions seen in the 1992 edition of AAMR's manual make the diagnostic process more complex, they also make the definition and classification process more relevant to instruction and the educational process than previous versions of the manual. Defining mental retardation as a function of the relationship between individual capacity and the environment and classifying mental retardation on the basis of the intensity of supports needed to address this reciprocal relationship (e.g., to intervene) have direct implications for instruction.

The shift toward a focus on constitutive aspects of the definition as relevant to education and the complexity of the operational (i.e., diagnostic) features of the definition likely contribute to the new definition's relatively limited use in education. However, from the viewpoint of providing educational services, the 1992 definition provides a powerful vehicle to begin to align the provision of educational services with the emerging supports paradigm in disability services.

UNDERSTANDING MENTAL RETARDATION

This chapter began by describing the changes in the ways that mental retardation is defined and understood. Because the educational process has relied on the psychometric traditions of assessment and testing for diagnosis, placement, and program design, issues of definition and evaluation are perhaps overemphasized. In focusing on issues such as defining mental retardation, even in the context of the functional model explored here, professionals may be guilty of not being able to see the forest for the trees. Defining mental retardation does not adequately help with understanding *people* with mental retardation; it does not sufficiently tell us *who* we are talking about when we refer to people with mental retardation. People with mental retardation do not identify themselves only on the basis of their disability, nor should professionals. Listen to

Mitchell Levitz, as quoted in Kingsley and Levitz (1994), as he talks about his life and who he is:

> On April 10th 1971, the birth of Mitchell Andrew Levitz was at the Peekskill Community Hospital and the parents of the child were Barbara and Jack Levitz. The Doctor told Barbara and Jack that the child had Down syndrome. This changed how they lived. I went to Lincoln Titus Elementary School up to fifth grade and I was in Cub Scouts and Webelos Scouts. I got an Arrow of Light award and played soccer with American Youth Soccer Organization on weekends. In middle school I had many teachers for different classes who helped me with many subjects. Some of the courses I took were math, history and sciences, chorus and art, physical education, and also speech therapy. I have been at Walter Panas High School since ninth grade. I have took most of the required courses and exams and only have the reading exam left to pass to get a regular diploma.
>
> At one time in my life, I felt that I had a memorable moment that was important in my life. It was my Bar Mitzvah.... Rabbi Josh Hammerman helped me and my two sisters to go through a time of studying and preparation.
>
> People make me feel important in life, especially my family with all of their love and support. Recently I went to Albany [New York] and Assemblyman George Pataki said to the whole entire Assembly and to the Speaker: "I would appreciate if you could welcome to the chamber this afternoon an extraordinary young man from my district. He is now a Junior at Panas High working as an intern in my district." I am very interested in politics and government. (pp. 15–18)

Reading the words of Mitchell Levitz, it is obvious that people with mental retardation are interested in politics and government, public service, religious life, relationships, and community activities. Or read the words of a person with mental retardation from a media campaign by The Arc, a national organization on mental retardation. One particular print ad features a man with mental retardation holding a baseball in his left hand and smiling at the camera. The text next to his sepia-tone picture states,

> They told me I was slow. Called me mentally retarded. And hid me from the world for 30 years. Then I was on my own, and scared of being different. But I learned I could do many things. Now I am a builder. Actor. Baseball fan and friend. And I tell myself and everyone who is different, "we are people first."

We need, then, to add the descriptors of baseball fan, actor, and friend to our understanding of who people with mental retardation are. Subsequent chapters in this book show that people with mental retardation are also lovers, spouses, and parents. More important, we need to hear the words of the man in the print ad for The Arc's media campaign—the words that have become the rallying call of the self-advocacy movement: *We are people first.* This is a slogan that has become, perhaps, too sanitized and too familiar to us. We talk about person-first language without remembering that there are people in the world who are identified and labeled by and discriminated against and stigmatized because of a narrow focus on only one aspect of their lives: their intellectual or cognitive capacity. People with mental retardation are, however, simply people, first and foremost.

Some individuals with mental retardation, like Mitchell Levitz, have an identified medical condition, such as Down syndrome, that is usually (though not always) associated with limitations in functioning. Other students are not identified as easily, and their support needs may be less intense. Some students with mental retardation have other limitations in functioning that affect their speech-language or motor skills, whereas some students' limitations are evident mainly in social contexts.

As a society, we have chosen to label people with mental retardation. It is worth remembering, however, that simply because we choose to categorize people according to certain characteristics does not make it so. Smith (1999) observed that discussions of mental retardation in the 20th century can be characterized as largely reflecting typological thinking, referring to the belief that individual differences diverge into underlying types or essences (Gelb, 1997). Smith noted that the core of the field of mental retardation is the assumption that somehow there is an "essence of mental retardation that eclipses all of the individual differences that characterize the people who are described by the term" (1999, p. 389). Smith continued by saying that perhaps it is time to abandon the term *mental retardation* because it may be simply a manifestation of the typological thinking that "inevitably creates a false and unhelpful categorization of people with very diverse needs and characteristics" (p. 391).

It is important to recognize that categorizing people as having disabilities or mental retardation has a significant impact on these individuals. Such efforts affect how people are perceived by society as a whole, what expectations are held about their capacity to participate in the mainstream of society, and how interventions are designed and implemented. Previous definitions and categorizations continued to perpetuate images of incapacity and dependency, of incompetence and helplessness. A marked decline in the percentage of students labeled as having mental retardation has occurred in many U.S. states, at least in part because parents and students themselves do not want to be stigmatized by having the label and work against that outcome.

When, as promoted in the 1992 AAMR definition, we focus our attention not on fixing the impairment in the individual but instead on identifying supports that can address the interaction between an individual's functional capacity and the social context, we move beyond stigma and stereotypes. When we focus on ability and enable students to capitalize on their capacities, we embark on a course of action that will enable us to better prepare students to navigate the uncertain waters of adulthood. Focusing on supports and not on individual impairments enables us to think creatively and to modify environments, to identify accommodations, to provide instruction, and to mobilize resources to provide students with mental retardation access to the general curriculum and, ultimately, to an education program that prepares them to become more self-reliant and self-sufficient.

ADDITIONAL READINGS

Defining Mental Retardation

Greenspan, S. (1997). Dead manual walking: Why the 1992 AAMR definition needs redoing. *Education and Training in Mental Retardation and Developmental Disabilities, 32,* 179–190.

Kingsley, J., & Levitz, M. (1994). *Count us in: Growing up with Down syndrome.* San Diego: Harcourt Brace & Co.

Luckasson, R., Coulter, D.L., Polloway, E.A., Reiss, S., Schalock, R.L., Snell, M.E., Spitalnick, D.M., & Stark, J.A. (1992). *Mental retardation: Definition, classification, and systems of supports.* Washington, DC: American Association on Mental Retardation.

MacMillan, D.L., Gresham, F.M., & Siperstein, G.N. (1993). Conceptual and psychometric concerns about the 1992 AAMR definition of mental retardation. *American Journal on Mental Retardation, 98*, 325–335.

Polloway, E.A., Smith, J.D., Chamberlain, J., Denning, C.B., & Smith, T.E.C. (1999). Levels of deficits or supports in the classification of mental retardation: Implementation practices. *Education and Training in Mental Retardation and Developmental Disabilities, 34*, 200–206.

Reiss, S. (1994). Issues in defining mental retardation. *American Journal on Mental Retardation, 99*, 1–7.

Understanding Mental Retardation

Blatt, B. (1987). *The conquest of mental retardation.* Austin, TX: PRO-ED.

Blatt, B., & Kaplan, F. (1966). Christmas in purgatory. New York: Allyn & Bacon.

Bogdan, R., & Taylor, S.J. (1994). *The social meaning of mental retardation: Two life stories.* New York: Teachers College Press.

Trent, J.W. (1994). *Inventing the feeble mind: A history of mental retardation in the United States.* Berkeley: University of California Press.

Wehmeyer, M.L., & Patton, J. (1999). *Mental retardation in the 21st century.* Austin, TX: PRO-ED.

Diagnosing Mental Retardation

Grossman, H.J., Begab, M.J., Cantwell, D.P., Clements, J.D., Eyman, R.K., Meyers, C.E., Tarjan, G., & Warren, S.A. (1983). *Classification in mental retardation* (8th ed.). Washington, DC: American Association on Mental Deficiency.

Jacobson, J.W., & Mulick, J.A. (1996). *Manual of diagnosis and professional practice in mental retardation.* Washington, DC: American Psychological Association.

Luckasson, R., Coulter, D.L., Polloway, E.A., Reiss, S., Schalock, R.L., Snell, M.E., Spitalnick, D.M., & Stark, J.A. (1992). *Mental retardation: Definition, classification, and systems of supports* (9th ed.). Washington, DC: American Association on Mental Retardation.

Experiencing Mental Retardation

Kingsley, J., & Levitz, M. (1994). *Count us in: Growing up with Down syndrome.* San Diego: Harcourt Brace & Company.

Schneider, J. (1998). *Waiting for home: The Richard Prangley story.* Grand Rapids, MI: William B. Eerdmans Publishing Co.

Smith, J.D. (1995). *Pieces of Purgatory: Mental retardation in and out of institutions.* Pacific Grove, CA: Brooks/Cole.

Walz, T. (1999). *The unlikely celebrity: Bill Sackter's triumph over disability.* Carbondale: Southern Illinois University Press.

Journals

Published by the American Association on Mental Retardation
  Mental Retardation
  American Journal on Mental Retardation
Published by the Council for Exceptional Children
  Education and Training in Mental Retardation and Developmental Disabilities

CHAPTER OBJECTIVES

1. Define *curriculum* and identify formal and informal curricula.
2. Define *curriculum design and planning* and describe theories that contribute to such efforts.
3. Discuss the application of universal design to curriculum design.
4. Identify educational and curricular supports and discuss their importance in the educational process.

KEY TERMS

Curriculum
Curriculum decision making
Formal and informal curricula
Curriculum design and planning
Universal design
Natural supports
Person-centered planning

2

Curriculum Decision Making and Educational Supports

TIM NOTICES A MYSTERIOUS FORCE-FIELD
AROUND HIS JOB COACH THAT
CO-WORKERS CANNOT PENETRATE.

C hapter 1 uses the terms *curriculum decision making* and *educational supports* to identify practices associated with excellence in education for students with mental
retardation. This chapter provides an overview of these two elements, and subsequent chapters supply more detail concerning curriculum decision making and the
design of educational supports.

WHAT IS CURRICULUM?

When considering the role of **curriculum decision making** in teaching students with
mental retardation, one should consider what is meant by the term **curriculum.** On the
surface, this seems a simple task, but on closer examination, there is much to consider.

Doll noted that "scholars in the curriculum field have sometimes become lost in
arguments about the semantics of curriculum definitions" (1996, p. 14). The several
dimensions of defining curriculum lead to contrasting opinions, including the degree to
which the curriculum is planned versus spontaneous; formal and informal aspects of the
curriculum; the magnitude, breadth, or scope of the curriculum; and the relationship
among content, process, and instructional activities within the curriculum. Sands,
Kozleski, and French (2000) summarized the literature on curriculum as referring to the
following alternatives:

- A plan for classes offered by a school
- Materials used to present information to students
- The subject matter taught to the students
- The courses offered in a school
- The planned experiences of the learners under the guidance of the school

Doll offered a working definition of *curriculum* as "the formal and informal content and
process by which learners gain knowledge and understanding, develop skills, and alter
attitudes, appreciations and values under the auspices of that school" (1996, p. 15).
Sands and colleagues (2000) identified a similar definition set forth by Hass and Parkay,
who defined *curriculum* as being "all of the experiences that individual learners have in
a program of education whose purpose is to achieve broad goals and related specific
objectives, which is planned in terms of a framework of theory and research or past and
present professional practice" (1993, p. 9). Both definitions identify curriculum as
broadly defined and as encompassing aspects of both formal and informal school experiences. Sands and colleagues referred to this distinction as the planned curriculum and
the experienced curriculum.

Sands et al. (2000) also distinguished between *curriculum* as the *what* and *instruction*
as the *how* in describing school processes and student experiences, whereas Doll's (1996)
definition includes instruction as part of the definition of curriculum. This text adopts
the distinction between curriculum and instruction as unique components of the educational experience; however, providing access to the general curriculum includes
changes in both curriculum design and decision making (i.e., the *what*) and instructional
strategies and methodologies (i.e., the *how*).

Doll's distinction between **formal and informal curriculum** is noteworthy:

Every school has a planned, formal, acknowledged curriculum, and also an unplanned, informal, or hidden one. The planned curriculum embraces content usually categorized within subjects and subject fields. The unplanned curriculum includes such varied experiences or engagements as advancing oneself inconsiderately in the cafeteria line, learning to like history, protecting one's front teeth from being pushed down hard on drinking fountains, finding new ways to beat the system, and resisting pressure to smoke marijuana. (pp. 14–15)

It is important that students experience both the formal and informal curriculum, a topic that is examined subsequently as part of a focus on issues regarding access to the general curriculum for students with mental retardation.

A focus on the curriculum as a target of design and decision-making activities is appropriate within the reconceptualization of mental retardation as presented in Chapter 1. Sands and colleagues (2000) noted the following:

Curriculum reform across both general and special education provides a unique opportunity for collaboration between school professionals, support personnel, students, families, and community members. In fact, *curriculum deficits, not student deficits, can become the common ground from which representatives of these groups can hold conversations and work collaboratively.* (pp. 19–20; italics added)

This distinction, in which the focus shifts from student deficits to deficits in the curriculum and its design and implementation, is important in the education of students with mental retardation and is consistent with a functional model described in Chapter 1. The curriculum is the context or the environment in which we, as educators, must examine the relationship between an individual student's functional limitations and his or her environment. Such activities must include key stakeholders in the educational process from the earliest design phases through the student-specific decision-making process. The demand is on the curriculum to become flexible enough to ensure that students with a wide array of cognitive and other capacities can have access to and, perhaps more important, progress and succeed within the context of the general curriculum.

CURRICULUM DESIGN

Here and throughout the text, the terms *curriculum design* and *curriculum decision making* have been used to refer to activities that are important for enabling students with mental retardation to gain access to the general curriculum. Although in many circumstances these terms can be used interchangeably, they are used here in reference to activities that differ primarily in scope. **Curriculum design** refers to the broader activity of *planning* the curriculum. This planning is often districtwide but also can be campuswide. Doll described curriculum design as follows:

A carefully conceived curriculum plan that takes its shape from 1) what its creators believe about people and their education and 2) how its creators would like to see their beliefs expressed. A curriculum design takes into account a number of interrelated and interdependent elements: what its creators want done, what subject matter they wish to use to fulfill the design's purposes, what instructional strategies they favor using, and how they will determine the success of feasibility of the design. (1996, p. 204)

Doll's use of the term *creator* in reference to curriculum design implies that the process of curriculum planning and design is intended to *create* a curriculum. Such activities are, invariably, conducted in groups or committees, and the outcomes of the process determine the district's or school's curriculum that teachers and others in the educational process are to teach. The curriculum-design process leads to the creation of the *general curriculum,* which is discussed in Chapter 3. The curriculum decision-making process, discussed in the following paragraphs and in subsequent chapters, is the process of coming to a judgment about the most appropriate and important content for an individual student's educational program. In the context of providing special education supports, such decisions are made by the IEP team.

To a large extent, professionals in the field of special education have operated outside of the context of the general curriculum, and special education teachers have been expected to design an appropriate curriculum for students with mental retardation on the basis of each student's unique educational needs. As Knowlton (1998) pointed out and as the U.S. Department of Education's mandate to expand access to the general curriculum suggests (for more information, see Chapter 3), it is no longer acceptable for the field of special education to operate wholly outside of the general curriculum. The consequences of doing so are reflected in the still overwhelmingly segregated system of education for students with mental retardation; in professionals' continued emphasis on deficits and handicapism reflected in the language we use (e.g., trainable, educable); and in our low expectations for students with mental retardation, as illustrated by Maureen's story in Chapter 1. It is necessary to reference both individual student needs and the general curriculum when making curriculum decisions for students with disabilities.

AN INCLUSIVE APPROACH TO CURRICULUM DESIGN

The curriculum design process involves and is influenced by competing social, cultural, political, and economic forces as well as the different orientations of national, state, and local school standards. National curriculum reform efforts since the 1990s have focused on creating school programs that address broad-based educational goals—academic, personal, social, and career-based domains, including both content and process goals. In addition, the need to personalize learning to respond to and support ethnic, linguistic, ability, and cultural diversity has been addressed widely. Proponents of the standards-based education movement (discussed in more detail in Chapter 3) are explicit about their beliefs that all students, including students with disabilities, can be held to higher educational standards and can achieve at levels higher than previously expected.

These broad calls for reform, flexibility, and personalization are closely aligned to the principles and values of inclusive education and imply that curriculum must address student characteristics that are not necessarily widespread in the education system. Pugach and Warger (1996b) summarized the necessary characteristics of a curriculum that responds to and supports student diversity and inclusive education: 1) a focus on in-depth coverage of content within meaningful contexts; 2) attention to students' abilities to think critically, manage their own learning, work collaboratively, foster peer relationships, and solve problems; 3) a focus on students' interests, needs, and previous experiences to guide curriculum design and implementation; and 4) an allowance for differences in the manner in which students interact with and learn from the curriculum and demonstrate their learning.

The mandates from the Office of Special Education Programs regarding access to the general curriculum serve as a vehicle to begin to realize the type of curriculum characteristics described by Pugach and Warger (1996b). Strong collaboration among all school professionals, students, families, support personnel, and community members is critical to designing and implementing this type of curriculum (see Chapter 10). Collaboration between general and special educators is especially important; general educators offer a rich and in-depth knowledge of academic content areas, and special educators are skilled in understanding and responding to learner variance and creating accommodations to meet learner strengths and needs. Curriculum design really can only achieve the type of outcomes desired if the perspectives and sets of expertise of both general and special educators are involved in the design process.

THEORIES DRIVING CURRICULUM DESIGN

Curriculum design is—more or less, depending on the particular effort—theory driven. Doll identified several theories that have been "posed to guide curriculum design in the future" (1996, p. 32). The approach to curriculum design advocated in this text embodies several of Doll's theoretical perspectives. First, Doll noted that curriculum planning should adhere to an *empowerment theory* of curriculum design that "focuses on making competent and confident curriculum planners of teachers, administrators, parents, and other citizens... [with] decision making power... granted to classroom teachers in particular" (p. 33). Doll also noted that this theoretical perspective "recognizes variations among pupils leading to the creation of special curricula; it also encourages individualization" (p. 33).

The second theoretical perspective embodied in this approach to curriculum design is the *education-in-balance* perspective, which emphasizes a balanced curriculum for individual learners that takes into account a variety of student circumstances and characteristics, such as socioeconomic background, gender, race, cognitive ability, and so forth. Both the empowerment theory and the education-in-balance perspective capture the essence of the need for individualized, person-focused, and capacity-driven curriculum design and decision making and are consistent with the implications of the functional model discussed in Chapter 1. Doll (1996) further noted that both of these theories lay the foundation for restructuring the way education is provided. This is clearly the case when one considers issues pertaining to inclusion, student-directed learning, or community-based instruction. In each of these cases, implementing best practices requires a change from a system that was designed with a segregated, teacher-directed, and school-centered focus. Thus, the third theoretical perspective influencing the process of curriculum design is the *transformation theory*, which suggests that for schools to succeed and for curricula to be effective, the structure or organization of the school—the school environment, school day, place of instruction, and so forth—needs to be transformed. Curricula then can be matched to optimal learning environments and circumstances.

A fourth theoretical perspective emerged in the 1990s and is playing a significant role in guiding curriculum design efforts for students with mental retardation and other disabilities. This perspective is the implementation of *universal design theory* within curriculum planning and design.

UNIVERSAL DESIGN AS CURRICULUM THEORY

The principle of universal design emerged, initially, from architecture. **Universal design** suggests, quite simply, that all buildings and environments should be accessible to all people (Moon, Hart, Komissar, & Friedlander, 1995). This principle subsequently was applied to the design and development of consumer products and assistive devices with the same intent—that such products and devices should be accessible to all people.

The principle of universal design was introduced to ensure that members of certain groups, such as people with disabilities or older adults, have access to the environment or products that could enhance their quality of life. Therefore, buildings are designed with ramps, wide doors, and accessible restrooms, or products are designed with simple controls and clearly comprehensible uses. The application of universal design makes the environment or product more accessible to *all* people and, in some cases, simpler to use. Readers will no doubt agree that a videocassette recorder that adheres to the principles of universal design and makes recording programs or other functions simple and easily accomplished would, in fact, benefit most of the population—not just individuals with mental retardation!

Given the emphasis of universal design principles on gaining access to environments and products, it seems logical that this principle be applied to assist in understanding how to gain access to curriculum. Researchers at the Center for Applied Special Technology noted

> The basic premise of universal design for learning is that a curriculum should include alternatives to make it accessible and applicable to students, teachers, and parents with different backgrounds, learning styles, abilities, and disabilities in widely varied learning contexts. The "universal" in universal design does not imply one optimal solution for everyone, but rather it underscores the need for inherently flexible, customizable content, assignments, and activities. (1998/1999)

Orkwis and McLane defined *universal design for learning* as "the design of instructional materials and activities that allows the learning goals to be achievable by individuals with wide differences in their abilities to see, hear, speak, move, read, write, understand English, attend, organize, engage, and remember" (1998, p. 9). The application of the values and design principles fundamental to universal design to curriculum planning and decision making communicates that the curriculum must be planned and designed in such a manner that it is accessible by all students, including students with mental retardation. The onus is on curriculum planners and designers to employ principles of universal design to ensure that students with a wide range of capacities can gain access to and advance in the curriculum. Unfortunately, this is too rarely the case, and although retrofitting the curriculum to provide access for all students may be the only option for educators working with students with mental retardation today, a concentrated effort to change the design and planning process is absolutely necessary if fundamental change is to occur. Designing a curriculum that is universally accessible for students with mental retardation is a complex task.

The implementation of the Americans with Disabilities Act (ADA) of 1990 (PL 101-336) posed similar challenges regarding how to provide individuals with disabilities with access to the environment (e.g., work, government services and utilities, transportation) equal to that provided to individuals without disabilities. Although people with mental retardation were clearly among the covered populations identified in the ADA, the law itself provided no specific provisions for people with mental retardation and no specific guidelines for how to achieve accessibility when more than a curb cut was needed. One answer from The Arc's question-and-answer sheet on the ADA illustrates this issue:

> Many individuals with mental retardation do not need special lifts to use public transportation. They might, however, need special assistance from bus drivers in embarking on the right bus and disembarking at the correct location. Bus driver training programs are often essential to successful bus transportation for many people with mental retardation. Another example would be employment-related training for businesses who could be potential employers of workers with mental retardation. (1995)

The idea of providing supports to implement the provisions in the ADA is apparent in this example. Training bus drivers does not change the person with mental retardation but, instead, alters the environment in which he or she lives, works, learns, or plays and, as such, provides the individual with enhanced access to that environment. For example, the Target store chain has provided cognitive supports in line with ADA requirements by implementing a wide array of design changes in their stores. These changes include alterations to the physical environment, such as wider aisles, handrails in restrooms, and wider doors as well as color-coded departments to make navigation through the store easier for people with cognitive disabilities. Other ways that Target implemented the ADA access provisions include making signs more visible and simpler to read or using graphic icons on the signs.

Essentially, principles of universal design must be applied to curriculum development and planning, and it is equally important that accommodations, modifications, and augmentations take into account cognitive access needs and not simply physical or sensory access needs.

CURRICULUM DECISION MAKING

Instead of creating a curriculum for a particular school district or building, teachers and other key stakeholders in the curriculum decision-making process (e.g., students, parents and family members, other educational professionals) should design an individualized education program for each student that takes into account both the student's needs and the general curriculum. To engage in curriculum decision making is to make decisions about the *content* of a student's educational program—the *what* of the educational process. As was indicated in the discussion of curriculum theory, this is an empowering process in which teachers, students, parents and family members, and others are charged with examining the student's functional needs; identifying barriers in the environment (including the curriculum); making decisions about instructional strategies, methods, and materials; and balancing the multiple demands inherent in the educational process for students with mental retardation. Chapter 4 describes a model that IEP teams can use to design educational programs (and make curriculum decisions) that ensure both access to the general curriculum and consideration of individual needs.

DESIGNING EDUCATIONAL SUPPORTS
FOR STUDENTS WITH MENTAL RETARDATION

Although up to now the term *supports* has been used generically, for the remainder of the text the terms *curricular supports* or *educational supports* are used or assumed. This is not because the nature of supports is fundamentally different in educational environments versus other service areas. Rather, the supports, in and of themselves, must be conceptualized within the context of the educational environment or the curriculum. When used as an adjective to modify *supports,* the term *curriculur* is used in its broadest sense as described previously and is generally synonymous with the term *educational supports.*

Jorgensen defined the construct of **natural supports** within the context of education as follows:

> Natural supports for school-age children with disabilities are those components of an educational program—philosophy, policies, people, materials and technology, and curricula—that are used to enable all students to be fully participating members of regular classroom, school, and community life. (1992, p. 183)

The degree to which supports should be natural has been a complex issue in disability services, particularly in providing supported employment for individuals with disabilities. The emphasis on natural supports came about as a reaction to problems with the professionalization of the field of disability services, particularly when the intent of such services was to enhance community inclusion. The emphasis in providing natural supports is that "relying on typical people and environments enhances the potential for inclusion more effectively than relying on specialized services and personnel" (Nisbet, 1992, p. 5). For example, in a natural supports model, a person's co-workers or his or her employer would act as the individual's job coach. The advantages to this are that the person with the disability may be viewed more as a part of the work environment than he or she would be if he or she was accompanied by someone from an external agency, it may be easier to fade levels of intensity of supports, and the person with disabilities may be more fully included in the work environment. The disadvantages are that the co-worker or employer may or may not have time for additional responsibilities or may not have the expertise to provide the individual with disabilities with needed technological support (e.g., task-analyzing a work skill to enable a person to learn the skill).

The AAMR (1992) framework, particularly as it is depicted in Figure 1.2, does not distinguish between natural and other supports, although both the levels of intensities of supports and the constellations of supports exemplified in Figure 1.2 reflect a preference toward natural supports and support designs that focus on enhancing individual capacity and the opportunity to self-direct learning and supports. In discussing the implications of the classification system to the field of education, the authors of the AAMR manual stated that "whereas the purpose of support is to advance and enrich the success of integration... natural, less intrusive supports that are still effective are preferred over artificial supports that may be less reliable or stigmatizing" (1992, p. 119). There should be a similar preference toward less intrusive or stigmatizing means of providing educational supports.

DESIGNING PERSONALIZED CURRICULAR SUPPORTS FOR STUDENTS WITH MENTAL RETARDATION

When discussing the design of curriculum and supports within the context of educating students with mental retardation, it is important to retain a vision of what is appropriate or desired for students with mental retardation. Knowlton (1998) proposed that the design of curricula and personalized curricular supports for students should be driven by the *three Rs* of personalized curricular support plans:

- The support should be *rational* with respect to its reliance on current performance data and future projections.
- It is *responsible* insofar as compliance with statutory policies and ethical principles is concerned.
- It is *responsive* to immediate and long-term issues in the lives of students with disabilities and their family members.

These three Rs "predicate meaningful, effective planning of curricular supports" (Knowlton, 1998, p. 96).

Teachers and administrators believe that a responsible curriculum for students with mental retardation embodies principles of individualization and personalized planning. In special education, this process has been a bottom-up affair, with the curriculum being derived from the instructional needs of the student. In addition, the Individuals with Disabilities Education Act (IDEA) Amendments of 1997 (PL 105-17) and the principles of best practice in the education of students with mental retardation have fostered participatory planning and consensus building among key stakeholders and have been outcomes-oriented. This outcomes orientation is reflected, for example, in the IDEA 1997 transition mandates, which identify a number of outcomes (e.g., employment, post-secondary education, recreation and leisure outcomes) to be derived from transition services. Knowlton described the process of developing appropriate curricular supports as

> [H]inging first on consensus-driven determination, among professionals, family members, and the student with developmental disabilities, of the degree of independence and style of life desired and then, on creative, longitudinal planning through which instructional programs, their goals and objectives, and the settings in which they will be provided are identified and sequenced. (1998, p. 95)

An educational program appropriate for students with mental retardation has been, and should remain, one in which the curriculum is individually designed and implemented with the identification and provision of continuously personalized supports toward the end of maximum independence and the highest quality of life. In addition, however, the starting point for that program needs to be the general curriculum. A discussion of what is meant by the term *general curriculum* and by the mandate to provide access to the general curriculum, and a discussion of ways in which teachers can ensure such access, is provided in Chapter 3. When considering, however, a vision for an appropriate curriculum for students with mental retardation, it is important to address the legitimate concern that this signals a return to a special education emphasis on remediation. The earliest approaches to educating students with mental retardation involved a remedial education focus—an attempt to increase student skills in reading, language arts, writing, and numeracy that, in essence, became a watered-down version of the general curriculum.

Unlike a watered-down version of the general curriculum, with improper emphasis on developmental prerequisites to academic skills, Knowlton (1998) suggested that effective curricular practices center on adult- and community-oriented modifications that can enhance the individual's ultimate functioning as an adult. The use of the general curriculum as a benchmark from which personalized modifications are determined is not for the purposes of thinning it, but rather of personalizing it so that the student is taught in a manner that is keyed to "ultimate independence and lifestyle quality on the basis of rational decisions, responsive programs, and responsible compliance" (Knowlton, 1998, pp. 99–100). For a variety of reasons, many of which are discussed in Chapter 3, engaging students with mental retardation with the general curriculum is a critical feature of an appropriate educational program, not to the exclusion of an individualized, person-centered, functional, and outcomes-oriented focus, but as a starting point for consideration in addressing the individually determined needs of the students.

DESIGNING OR IDENTIFYING EDUCATIONAL SUPPORTS

The design or identification of any support, be it an instructional experience or linking a person with a co-worker to provide support, begins with an assessment. Chapter 7 introduces an *empowerment evaluation* framework that involves the "use of concepts, techniques and findings to foster improvement and self-determination" to drive individual and program assessment activities (Fetterman, 1996, p. 4). According to Fetterman, empowerment evaluation has "an unambiguous value orientation, designed to help people help themselves and improve their programs using a form of self-evaluation and reflection" (p. 5). It is, by necessity, a collaborative group activity with a focal point on the individual as an evaluator as well as an evaluatee, thus emphasizing self-evaluation and self-directed assessment. Similarly, assessment focused on designing or identifying supports needs to have the same unambiguous orientation toward enabling people to help themselves. Such assessment should be future-oriented, should employ multiple measurement techniques that include participant self-report indicators, and should involve key stakeholders in the process.

In addition, such assessments should have ecological validity. If the focus in educating students with mental retardation is on the interaction between functional limitations and the social and environmental context, then assessment needs to evaluate that interaction. Such evaluations examine the demands of the environment; the capacity of the individual to respond to those demands; and the types of actions that could, in essence, close whatever gap exists between those two. Such actions could include modifying the environment to change the demands on the individual to help him or her succeed in that environment, teaching skills to meet the demands of the environment, identifying ways that existing resources or additional resources could help bridge the gap, determining if a particular device could help, and so forth.

Knowlton (1998) noted that a **person-centered planning** approach is one in which individualized supports can be designed. The curriculum decision-making and educational support design process, as conducted by the IEP team, should incorporate components of both person-centered and student-directed planning, as discussed in detail in Chapter 6. However, by way of introduction, Knowlton identified the goals of person-centered approaches as "to recognize the person's abilities and future aspirations and to reach consensus concerning the necessary supports and services" (p. 101). These models provide a structure for cooperative problem solving and decision making and are particularly valuable for identifying educational supports for a number of reasons. Unlike traditional educational decision-making models, the person-centered processes emphasize the active involvement of a wide array of participants in the decision-making process, particularly key stakeholders such as parents or family members and the student him- or herself. Because the concept of educational supports is portrayed as a broad array of resources and strategies that lead to inclusion, the larger number of people involved in the decision-making process increases the potential that a particular support option will be identified. Although the inclusion of, for example, a speech-language therapist on the team might ensure that options related to commercial devices that would augment a communication problem would be explored, it is important not to think only in terms of professional or "expert" input in the support design process. There are a myriad of other resources or strategies that people (e.g., family members, neighbors) can provide that would serve as supports, many of which occur naturally.

A second benefit to a person-centered approach is that, almost without exception, these processes begin with visioning or dreaming activities that emphasize the student's strengths and capacity and focus attention on the hopes and wishes of the student and his or her family. The process focuses on creativity and brainstorming, encouraging participants to try to approach problems from different angles. It is not too hard to imagine that in such a climate, team members might be able to identify more, and more creative, solutions to overcome barriers and provide supports than might otherwise occur. The challenge in the implementation of such processes is to ensure that the general curriculum and its potential is included in the decision-making process.

SUMMARY

This chapter has focused on the underlying theoretical perspectives and overarching principles of curriculum design, curriculum decision making, and the design of educational supports that enable students to receive an appropriate IEP within the context of the general curriculum. If students with mental retardation are to gain access to and progress in the general curriculum, it is necessary that curriculum design and planning efforts embody several theoretical perspectives, particularly that of *universal design*. The implementation of principles of universal design to curriculum access and access to the general curriculum itself are the focus of subsequent chapters. However, it is important to reemphasize the centrality of the *empowerment theory* to this approach. That is, the solution to the problem of how to provide both an appropriate IEP and access to the general curriculum for students with mental retardation lies in enabling teachers (among other key stakeholders) to take a creative, problem-solving approach to curriculum decision making and educational supports design. There are, certainly, standard solutions to problems that could be applied in a template-matching process (e.g., student with certain types of expressive communication disorders can benefit from certain types of alternative communication devices), but in the end such a process is destined to fall short. First, such efforts are almost inevitably deficits-oriented (matching deficits with ways to fix the deficits) and, more important, simply cannot take into account the range of student needs and capacities or the potential resources or strategies that could provide support. The solution to the problem of providing an excellent education for students with mental retardation rests not in standardized processes prescribed by experts in the field but instead in the creative energy of teachers, students, parents and family members, and others involved in curriculum decision making and identification of educational supports.

Unless the curriculum is planned or designed with the principles of universal design in mind, it will be much more difficult to make curriculum decisions and design educational supports within the context of the general curriculum. This text focuses on the microlevel of the IEP decision-making process and the student's educational program. In so doing, the intention is not to negate the importance of macrolevel issues such as curriculum planning and design in the success of students with mental retardation. Educators who provide educational services and supports for students too often do not have the luxury to wait until a curriculum meets their needs and is designed with all students in mind. To the extent that the curriculum-design process too often excludes students with mental retardation, the discipline, as a whole, has become too far removed from the general curriculum.

ADDITIONAL READINGS

Curriculum and Curriculum Design in Education

Doll, R.C. (1996). *Curriculum improvement: Decision making and process* (9th ed.). Needham Heights, MA: Allyn & Bacon.

Glatthorn, A.A. (1995). *Content of the curriculum* (2nd ed.). Alexandria, VA: Association for Supervision and Curriculum Development.

Morrison, G.S. (1993). *Contemporary curriculum K–8*. Needham Heights, MA: Allyn & Bacon.

Tanner, D., & Tanner, L. (1995). *Curriculum development: Theory into practice* (3rd ed.). Upper Saddle River, NJ: Prentice Hall.

Wiggins, G., & McTighe, J. (1999). *Understanding by design*. Alexandria, VA: Association for Supervision and Curriculum Development.

Curriculum Design and Decision Making in Special Education and Mental Retardation

Cipani, E.C., & Spooner, F. (1994). *Curricular and instructional approaches for people with severe disabilities*. Needham Heights, MA: Allyn & Bacon.

Ferguson, D.L. (1987) *Curriculum decision making for students with severe handicaps: Policy and practice*. New York: Teachers College Press.

Hickson, L., Blackman, L.S., & Reis, E.M. (1995). *Mental retardation: Foundations of educational programming*. Boston: Allyn & Bacon.

Sands, D.J., Adams, L., & Stout, D.M. (1995). A statewide exploration of the nature and use of curriculum in special education. *Exceptional Children, 62,* 68–83.

Sands, D.J., Kozleski, E., & French, N. (2000). *Inclusive education in the 21st century*. Belmont, CA: Wadsworth Publishers.

Universal Design in Education

Bowe, F.G. (2000). *Universal design in education: Teaching nontraditional students.* Westport, CT: Bergin & Garvey.

Orkwis, R., & McLane, K. (1998, Fall). *A curriculum every student can use: Design principles for student access.* ERIC/OSEP Topical Brief. Reston, VA: Council for Exceptional Children.

Natural Supports

Bradley, V.J., Ashbaugh, J.W., & Blaney, B.C. (1994). *Creating individual supports for people with developmental disabilities: A mandate for change at many levels.* Baltimore: Paul H. Brookes Publishing Co.

Nisbet, J. (Ed.). (1992) *Natural supports in school, at work, and in the community for people with severe disabilities.* Baltimore: Paul H. Brookes Publishing Co.

CHAPTER OBJECTIVES

1. Define what is meant by the *general curriculum* in the Individuals with Disabilities Education Act (IDEA) Amendments of 1997 (PL 105-17), and discuss factors that contribute to that definition.
2. Discuss the relationship between the access to the general curriculum requirements as stated in the IDEA Amendments of 1997 and standards-based reform.
3. Identify the assumptions of standards-based reform efforts and the positive and negative potential consequences of such reform efforts.
4. Define what is meant by *access to the general curriculum*.

KEY TERMS

General curriculum
Access to the general curriculum
Formal and informal curriculum
Standards-based reform
High-stakes testing

3

Conceptualizing Access to the General Curriculum

HOW MANY STUDENTS ARE FALLING
THROUGH THE CRACKS?

In the first two chapters, this text refers to gaining access to the general curriculum as a desirable outcome for students with mental retardation. This chapter reviews what is meant by the *general curriculum* and, subsequently, what is entailed in gaining access to that curriculum.

Ensuring that students have access to the general curriculum is a key feature of the Individuals with Disabilities Education Act (IDEA) Amendments of 1997 (PL 105-17). In testimony on June 20, 1995, before the U.S. House Committee on Economic and Education Opportunities, Subcommittee on Early Childhood, Youth and Families, then Secretary of Education Richard Riley made the following comments with regard to the Department of Education's then draft proposal for the reauthorization of IDEA:

> Our second principle is to improve results for students with disabilities through higher expectations and access to the general curriculum. We know that most children work harder and do better when more is expected of them—whether it be in the classroom, doing their homework, or doing the dishes. Disabled students are no different. When we have high expectations for students with disabilities, most can achieve to challenging standards—and all can achieve more than society has historically expected. However, not all schools presently have high expectations for these students, and not all schools take responsibility for the academic progress of disabled students.
>
> Our proposal would create an improved IEP process focused on educational results. The new IEP would include meaningful annual objectives for the student. Unless the IEP indicates otherwise, it would focus on access to the general curriculum, in which children with disabilities would have the opportunity to meet the same challenging standards as other students.

Chapter 1 has provided an overview of the impact of changes in the way society defines and views disability on expectations for individuals with disabilities. These same themes of raising expectations clearly were the driving force in the inclusion of language pertaining to access to the general curriculum in the IDEA Amendments of 1997. This was emphasized in the ceremony held at the signing of the amendments, during which a young man with a disability named Joshua Bailey made a few comments. Bailey, who was then a senior in high school, said the following:

> I am someone who insists on having that chance. . . . When I entered high school, I had a discussion with one of my advisors, who said that I should take courses that I could handle easily. I looked him right in the eye and said, "No thanks. I'll take the tough courses and do my best." And I have. Next September, when I return to school, I will take seven classes. They are advanced placement American History, accelerated English III, accelerated Algebra II, accelerated Chemistry, Latin III, Drafting III, and psychology/sociology. Like I said—we can learn. My advisor wasn't trying to put me down. Maybe he was being a little overprotective. Sometimes people just don't understand what we need. [See Appendix A for a transcript of the entire speech.]

The IDEA Amendments of 1997, as passed by Congress, included statutory and regulatory language pertaining to providing access to the general curriculum. Fundamentally, the IDEA amendments of 1997 require that students' IEPs include

- A statement of how the child's disability affects the child's involvement with and progress in the general curriculum

- A statement of measurable goals to enable the child to be involved with and progress in the general curriculum

- A statement of the services, program modifications, and supports necessary for the child to be involved in and progress in the general curriculum

These regulations lead to three logical questions: What is the *general curriculum?* What constitutes *access* to the general curriculum? How is access to the general curriculum achieved for students with disabilities?

WHAT IS THE GENERAL CURRICULUM?

Although there are many meanings to and definitions of the term *curriculum* (see Chapter 2), for the purposes of IDEA, the answer to the question "What is the general curriculum?" seems straightforward. The IDEA regulations state that the term **general curriculum** refers to "the same curriculum as for nondisabled children" (Federal Register, 1999, p. 12592). However, as straightforward as this may appear to be, it does not address the nuances of *curriculum.* For example, does this requirement to ensure access to the "same curriculum as nondisabled children" refer both to the formal and informal aspects of curriculum? Might schools meet these requirements strictly through the informal aspects of curriculum? Certainly the way in which access to the curriculum is achieved depends on whether this refers to both curricular components. The following sections highlight issues to take into account when defining the general curriculum.

Formal versus Informal Curriculum

There are several reasons to believe that the language in IDEA pertaining to **access to the general curriculum** refers, principally, to students having access to the formal curriculum. It is also clear that IDEA 1997 intends that students with disabilities benefit from both formal and informal components of the curriculum.

First, in addition to emphasizing access to the general curriculum as a means of encouraging high expectations for all students with disabilities, IDEA and the subsequent legislation also emphasize measures of accountability and the establishment of high expectations: Students with disabilities are included in state- and districtwide assessments, and IDEA is easily aligned with state and local education improvement efforts. Such assessments almost exclusively focus on the formal curriculum presented to students and not the informal aspects of the curriculum.

Second, IDEA emphasizes educating students with disabilities in the least restrictive environment and states a clear preference for students with disabilities receiving their education in the general classroom. A primary reason for including students with disabilities in general classrooms is that they can experience the benefits of the informal curriculum and the myriad of experiences needed for social competence and community inclusion. Thus, one of the core assumptions of this preference is the importance of gaining access to the informal curriculum. Therefore, although the access to the general curriculum mandate might be interpreted as referring to the formal curriculum, it is clear that in the context of the IDEA mandates that educators need to ensure access to both the **formal and informal curriculum.** Although this text focuses primarily on the formal curriculum in many of the subsequent chapters, it does not advocate for the exclusion of a focus on the informal curriculum. We, the authors, believe that students with mental retardation need to receive their education within the context of the typical classroom and in so doing, have access to the informal curriculum.

Locally Determined General Curriculum

By defining *the general curriculum* as "the same curriculum as for nondisabled children," the federal government kept the definition of *general curriculum* quite broad, even based on the assumption that it refers only to the formal curriculum. This was, no doubt, purposeful because there are strongly held beliefs on the part of some citizens concerning the role of the Department of Education in determining curricular content. The law clearly intends for the general curriculum to be determined locally. Thus, when discussing access to *the* general curriculum, we must regard the *the* as referring to *the local school district's* general (versus specialized) curriculum and not *The* as in *The General Curriculum*, referencing a particular official curriculum or curriculum standard.

Explicit versus Implicit Content

Identifying the formal curriculum as the reference point for defining the general curriculum provides some narrowing of the focus for curriculum decision makers. However, it should be noted that there are both explicit and implied components of the formal curriculum. Practitioners tend to think more in terms of the explicit components, that is, those that are clearly articulated in standards or materials (e.g., learning to work long division problems, identifying state capitals), when thinking of the formal curriculum. Sometimes, however, there are skills, capacities, and knowledge that may not be a specified end but are taught, implicitly, as the means to the end. For example, a sixth-grade standard in science from the *Texas Essential Knowledge and Skills* (TEKS; Texas Education Agency, 1996) science standards states that one important outcome regarding science concepts is that

> The student knows that there is a relationship between force and motion. The student is expected to
> 1. Identify and describe the changes in position, direction of motion, and speed of an object when acted on by force
> 2. Demonstrate that changes in motion can be measured and graphically represented
> 3. Identify forces that shape features of the Earth including uplifting, movement of water, and volcanic activity

The explicit component of this curriculum is that students will understand the concepts of force and motion and gain knowledge about facts pertaining to the relationship between these two constructs. The implicit aspect of the curriculum is that students will learn (or, more likely at this phase, have reinforced) the cognitive and problem-solving skills used in the scientific method. Students learn both about force and motion (i.e., explicit outcomes) and, through the process, how to engage in inquiry through the scientific method (i.e., implicit outcome).

While the informal curriculum is driven primarily by the social milieu or context of the school and is more spontaneous and unplanned, the formal curriculum, including its implicit aspects, is planned. To return to the previous example, teachers are intentional and thoughtful about teaching the scientific process, even in the context of teaching about force and motion. Teachers are aware of the myriad of implicit skills, concepts, and knowledge that are imbedded in the formal curriculum, and it is important for teachers to think in terms of both the explicit and implicit aspects of the formal curriculum as it pertains to gaining access to the general curriculum for students with mental retardation. Although students may have difficulty with achieving all that is circumscribed in the explicit portion of the formal curriculum, through purposeful curriculum decision making and the design of supports, those same students may be able to gain access to the general curriculum by focusing on the implicit components of that curriculum.

Standards-Based School Reform

The final piece of the puzzle to consider when defining the general curriculum is that in most states what is seen as the general curriculum (i.e., the formal curriculum that is provided to all children) is derived from or, at the least, is referenced to state and local performance and content standards. The idea of setting standards as a form of educational reform is not new, but since the focus on establishing national standards on which to base a national assessment in the early 1990s, standards-based reform has become the dominant format for public school improvement efforts in the United States.

Sykes and Plastrik (1993) noted that several meanings of the term *standard* influence the idea of **standards-based reforms**. A *standard* is an exemplar that serves as a measure of value, weight, or some other quality. For example, Greenwich Mean Time is a *standard* for measuring chronological time. *Standard* denotes that an established value, weight, or quality becomes the comparison point for all other similar entities. Setting educational standards, therefore, establishes exemplars with which to compare (e.g., measure) educational progress. The term *standard* also implies correctness or perfection, such as might be found in a religious book of standards (Sykes & Plastrik, 1993). At a similar, though secular, level, the term *standard* is used to refer to the attainment of a level of excellence or a high-quality outcome (Sykes & Plastrik, 1993). "Setting the bar higher," a cliché that refers to raising the bar over which track and field athletes attempt to jump or vault, is a typical cliché associated with establishing standards of excellence or high quality. Fittingly, the mechanisms by which such bars are held aloft are literally referred to as *standards*.

The process of setting standards as a means of facilitating change in the educational system involves the establishment of content or performance outcomes that serve as exemplars of high-quality outcomes of the educational process. The establishment of such standards, the development and implementation of curricula to enable students to attain these standards, and the alignment of standards and curricula with testing to determine student progress toward meeting the standards form the essential components of what is referred to as *standards-based reform*. The Committee on Goals 2000 and the Inclusion of Students with Disabilities (1997), established through the auspices of the Goals 2000: Educate America Act of 1994 (PL 103-227) to "conduct a comprehensive study of the inclusion of children with disabilities in school reforms..." (p. 2), defined *standards-based reform* as "an approach to education reform that sets standards of performance in designated subject areas as a means of strengthening the content of school curricula, increasing the motivation and effort of students, teachers and school systems, and thereby improving student achievement" (p. 253).

It is, however, inaccurate to refer to standards-based reform as if it were a single approach or method of reform. Sykes and Plastrik (1993) identified at least three models of reforms in which standards are applied or utilized—the systemic reform model, the professional model, and the reform network model. The systemic reform model "proposes that policymakers and educators collaborate in developing and coordinating an array of policy instruments aimed at providing firm guidance for teaching and learning" (Sykes & Plastrik, 1993, p. 8). The starting point for such efforts are content standards that "define the curriculum" and performance standards that "define what students should learn" (p. 8). Such standards are then combined, in a variety of ways, with the school's vision and goals; instructional efforts that include curriculum design to achieve these standards; teacher training, ongoing education, and licensure; administrative oversight of instructional activities; and student or teacher assessment or evaluation procedures. Sykes and Plastrik noted several intents or effects of the systemic reform model. The first intent is to direct instructional activities to align with the multiple policy changes, from standards to evaluation. A second intent of such reform is to focus the curriculum to "delimit the work of teachers and students to a manageable core of widely shared learning outcomes" (p. 9). Third, the systemic reform model attempts to change how teachers teach and, thus, what and how children learn. Fourth, systemic reform is intended to motivate students through the linkages between performance outcomes and a "wider array of stakes and postschool futures" (p. 10).

Because the systemic reform model, or at least components of this model, is the dominant school reform agenda in today's school improvement movement, it is worth noting the potential benefits and pitfalls of the intent or effects of the systemic reform model for students with disabilities. The benefits are that students with disabilities would, through such efforts, have access to a challenging curriculum, be held to high expectations, and fall within the accountability system and not excluded or marginalized. In its broadest format, the systemic reform model addresses multiple aspects of the educational experience, from instructional content and strategies to teacher training, and the overarching intent is to change the teaching and learning processes. It is likely that, as a field, educators who work with students with mental retardation could improve instruction if they were provided with ongoing training and support to learn and implement a wide variety of instructional strategies and teaching models.

The pitfalls of the systemic reform model include unintended consequences from the misapplication of systemic reforms or the overemphasis of certain components to the exclusion of others. When **high-stakes testing**—tests that have meaningful, and often serious, consequences for students or educators, such as grade retention or promotion, graduation, loss of school funding, and so forth—is linked to content and performance standards and students, teachers, and schools alike become accountable for improving scores on such tests, the effect of systemic reform efforts could be to substantially narrow the curriculum instead of focusing it. For example, if standards and high-stakes testing emphasize only the core academic content areas, the efforts of teachers, building administrators, and others will be focused primarily on those areas. This may result in the exclusion of other important content areas, such as preparing students for the transition from school to work or addressing other functional needs of students with mental retardation.

In addition, although the premise that higher stakes motivate students to achieve may be applicable for some segments of the school population, for others, the establishment of high stakes may have the opposite effect and may actually limit a student's motivation to stay in school. Implementing high stakes assessments and limiting the curriculum to core content areas may result in even higher dropout rates because students who are already having difficulty with achieving experience more failure, are presented only with options such as being retained or attending weekend or summer school programs, or are excluded from graduation as a result of failure on a high-stakes test. Sykes and Plastrik (1993) noted that high-stakes accountability mechanisms may be a problem for all students, not just for students with disabilities:

> If such standards are attached to powerful stakes such as progress through and graduation from school, admission to higher education and access to employment opportunities and training, the consequences will lay bare and potentially exacerbate our society's continuing, unresolved, and systemic inequities. Furthermore, much evidence indicates that the imposition of external, high-stakes accountability produces negative effects on student motivation and on the character of teaching. (p. 21)

The other two models that fall under the rubric of standards-based reform are what Sykes and Plastrik (1993) referred to as the professional model and the reform network model. The professional model focuses on the development of standards in the licensure and advanced certification of teachers and on program accreditation. This model is more concerned with enhancing professionalism and professional competency through the development of standards than on reforming curriculum or content, per se. The standards developed in the professional model guide how various professionals and support roles are fulfilled and how assessment, curriculum, and instructional practices are implemented with students. Zemelman, Daniels, and Hyde (1993) offered examples of the qualities of professional standards of curriculum that have been recommended for general and special educators who support inclusive education:

- *Authentic and meaningful:* Connects to students' lives, such as dividing pizza or cake rather than working problems in a math textbook
- *Student-centered:* Considers the interests, preferences, concerns, and questions that students bring to the learning context and allows students to apply the skills of choice making, negotiating, conflict resolution, and collaboration to arrive at common ground
- *Experiential:* Incorporates activities that are related to authentic, naturally occurring, real-world experiences through direct or simulated activities rather than through transmission models
- *Foster collaboration and positive relationships among students:* Allows children to learn from and with others, working toward the ability to develop problem-solving skills, social skills, and communication skills
- *Value partial participation:* Values the contributions of all students, even if some students may only be capable of carrying out portions of skills or activities independently

- *Chronologically and developmentally appropriate:* Provides experiences that reflect both age-appropriate materials and goals and an understanding of the students' cognitive, affective, physical, and communicative abilities over time

- *Future oriented:* Provides students with the "big picture" so that they are prepared for future environments, expectations, norms, and rules

- *Focused on self-determination:* Creates clear expectations and opportunities for students to learn how to direct their own learning, understand their strengths and needs, and communicate their choices and needs to others

Once specified, standards for professional practice should be modeled, practiced, and applied to building- and classroom-level curriculum decisions, implementation, and evaluations.

The final standards-based reform model, the reform network model, focuses more attention on the contextual variables associated with learning, including family involvement, the community's commitment to and capacity to support education, and, particularly, the culture or climate of the school. Proponents such as Sarason (1996) and Sizer (1992) approach these reform efforts on a school-by-school and campus-by-campus basis. Instead of creating a standardized system, they focus on schools as organizational entities and emphasize diversity between schools, look for gradual changes that occur by addressing school climates and cultures, and use standards to provide direction for operating schools while leaving plenty of room for individualization (Sykes & Plastrik, 1993).

Standards-Based Reforms and Students with Disabilities

The Committee on Goals 2000 and the Inclusion of Students with Disabilities (1997) reached two conclusions in their analysis of the policy frameworks undergirding the implementation of standards-based reform for all students and for students with disabilities: 1) the expectations of those advocating standards-based reforms currently exceed the limits of existing professional practice and expert knowledge; and 2) the professional and technical problems associated with standards-based reform are compounded when it is melded with special education. These committee members further stated that

> The broad range of people involved in the educational enterprise need to understand and agree on what the phrase "all students can learn to high standards" really means. Survey data from teachers and the public suggest that, at a symbolic level, the idea is accepted. But there is considerably less agreement about its operational meaning—how the idea should be applied to individual students and implemented in classrooms, and what consequences should be imposed for nonattainment of the standards. (p. 66)

The committee recommended several ways to make decisions about designing defensible standards for students with disabilities. Such a decision-making process would need to consider the following:

1. Do content standards represent skills critical to the individual's success once he or she leaves school?

2. Do content standards represent critical skills appropriate for the age of the student?

3. Can the curriculum of the content standards be fully taught to the students without jeopardizing their opportunity to master other critical, functional behaviors?

These three questions are examples of how curriculum planning and design should proceed according to principles of universal design. In their final recommendations, the Committee on Goals 2000 and the Inclusion of Students with Disabilities (1997) further illustrated the need for links between standards/curriculum development and universal design. The committee accepted the principles that all students should have access to challenging standards and that there is merit in an accountability system that includes students with disabilities. States and localities that decide, however, to "implement standards-based reforms should design their common content standards, performance standards, and assessment to maximize participation of students with disabilities" (p. 197).

The committee recommended that although the presumption should be that each student with a disability will participate in the state or local standards, participation for any given student may require alterations to the common standards and assessments. There are, however, several problems with alternative standards. First, there is the perception that *alternative standards* simply means *lower standards*. Many proponents of standards-based reform are not willing to change standards because of the potential for such alterations to begin the slippery slope back to low expectations for student achievement. In addition, there is an inherent contradiction in setting standards as exemplars of high quality and then setting additional or alternative standards.

Finally, the committee recommended that the IEP process should be strengthened to become the formal mechanism for deciding how individual students with disabilities participate in standards-based reforms. The model presented in Chapter 4 illustrates just such a decision-making process.

High-Stakes Testing and Students with Disabilities
As previously implied, perhaps the most difficult component of standards-based reform is the link between standards and high-stakes testing. The consequences of this link are of most concern, particularly for students with disabilities. Because the potentially negative consequences of standards-based reform with high-stakes testing have already been covered, this section concentrates on the degree to which such testing is appropriate at all as a strategy to be employed with students with disabilities. The National Research Council's Board on Testing and Assessment formed a committee, the Committee on Appropriate Test Use (CATU; 1999), to examine the appropriateness of high-stakes testing for all students, including students with disabilities. This committee came to a number of conclusions and recommendations about the use of high-stakes tests for all students. First, they concluded that high-stakes tests should be used only *after* implementing changes in teaching and curriculum that ensure that students have been taught the knowledge and skills that will be tested. Given that a stated intent of standards-based school reform is to change instruction and learning by *first* setting high standards, one cannot assume *a priori* that students have received instruction that ensures that they have been taught the particular content or skill area. The committee's report states this by recommending that "a test may appropriately be used to lead curricular reform, but it should not also be used to make high stakes decisions about individual students until test users can show that the test measures what they have been taught" (1999, p. 278).

In addition, CATU recommended that scores from large-scale assessments should never be the only source of information used to make promotion, retention, or other high-stakes decisions and that the consequences of doing poorly on tests should not be limited to simple either-or options (e.g., graduation, retention); instead, poor performances should indicate a need to focus on early intervention and remediation strategies. Specifically with regard to students with disabilities, the committee suggested that more research is needed to find methods for enabling students with disabilities to participate in large-scale assessments in ways that provide valid information. The committee expressed concern over the validity of using high-stakes or statewide accountability tests with students with disabilities, who rarely are included in norming samples. After expressing the need for accommodations and individualized interpretations of scores, the committee noted, "Because a test score may not be a valid representation of the skills and achievements of students with disabilities, high stakes decisions about these students should consider other sources of evidence, such as grades, teacher recommendations, and other examples of student work" (1999, p. 295).

The findings from both the Committee on Goals 2000 and the Inclusion of Students with Disabilities, which examined standards-based reform for students with disabilities, and CATU, which examined the inclusion of students with disabilities in high-stakes testing, are remarkably similar: Little is known about the impact of using standards-based reform to drive educational reform for students with disabilities, and the risks inherent in combining standards with high-stakes testing seem evident and potentially quite harmful.

This text proceeds, therefore, under the belief that the issue of access to the general curriculum needs to be separated from high-stakes testing in order to ensure both access to a challenging curriculum and an individualized instructional program. The establishment of high standards for all students, although admittedly vague, does not hold the threat inherent in high-stakes testing, especially if these standards are developed with an eye toward universal design. Holding students to high expectations through the establishment of content or performance standards can, presumably, bring positive changes to education if those standards bear in mind issues of functional needs and flexibility and are not yoked to high-stakes testing over a narrow curricular domain.

IDEA and its amendments do not speak to this separation and, indeed, require that all children be included with adequate modifications in general state and local assessments or included in the accountability process through an alternate assessment. However, ensuring both access to the general curriculum and to a truly individualized education is consistent with the intent of IDEA, while sacrificing the latter in the name of high-stakes testing seems inconsistent. Decisions about student participation in testing, test modifications, and accountability through alternate assessment processes are to be made by the IEP team and should be a component of the design of educational supports.

WHAT CONSTITUTES ACCESS TO THE GENERAL CURRICULUM?

Turning our attention to the meaning of *access*, it would seem apparent to any educator who has examined state or local performance standards, administered assessments driven by such standards, or who is familiar with the general curriculum that there are standards that some students with mental retardation simply will not attain, regardless of high or low expectations. Although such standards vary widely from state to state, they often involve learning complex constructs and applying higher order cognitive skills and strategies. Is it the intent of the federal law that the educational program of a student with disabilities start and stop with the general curriculum?

For a variety of reasons, the obvious answer to this must be *no*. First, imposing an externally mandated curriculum on students with disabilities flies in the face of the IEP requirements for students with disabilities mandated in IDEA. Individualization is a hallmark of disability policy in the United States (Turnbull & Turnbull, 2000), and a focus on educational supports and services to meet each student's unique educational needs is at the core of IDEA and special education practice. Knowlton, calling individualization a "tenet of special education as old as the field itself" (1998, p. 96), succinctly stated that "a curriculum appropriate to the needs of students with developmental disabilities is one from which programs are personalized continuously for any one student toward the ends of maximum independence and the highest possible lifestyle quality" (p. 95).

A student's educational program, then, is intended to be individually determined on the basis of unique learning needs and driven by the locally determined general curriculum. The regulations for the 1997 amendments to IDEA address this by noting that

> [A] description of how a child's involvement in the general curriculum is a statutory requirement and cannot be deleted. The requirement is important because it provides the basis for determining what accommodations the child needs in order to participate in the general curriculum *to the maximum extent appropriate* [italics added]. (Federal Register, 1999, p. 12592)

In an additional comment related to the statutory language pertaining to access to the general curriculum, the regulations for the 1997 amendments to IDEA stated:

> In order to ensure full access to the general curriculum, it is not necessary to amend [the statutory language] to clarify that a child's involvement in the general curriculum must be to the "maximum extent appropriate to the needs of the child." The individualization of the IEP process, together with the new requirements related to the general curriculum, should ensure that such involvement and progress is "to the maximum extent appropriate to the needs of the child." (Federal Register, 1999, p. 12592)

It is clear that IDEA intended that an appropriate educational program for students with disabilities involves the design of an IEP that is derived from the general curriculum to the maximum extent appropriate. The decision regarding what is *appropriate* should be made by the IEP team. For purposes of the current discussion, the word *maximum* should be emphasized as much as the word *appropriate*. The clear mandate is to maximize the students' interaction with the general curriculum. Section 300.347(a)(3) in IDEA 1997 requires that the IEP include the following:

> A statement of the special education and related services and supplementary aids and services to be provided to the child, or on behalf of the child, and a statement of the program modifications or supports for school personnel that will be provided for the child
>
> i. to advance appropriate toward attaining the annual goals;
> ii. to be involved and progress in the general curriculum;
> iii. to be educated and participate with disabled and nondisabled children.... (Federal Register, 1999, p. 12592)

Of course, the mandate to consider involvement *to the maximum extent* is no assurance of actual involvement. One only has to note that the language in IDEA 1997 pertaining to removal from the general classroom states that each child should be educated with typically developing children "to the maximum extent appropriate"; however, it remains the case that most students with mental retardation are removed from the general classroom most of the time (Report to Congress on the Implementation of IDEA, 1999).

Where Is Access to the Curriculum Provided?

At the risk of oversimplifying more than 15 years of research, model programs, strategies, and policy efforts to promote inclusion, the overwhelming emphasis in the movement toward inclusion has been on the *place* where students receive their education. There remains a critical need to address the issue of place in the education of students with disabilities. Technically speaking, however, the mandate to provide access to the general curriculum does not speak to the issue of place but instead focuses the question of educational merit on *what*. A student may have access to the general curriculum in environments other than the general classroom. And, although this is not inaccurate as a legal stance, this does not appear to be the intent of the U.S. Department of Education, which emphasizes that students with mental retardation can and should be provided access to the general curriculum through the general education classroom. Nevertheless, it is time to move the discussion from *where* to *what* by answering the *where* question as, to paraphrase IDEA 1997's definition of the general curriculum, the same *educational environment* as for nondisabled children.

HOW IS ACCESS TO THE GENERAL CURRICULUM ACHIEVED?

The regulations to the 1997 amendments to IDEA use the term *access to the general curriculum;* the statutory language in IDEA 1997 does not. Instead, the law itself states that educational services, supports, modifications, and goals should ensure that students *progress* in the general curriculum. Just as research has shown, over the years, that a student's presence in the classroom does not guarantee that he or she will be meaningfully included (e.g., part of the social network), so too should the field note that simply having access to the general curriculum is likely insufficient. IEP teams are charged with ensuring a student's progress in the general curriculum and not just documenting the presence of the curriculum in a student's educational program.

Gaining Access to the General Curriculum

The key components to ensure that students with mental retardation gain access to and progress in the general curriculum, as well as the chapters in this book that address these specific components, include the following:

1. The implementation of a planning process to ensure that the design of a student's IEP is based on the general curriculum, takes into account the student's unique

learning needs (e.g., curriculum decision making; Chapter 4) and involves key stakeholders as meaningful partners (Chapters 5, 6, and 10)

2. The schoolwide implementation of universally designed curricular materials (Chapter 16) and high-quality instructional methods and strategies that challenge all students (Chapters 8 and 9)

3. The implementation of instructional decision-making activities focused at the lesson, unit, and classroom level to ensure that students can progress in the curriculum (Chapter 4)

4. The design and implementation of additional curricular content and instructional strategies to ensure progress for students with learning needs that are not met by schoolwide efforts (Chapters 11, 12, 13, 14, and 15)

5. The implementation of student and program evaluation processes that focus on personal outcomes (Chapter 6)

Figure 3.1 summarizes the key elements of these components, which involve three levels of action (i.e., planning, curriculum, and instruction) that are affected by three

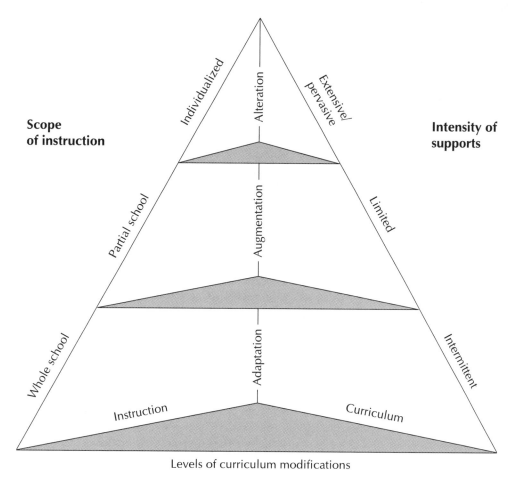

Figure 3.1.   Multilevel focus for gaining access to the general curriculum.

levels of intensities of supports (i.e., intermittent, limited, and extensive/pervasive), three levels of scope of instruction (i.e., whole school, partial school, and individualized), and three levels of curriculum modifications (i.e., adaptation, augmentation, and alteration). The subsequent chapters, as referenced previously, provide detail to implement this course of action. (Appendix B includes a fact sheet on access to the general curriculum that reflects part of the framework suggested in this text.)

SUMMARY

We have suggested that the mandate in the 1997 amendments to IDEA to provide access to the general curriculum stands with the act's emphasis on inclusion to require that educators take into account all aspects of both the formal and informal curriculum; however, the mandate for access to the general curriculum is more applicable to the formal curriculum. The formal aspect of the curriculum includes that which is both explicit and implicit, the latter of which may be particularly important for gaining access for students with mental retardation. The general curriculum is clearly intended to be locally determined, and IDEA 1997 clearly mandates that students should progress in the general curriculum. The challenge is to ensure that students with mental retardation gain access to and progress in the general curriculum while still receiving an education that meets their unique learning needs. Chapter 4 introduces a decision-making process that enables IEP teams to accomplish this.

ADDITIONAL READINGS

Access to the General Curriculum

Association for Supervision and Curriculum Development. (2000). *Educating students with disabilities*. Alexandria, VA: Author. (An ASCD InfoBrief available at http://www.ascd.org/frame-infobrief.html).

Standards-Based Reform

Northwest Regional Education Laboratory. (1999). *Catalog of school reform models*. Portland, OR: Author. (Available: http://www.nwrel.org/scpd/natspec/catalog/index.html).

Ohanian, S. (1999). *One size fits few: The folly of educational standards*. Portsmouth, NH: Heinemann.

Rothman, R. (1995). *Measuring up: Standards, assessment, and school reform*. San Francisco: Jossey-Bass.

Tucker, M.S., & Codding, J.B. (1998). *Standards for our schools: How to set them, measure them, and reach them*. San Francisco: Jossey-Bass.

U.S. Department of Education. (1983). *A nation at risk: The imperative for educational reform*. Washington, DC: Author. (Available: http://www.ed.gov/pubs/NatAtRisk/index.html).

U.S. Department of Education. (1993). *School-based reform: Lessons from a national study. A guide for school reform teams*. Washington, DC: Author. (Available: http://www.ed.gov/ pubs/Reform/index.html).

U.S. Department of Education. (1997). *Standards: Making them useful and workable for the education enterprise*. Washington, DC: Author. (Available: http://www.ed.gov/pubs/Standards/).

Standards-Based Reform and Students with Disabilities

Committee on Goals 2000 and the Inclusion of Students with Disabilities. (1997). *Educating one and all: Students with disabilities and standards-based reform.* Washington, DC: National Academy Press.

Glatthorn, A.A., & Craft-Trip, M. (2000). *Standards-based learning for students with disabilities.* Larchmont, NY: Eye on Education.

High-Stakes Testing

Committee on Appropriate Test Use (1999). *High stakes.* Washington, DC: National Research Council.

Sacks, P. (1999). *Standardized minds: The high price of America's testing culture and what we can do to change it.* Cambridge, MA: Perseus Books.

Appendix A

REMARKS OF JOSHUA BAILEY AT THE INDIVIDUALS WITH DISABILITIES EDUCATION ACT AMENDMENTS SIGNING CEREMONY, JUNE 4, 1997

Thank you, Assistant Secretary Heumann. I enjoyed your remarks about your mother. I'm proud of my mother, too. And I would like you all to meet her, as well as my sister, Sarah.

Mr. President, Secretary Riley, members of Congress, ladies and gentlemen: My fellow students here today are deeply honored to represent America's disabled students at this historic ceremony. We thank you for giving us the opportunity to get a good education and to have a bright future. I know that in years to come, we will make you very proud of us. We want you to know that we can learn, and learn just as well as anybody. All we need is the appropriate help and the chance.

I am someone who insists on having that chance. I have a learning disability called dyslexia. Learning disabilities account for over half of all disabilities served by IDEA. When I entered high school, I had a discussion with one of my advisors, who said that I should take courses that I could handle easily. I looked him right in the eye and said, "No thanks. I'll take the tough courses and do my best." And I have. Next September, when I return to school, I will take seven classes. They are advanced placement American History, accelerated English III, accelerated Algebra II, accelerated Chemistry, Latin III, Drafting III, and psychology/sociology. Like I said—we can learn. My advisor wasn't trying to put me down. Maybe he was being a little overprotective. Sometimes people just don't understand what we need.

As one teacher said about me, "He's the first dyslexia student I've ever taught." I think I was the first one she ever knew about. But I have found that teachers and others are willing to learn. They have good hearts, and they want to help—they just need to know how. I think IDEA will help make that possible. Most importantly, it will let people know that we exist. It will tell them that we can learn to higher standards if we get what we need and if principals, teachers, parents, and students all work together.

The IDEA will be especially helpful to teachers, and I know from my own experience how important that is. I held an inservice program on dyslexia for general education teachers, and I know what a terrific job teachers can do when they have the right tools. Ladies and gentlemen, it is my prayer that all students—regardless of their abilities and disabilities—will have the opportunity to succeed and become contributors to this great nation.

(From U.S. Department of Education, Office of Special Education web page. Available: http://www.ed.gov/offices/OSERS/IDEA/speech_3.html.)

Appendix B

CURRICULUM ACCESS AND
UNIVERSAL DESIGN FOR LEARNING

What Is Curriculum Access?

Under the 1997 IDEA reauthorization, all students, regardless of their abilities, must be given the opportunity to become involved with and progress in the general education curriculum. Every student must have access to what is being taught. Providing access, however, involves much more than supplying every student with a textbook or a computer. Teachers must ensure that students are actively engaged in learning; that is, the subject matter is cognitively challenging them, regardless of their developmental level.

Students with disabilities can be blocked from this interaction because of an inflexible text that may inadvertently create physical, sensory, affective, or cognitive barriers. Even though they may have the same tools as everyone else, they do not truly have equal access to the curriculum. But there are several strategies educators can employ to give these students access, including using a curriculum that has been universally designed for accessibility.

What Is Universal Design for Learning?

To accommodate students' individual needs and to give them the opportunity to progress in content areas, educators traditionally have adapted or altered the textbook or tests. Typical accommodations are Braille or recorded texts for visually impaired students, captioned materials for hearing-impaired students, and customized supplementary materials or alternative texts that address cognitive disabilities. In most classrooms, these accommodations are added to the standardized curriculum much as a wheelchair ramp is added to a building where stairs formerly provided the only access.

Just as after-the-fact architectural accommodations are often awkward and expensive, after-the-fact curriculum adaptations can be time consuming to design and difficult to implement in classrooms of diverse learners. A more efficient way to provide student access is to consider the range of user abilities at the design stage of the curriculum and incorporate accommodations at that point. This "built-in" access for a wide range of users, those with and without disabilities, is the underlying principle in universal design.

In terms of curriculum, universal design implies a design of instructional materials and activities that allows learning goals to be attainable by individuals with wide differ-

This ERIC Digest publication was written by Raymond Orkwis. ERIC Digests are in the public domain and may be freely reproduced and disseminated. This publication was prepared with funding from the U.S. Department of Education, Office of Special Education Programs (OSEP), under Contract No. ED-99-CO-0026. The opinions expressed in this report do not necessarily reflect the positions or policies of OSEP or the Department of Education.

ences in their abilities to see, hear, speak, move, read, write, understand English, attend, organize, engage, and remember. Such a flexible, yet challenging, curriculum gives teachers the ability to provide each student access to the subject area without having to adapt the curriculum repeatedly to meet special needs.

The essential features of universal design for learning have been formulated by the Center for Applied Special Technology (CAST) into three principles:

- The curriculum provides multiple means of representation. Subject matter can be presented in alternate modes for students who learn best from visual or auditory information, or for those who need differing levels of complexity.

- The curriculum provides multiple means of expression to allow students to respond with their preferred means of control. This accommodates the differing cognitive strategies and motor-system controls of students.

- The curriculum provides multiple means of engagement. Students' interests in learning are matched with the mode of presentation and their preferred means of expression. Students are more motivated when they are engaged with what they are learning.

How Is Universal Design for Learning Being Implemented?

Teachers who want to begin implementing universal design must begin by using curricular materials that are flexible. Although digital materials are not the only way to deliver a universally designed curriculum, they allow the greatest flexibility in presentation. They can be easily customized to accommodate a wide range of student abilities, but the teacher and the students must know how to use them. The mere presence of good software programs in the classroom does not guarantee that they will provide needed access.

The access provided by universal design for instructional materials does not mean that students are accommodated by lowering the standards, finding "the least common denominator," or otherwise "dumbing down" the curriculum. In fact, the curriculum must remain at a sufficient level of difficulty if students are to progress in it. For example, a software program for beginning readers can have different settings for the speed at which the information is presented and highlighted (multiple representations). It can be controlled with vocal commands, single switch controls, or alternate keyboards (multiple expressions). It can request different levels of feedback from students, from having them repeat the sounds of letters and words to creating their own stories using the vocabulary words they've learned (multiple engagements). These accommodations allow the necessary flexibility for student access and the necessary challenge for learning.

Is There Support for a Universal Design Curriculum?

Many teachers are already working in environments with varying degrees of inclusiveness, effectively teaching students with and without disabilities in the same classroom. Many general and special educators now collaborate on curriculum and prepare adaptations for special needs in their classes. These teachers have already taken the first step toward implementing universal design goals in their classrooms.

As the demographics of classrooms continue to change and there is more need for adapted materials, curriculum developers, particularly those who produce instructional software, are considering the advantages of universal design. With the federal government and states pushing for schools to incorporate more technology-based teaching tools in the classroom, understanding the foundations of universal design for curriculum access can help guide teachers into implementation.

How Can I Find Out More about Universal Design for Learning?

Several groups are working on universal design issues as they relate to curriculum access:

- CAST is an educational organization that explores how technology can be used to expand opportunities for all people, including those with disabilities. Their web site contains much information about universal design for learning and accessibility, including an elaboration of the three essential curricular principles of universally designed curricula. CAST, 39 Cross Street, Suite 201, Peabody, MA 01960; 978-531-8555; e-mail: cast@cast.org; http://www.cast.org.

- The ERIC/OSEP Special Project of the ERIC Clearinghouse on Disabilities and Gifted Education (ERIC EC) has published *A Curriculum Every Student Can Use: Design Principles for Student Access,* a topical brief on universal design for learning. It is available from the Clearinghouse or on the Internet at http://ericec.org/osep/udesign.htm. ERIC Clearinghouse on Disabilities and Gifted Education, 1920 Association Drive, Reston, VA 21091-1589; 800-328-0272.

- *Research Connections* is a biannual review of special education research sponsored by the U.S. Department of Education's Office of Special Education Programs (OSEP) and published by ERIC EC. The Fall 1999 issue focuses on universal design and access to the general education curriculum. A related issue, from Fall 1998, describes research in integrating technology in the curriculum to improve opportunities for students with learning disabilities. These free publications can be requested from the Clearinghouse or found at its web site.

- The Trace Center is a research, development, and resource center that focuses on increasing access to computers and information technologies for people with disabilities. The Center's web site includes a section called "Designing a More Usable World," which employs universal design features. Trace Research & Development Center, University of Wisconsin–Madison, 5901 Research Park Boulevard, Madison, WI 53719-1252; (608) 262-6966; e-mail: web@trace.wisc.edu; http://trace.wisc.edu.

- EASI (Equal Access to Software and Information) is a project of the Teaching, Learning, and Technology Group, an affiliate of the American Association for Higher Education. EASI provides information and guidance in the area of access-to-information technologies by individuals with disabilities. In conjunction with the Rochester Institute of Technology, EASI conducts online workshops on access issues. Contact EASI c/o TLT Group, PO Box 18929, Rochester, NY 14618; (716) 244-9065; e-mail: easi@tltgroup.org; http://www.rit.edu/~easi/.

CHAPTER OBJECTIVES

1. Identify curricular modifications to promote access to the general curriculum.
2. Discuss how to determine an appropriate education for students with mental retardation.
3. Apply a decision-making model to enable IEP teams to make decisions about an appropriate education program for students with mental retardation.
4. Identify instructional strategies that provide ways to adapt the curriculum.
5. Identify self-regulation, self-management, and student-directed learning strategies that can be employed to augment the curriculum.

KEY TERMS

Curriculum adaptation
Curriculum augmentation
Curriculum alteration
Appropriate education
  program
Assistive technology
Content enhancement
Teaching devices
Advance organizers
Scaffolding
Social-constructivist
  model

Learning strategies
Self-regulation
Self-management
Student-directed learning
Self-instruction
Self-monitoring
Self-evaluation
Self-reinforcement
Self-determination

4

Achieving Access to the General Curriculum

MRS. KING SPORTS HER
WORN SOFTBALL CAP AS A REMINDER
THAT INDIVIDUALIZING TO MEET
UNIQUE STUDENT NEEDS IS
OLD HAT TO GOOD TEACHERS.

C hapter 3 identifies the key components for ensuring that students with mental retardation gain access to and progress in the general curriculum. Because designing the student's formal curriculum should be the first step in the education process, the first activity is the implementation of a planning process to ensure that a student's educational program is designed on the basis of the general curriculum, takes into account the student's unique learning needs, and involves key stakeholders as meaningful partners. This chapter introduces a decision-making model that provides a framework for individualized education program (IEP) teams to use to make curriculum decisions. This model employs three components of curriculum decision making—curriculum adaptation, augmentation, and alteration—that enable IEP teams to ensure that a student's educational program is driven by both the general curriculum and the student's unique needs and provides an overview of strategies for adapting, augmenting, and altering curriculum. Chapter 5 provides greater detail about the IEP team and the IEP process, including the identification of other educational supports.

CURRICULUM MODIFICATIONS TO ENSURE ACCESS

When three levels of curriculum modifications, *adaptation, augmentation,* and *alteration,* are considered on a step-by-step basis, they provide a framework to support IEP teams in making curriculum decisions. The purpose of curriculum modification is to "more closely *align* the cognitive, affective, communicative, and physical/health demands of *the curriculum to the capacities, strengths, and needs of students*" (Sands, Kozleski, & French, 2000, p. 70; italics added).

Although the term *modification* is used, each level of modification does not involve changing the content of the curriculum. In fact, the first two levels of modification discussed—adaptation and augmentation—do not change content at all; rather, they change the way that content is represented in the material, the way that the content is presented by the teacher, and the way that students engage with and respond to the material, in addition to adding or expanding the curriculum to ensure success. It should be reemphasized that the current discussion refers not to *instructional* decision making or implementation but to levels of *curriculum* modification that enable students to receive as much content from the general curriculum as possible before altering the content to include unique or individually determined needs.

Curriculum Adaptation

Curriculum adaptation refers to any effort to modify the representation or presentation of the curriculum or to modify the student's engagement with the curriculum to enhance access and progress. Orkwis and McLane noted that

> Access to the curriculum begins with a student being able to interact with it to learn. For students with disabilities, an inability to interact with the curriculum, because of physical, sensory, or cognitive barriers, can be the first stumbling block on the path toward the goal of competence. (1998, p. 1)

Adapting the way that curriculum content is represented refers to modifying the way in which the information in the curriculum is depicted or portrayed. Most curriculum content is delivered in print, usually textbooks, workbooks, and worksheets. There are a number of ways to change that representation, including changing font size and using graphics. For example, students who have difficulty with reading and comprehending large blocks of text might benefit from changing that same information into an outline, depicting information in more manageable chunks, or highlighting key elements in the text.

Using Internet-based technologies to represent information has considerable utility. When students are provided with information on a web site instead of in a textbook, they can alter the size or color of the font themselves using their browser, or, often, such information can be more easily adapted to provide graphic, pictorial, or iconic representations. In addition, key themes, words, or ideas can be hyperlinked on web sites, leading students to yet another layer of information about that topic. Such adaptations are presented in Chapter 16.

Adaptations in curriculum presentation modify the way teachers convey or impart information. Historically, curriculum presentation has been through written (e.g., chalkboards, overheads) or verbal (e.g., lectures) formats. These primary means of presentation have drawbacks for many students who read ineffectively, do not read at all, or have difficulty with attending to or understanding lecture formats. There are a variety of ways to change the presentation mode, from using film or video sources, to reading or playing an audiotape of written materials, to providing web-based information through the use of text-reader programs, to providing digitized audio or video transmissions that accompany whatever representation means is used.

Curriculum adaptations also alter the ways in which students engage with and respond to the curriculum. The most typical means of student engagement within the curriculum involve written responses, such as worksheets or exams, or, perhaps less frequently, oral responses or reports. However, students may respond to or engage the curriculum in a number of other ways, including "artwork, photography, drama, music, animation, and video" (Center for Applied Special Technology, 1998–1999), that would enable students to express their ideas and demonstrate their knowledge.

Curriculum Augmentation

Curriculum augmentation involves enhancing the standard curriculum with "metacognitive or executive processing strategies for acquiring and generalizing the standard curriculum" (Knowlton, 1998, p. 100). Knowlton identified several augmentation practices, including target cognition (Belmont & Mitchell, 1987; Borkowsi, Weyhing, & Turner, 1986) and self-regulation (Mithaug, 1993; Schunk & Zimmerman, 1994, 1998). These augmentations do not change the curriculum but, rather, add to or augment the curriculum to provide students with strategies for success. Subsequent sections explore self-directed learning strategies, self-management, and self-regulation strategies as essential components of gaining access to the general curriculum.

Far and away the most visible means of providing access to the general curriculum for students with disabilities are technology based. These adaptations can benefit students with mental retardation as well but in and of themselves are not sufficient to ensure access to and progress in the curriculum. Instead these *adaptations* must occur parallel with curriculum *augmentation,* in which students are taught how to problem solve, make decisions, self-regulate and self-manage behavior, and so forth.

Curriculum Alteration

The final option available to curriculum decision makers is **curriculum alteration**. Knowlton (1998) identified life skills curricula and vocational curricula (i.e., career/vocational education, work study) as examples of alternative curricula. Knowlton also noted that "while it is tempting to view an altered curriculum as a 'functional curriculum,' any curricular plan for a student with developmental disabilities must function ultimately as the delineation of knowledge and skills necessary for maximum independence and lifestyle quality" (p. 100). In essence, the challenge is to use curriculum adaptation and augmentation practices combined with instructional decision making and the design of educational supports to make the general curriculum functional, a process made easier when that curriculum is planned or designed with the principles of universal design in mind. Although an altered (or, quite frequently, an alternative) curriculum is the most common modification made in the education of students with mental retardation, most alternative curricula are not designed in adherence with principles of universal design and, in essence, serve as a barrier to access. As discussed previously, it is not the intent of the 1997 IDEA amendments that students with mental retardation should have "access to the general curriculum" at the cost of an appropriate education. As such, there may be circumstances under which curriculum alteration should occur. However, such alterations should be made within the context of age-appropriate, inclusive environments. For example, a student who still needs to learn to tie his or her shoes when his or her peers have already mastered such a task can do so in the naturally occurring context of dressing before and after gym class.

A MODEL TO PROMOTE ACCESS TO AND PROGRESS IN THE GENERAL CURRICULUM

The model depicted in Figure 4.1 is a flowchart that IEP teams can use to make decisions about a student's educational program. The flowchart includes input from the two primary contributors to an *appropriate* education program: the general curriculum, typically determined by state or local standards, and an individually determined curriculum, which is derived from a student's unique needs. The idea of an **appropriate education program** is one that has been an integral part of the public law mandating equal access for students with disabilities. In fact, one of the original purposes of the Education for All Handicapped Children Act of 1975 (PL 94-142) was to codify the position that all students with disabilities have a right to a free, appropriate public education (Turnbull & Turnbull, 2000). What defines an *appropriate education* can vary. Turnbull and Turnbull (2000) noted that IDEA itself defines an *appropriate education* as special education and related services that 1) are provided at public expense, under public direction and supervision, and without charge; 2) meet the standards of the state education agency; and 3) include appropriate preschool, elementary school, and secondary school education.

IDEA's definition of an *appropriate education* is, in essence, a procedural one. An appropriate education is one that conforms to IDEA's process that, the presumption is, will produce an acceptable result for the student. In a landmark decision regarding exactly what constituted an *appropriate education,* the Supreme Court determined in Board of Education v. Rowley (1982) that an appropriate education, as mandated by

IDEA, did not equate with the outcome of maximum benefit or achievement for students. However, the court also indicated that "it would do little good for Congress to spend millions of dollars in providing access to a public education only to have the handicapped child receive no benefit from that education" (Turnbull, 1986, p. 279).

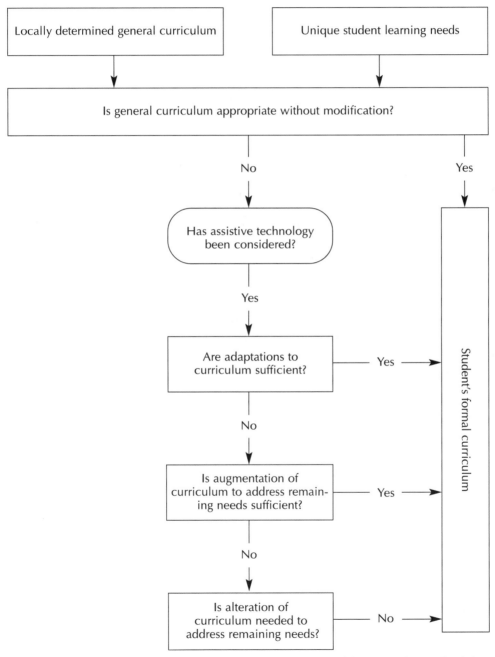

Figure 4.1. A model for designing general curricula to allow students with mental retardation access to the general curriculum.

As such, in the Board of Education v. Rowley (1982) decision, the Supreme Court set a standard for an *appropriate education* as being one from which a student might derive some benefit. The court decision does not require proof of benefit but instead requires proof that the process in IDEA was implemented and services and supports were provided in such a manner that the individually determined program can be said to have been designed to provide educational benefit.

Another definition of an appropriate education, also derived from IDEA, is an *individualized education*. Under IDEA, each student must have an IEP (in kindergarten through 12th grade) or an individualized family service plan (IFSP; if he or she is in preschool) that meets the student's educational or learning needs. This sense of *appropriate* coupled with *individualized* is also found in the Rowley decision and provides further confirmation that the value for individualization in curriculum decision making for students with mental retardation cannot and should not be abandoned. In all, the appropriate education program identified in Figure 4.1 embodies the intent of both IDEA and the Rowley case for an IEP while still providing access to the general curriculum.

The model in Figure 4.1 contains a number of assumptions that underlie its use. First, it assumes the presence of a *general curriculum* that describes the formal content (the *what* of the educational experience) for all students. Until the advent of the national focus on standards-based reform, many states and local districts did not have a general curriculum, and often the curriculum they had was synonymous with or determined by instructional materials (e.g., textbooks, workbooks). This situation seems less likely now, as virtually all state education agencies have developed or are in the process of developing state standards or benchmarks intended to drive school reform efforts.

The model in Figure 4.1 does not, however, assume that the general curriculum is designed with the needs of a diverse student population in mind. Although it is necessary to design curricula according to principles of universal design so that all students can benefit, the decision-making model in Figure 4.1 does not rely on the existence of a universally designed curriculum.

The decision-making process outlined in the model in Figure 4.1 *begins* with the general curriculum and takes into account individual student needs. Most models for curriculum decision making for students with mental retardation begin not with the general curriculum but, instead, with individually determined content needs. In some cases, efforts are made to overlay or map these individually determined needs onto the general curriculum or, more frequently, fit them into the routine of the typical school day. Often, the result from this is an alternative curriculum that does not coincide with the general curriculum. If this alternative curriculum is of high quality, this may not be overly problematic. When the alternative curriculum is of questionable quality and based on low expectations and stereotypes, however, simply mapping a student's individual needs onto the general routine of the day does not raise expectations for the student or ensure access to a challenging curriculum. By beginning with the general curriculum, then working through the three levels of modifications suggested, IEP teams will work from high standards and high expectations toward individualization.

The model assumes that students vary according to the degree to which they require curriculum modifications. For some students, the general curriculum is the most appropriate *formal curriculum* without modification. Other students need curriculum adaptations in addition to schoolwide adaptations to progress, whereas others need a combination of adaptations and curriculum augmentation. Finally, some students need a combination of all three curriculum modifications to succeed. When making decisions about adaptation, augmentation, and alteration, both the content and demands of the curriculum and the needs and strengths of the student must be considered.

The model outlined in Figure 4.1 incorporates the mandate given in the IDEA Amendments of 1997 that **assistive technology (AT)** be considered for all students with disabilities. AT is important at two levels. Obviously, the use of AT devices is a primary focus in the design of curriculum adaptations. Before using it as a means to adapt the curriculum, however, AT might be used to *remove* the barrier that is introduced by a disability and, in turn, negate the need to adapt the curriculum. For example, providing large-print materials is a curriculum adaptation in that it changes something about the curriculum itself (i.e., the representation of the information by larger text size). However, if through an assistive device, even one as simple as eyeglasses, the student is enabled to *see* typical size print, the use of AT provides access to the curriculum without engaging in curriculum modifications.

By linking the use of AT to the curriculum decision-making process, decisions about technology-based supports can be grounded in individual student needs *and* in the general curriculum—not just in one or the other. This is an important component for students with mental retardation, who often do not have access to technology that is cognitively accessible (Wehmeyer, 1998, 1999). The consideration of AT needs to be a part of the decision-making process related to other components of the educational program as well, such as student involvement in standardized testing, student age of majority mandates, and other IEP team decisions discussed in Chapter 5.

STRATEGIES FOR ADAPTING THE CURRICULUM

As stated previously, curriculum adaptations are efforts to change the representation or presentation of the curriculum or to modify a student's engagement with the curriculum to enhance his or her access and progress. Technology-driven ways to adapt the curriculum are discussed in Chapter 16. Beyond the use of technology to make adaptations, a number of strategies warrant consideration.

Orkwis and McLane (1998) provided examples of curriculum adaptations in curricular presentation and representation as well as in student engagement. For example, one adaptation these authors recommended to address cognitively based barriers by using multiple means of representation or presentation involved the incorporation of *summaries of big ideas* to improve access for some students and provide emphasis for other students, noting that some key concepts are inaccessible due to the linguistic complexity of the content's representation. Orkwis and McLane's suggestion for summarizing is similar to aspects of **content enhancement** practices (Deshler, Ellis, & Lenz, 1996). Bulgren and Lenz defined *content enhancement* as a means "to select *critical features* of the *content* and *transform them* in such a manner that promotes learning" (1996, p. 442). Content enhancement strategies modify some aspect of the curriculum to promote learning without changing the content itself. Bulgren and Lenz discussed the term **teaching device,** which is "an instructional technique or a tactic...associated with facilitating organization and understanding, recalling, and applying information" (p. 445), and identified a number of them. These teaching devices, listed in Table 4.1, provide excellent examples of non–technology-based curriculum adaptations.

A quick look at Table 4.1 illustrates that much of what is considered *good teaching* is already geared at curriculum adaptation. Bulgren and Lenz (1996) identified multiple means of representation and presentation of curricular content (e.g., visual, verbal) and

Table 4.1. Teaching devices for use in content enhancement

Device type	Verbal presentation mode	Visual presentation mode

Organize	Summarization
	Chunking
	Advance organizer
	Post organizer
	Verbal cues about
	  organization
		Outline
		Web
		Hierarchical graphic
		  organizer
		Table
		Grid
		Flowchart

Promote understanding	Analogy Synonym Antonym Example Comparison Metaphor Simile	Symbol Concrete object Picture Model Diagram
Describe	Current events Past events Fictional story Hypothetical scenario Personal story	Film Filmstrip Video
Demonstrate	Role play Dramatic portrayal	Physical gesture or movement Moveable objects Demonstration
Promote recall	Acronyms Keywords	Visual images Sketches

From Bulgren, J., & Lenz, B.K. (1996). Strategic instruction in the content areas. In D.D. Deshler, E.S. Ellis, & B.K. Lenz (Eds.), *Teaching adolescents with learning disabilities: Strategies and methods* (2nd ed., p. 446). Denver, CO: Love Publishing Company; adapted by permission.

then identified "teaching devices" in these means of representation and presentation across five general uses: to organize information, to promote understanding or clarify, to describe, to demonstrate, and to promote recall. For example, presenting content information by providing examples or comparisons to promote a student's understanding of a construct is a means of curriculum adaptation. Likewise, using a table or a graph to present information is a visual means of presenting information to assist in learning.

Advance Organizers

A frequently noted curriculum adaptation is the use of advance organizers. Derived from the work of Ausubel (1960) to promote meaningful rather than rote learning of verbal material, an **advance organizer** is a "tool to provide ideational scaffolding for the incorporation and retention of more detailed and differentiated materials" (Bulgren & Lenz, 1996, p. 448). Peleg and Moore described an advance organizer as "an introduction presented to learners before the material to be taught containing an overview of the structure of the unit and creating a connection between the new material to be learned and information already learned" (1982, p. 621). Such organizers can be presented in multiple mediums, in written or oral formats, or through digitized means. Bulgren and Lenz (1996) noted that research shows that advance organizers can promote learning for students with low levels of achievement; however, teachers should be aware of several issues when working with students with cognitive disabilities. These issues include research findings that students with learning disabilities do not independently recognize or use advance organizers (Lenz, Alley, & Schumaker, 1987) and benefit primarily when the organizers are made explicit and students are actively prompted to use them (Bulgren, Schumaker, & Deshler, 1988; Lenz et al., 1987).

A limited number of research studies have been conducted on the efficacy of the use of advance organizers with students with mental retardation, with mixed, although generally promising, results. In the earliest published study, Peleg and Moore (1982) found that when students with mild mental retardation were instructed using advance oral and written organizers, the oral organizer seemed detrimental to the student's learning, whereas the written organizer helped the student's learning, though not significantly.

Subsequent research was more encouraging. Reis (1986) found that advance organizers in the form of knowledge statements (i.e., statements that define certain concepts in the content in advance) and purpose statements (i.e., statements that provide students with a description of what they were supposed to listen for in particular) improved the comprehension of students with and without mental retardation. All of the students who used advance organizers performed better in the knowledge plus purpose statements condition than in all of the other conditions (i.e., knowledge statement only, purpose statement only, no advance organizer). In addition, using only knowledge statements or purpose statements was more positive than using no advance organizers at all. Although there were group differences in comprehension scores (e.g., on average, students without mental retardation answered more questions than students with mental retardation), there were no differences in the groups with regard to the benefits derived from using the advance organizers. Chang (1986) found that the use of advance organizers prior to viewing a film facilitated comprehension for students with and without mental retardation, with no differential effects based on disability (i.e., students with mental retardation benefited as much from the advance organizers as students without mental retardation).

The few studies examining the potential utility of advance organizers for students with mental retardation provide only limited information about their viability with this population; however, given this strategy's prominence in the field of learning disabilities as an effective way to adapt the representation and presentation of the curriculum, it is important to consider this approach more seriously. Moreover, most of the research in this area has been conducted to examine hypotheses related to strategy use in general by people with mental retardation. As such, there have not been extensive efforts to examine the types of advance organizers that might be effective, other than to suggest that oral or verbal organizers may not be the best means. The advent of computer-based technologies provides newer and potentially more powerful options for advance organizers for all students, particularly for students with mental retardation.

Scaffolding

As another example of a curriculum adaptation, Orkwis and McLane (1998) suggested using **scaffolding**—temporary support for learning that is gradually reduced—to promote learning and to reduce barriers to the student's engagement with and response to the curriculum. They suggested ensuring that all steps in the expression process are explicitly stated for students and taught if necessary and that scaffolding is provided as needed.

The idea of using scaffolding as an instructional tool derives from a constructivist perspective on the educational process, which posits that "teaching and learning has changed to a conception that students actively construct their own knowledge and understanding" (Roehler & Cantlon, 1997, p. 8) through active involvement in learning. A **social-constructivist model** of learning is one that has relevance to the reconceptualization of mental retardation as a function of the outcome between functional limitations and the environment. Drawing from the theoretical formulations of Vygotsky (1978) and others, Roehler and Cantlon's perspective suggests that all knowledge is social in nature and that learning occurs in the context of social interactions. Roehler and Cantlon described learners within this framework as

> Active risk takers who accept challenges and understand how and why to learn. They are given opportunities to restructure information in ways that make sense to them. Learners connect new materials with their previously known information. They generate questions and comments as information becomes internalized. Learners first experience active problem-solving activities with others but gradually become independent problem solvers. Initially, the teacher or more knowledgeable person controls and guides the learners' activities. Eventually, the teacher and learners share the responsibilities, with the learners taking the lead. (p. 8)

The social-constructivist model of learning shares certain themes with student self-regulated or self-directed learning. Schunk noted that

> Current theories of learning and motivation portray students as individuals who formulate achievement goals, selectively attend to events, engage in activities, and employ strategies they believe will help them attain goals, process information in meaningful ways...and create and maintain a positive psychological climate for accomplishing goals. (1994, p. 3)

Stark differences become evident when these descriptions of learners and learning are contrasted with the traditional educational experiences of students with mental retardation. Most students with mental retardation have not been taught to set goals, solve problems, or self-regulate learning. Traditional models of teaching employed with students with mental retardation have been largely teacher-directed and highly structured (Wehmeyer, Palmer, Agran, Mithaug, & Martin, 2000).

Within the context of a constructivist approach to education, *scaffolding* refers to "controlling those elements of the task that are initially beyond the learner's capability, thus permitting him to concentrate upon and complete only those elements that are within his range of competence" (Wood, Bruner, & Ross, 1976, p. 89). Scaffolding "characterizes the social interaction between students and teachers" (Roehler & Cantlon, 1997, p. 9) and it may be that factor, the broader focus on scaffolding as an outcome of social interaction, that distinguishes it from the practice of providing prompts, which are usually designed to be as unobtrusive as possible. The delivery of scaffolded instruction, noted Roehler and Cantlon, requires the establishment of a "shared understanding of the task," which is accomplished by

> Creating a balance of support and challenge. Support is provided through scaffolding; challenge is provided through learner interest in completing the task. Learners are given opportunities to act like they know how to complete a task before they actually do. (p. 9)

Like the delivery of prompts, however, the objective in providing scaffolded instruction is to provide the least amount of scaffolding necessary and to withdraw that level of support as soon as possible. Scaffolded learning provides students with the means to experience success by completing a task. For students with mental retardation, the process of scaffolded learning may be the key to their progress in the general curriculum.

These are only a sampling of the strategies that can be used to adapt the curriculum. More examples are discussed in a subsequent chapter on teaching strategies in inclusive environments.

STRATEGIES FOR AUGMENTING THE CURRICULUM

Curriculum augmentation refers to the process of augmenting or expanding the curriculum in such a manner as to teach students skills or strategies that enable them to more effectively interact with and, presumably, progress in the general curriculum.

Strategy Instruction

At the core of this effort is the use of strategy instruction or learning strategies that enable students to learn more effectively. Knowlton (1998) identified the **learning strategies** approach as central to a "learning to learn" approach and, as such, as critical to the curriculum augmentation process. Rosenthal-Malek and Bloom defined cognitive strategies as "cognitive operations, over and above the processes directly involved in carrying out a task, that help the student to attack a problem more effectively" (1998, p. 139). Learning strategies are identified as those techniques that focus cognitive and behavioral actions on a learning task—in essence teaching strategies that, in turn, enable a student to learn content or acquire new skills.

Instructional activities derived from a cognitive approach focus on teaching students cognitive strategies to enhance their interaction with the learning materials and environment. Ellis and Lenz described a cognitive approach to teaching as "based on providing instruction consistent with how a student thinks in the context of learning tasks" (1996, p. 12). The assumptions inherent in a cognitive approach are that students construct learning through interactions with the environment, that the learner is an active component who *makes* learning occur, and that the educational process needs to provide experiences that enable learners to construct new meanings (Ellis & Lenz, 1996). Most models of learning forwarded by cognitive theorists and through information processing models propose components of learning that involve metacognition or metarepresentation (i.e., thinking about thinking or thinking about how other people think or will act), self-regulation, and the role of *executive processes* in the organization and application of other cognitive functions or processes. The executive processes focus attention, memory, and cognitive processes (thinking) to address problems and identify strategies (Rosenthal-Malek & Bloom, 1998). For additional resources on cognitive approaches to education, see the *Additional Readings* section at the end of this chapter.

Borkowski and colleagues (Borkowski & Cavanaugh, 1979; Borkowski & Day, 1987; Borkowski et al., 1986) have explored the teaching of strategies to students with mental retardation. Borkowski et al. (1986) emphasized that students with mental retardation differ widely in their capacity to acquire strategies and transfer that learning to other environments. Instead of assuming that all students with mental retardation will succeed in the use of such strategies or, conversely, assuming that students with mental retardation cannot use such strategies because of their cognitive limitations, these authors recommend being purposeful and explicit about the importance for students to use such strategies and to be equally explicit about prompting students to apply such strategies. This is similar to the recommendations made by Bulgren and Lenz (1996) with regard to the use of advance organizers for students with cognitive disabilities.

By and large, a cognitive or learning strategies approach to the education of students with mental retardation has been examined only in the context of teaching academically oriented content and has been posed as, essentially, antithetical to a functional or life skills approach. There are legitimate concerns with the cognitive or learning strategies approach as it has been applied to students with mental retardation. Polloway, Patton, Epstein, and Smith (1989) noted that in cases in which a cognitive strategies approach is used exclusively for students with mental retardation, there is a tendency to narrow the curriculum, especially with regard to functional skills instruction. This concern echoes previously discussed concerns about the role of the general curriculum in the instruction of students with mental retardation and can be addressed in the same manner. Also, there are concerns about the utilization of cognitive-based instructional strategies with a population of students whose primary limitation is, in fact, cognitive in nature.

The hesitancy to apply cognitive strategies in instruction for students with mental retardation stems from a number of historic aspects of the field of mental retardation and from application of definitions of mental retardation. First, students with mental retardation historically have been taught using primarily, and often exclusively, behavioral techniques. Thus, teachers of students with mental retardation have, by and large, received their training in this theoretical area, often to the exclusion of other perspectives. Second, there has been a presumption of incompetence related to the label *mental retardation* that harkens back to the impairments model discussed in Chapter 1. This has affected educators and students in two ways: 1) As a result of historical perceptions of mental retardation, educators (and other stakeholders) may hold low expectations for student success in learning cognitive strategies and, as such, may opt not to use such strategies; and 2) cognitive theorists often have placed *mental age* limitations or parameters on their estimation of the utility of cognitive strategies, which in turn probably limited their application to students with mental retardation.

This is, however, one more area in which a different definition of mental retardation and a changing view of disability might affect instruction for students with mental retardation. When the emphasis in definition is placed on the interaction between the functional capacity of the student and the environment, as in the functional model described previously, then the potential utility of cognitive strategies as ways for a student to interact with his or her learning environment to make progress becomes more apparent. The benefits of broadening our perception of mental retardation from an impairment of the individual to an interaction between the individual and his or her environment is evident in, for example, the field's growing interest in and focus on self-determination. Promoting self-determination requires that students be taught problem-solving, decision-making, or goal-setting strategies that allow them to learn more effectively (Sands & Wehmeyer, 1996; Wehmeyer, Agran, & Hughes, 1998).

There is a need for more research on cognitive strategies and learning strategies as they apply to students with mental retardation and, likely, a need for the development of new or revised strategies that are beneficial to students with mental retardation.

Rosenthal-Malek and Bloom (1998) identified a number of cognitive or learning strategies that might be applicable to students with mental retardation or developmental disabilities, and each is defined briefly in Table 4.2.

The differences between these augmentation strategies and the teaching devices listed in the section on curriculum adaptation are the locus of operation. Teaching devices are ways that teachers present or represent information to facilitate student learning. Learning strategies involve actually teaching students to employ some strategy to learn the curricular content. For example, a teacher could use rhymes in the presentation of materials (adaptation) or could teach students to create their own rhymes (augmentation) to facilitate learning. Advance organizers can be used to both adapt and augment the curriculum. For example, a student might be provided an outline of a chapter prior to reading it so that he or she might be better prepared to identify the key elements in the chapter. This would be an example of curriculum adaptation as it affects student engagement with the curriculum and, in essence, changes the way the material is presented (outline format versus or in addition to narrative format). Conversely, teaching a student to read, outline, and then reread a chapter as a strategy to help him or her identify key elements and better comprehend the material is, in essence, a means of augmenting the curriculum, in that students are taught a learning strategy to enable them to gain access to the curriculum.

One of the benefits of using learning strategies is their impact on generalization. Cognitive theorists define *generalization* as the "spontaneous use of a cognitive strategy in a unique situation" (Rosenthal-Malek & Bloom, 1998, p. 139). Cognitive or learning strategies emphasize providing a student with strategies and knowledge to adapt to new situations and solve unique or novel problems. Instead of simply learning skills that may or may not generalize to other circumstances, students learn strategies that they can apply to a wide array of problems and situations.

Table 4.2. Cognitive or learning strategies appropriate for students with mental retardation

Strategy domain	Specific strategy	Definition
Rehearsal strategies	Shadowing	Teaching students to repeatedly read aloud a written section, vocalize thinking (think aloud), or repeat information presented orally verbatim
	Verbatim notes	Teaching students to copy sections of text in order to rehearse information
Encoding and retrieval strategies	Organization and elaboration	Teaching students to organize information to facilitate learning or form additional links with information
	Graphic organizers	Teaching students to use visual representations of concepts or topics
	Semantic mapping	Teaching students to brainstorm about words related to specific vocabulary words
	Question–answer relationships	Teaching students how to ask questions in order to better understand a specific text
	Mnemonics	Teaching students to form associations between content areas
	Key word method	Teaching students to associate specific images with particular words or constructs
	Rhymes	Teaching students to create rhymes to enhance memorization

Source: Rosenthal-Malek and Bloom (1998).

Self-Regulation, Self-Management, and Student-Directed Learning Strategies

An emphasis on the use of strategies to create *active learners* is also found in the research on self-regulation and self-regulated learning. Whitman defined **self-regulation** as

> A complex response system that enables individuals to examine their environments and their repertoires of responses for coping with those environments to make decisions about how to act, to act, to evaluate the desirability of the outcomes of the action, and to revise their plans as necessary. (1990, p. 373)

Zimmerman defined *self-regulation* as the degree to which "individuals are metacognitively, motivationally, and behaviorally active participants in their own learning process" (1994, p. 3). Schunk defined *self-regulated learning* as the "process whereby students activate and sustain cognitions, behaviors, and affects that are systematically oriented toward the attainment of goals" (1994, p. 75). Together, the use of strategies to promote self-regulation and self-regulated learning provides another means of augmenting the curriculum.

Bandura (1986) and other social cognitive theorists view self-regulation as having three components: self-observation (i.e., attentiveness to aspects of one's behavior), self-judgment (i.e., comparing present performance with one's goal), and self-reaction (i.e., evaluations about performance). Whereas cognitive or learning strategies teach students "learning to learn" tactics designed to enable them to learn more effectively, self-regulation or self-regulated learning strategies teach students to direct the learning process by regulating their behavior. Although learning strategies emphasize cognitive processes, self-regulation strategies emphasize both cognitive and behavioral processes. Teaching students to self-regulate learning typically involves teaching students several self-management or student-directed learning strategies. **Self-management strategies** or **student-directed learning strategies** are behavioral strategies that enable students to manage or direct elements of their own behavior (Agran, 1997). These strategies also have been hypothesized to enhance generalization, in which generalization is defined more in terms of the replication of behaviors to different or new environments.

Using such strategies shifts the emphasis from providing teacher-directed instruction to enabling a student to regulate his or her own behavior. A variety of strategies have been used to teach students, including students with significant disabilities, how to manage their own behavior. Among the most commonly used student-directed learning strategies are permanent prompts, self-instruction, self-monitoring, and self-reinforcement.

Permanent Prompts *Permanent prompts* are visual or picture cues that students use to guide their behavior. They have been used with individuals with mental retardation to teach lengthy and complex task sequences (Bambara & Cole, 1997; Wacker & Berg, 1993) and to promote on-task behavior and independent work performance (MacDuff, Krantz, & McClannahan, 1993; Mithaug, Martin, Agran, & Rusch, 1988).

Self-Instruction **Self-instruction** involves teaching individuals to provide their own verbal cues prior to the execution of target behaviors. Individuals with mental retardation have been taught to use this strategy to solve a variety of work problems (Agran & Moore, 1994; Hughes & Rusch, 1989); to complete complex, multistep sequences (Agran, Fodor-Davis, & Moore, 1986); and to generalize desired responses across changing work environments (Agran & Moore, 1994). Self-instruction allows an individual to provide him- or herself with sufficient verbal information to cue a response—information that might otherwise not be provided by a service provider.

Self-Monitoring **Self-monitoring** involves teaching students to observe whether they have performed a targeted behavior and whether their response meets existing criteria. Among several applications reported in the research literature are the effects of self-monitoring on facilitating job-task changes (Sowers, Verdi, Bourbeau, & Sheehan, 1985) and evaluating how often a task was completed (Mace, Shapiro, West, Campbell, & Altman, 1986). Teaching someone to monitor his or her own behavior may produce a desired change without another intervention.

Self-Reinforcement *Self-reinforcement* involves teaching individuals to administer consequences to themselves (e.g., verbally telling themselves they did a good job) and provide themselves with reinforcers that are accessible and immediate. Given access to self-administered reinforcement, behavior change may be greatly facilitated.

Research in education and vocational rehabilitation has shown that student-directed learning strategies—specifically self-monitoring, self-instruction, and self-reinforcement—are as successful as or more successful than teacher-directed learning strategies and that self-management strategies are effective means to increase independence and productivity. (See Martin, Burger, Elias-Burger, & Mithaug [1988] for a comprehensive overview of the research literature prior to 1986.)

Self-monitoring procedures have been shown to improve the motivation and performance of students with disabilities. Malone and Mastropieri (1992) determined that under a self-monitoring condition, middle school students with learning disabilities performed better on reading comprehension transfer tasks than peers who did not self-monitor. McCarl, Svobodny, and Beare (1991) found that teaching three students with mental retardation to record progress on classroom assignments improved on-task behavior for all students and increased productivity for two of the three students with mental retardation.

Kapadia and Fantuzzo (1988) used self-monitoring procedures to increase attention to academic tasks for students with developmental disabilities and behavior problems. Lovett and Haring (1989) showed that self-monitoring activities enabled adults with mental retardation to improve task completion of daily living activities. Chiron and Gerken (1983) found that students with mental retardation who charted progress on school reading activities showed significant increases in their reading levels. Trammel, Schloss, and Alper (1994) found that self-monitoring (graphing progress on a chart) and student-directed goal setting enabled students with learning disabilities to increase the number of assignments they completed successfully.

The use of self-instruction also has proven to be beneficial for individuals with disabilities. As stated previously, *self-instruction* refers to "verbalizations an individual emits to cue, direct or maintain his or her own behavior" (Agran et al., 1986, p. 273), although several authors reported self-instructional strategies in which students think through the strategies instead of verbalizing them. A number of studies have found that self-instruction training is a useful technique for increasing job-related skills of individuals with mental retardation (Agran et al., 1986; Hughes & Petersen, 1989; Rusch, McKee, Chadsey-Rusch, & Renzaglia, 1988; Salend, Ellis, & Reynolds, 1989). Graham and Harris (1989) found that a self-instructional strategy improved the essay composition skills of students with learning disabilities. Agran, Salzberg, and Stowitschek (1987) found that self-instructional strategies increased the percentages of initiations with a work supervisor when employees—five individuals with mental retardation—ran out of work materials or needed assistance.

Schunk (1981) showed that students who used **self-evaluation** by verbalizing cognitive strategies related to evaluating their study and work habits had increased math achievement scores. Brownell, Colletti, Ersner-Hershfield, Hershfield, and Wilson (1977) found that students who determined their own performance standards demonstrated increased time on-task when compared with students operating under imposed standards.

Self-reinforcement also leads to increased performance. Lagomarcino and Rusch (1989) used a combination of self-reinforcement and self-monitoring procedures to improve the work performance of a student with mental retardation in a community environment. Moore, Agran, and Fodor-Davis (1989) used a combination of student-directed learning strategies, including self-instruction, goal setting, and self-reinforcement, to improve the production rate of workers with mental retardation.

Self-Determination to Promote Augmentation

A final means of expanding the curriculum to provide access is to enhance student self-determination. **Self-determination** refers, in essence, to assuming control over one's life and one's destiny. Self-regulation is one essential characteristic of self-determined behavior, and promoting self-regulation is a critical aspect of promoting self-determination. In addition, however, a focus on promoting self-determination includes efforts to enhance goal setting, problem-solving, and decision-making skills, self-awareness, and self-advocacy and leadership skills. Like student-directed learning strategies, promoting self-determination focuses on student control or direction over the learning process and is goal oriented. Efforts to enhance self-determination, however, are more global in nature, emphasizing efforts to enhance individual capacity, modify or create environments that promote causal agency, and design supports or accommodations to ensure control and choice. Chapter 14 addresses self-determination in greater detail.

ALTERING THE CURRICULUM: TOWARD FUNCTIONALITY

As one of three ways to modify the curriculum, curriculum alterations provide the means to ensure an appropriate education for students when the general curriculum falls short with regard to unique student needs. Processes leading to curriculum alteration are already widely used in the education of students with mental retardation. Polloway et al. (1989) described several curricular approaches that lead to functionality, including a vocational training emphasis, career education curricula, adult outcomes orientations, and life skills curricular approaches. Each of these curricular approaches emphasizes the identification of individual student needs and the design of instructional activities to achieve those needs. To the degree that such approaches are seen as (or actually are) antithetical to the general curriculum is as much an indictment of the general curriculum as a shortfall of educational programming for students with mental retardation. That is, one should not have to choose between educational experiences that lead to individually determined, adult- and career-oriented, and life skills–focused outcomes and the general curriculum. Instead, the general curriculum needs to address these key areas so that functionality is included in the general curriculum. Employing design principles inherent in universal design (Chapter 2) can, in fact, lead to such an outcome.

In many cases, specific educational practices and experiences are linked to these curricular approaches. For example, it is generally accepted that effective transition services and supports will incorporate community-based learning experiences. In fact, the educational programs of students with mental retardation whose support needs are more intense will be more and more community-based as the student ages, such that by ages 18–21, students may spend the majority of their instructional day in the community. Once again, however, it should be noted that there are educational models for all students that employ community-based learning experiences (Gardner, 1993) and that the solution to the perceived problem of functional curriculum versus general curriculum lies in promoting a more individually determined curriculum for all students, complete with learning experiences such as community-based instruction. Such compromises are not incompatible with standards-based reform in theory as much as in the way standards-based reforms are often implemented.

SUMMARY

This chapter began by emphasizing that achieving progress in the general curriculum for students with mental retardation requires the multilevel focus depicted in Figure 3.1. In addition to focusing on curriculum planning and design (i.e., ensuring that curriculum is designed based on principles of universal design), there needs to be a focus on curriculum decision making that considers curriculum adaptations and augmentations before considering curriculum alterations. The decision-making process presented in Figure 4.1 provides a step-by-step process for making curriculum decisions on the basis of the general curriculum and unique student learning needs.

Curriculum adaptations refer to efforts to alter or change the presentation, representation, or student engagement with the curriculum. By and large, the emphasis in the field has been on the role of technology to provide access by adapting curricular materials. Although such use of technology has promise, as discussed in Chapter 16, there are other curriculum adaptations that warrant consideration, including the use of scaffolding and advance organizers. In fact, it is important to consider whole-school implementation of these types of adaptations so as to minimize the degree to which students with disabilities, including students with mental retardation who have intermittent support needs, need to receive *special* intervention. Moreover, curriculum adaptations, technological or otherwise, will likely not suffice in and of themselves to ensure that students with mental retardation make progress in the general curriculum; therefore, IEP teams and curriculum decision-makers must consider ways to augment the curriculum to provide students with the opportunity to learn strategies that better enable them to interact with and progress in the curriculum. Only then will it be necessary to consider adding content to the curriculum. Once whole-school instructional practices are in place (an educational support design issue) and the student's IEP team has designed the curriculum based on the process depicted in Figure 4.1, the attention will then turn to other aspects of designing educational supports, including instructional decision making (classroom, unit, and lesson-level instructional decisions are discussed in Chapter 5) and the design and implementation of other educational supports.

ADDITIONAL READINGS

Cognitive or Learning Strategy Instruction: General

Brooks, J.G., & Brooks, M.G. (1999). *In search of understanding: The case for constructivist classrooms.* Alexandria, VA: Association for Supervision and Curriculum Development.

Cole, R.W. (1995). *Educating everybody's children. Diverse teaching strategies for diverse learners: What research and practice say about improving achievement.* Alexandria, VA: Association for Supervision and Curriculum Development.

Pressley, M.J., & Burkell, J. (1990). *Cognitive strategy instruction that really improves children's academic performance.* Cambridge, MA: Brookline Books.

Cognitive or Learning Strategy Instruction: Students with Disabilities

Deshler, D.D., Ellis, E.S., & Lenz, B.K. (Eds). (1996). *Teaching adolescents with learning disabilities: Strategies and methods* (2nd ed.). Denver, CO: Love Publishing Company.

Harris, K.R., Graham, S., Deshler, D., & Pressley, M. (1997). *Teaching every child every day: Learning in diverse schools and classrooms.* Cambridge, MA: Brookline Books.

Hogan, K., & Pressley, M. (1997). *Scaffolding student learning: Instructional approaches and issues.* Cambridge, MA: Brookline Books.

Pressley, M.J., & Woloshyn, V. (1995). *Cognitive strategy instruction that really improves children's academic performance.* Reston, VA: Council for Exceptional Children.

Self-Regulation, Self-Regulated Learning, and Student-Directed Learning

Agran, M. (1997). *Student-directed learning: Teaching self-determination skills.* Pacific Grove, CA: Brooks/Cole.

Mithaug, D. (1993). *Self-regulation theory: How optimal adjustment maximizes gain.* Westport, CT: Praeger.

Pintrich, P.R. (1995). *Understanding self-regulated learning.* San Francisco: Jossey-Bass.

Schunk, D.H., & Zimmerman, B.J. (Eds). (1994). *Self-regulation of learning and performance: Issues and educational applications.* Mahwah, NJ: Lawrence Erlbaum Associates.

Schunk, D.H., & Zimmerman, B.J. (Eds). (1998). *Self-regulated learning: From teaching to self-reflective practice.* New York: The Guilford Press.

Zimmerman, B.J., Bonner, S., & Kovach, R. (1996). *Developing self-regulated learners: Beyond achievement to self-efficacy.* Washington, DC: American Psychological Association.

CHAPTER OBJECTIVES

1. Discuss the individualized education program (IEP) process and the role of the IEP team in both curriculum decision making and the design of educational supports.
2. Define *person-centered planning*, and identify the features that distinguish it from other planning processes.
3. Discuss student-directed planning and its importance in achieving access to the general curriculum.
4. Identify developmentally appropriate and age-appropriate practices and discuss their importance for students with mental retardation.

KEY TERMS

Individualized education program (IEP)
Age of majority
Person-centered planning
Student-directed planning
Test accommodations
Alternate assessments
Developmentally appropriate practice
Mental age–chronological age discrepancy

5

Person-Centered and Student-Directed Planning

SPECIAL EDUCATION STUDENTS TURN TO GAMBLING TO AVOID THE BOREDOM OF AGE-INAPPROPRIATE ACTIVITIES.

D etermining an appropriate formal curriculum is one of the most important goals of a student's individualized education program (IEP) team in facilitating access to the general curriculum, but it is not their only role. This chapter explores the IEP team and its other responsibilities related to designing educational supports that ensure access to the general curriculum.

THE IEP TEAM

Chapter 4 contains a description of a decision-making model that IEP teams could use to make decisions about a student's formal curriculum. The determination of a student's formal curriculum, however, is only one—albeit crucial—component in the design of an appropriate educational program for a student. In addition to identifying the content of a student's educational program, the IEP team is charged with numerous other responsibilities.

The fundamental purpose of the IEP team under IDEA is to design an IEP for each student. The Office of Special Education and Rehabilitation Services (OSERS) called the IEP the "cornerstone of a quality education for each child with a disability" and noted that the IEP "creates an opportunity for teachers, parents, school administrators, related services personnel, and students... to work together to improve educational results for children with disabilities" (2000, p. 1).

What is meant by the **individualized education program** that IEP teams are to design? At the broadest level, an education program is, as implied by the word *program,* a plan of procedures for a student's education. It is a plan for the totality of the student's educational experience. In IDEA, however, the IEP is more than just a plan; it is a written, legal document describing the services and supports to be provided to the student. IDEA has numerous requirements with regard to what a student's IEP must contain, including showing how the student will be involved in the general curriculum and the extent, if any, to which the student will not participate with students without disabilities in a general classroom. The IEP also must list supplementary aids and services to be provided to the child and identify program modifications or supports for school personnel so that the child will advance appropriately toward annual goals, progress in the general curriculum, participate in extracurricular activities, and be educated with his or her peers (The Arc, 1999).

The IEP team should consist of a wide array of stakeholders who meet at least annually at a student's IEP meeting. The IEP meeting was intended by IDEA to be a collaborative *decision-making* meeting in which the IEP team comes to a decision about a student's individually determined educational program. Most decision-making models have sequential steps through which a decision maker must proceed. These steps are 1) to identify the options available, 2) to identify the consequences of implementing each option—the risks and benefits associated with that implementation, 3) to weigh the benefits and risks with individual preferences and priorities, and 4) to select a particular option. Through a systematic process, IEP teams are, essentially, charged with making decisions about the curriculum and about educational supports. Included in the category of educational supports, design and decision making are actions that put the curriculum decision-making process into action, including a placement decision, instructional decision making (a shared function with the student's teachers or teacher), decisions about accommodations and environmental modifications, and an evaluation plan that includes IEP goals and objectives. It is not desirable for the IEP team to micromanage the instructional process; instead, it should make curriculum and instructional decisions to lay a framework on which teachers can expand with building- and classroom-level curricular and instructional decisions. Three subsequent chapters discuss the classroom-level processes, including creating a learning community (Chapter 7), making building- and classroom-level instructional and curriculum decisions (Chapter 8), and implementing instructional strategies in inclusive settings that benefit all children (Chapter 10).

Returning, however, to the notion that IEP teams should be decision-making bodies, there is considerable evidence, largely focused on the difficulty of meaningfully involving parents, that suggests that these meetings too often do not involve decision making. Instead, some schools approach the IEP meeting as an *information and instruction meeting*, in which the meeting exists so that one group (i.e., school personnel) can give information (i.e., about the predetermined educational program) to another group (e.g., parents, students). Such meetings are built on an *educator as expert* model, in which the meeting leader deems to know something that the other team members do not. Other schools take the approach of the IEP meeting as a *consultation meeting*, in which the opinions or advice of various parties (e.g., parent, student, agency, provider) are solicited and then considered for incorporation into a final decision or educational program. The problem with the consultation model is that the person or agency who sets up the meeting—in this case the school—is still in charge of the decisions, and the opinions or advice that are gathered in such a meeting can be heeded or discarded. Still other schools view IEP meetings as *team-building meetings*, in which stakeholders are brought together to get the team excited about the educational program, which has been determined by and large prior to the meeting. None of these models embody the deliberative and evaluative process inherent in decision-making meetings and in reaching group decisions.

The 1997 IDEA amendments put into place several new requirements that reiterate the intent of the IEP meeting as a decision-making meeting. The need for IEP team members to be deliberative and to apply a decision-making model to the curriculum decision-making process has been discussed previously. This decision-making process leads to decisions about placement, instruction, accommodations and environmental modifications, and program evaluation. The *age-of-majority* requirements added in the 1997 amendments to IDEA (which concern the transfer of rights accorded through IDEA from parents to students at the **age of majority**) require that IEP teams make decisions about how best to prepare students to provide informed consent and to assume greater responsibility for decisions about their own education programs. In addition, IEP teams must make decisions pertaining to student involvement in statewide assessments and about modifications needed to ensure that process.

Too often, IEP meetings and teams are configured in a way that makes deliberative action unlikely, if not impossible. If the field of special education is to respond to the IDEA 1997 amendments' mandates for access to the general curriculum, change must start with the planning and decision-making process. Specifically, IEP meetings need to become truly deliberative, decision-making meetings, and all IEP team members, including the student with mental retardation, need to be supported to participate fully in the process. Such an effort will, by necessity, need to become more person-centered and student-directed. Person-centered and student-directed planning are summarized briefly in the following sections and are followed by an examination of models and efforts to merge these planning processes into a system by which decisions can be made about educational supports. The chapter concludes with a return to the primary outcomes—decisions about placement, instruction, accommodations and environmental modifications, and program evaluation—of the IEP meeting as a decision-making process.

PERSON-CENTERED PLANNING

Person-centered planning approaches share common beliefs and attempt to put those beliefs into a planning framework (see *Additional Readings* for examples and resources). Such beliefs include the following:

- All individuals, regardless of the type or severity of their disability, benefit from services and supports in their communities, and through such supports, these individuals benefit the community itself (Everson, 1996).
- Direction in shaping the planning process and formulating plans should come from the individual.
- Personal social relationships in support of the individual are of primary importance, leading to an emphasis on involvement of family and friends in the planning process.
- Capacities and assets rather than limitations and deficiencies are the focus.
- Environments, supports, and services that are available in the community are emphasized as opposed to disability-specific supports and services (O'Brien & Lovett, 1993).

Schwartz, Jacobson, and Holburn (2000) used a consensus process to define *person-centeredness*. This effort provides a useful picture of the values underlying person-centered planning as it exists today. Specifically, Schwartz and colleagues identified eight hallmarks of a person-centered planning process:

1. The person's activities, services, and supports are based on his or her dreams, interests, preferences, strengths, and capacities.
2. The person and people important to him or her are included in lifestyle planning and have the opportunity to exercise control and make informed decisions.
3. The person has meaningful choices, with decisions based on his or her experiences.
4. The person uses, when possible, natural and community supports.
5. Activities, supports, and services foster skills to achieve personal relationships, community inclusion, dignity, and respect.
6. The person's opportunities and experiences are maximized, and flexibility is enhanced within existing regulatory and funding constraints.
7. Planning is collaborative and recurring and involves an ongoing commitment to the person.
8. The person is satisfied with his or her relationships, home, and daily routine.

The beliefs illustrated in these two lists of what constitutes *person-centeredness,* when operationalized in a strategic planning process, provide a means to ensure that the planning process reflects the assumptions held in redefining mental retardation as discussed in Chapter 1. The focus in such processes is not on fixing or changing the individual but instead on identifying and designing supports that enable the person to participate in his or her community. Table 5.1 compares person-centered planning with traditional educational planning processes.

Adopting a person-centered planning focus is important to the education of students with mental retardation for a variety of reasons. First, the process is stakeholder driven and community focused. Second, team members commit to meeting as often as necessary instead of just at one-shot annual meetings. Third, the focus is on student capacity, and the process is future oriented. Finally, such a process allows for a deliberative, decision-making oriented process.

One frequently cited limitation to person-centered planning is the amount of time required to engage in this level of individualization and collaboration. This barrier can be removed by implementing the types of planning, curricular and instructional supports, and activities identified in Figure 3.1. When there is schoolwide implementation of adapted curricular materials (see Chapter 16) and positive behavioral supports (see Chapter 11) and when all teachers employ classroom decision-making strategies (see Chapter 8) and adapt and augment the curriculum with strategies to ensure that all children progress in the curriculum (see Chapters 3 and 15), the need for highly intensive individualized planning is reduced. Obviously, the majority of students in a school do not require an IEP or an IEP meeting. When schoolwide and classroomwide supports and activities are implemented, the unique needs of a number of students with mental retardation who require limited or intermittent supports will be addressed, thus eliminating the need for longer, more intensive IEP meetings. It would still be necessary to meet at least annually to design the student's IEP, and the IEP team should continue to

Table 5.1. Traditional education planning and person-centered planning

Traditional education planning	Person-centered planning
A multidisciplinary team of professionals meets annually with parents to plan students' IEPs.	Stakeholders (e.g., student, parents, family members) form a *circle of support* and meet as frequently as needed to develop and implement a future vision for the student.
Transdisciplinary assessment is conducted using standardized and nonstandardized assessments, and the data are interpreted by the IEP team.	The *circle of support* gathers, organizes, and manages assessment information from a wide array of sources and organizes that information into a personal profile, usually using visual maps and graphic images.
The student is invited to participate if he or she is of transition age or if it is otherwise deemed appropriate by the team.	The student is the focal point for the planning process, and the circle of support defines a role for the student and helps him or her to assume that role.
Parents are invited to participate in the IEP meeting and in the development of the plan.	Parents, other family members, friends, and general community members define the personal profile, outline future visions, and identify how service providers can support.
An IEP is generated.	A future vision is identified, and an action plan is put into place to drive subsequent action.

Source: Everson (1995).

use the model presented in Chapter 4 to make decisions about the program. Such meetings can retain the essence of person-centered planning meetings even if repeated meetings are not necessary. The meetings should continue to be student driven as well. The more time-intensive meetings are, as such, necessary only for students whose support needs are identified as extensive or pervasive.

STUDENT-DIRECTED PLANNING

The educational experience of most students, particularly students with disabilities, can often be described as a one-way street. Students are *recipients* of instructional programs that are almost uniformly *teacher-delivered* and based on plans and decisions *made by others,* including the student's teacher and parents, administrators, school board members, and state legislators. There is no doubt in the minds of most students about who is in control when they are in school. Sarason described the typical classroom:

> Our usual imagery of the classroom contains an adult who is "in charge" and pupils who conform to the teacher's rules, regulations and standards. If students think and act in conformity to the teacher's wishes, they will learn what they are supposed to learn. (1990, p. 78)

IDEA contains language that requires all IEPs of students ages 16 and older who receive special education services to include a statement of needed transition services. IDEA also mandates student involvement in transition planning, stating that needed transition services *must* be based on student preferences and interests. This is **student-directed planning**. Although the statutory language of IDEA requires student involvement in the IEP meeting "when appropriate," the regulations regarding student involvement in transition planning are clear and unambiguous. These regulations state that if one of the purposes of an IEP meeting is to consider transition services, then the school must include the student in the meeting (Sec. 300.344[c]). The regulations then point out that "for *all students who are 16 years or older,* one of the purposes of the annual meeting *will always be the planning of transition services,* since transition services are a required component of the IEP for these students" (Sec. 300.344, Note 2; italics added). The IDEA Amendments of 1997 lowered the age at which transition must be discussed to 14, requiring that a statement of transition services be included and updated annually once a student turns 14. In other words, schools must invite all students ages 14 and older to planning meetings, and decisions made about students' transition services must be based on the students' preferences and interests.

Although IDEA mandates do not state so directly, the clear intent of the student-involvement language in IDEA was to ensure that students with disabilities have a meaningful voice in the process of making decisions about their futures. Wehmeyer and Ward (1995) argued that the student involvement language places the intent and spirit of IDEA in line with requirements for consumer choice and involvement in planning found in other civil rights legislation, like the Americans with Disabilities Act of 1990 (PL 101-336).

As a result of specific language in IDEA, a growing number of processes and resources have been designed to promote active student involvement in education and transition planning (see *Additional Readings* at the end of this chapter). Similar to the belief system that undergirds person-centered planning, the student-directed planning processes strive to put the student at the center of the decision-making process, in some cases focusing on enabling students to chair their own IEP meetings (Martin & Marshall, 1995). Student-directed planning processes and materials tend to focus on building student capacity to engage and succeed in the planning process. Thus, the focus for most student-directed planning efforts is on building students' capacity to set goals, solve problems, communicate effectively, and develop other skills that lead to students assuming control over the planning process as well as to providing students with opportunities to assume such control.

PERSON-CENTERED, STUDENT-DIRECTED IEP MEETINGS

To ensure that the education programs of students with mental retardation are individualized and driven by the general curriculum and by unique student learning needs, the IEP process needs to embody principles of both person-centered and student-directed planning. Although these two types of planning processes are identified as distinct from one another, they are relatively similar. However, in our estimation, there has not been as much overlap between the two processes as there should be. There is no question that, at this point in time, most practitioners of person-centered planning view the promotion and enhancement of self-determination and self-direction as both a core value and an anticipated outcome of the process. Given the hallmarks of person-centered planning identified by Schwartz and colleagues (2000), it is not hard to see why person-centered planning and student-directed planning are viewed as closely related, if not synonymous.

However, on close examination, person-centered planning processes differ from student-directed or self-directed planning processes in the priority they assign to various values. To some degree, the ingredients are the same, but they are mixed in different ways and proportions. For example, person-centered planning emphasizes the role of significant others, whereas student-directed planning processes emphasize building student capacity to set or track goals or make decisions.

Although it is inaccurate to imply a stark contrast between the two processes, the different values for various components of planning do have different effects on promoting self-determination. Cross, Cooke, Wood, and Test (2000) examined the effects of two planning processes, the McGill Action Planning System (MAPS; Vandercook, York, & Forest, 1989) and the ChoiceMaker process (Martin & Marshall, 1996), on the self-determination of adolescents with disabilities. Both processes resulted in enhanced self-determination (as measured by student-report and teacher-report indicators), but the ChoiceMaker process (which includes the "Self-Directed IEP" process) had larger effects than the MAPS process on self-determination. The generalizability of the study's findings was limited by sample size (five students per group). Although both processes were beneficial for students, it appeared that the ChoiceMaker process was more beneficial in promoting self-determination because of the focus on capacity building in the student-directed process.

A number of variables likely account for why person-centered planning and student-directed planning emphasize different components. One such variable has been the populations to whom these processes have been applied. Person-centered planning emerged from efforts to plan for (and largely remains a process employed with) individuals with cognitive, developmental, or multiple disabilities requiring extensive and pervasive supports. Conversely, most student-directed planning processes have focused on students with limited support needs.

Our own research has shown that teachers of students requiring extensive or pervasive supports believe that their students would not benefit from instruction in areas such as problem solving, decision making, or goal setting because of the limitations inherent in their students' disabilities (Wehmeyer, Agran, & Hughes, 2000), reflecting a societal belief that teaching or promoting those specific skills is secondary in value to ensuring that the person has choices and can express preferences. Although no research exists regarding the efficacy of merging person-centered and student-directed planning processes to plan the education programs of students with mental retardation, there is a small, but growing, literature base on the use of person-centered planning processes in the context of making decisions about a student's educational program. Flannery et al. (2000) evaluated the effect of training IEP team members on person-centered planning in a variety of planning outcomes and found that the person-centered planning process increased the number of nonpaid individuals scheduled to provide support to students and resulted in higher satisfaction with the planning process for educators, students, and parents. This outcome illustrates the importance of adopting a person-centered process if the field is to move from a deficits model of mental retardation to a supports model.

Miner and Bates (1997) also examined the effect of person-centered planning activities on the IEP process and concluded that person-centered planning resulted in significant improvement in parental participation in the IEP process. Parents described feelings of increased preparedness, participation, and student participation and preparedness to discuss action steps. Hagner, Helm, and Butterworth (1996) conducted a qualitative study of person-centered planning within the context of educational planning for six students with mental retardation. Participants reported that they found the process valuable and "felt energized" through the process (p. 168). Hagner and colleagues (1996) found, however, that unlike similar reports for adults with mental retardation, there was only partial control of the planning by the focal student and limited involvement by community participants. These authors noted that "during meetings, focal individuals were reluctant to forthrightly dispute what parents, friends, and professionals said" (p. 169) and recommended that person-centered planning focus more on teaching self-advocacy skills, a recommendation consistent with the merger of person-centered and student-directed processes. Choosing Outcomes and Accommodations for Children (COACH; Giangreco, Cloninger, & Iverson, 1998) is an example of person-centered planning as applied to education and embodies many components found in student-directed planning processes.

Examples of the use of person-centered planning to make education decisions come largely from the literature on transition services and transition planning. A similar need exists, however, for the educational decision-making process for young children. The Education for the Handicapped Act Amendments of 1986 (PL 99-457) established two new programs, the Infants and Toddlers with Disabilities Program for children from birth to 2 years of age and the Preschool Program for children from 3 to 5 years of age. These new programs, in essence, extended the provisions of Part B of the act, which focused on children between 6 and 21 years of age, to include children between birth and 5 years of age. Planning for the education of young children was to be accomplished by an individualized family service plan (IFSP) that contained information about the child's levels of development and family resources, priorities, and concerns; a statement of major outcomes expected for the child and his or her family; timelines and criteria for determining progress; needed services and supports; a statement of the natural environment in which services and supports will be provided; and procedures for the transition from early intervention to preschool and preschool to Part B services (Smith & McKenna, 1994).

The difference between the IFSP process and the IEP process is evident in the focus of their names. The IEP refers to an educational program, whereas the IFSP refers to a process to provide family supports and services. Parents and family members often express shock and dismay about the differences between planning meetings conducted in early intervention and Part C preschool programs and the IEP planning process that begins in elementary school, principally because the former employs what is essentially a person-centered focus, whereas the latter does not. By making the IEP process more person-centered, schools can begin to bridge the gap between the IFSP process and the IEP process. As students age, however, the focus only on developing an IEP needs to change to a family and student support plan. In fact, perhaps the ideal to strive for is to develop an individualized family and student support plan (IFSSP).

IEP MEETING OUTCOMES: EDUCATIONAL SUPPORTS

By employing more person-centered, student-directed planning, the IEP process can become more deliberative and decision-focused. Through such a process, IEP teams need to make a wide array of decisions, beginning with a decision about the curricular content for a student's educational program. Once the IEP has been determined, IEP teams need to make decisions about educational supports to implement the program. As mentioned previously, two of these supports, instructional decisions and program evaluation decisions, are discussed extensively in subsequent chapters. In addition to these two areas, however, IEP teams must consider other decisions related to the design of educational supports. These decisions include placement, accommodations and environmental modifications, **test accommodations** and **alternate assessments,** and developmentally and age-appropriate instruction.

Placement

One of the most visible, and often difficult, decisions to be made during an IEP meeting is the student's placement—deciding *where* a student will receive his or her education. Once again, the values-based emphasis of this text is that students with mental retardation should receive their educational program in the context of the general classroom. Under circumstances discussed in Chapter 14, older students with mental retardation need to receive an increasingly higher proportion of educational services outside of the school building context. However, if done within the context of educational reform efforts that emphasize community-based and community-referenced learning for all students, this does not need to be a pull-out model in which only students with mental retardation leave the general classroom for services.

Too often, decisions about a student's placement precede decisions about the actual program and are based on the student's diagnosis or on what programs are available for students with that diagnosis. This is unacceptable. For all students, the decision about the context in which they receive their instruction needs to be a function of the decision about what they will learn. Too often, this has not been the case for students with mental retardation who continue to receive their educational services in segregated environments, despite decades of focus on inclusion in the general classroom. The *21st Annual Report to Congress on the Implementation of IDEA* (Office of Special Education Programs [OSEP], 1999) illustrates this dilemma. Table 5.2 identifies the percentage of children across all disability categories between the ages of 6 and 21 who received their educational services in one of several educational environments. These environments are identified in IDEA and defined accordingly to include

- General classroom: includes students who receive the majority of their educational program in a general classroom and receive special education and related services outside the general classroom for less than 21% of the school day
- Resource room: includes students who receive special education and related services outside the general classroom for at least 21% but no more than 60% of the school day
- Separate classroom: includes students who receive special education and related services outside the general classroom for more than 60% of the school day
- Separate school: includes students who receive education in private and public separate day schools for students with disabilities for more than 50% of the school day
- Residential facility: includes students who receive education in a public or private residential facility, at public expense, for more than 50% of the school day
- Homebound/hospital environment: includes students placed in and receiving special education in hospital or homebound programs

As can be seen in Table 5.2, 45% of all students with disabilities are served in the general classroom (i.e., not outside of the general classroom for more than 21% of the day); 28% of all students with disabilities are served in resource classrooms, and only 21% of students with disabilities are served in separate classrooms. As indicated in Table 5.3, however, the dominant educational environment for students with mental retardation remains the separate classroom, with 54% of all students with mental retardation receiving their education in this environment. Only 10% of students with mental retardation receive their education primarily in the general classroom, and 7% of all students with mental retardation receive their education in a separate public or private facility.

Certainly, some of these statistics might be accounted for by the fact that as students with mental retardation get older, they are more likely to be provided educational services in the community, with students ages 18–21 often served outside the public school building (see Chapter 14). However, this notion is quickly dismissed by examining the OSEP data for students ages 6–11 with mental retardation, as depicted in Table 5.4, which shows that the percentage of students with mental retardation this age receiving their education in separate classrooms is almost the same (55%) as for all students with mental retardation, even though a slightly higher percentage of students with mental retardation this age are being served in the general classroom (13%).

Why do an overwhelming number of students with mental retardation receive their education in segregated environments, even after years of advocacy toward inclusion in the general classroom? To explain this, one must return to the discussion in Chapter 1 of the low expectations and negative stereotypes associated with the label of mental retardation. Ultimately, the educational placement process for students with mental retardation has not been contingent on the curriculum decision-making process but instead on preexisting school programs and the availability of services within the often narrowly defined parameters of those programs. Once more, if the educational process is to be responsive to the IDEA Amendments of 1997 mandates to provide access to the general curriculum, the educational placement decision must be decoupled from the student's label and tied to the instructional needs of his or her educational program.

This leads to the question of exactly what the optimal educational environment is for students with mental retardation. Chapter 14 addresses issues pertaining to community-based instruction and the inherent conflict between being included in the general classroom and receiving educational services that are functional and individualized. However, in moving the discussion from *where* a student with mental retardation should receive his or her educational program to *what* is in that program, there is no intent to minimize the importance of the educational environment as a critical educational support. The importance of creating learning communities for all students is discussed in Chapter 7, and an in-depth discussion of issues pertaining to the classroom environment as an educational support is included in that chapter. However, over and above the importance of teachers creating learning communities and learning environments in which all students can succeed is the necessity to provide all students with the opportunity to learn in environments that emphasize their strengths and maximize their learning. Although the standards-based school reform movement has been the dominant reform applied across the country, it is not by any means the only reform model available. Many reform models emphasize learning outside of the traditional classroom as well as changes in the way that the general classroom is structured. Schools configured around developmental psychologist Howard Gardner's multiple intelligences (MI) theory, for example, emphasize critical ecological factors that affect learning, including learning oriented around community-based projects (Armstrong, 1994; Gardner, 1993). Gardner and Blythe described a school day based on MI theory and noted that during the second half of the school day "students and teachers venture out into the community for further contextual exploring and learning" (1993, p. 76).

Indeed, even versions of standards-based reform models emphasize the environment as an important support for learning. Sykes and Plastrik (1993) identified the *reform network model* as a version of standards-based reform that focuses standards setting at the level of the school site. Within this model, the school is understood as an organization whose structure affects teaching and learning. Consequently, the "design and effectiveness of the organization's structure and climate can greatly help or hinder the quality of instruction and curriculum and learning outcomes" (p. 22). School reform models within the *reform network* idea, including those proposed by Sizer (1992) and Comer (1988), emphasize school–community relationships and inclusive learning experiences as critical to success.

Accommodations and Environmental Modifications

IEP teams must make decisions about the use of accommodations and other environmental modifications. The decision-making model described in Chapter 4 with relation to decisions about the student's curricular content included consideration of the use of assistive technology at two levels. The first level is the use of such technology to ameliorate the impact of the student's disability and to minimize or eliminate the need to modify the curriculum. At the simplest level of technology, wearing eyeglasses will likely correct impairments in a student's vision and, consequently, eliminate the need for a curriculum adaptation such as large-print materials. The second level of assistive tech-

Table 5.2. Percentages of children ages 6–21 served in different educational environments under IDEA, Part B, during the 1996–1997 school year: All disabilities

State	Regular classroom	Resource room	Separate classroom	Public separate facility	Private separate facility	Public residential facility	Private residential facility	Home/hospital environment
Alabama	41.27	41.11	15.44	1.06	0.09	0.48	0.27	0.27
Alaska	57.42	30.85	10.06	1.46	0.05	0.02	0.09	0.06
Arizona	46.14	32.87	17.54	1.33	1.14	0.57	0.19	0.23
Arkansas	39.44	43.76	14.15	0.25	0.72	0.00	1.11	0.57
California	52.64	20.99	22.67	1.06	1.73	0.20	0.23	0.48
Colorado	71.14	16.04	8.66	1.48	0.37	0.64	0.97	0.69
Connecticut	56.69	20.23	17.18	1.62	2.81	0.14	1.16	0.19
Delaware	23.70	63.62	7.37	4.06	0.15	0.48	0.00	0.61
District of Columbia	17.19	21.35	38.52	11.61	11.33	0.00	0.00	0.00
Florida	38.55	25.12	32.82	2.18	0.23	0.50	0.00	0.60
Georgia	36.85	34.86	27.02	0.68	0.01	0.42	0.07	0.08
Hawaii	44.23	34.21	20.11	0.25	0.24	0.41	0.18	0.39
Idaho	67.49	23.54	7.20	0.68	0.09	0.51	0.20	0.31
Illinois	36.10	29.83	27.29	3.68	2.00	0.35	0.31	0.43
Indiana	59.72	14.40	23.83	0.82	0.02	0.49	0.33	0.38
Iowa	56.40	27.00	13.46	2.07	0.00	0.81	0.19	0.08
Kansas	61.19	24.80	11.38	1.46	0.19	0.45	0.20	0.34
Kentucky	47.40	34.53	16.51	0.39	0.13	0.53	0.15	0.37
Louisiana	35.15	20.65	40.93	0.89	0.13	1.27	0.04	0.94
Maine	51.38	34.03	11.92	0.66	0.81	0.06	0.79	0.35
Maryland	43.87	23.93	24.49	3.67	2.55	0.55	0.60	0.35
Massachusetts	65.78	13.16	14.43	1.77	3.33	0.0	0.80	0.74
Michigan	48.10	23.83	23.21	4.31	0.0	0.16	0.09	0.30
Minnesota	65.25	21.51	7.73	3.78	0.29	0.77	0.44	0.24
Mississippi	35.22	37.95	24.85	0.50	0.06	0.66	0.03	0.72
Missouri	40.68	39.71	16.10	2.40	0.48	0.39	0.03	0.21
Montana	55.82	32.08	9.66	0.89	0.13	0.58	0.58	0.26
Nebraska	64.15	22.65	10.29	1.67	0.27	0.34	0.11	0.52
Nevada	45.74	41.54	10.11	2.13	0.00	0.11	0.01	0.36
New Hampshire	51.49	25.23	17.20	2.36	1.55	0.31	1.54	0.32

New Jersey	46.43	25.46	19.18	2.84	5.02	0.36	0.06	0.65
New Mexico	33.91	29.87	34.09	0.93	0.01	0.53	0.06	0.60
New York	42.35	13.05	33.65	6.64	2.12	0.69	1.10	0.40
North Carolina	58.33	22.11	17.06	1.17	0.24	0.48	0.20	0.42
North Dakota	78.86	14.14	5.26	0.30	0.22	0.48	0.40	0.34
Ohio	61.47	24.89	8.37	3.75	0.00	0.46	0.00	1.06
Oklahoma	49.78	35.48	12.93	0.64	0.16	0.50	0.11	0.40
Oregon	70.39	18.96	6.52	1.10	1.18	1.28	0.14	0.43
Pennsylvania	37.78	31.00	26.59	1.85	1.61	0.72	0.23	0.23
Puerto Rico	6.03	59.31	26.21	3.89	1.98	0.12	0.06	2.40
Rhode Island	50.40	18.93	25.32	0.70	2.03	0.70	1.26	0.66
South Carolina	35.03	37.82	24.88	0.92	0.05	0.49	0.06	0.74
South Dakota	64.61	25.10	6.71	0.52	0.78	0.75	1.36	0.16
Tennessee	46.14	32.44	18.35	0.86	0.60	0.17	0.01	1.44
Texas	25.58	50.79	21.55	0.87	0.01	0.12	0.00	1.09
Utah	44.20	31.94	20.70	2.43	0.0	0.38	0.0	0.34
Vermont	83.77	7.14	4.04	1.23	1.22	0.16	1.52	0.92
Virginia	41.73	31.65	23.97	0.87	0.59	0.67	0.24	0.29
Washington	50.59	32.54	15.41	0.61	0.22	0.12	0.02	0.48
West Virginia	47.65	35.33	16.11	0.23	0.02	0.27	0.03	0.37
Wisconsin	38.09	41.94	18.27	0.91	0.07	0.48	0.03	0.21
Wyoming	55.88	32.83	8.82	0.36	0.26	0.88	0.56	0.41
American Samoa	51.99	30.28	17.74	0.00	0.00	0.00	0.00	0.00
Guam	29.21	37.27	31.14	1.36	0.40	0.06	0.57	0.00
Northern Marianas	74.92	16.08	8.68	0.00	0.00	0.00	0.00	0.32
Palau	36.00	44.80	17.60	0.00	0.00	0.00	0.00	1.60
Virgin Islands	16.33	31.12	49.56	0.00	0.65	0.00	1.21	1.13
Bureau of Indian Affairs	40.60	48.96	8.22	0.48	0.01	0.23	1.31	0.19
United States and outlying areas	45.74	28.51	21.42	2.08	1.01	0.42	0.28	0.54
50 states, District of Columbia, and Puerto Rico	45.75	28.47	21.43	2.09	1.01	0.42	0.28	0.54

Data based on the December 1, 1996, count, updated as of September 1, 1998. Any discrepancy in the total percentage for each entry is the result of rounding to two decimal places.

Source: U.S. Department of Education, Office of Special Education Programs, Data Analysis System (DANS).

Table 5.3. Percentage of children ages 6–21 served in different educational environments under IDEA, Part B, during the 1996–1997 school year: Mental retardation

State	Regular classroom	Resource room	Separate classroom	Public separate facility	Private separate facility	Public residential facility	Private residential facility	Home/hospital environment
Alabama	6.69	48.28	42.42	2.19	0.08	0.07	0.09	0.18
Alaska	13.00	35.55	51.04	0.28	0.00	0.14	0.00	0.00
Arizona	7.96	20.15	67.39	2.89	1.28	0.00	0.06	0.25
Arkansas	11.09	51.40	33.74	0.02	1.46	0.00	1.63	0.67
California	5.25	12.59	72.25	6.31	1.91	0.00	0.09	1.60
Colorado	35.19	25.69	37.68	0.41	0.06	0.54	0.10	0.32
Connecticut	10.06	21.59	59.62	4.91	2.96	0.20	0.63	0.03
Delaware	4.80	58.06	23.23	12.97	0.50	0.33	0.00	0.11
District of Columbia	1.62	4.52	58.14	25.06	10.66	0.00	0.00	0.00
Florida	2.73	7.59	79.51	9.37	0.14	0.19	0.00	0.45
Georgia	5.98	25.45	67.18	0.64	0.01	0.50	0.07	0.17
Hawaii	17.25	34.39	48.15	0.00	0.0	0.11	0.0	0.11
Idaho	31.85	39.97	26.83	0.98	0.14	0.00	0.17	0.07
Illinois	7.51	5.93	70.00	10.19	5.49	0.18	0.56	0.12
Indiana	13.72	13.60	69.97	1.86	0.00	0.21	0.24	0.38
Iowa	36.45	34.22	26.50	2.36	0.00	0.32	0.11	0.04
Kansas	20.00	30.97	45.58	1.68	0.39	0.35	0.85	0.18
Kentucky	20.63	50.78	27.82	0.20	0.06	0.04	0.04	0.43
Louisiana	2.70	9.56	81.60	2.41	0.47	2.28	0.05	0.92
Maine	7.56	36.15	53.03	0.72	1.99	0.00	0.32	0.24
Maryland	6.91	14.49	57.77	17.88	2.20	0.07	0.42	0.26
Massachusetts	24.33	20.71	48.25	1.66	3.49	0.0	1.21	0.35
Michigan	7.81	16.71	62.01	13.18	0.0	0.07	0.05	0.18
Minnesota	20.91	39.57	31.10	7.70	0.14	0.14	0.17	0.27
Mississippi	2.55	29.64	64.28	1.21	0.01	1.17	0.08	1.07
Missouri	3.07	21.96	58.41	15.10	0.61	0.25	0.08	0.52
Montana	17.88	32.82	47.47	0.15	0.15	0.59	0.59	0.37
Nebraska	26.92	40.54	27.79	3.56	0.19	0.30	0.26	0.44
Nevada	7.79	35.09	43.07	13.74	0.00	0.06	0.06	0.18
New Hampshire	24.33	23.58	41.69	4.82	3.00	0.11	1.71	0.75

New Jersey	2.16	16.83	48.66	16.98	12.67	1.32	0.17	1.21
New Mexico	7.42	14.12	77.45	0.58	0.05	0.00	0.00	0.39
New York	6.24	7.54	56.66	25.34	3.03	0.13	0.66	0.41
North Carolina	14.92	34.97	45.65	3.09	0.68	0.10	0.15	0.44
North Dakota	31.37	41.30	25.26	0.16	0.16	0.24	0.56	0.95
Ohio	20.00	61.99	16.56	0.63	0.00	0.51	0.00	0.31
Oklahoma	11.12	43.08	44.24	0.80	0.18	0.20	0.08	0.29
Oregon	29.64	27.66	39.30	1.79	0.72	0.32	0.13	0.43
Pennsylvania	5.89	28.80	58.68	5.61	0.43	0.17	0.16	0.26
Puerto Rico	1.85	36.19	50.60	7.56	1.84	0.15	0.14	1.66
Rhode Island	2.95	5.25	80.02	0.55	9.39	0.18	1.29	0.37
South Carolina	6.59	27.94	61.25	2.32	0.01	0.47	0.10	1.32
South Dakota	17.54	49.53	26.55	1.01	2.15	0.40	2.76	0.07
Tennessee	7.71	33.98	55.42	1.37	0.95	0.03	0.03	0.51
Texas	1.49	14.67	78.29	3.95	0.05	0.69	0.01	0.85
Utah	4.77	13.16	73.56	8.08	0.0	0.03	0.0	0.40
Vermont	72.71	11.91	12.72	0.52	0.67	0.00	0.74	0.74
Virginia	2.34	22.18	72.64	1.11	0.45	0.62	0.24	0.42
Washington	15.76	41.36	41.65	0.92	0.15	0.05	0.03	0.08
West Virginia	6.74	39.75	52.62	0.30	0.01	0.00	0.04	0.53
Wisconsin	6.45	30.86	58.86	2.92	0.05	0.51	0.07	0.27
Wyoming	7.96	38.68	46.91	1.10	0.14	4.12	0.69	0.41
American Samoa	0.00	0.00	100.00	0.00	0.00	0.00	0.00	0.00
Guam	9.24	26.89	59.66	2.52	0.00	0.00	1.68	0.00
Northern Marianas	64.86	18.92	13.51	0.00	0.00	0.00	0.00	2.70
Palau	16.67	0.00	66.67	0.00	0.00	0.00	0.00	16.67
Virgin Islands	1.12	31.25	66.96	0.00	0.22	0.00	0.22	0.22
Bureau of Indian Affairs	14.92	60.59	16.39	4.42	0.00	0.00	3.31	0.37
United States and outlying areas	10.50	28.44	54.19	4.94	0.92	0.31	0.21	0.49
50 states, District of Columbia, and Puerto Rico	10.50	28.41	54.21	4.94	0.92	0.31	0.21	0.49

Data based on the December 1, 1996, count, updated as of September 1, 1998. Any discrepancy in the total percentage for each entry is the result of rounding to two decimal places.

Source: U.S. Department of Education, Office of Special Education Programs, Data Analysis System (DANS).

Table 5.4. Percentage of children ages 6–11 served in different educational environments under IDEA, Part B, during the 1996–1997 school year: Mental retardation

State	Regular classroom	Resource room	Separate classroom	Public separate facility	Private separate facility	Public residential facility	Private residential facility	Home/hospital environment
Alabama	8.07	43.13	47.32	1.27	0.06	0.03	0.08	0.05
Alaska	14.64	40.50	44.55	0.31	0.00	0.00	0.00	0.00
Arizona	11.63	23.50	62.05	1.53	1.08	0.00	0.00	0.21
Arkansas	12.54	49.51	36.00	0.00	1.32	0.00	0.44	0.18
California	8.12	10.27	74.86	4.63	0.97	0.00	0.03	1.13
Colorado	44.50	25.36	29.89	0.08	0.00	0.00	0.00	0.17
Connecticut	14.57	17.40	63.88	2.76	1.19	0.00	0.19	0.00
Delaware	6.91	57.87	24.71	10.37	0.00	0.00	0.00	0.13
District of Columbia	1.42	3.77	64.62	23.58	6.60	0.00	0.00	0.00
Florida	3.21	8.45	81.62	6.20	0.10	0.04	0.00	0.38
Georgia	7.38	25.39	66.22	0.57	0.00	0.24	0.04	0.16
Hawaii	25.06	30.73	44.21	0.00	0.00	0.00	0.00	0.00
Idaho	44.12	39.86	15.50	0.51	0.00	0.00	0.00	0.00
Illinois	9.26	5.44	75.05	5.65	4.29	0.02	0.20	0.09
Indiana	17.98	12.62	68.24	0.81	0.01	0.01	0.16	0.17
Iowa	41.22	34.50	23.29	0.81	0.00	0.08	0.08	0.02
Kansas	30.30	30.26	39.00	0.09	0.13	0.04	0.13	0.04
Kentucky	24.51	53.05	21.93	0.15	0.04	0.01	0.03	0.28
Louisiana	3.66	11.64	81.24	1.99	0.20	0.76	0.02	0.48
Maine	9.51	38.28	48.96	0.23	3.02	0.00	0.00	0.00
Maryland	8.59	15.49	62.43	12.06	1.06	0.00	0.04	0.34
Massachusetts	28.22	18.13	50.66	0.66	1.83	.	0.34	0.14
Michigan	10.48	17.95	63.45	7.79	.	0.08	0.01	0.24
Minnesota	30.62	44.84	21.11	3.03	0.05	0.00	0.02	0.32
Mississippi	3.19	22.41	72.25	1.31	0.00	0.42	0.00	0.42
Missouri	3.76	23.41	61.21	10.96	0.18	0.04	0.06	0.37
Montana	20.39	42.36	35.68	0.18	0.18	0.35	0.35	0.53
Nebraska	37.29	38.26	21.56	2.14	0.00	0.08	0.17	0.50
Nevada	9.93	43.80	38.39	7.74	0.00	0.00	0.00	0.15
New Hampshire	22.42	24.55	44.55	5.15	1.82	0.00	1.21	0.30

New Jersey	2.94	15.72	57.32	13.16	8.88	1.15	0.00	0.83
New Mexico	7.68	17.75	73.77	0.66	0.00	0.00	0.00	0.13
New York	7.66	6.84	70.20	11.54	3.17	0.02	0.35	0.22
North Carolina	22.32	33.59	40.98	2.10	0.76	0.00	0.08	0.17
North Dakota	46.71	32.72	19.14	0.41	0.00	0.00	0.21	0.82
Ohio	21.77	59.43	18.19	0.54	0.00	0.00	0.00	0.07
Oklahoma	12.49	41.88	44.73	0.51	0.15	0.05	0.00	0.18
Oregon	42.88	23.88	31.22	1.01	0.50	0.14	0.29	0.07
Pennsylvania	5.51	26.12	63.91	3.87	0.22	0.08	0.03	0.25
Puerto Rico	1.42	46.18	48.67	2.14	1.07	0.00	0.00	0.51
Rhode Island	3.70	5.09	85.42	0.00	5.56	0.00	0.23	0.00
South Carolina	6.45	27.27	63.78	1.75	0.01	0.14	0.04	0.56
South Dakota	25.34	54.45	19.01	0.51	0.34	0.00	0.34	0.00
Tennessee	10.14	34.56	54.11	0.59	0.31	0.00	0.00	0.28
Texas	2.50	20.58	74.64	1.61	0.06	0.03	0.01	0.58
Utah	6.35	17.16	75.30	1.11	0.00	0.00	0.00	0.08
Vermont	86.27	9.15	2.99	0.00	0.70	0.00	0.35	0.53
Virginia	2.24	13.52	82.73	0.87	0.15	0.04	0.05	0.40
Washington	19.48	44.25	35.70	0.37	0.14	0.00	0.03	0.03
West Virginia	8.43	37.34	53.72	0.13	0.00	0.00	0.00	0.38
Wisconsin	8.99	33.11	55.19	2.21	0.02	0.28	0.00	0.20
Wyoming	11.82	46.62	39.86	0.00	0.34	0.34	0.34	0.68
American Samoa	0.00	0.00	100.00	0.00	0.00	0.00	0.00	0.00
Guam	16.13	58.06	25.81	0.00	0.00	0.00	0.00	0.00
Northern Marianas	75.00	6.25	18.75	0.00	0.00	0.00	0.00	0.00
Palau	0.00	0.00	0.00	0.00	0.00	0.00	0.00	0.00
Virgin Islands	1.68	35.29	63.03	0.00	0.00	0.00	0.00	0.00
Bureau of Indian Affairs	22.61	64.75	9.20	3.45	0.00	0.00	0.00	0.00
United States and outlying areas	13.35	27.81	54.86	2.93	0.62	0.07	0.07	0.29
50 states, District of Columbia, and Puerto Rico	13.34	27.77	54.91	2.93	0.62	0.07	0.07	0.29

Data based on the December 1, 1996, count, updated as of September 1, 1998. Any discrepancy in the total percentage for each entry is the result of rounding to two decimal places.

Source: U.S. Department of Education, Office of Special Education Programs, Data Analysis System (DANS).

nology use, described in Chapter 4 and detailed in Chapter 16, is as a means to modify the curriculum through adaptations that change the presentation or representation of the curriculum or the student's interaction with that curriculum. These uses involve modifications to the curriculum or, in the case of the eyeglasses, interventions to modify the student's capacity to interact with the curriculum. Another class of modifications, however, focuses on the environment and accommodations or environmental modifications that may be necessary to ensure student success and progress. The IEP team is charged with making decisions about the accommodations and environmental modifications that are necessary for the student to have physical or cognitive access to the school building and the classroom. Chapter 2 discussed some types of accommodations related to cognitive access, including signage and color coding. The IEP team also is required to determine whether the student needs accommodations to participate in statewide or districtwide tests or whether the student can instead take an alternate assessment. These issues are discussed in the next section.

Test Accommodations and Alternate Assessments

In an August 24, 2000, memorandum to state directors of special education across the country, Judith Heumann, former Assistant Secretary of Education, noted that because assessment in education is often associated with direct benefits to students (e.g., promotion, graduation) and is an integral aspect of educational accountability systems related to student progress and school performance, to exclude students with disabilities from such assessments solely on the basis of disability would be a violation of several civil rights acts, including Section 504 of the Rehabilitation Act of 1973 (PL 93-112) and the Americans with Disabilities Act of 1990 (PL 101-336). Her OSEP memorandum is explicit in the intent of IDEA to involve students with disabilities in statewide or districtwide assessment. The memo stated that

> Although IDEA makes no specific reference as to how States include children with disabilities in the State accountability system, the IDEA requires States to establish performance goals and indicators for children with disabilities—consistent to the maximum extent appropriate with other goals and standards for all children established by the State—and to report on progress toward meeting these goals. (p. 4)

Furthermore, states must use information about the performance of children with disabilities on statewide and districtwide assessments to revise their state improvement plans to, in turn, improve the performance of students with disabilities on these assessments.

The IEP team must determine how, not whether, a child participates in statewide and districtwide assessments. Again, the memorandum is quite clear about this, stating that the only students with disabilities who are exempted from participation in general statewide and districtwide assessments are students with disabilities convicted as adults under state law and incarcerated in adult prisons. The IEP team must determine whether any modifications in test administration are needed for the student to participate in the statewide or districtwide assessment. If the IEP team determines that the student cannot participate in a specific statewide or districtwide assessment, it must state why that assessment is not appropriate and how that student will be assessed.

State and local education agencies (SEAs and LEAs) must provide alternate assessments for those students for whom test accommodations are not sufficient to enable them to participate in the typical statewide or districtwide assessment. Those alternate assessments had to be established no later than July 1, 2000. According to OSEP and IDEA, alternate assessments need to be aligned with the general curriculum standards set for all students. The OSEP memorandum stated repeatedly that the "purpose of an alternate assessment should match at a minimum the purpose of the assessment to which it is intended to serve as an alternate" (p. 10).

As such, IEP teams need to decide which, if any, modifications or accommodations would enable a student with mental retardation to participate in the statewide or districtwide assessment and, if they are unable to identify any such modifications and accommodations, to decide if the student should participate in an alternate assessment.

Developmentally and Age-Appropriate Instruction

A final issue that IEP teams need to consider in making curriculum decisions and designing educational supports is that their efforts should be conducted within the context of **developmentally appropriate practice** and with the use of age-appropriate activities. These two issues, one important in early childhood education and the other more focused with older students, share common themes and directions for IEP teams. The National Association for the Education of Young Children (NAEYC) defined *developmentally appropriate practice* as applying to educational programs that provide instruction and learning activities consistent with a child's developmental needs and that focus on child-initiated, child-directed, and teacher-supported activities. According to the NAEYC position statement on *Developmentally Appropriate Practice in Early Childhood Programs Servicing Children from Birth through 8*, such practice depends on three kinds of information:

1. What is known about child development and learning
2. What is known about the strengths, interests, and needs of each child
3. What is known about the social and cultural context in which children live (1997, pp. 4–5)

The gist of developmentally appropriate practice is the idea that "in real life children learn many different things from a naturally occurring experience" (Hutinger, 1994, p. 60). Instruction, then, 1) should be referenced to naturally occurring experiences; 2) should be based on knowledge about child development and learning; 3) should take into account student strengths, interests, and needs; and 4) should respond to the social and cultural context in which children live. The themes of addressing instruction and mental retardation as a function of the interaction between the disabling condition and the environment or context were repeated throughout the first chapter and resonate when considering developmentally appropriate practices. Likewise, themes around natural learning environments reflect practice in community-referenced planning and community-based learning (see Chapter 13), and issues of focusing on student strengths, interests, and needs mirror issues concerning student-directed planning, discussed previously in this chapter, as well as themes in self-determination (see Chapter 15).

Linking instruction to *developmentally appropriate* activities, however, has a controversial history in the education of students with mental retardation—a history that drove the focus on the need for *age-appropriate* instruction. Researchers seeking to understand human cognitive, social, and behavioral development have differing theories about the developmental trajectories in child development and whether developmental paths are uniform across all children in all contexts. In the field of mental retardation, the theory of invariant developmental paths has been debated (Hodapp, Burack, & Zigler, 1990). Researchers have posed competing theories about whether the developmental path experienced by people with mental retardation is similar to that experienced by children who develop typically or whether it is qualitatively different. A feature of this debate focused on the **mental age–chronological age discrepancy**. Mental age is a psychological construct that emerged from the realm of intelligence testing. Early intelligence tests resulted in a mental age determination that, when divided by the chronological age and multiplied by 100, resulted in a mental quotient or, eventually, intelligence quotient (IQ). Revised editions of tests such as the Stanford-Binet yielded a mental age, and conversion charts were used to calculate an IQ score based on mental age and chronological age.

A developmental approach to the education of students with mental retardation became associated with and interpreted as providing educational activities for the student that were consistent with or aligned with that student's mental age. Therefore, many adolescents with mental retardation were engaged in activities that were chronologically age-inappropriate but tied theoretically to the student's supposed mental age. Brown et al. illustrated this with the following anecdote:

> For years professionals have told parents, "Yes, Mr. Jones, your child is 20 years old and will complete school in 10 months, but he has a mental age of 4. That is why we are teaching him to sing, "When you're happy and you know it clap your hands"; that is why we are teaching him to touch long as opposed to short, to touch big as opposed to little, and to touch a card with four pennies taped to it." (1979, p. 81)

In addition to the concern with the mental age–chronological age discrepancy hypothesis, Brown and colleagues (1979) identified two other hypotheses that are linked to a developmental perspective that have had similar impacts on the education of older students with more significant disabilities. They are

- The earlier stage hypothesis: The student is developmentally functioning at an earlier stage or level, and instruction must be focused on moving the student to the next level.

- The "not ready for" hypothesis: The student is not ready socially, emotionally, intellectually, physically, and so forth to perform functional skills and must progress through a linear sequence of prerequisite skills before learning the functional skills.

The problem with applying these hypotheses to the education of students with mental retardation was, as Brown and colleagues pointed out, that students never acquired functional knowledge and skills that led to outcomes that were meaningful in their lives. However, as efforts to provide intensive supports in workplaces (e.g., supported employment), independent living (e.g., supported living), social and leisure environments, and other areas were combined with instruction on needed skills in community-based, ecologically valid environments (see Chapter 14), it became evident that independent of developmental level, mental age, or prerequisite skills, young people with mental retardation could succeed in these adult environments. Moreover, it became readily apparent that enabling young people with mental retardation to engage in age-appropriate activities accomplished an added benefit of changing the way others perceived these students (e.g., as an eternal child playing with a toy versus a person with adult interests).

Are these two philosophies incompatible? Do IEP teams have to choose between pursuing the attainment of developmental milestones or ignoring such information and focusing only on age-appropriate activities? The most fruitful path lies somewhere in the middle. By ignoring knowledge about child development, educators might deprive younger children of natural experiences that are important for progress and miss out on knowledge that would provide direction for gaining access to the general curriculum for older students. For example, Doll, Sands, Wehmeyer, and Palmer (1996) used research in child development to identify a likely sequence in the emergence of self-determination. This, in turn, provided useful information for teachers working with students with cognitive disabilities about when to focus on particular component elements of self-determined behavior, whether that would be a focus on choice making and the expression of preferences in early elementary school, a focus on identifying basic problems and solutions in late elementary school, or providing instruction about decision making on meaningful issues (e.g., substance use, relationships, career decisions). Knowledge about the development of self-determination can, in fact, be applied to provide access to the general curriculum.

The use of information about development to identify a likely sequence of skills (and, as such, to identify a likely scope and sequence of instruction) is not the same as making curriculum decisions about students based solely on hypotheses such as mental age. When students do vary in their attainment of developmental milestones, this can be a signal to provide adaptations or accommodations that enable the student to achieve those milestones and can provide the springboard for developing age-appropriate activities that promote progress in the student's educational program.

SUMMARY

The IEP team has been an important component of the special education enterprise since its inception with the passage of the Education for All Handicapped Children Act of 1975 (PL 99-457). This has not changed with subsequent reauthorizations of that act; if anything, the IDEA Amendments of 1997 expanded the role of the IEP team. It is clear that the IEP team is intended to be a decision-making body that reaches decisions about a wide variety of issues pertaining to the student's formal and informal education program. In too many cases, however, such meetings are not deliberative and are not based on a group decision-making process. If students with mental retardation are to achieve access to and progress in the general curriculum, the IEP process needs to change to become more inclusive and deliberative. The decision-making model described in Chapter 4 provides a structure or format by which the design of the student's formal curriculum can occur. Such a process should be implemented within the context of a meeting that incorporates principles from both person-centered and student-directed planning processes in order to ensure meaningful involvement on the part of all stakeholders. Such a merger creates a context in which students and families can dream about their futures and set goals that enable them to reach such dreams as well as to identify skills and knowledge necessary for students with mental retardation to meet these goals. The IEP team can then use information from this deliberative decision-making process centered around the general curriculum and the student's unique learning needs to make other decisions, including placement decisions.

The place where students can have the greatest access to the general curriculum is in the context of the general classroom. Students with more intensive support needs must spend proportionally more of their school day in community-based environments (see Chapter 14) as they get older; however, if other students without disabilities are learning in the community as well, this can become part of the educational context for all students. Finally, IEP teams need to consider how to ensure that students with mental retardation are included in procedures that are used for accountability purposes by schools. Such processes, however, must be designed such that they can show progress for all students, not just a few. As discussed in Chapter 3, it is our strong assertion that many high-stakes tests do not meet this criteria and create barriers to access of education for many students, including students with disabilities. Chapter 8 discusses the potential of using portfolio assessments to determine progress, and professionals and advocates alike who are concerned with the education of students with mental retardation must become involved with advocates for other children who are similarly disenfranchised by high-stakes testing to make the process more equitable and accountable for all students.

ADDITIONAL READINGS

The IEP and IFSP Team and Process

Bateman, B., & Linden, M.A. (1998). *Better IEPs: How to develop legally correct and educationally useful programs.* Reston, VA: Council for Exceptional Children.

Council for Exceptional Children (CEC). (1999). *IEP team guide.* Reston, VA: Author.

Office of Special Education and Rehabilitation Services (OSERS). (2000). *A guide to the individualized education program.* Washington, DC: Author. (Available http://www.ed.gov/offices/ OSERS/OSEP/IEP_Guide/)

Woods-Cripe, J.J., & Crabtree, J. (1995). *A family's guide to the Individualized Family Service Plan (videotape).* Baltimore: Paul H. Brookes Publishing Co.

Person-Centered Planning

Giangreco, M., Cloninger, C.J., & Iverson, V.S. (1998). *Choosing outcomes and accommodations for children (COACH): A guide to educational planning for students with disabilities* (2nd ed.). Baltimore: Paul H. Brookes Publishing Co.

Mount, B. (1988). *Interactive planning: New tools for collaborative planning in complex environments.* New York: Graphic Futures.

Mount, B., & Zwernik, K. (1988). *It's never too early. It's never too late. A booklet about personal futures planning* (Publication #421-88-109). St. Paul, MN: Governor's Planning Council on Developmental Disabilities.

O'Brien, J., & O'Brien, C.L. (n.d.). *The politics of person-centered planning.* Syracuse, NY: Center for Human Policy.

Schwartz, A.A., Jacobson, J.W., & Holburn, S. (2000). Defining person-centeredness: Results of two consensus methods. *Education and Training in Mental Retardation and Developmental Disabilities, 35,* 235–258.

Student-Directed Planning

Halpern, A., Herr, C.M., Wolf, N.K., Doren, B., Johnson, M.D., & Lawson, J.D. (1997). *NEXT S.T.E.P.: Student transition and educational planning.* Austin, TX: PRO-ED.

Martin, J.E., & Marshall, L.H. (1995). *ChoiceMaker: Self-directed IEP.* Longmont, CO: Sopris West.

Wehmeyer, M.L., & Kelchner, K. (1995). *Whose future is it anyway? A student-directed transition planning program.* Arlington, TX: The Arc of the United States.

Wehmeyer, M.L., & Sands, D.J. (1998). *Making it happen: Student involvement in education planning, decision making and instruction.* Baltimore: Paul H. Brookes Publishing Co.

IDEA Age-of-Majority Issues

Lindsey, P., Wehmeyer, M.L., Martin, J., & Guy, B. (in press). Age of majority and mental retardation: A position statement of the Division on Mental Retardation and Developmental Disabilities. *Education and Training in Mental Retardation and Developmental Disabilities.*

Alternate Assessment and Test Accommodations

Bryant, D.P., Patton, J.R., & Vaughn, S. (1999). *Step by step guide for including students with disabilities in state and district-wide assessments.* Austin, TX: PRO-ED.

Council for Exceptional Children (CEC). (2000). *Making assessment accommodations: A toolkit for educators.* Reston, VA: Author.

Elliott, S.N., & Braden, J.P. (2000). *Educational assessment and accountability for all students.* Reston, VA: Council for Exceptional Children.

Kleinert, H., & Klearns, J. (2000). *Alternate assessment: Measuring outcomes and supports for people with disabilities.* Baltimore: Paul H. Brookes Publishing Co.

Thurlow, M.L., Elliott, J.L., & Ysseldyke, J.E. (1998). *Testing students with disabilities: Practical suggestions for complying with district and state requirements.* Reston, VA: Council for Exceptional Children.

Thurlow, M.L., Ysseldyke, J.E., & Olsen, K. (2001). *Self-study guide for the development of statewide assessments that include students with disabilities.* Minneapolis, MN: National Center on Educational Outcomes. (Available: http://www.coled.umn.edu/nceo/OnlinePubs/Self_Study_Guide.html)

Developmentally and Age-Appropriate Instruction

Dunn, L., & Kontos, S. (1997). *Developmentally appropriate practice: What does research tell us?* Champaign, IL: ERIC Clearinghouse on Elementary and Early Childhood Education (ERIC). (Available: http://ericec.org/pubs/digests/1997/dunn97.html)

Brown, L., Ford, A., Nisbet, J., Sweet, M., Donnellan, A., & Gruenewald, L. (1983). Opportunities available when severely handicapped students attend chronological age appropriate regular schools. *Journal of The Association for Persons with Severe Handicaps, 8,* 16–24.

Hart, C.H., Burts, D.C., & Charlesworth, R, (1997). *Integrated curriculum and developmentally appropriate practice: Birth to eight.* Albany: State University of New York Press.

Horst, G., Hill, J.W., Wehman, P., & Bailey, C. (1981). Developing age-appropriate leisure skills in severely handicapped adolescents. *Teaching Exceptional Children, 14*(1), 11–15.

National Association for the Education of Young Children (NAEYC). (1997). *Position statement on developmentally appropriate practice in early childhood programs servicing children from birth through 8.* Washington, DC: Author. (Available: http://www.naeyc.org/resources/position-statements/daptoc.htm)

Wehman, P., Schleien, S., & Kiernan, J. (1980). Age appropriate recreation programs for severely handicapped youth and adults. *Journal of The Association for Persons with Severe Handicaps, 5,* 395–407.

CHAPTER OBJECTIVES

1. Define *program evaluation*, and discuss purposes for conducting such evaluations.
2. Identify the differences between student evaluation and program evaluation.
3. Discuss how personal outcome indicators differ from previous indicators of quality services and supports.
4. Compare and contrast how individualized and personalized supports might differ.
5. Describe empowerment evaluation and discuss how it differs from traditional program evaluation processes.

KEY TERMS

Program evaluation
Student evaluation
Personal outcomes
Empowerment evaluation
Individualized or personalized supports

6

Program Evaluation

Empowerment Evaluation and Personal Outcomes

A mong the duties of the individualized education program (IEP) team is determining the means by which a student's education program is evaluated. This is
done, principally, through the establishment of goals, which become one portion
of the accountability mechanism inherent in the IEP process. The IEP document itself
forms a contract for the actual services to be provided and the first level of accountability is whether the school is, indeed, providing these services and supports. The establishment of goals that include measurable indicators of student progress provides a
second level of accountability; however, legal rulings from the Board of Education v.
Rowley onward have indicated that a lack of progress is not necessarily an indication of
an inappropriate educational program. Nevertheless, the IDEA Amendments of 1997
discuss progress in the general curriculum as a desired outcome and require that IEP
teams document such student progress.

FROM STUDENT EVALUATION TO PROGRAM EVALUATION

Although the establishment of goals and criteria to measure student progress has always
been a primary function of the IEP process, **program evaluation** has rarely been conducted. That is, **student evaluation** has been the norm, and any failure to achieve established goals has been interpreted as a problem with or for the student. If, however,
mental retardation is defined as a function of the interaction between the student's
functional limitation and the social context, then it is no longer possible to operate
within an evaluation process that focuses *only* on the student and his or her impairments. Instead, it is necessary to consider the context or the environment, in this case
the student's education program (i.e., the totality of the student's educational experience), as the subject for evaluation. It is critical that we move from student-focused to
program-focused evaluations.

Program evaluation refers, quite simply, to efforts to evaluate the efficacy and utility of a given program. The referent *program* could be anything from the student's educational services and supports to an agency's effectiveness. Whereas student-focused
evaluation efforts are limited to examining student progress on predetermined goals, program evaluation is, by definition, a broader and more encompassing activity. Owens
(1988) identified three general purposes for conducting program evaluation. The first
purpose is to provide stakeholders in the program with information about the program's
plans, activities, and outcomes that can contribute to the modification and improvement
of the program. In the case of a student's education program, the stakeholders who are
integral to the program include the student, his or her family, school personnel, community members, and, generally, members of the IEP team. The second purpose is to
provide whatever information is needed to inform external audiences about the efficacy
of the program. Although this purpose is most salient to programs that are funded via
external sources, such as grant projects, it is relevant to keep in mind that the educational
enterprise has multiple funders, from taxpayers in the local community, to the state education agency, to the federal education department. One of the primary reasons for the
public's growing dissatisfaction with America's education system has been the sense that
the system has not been accountable with regard to both student outcomes and taxpayer
expenditures. As such, being able to provide information to document the effectiveness
of a program is a critical feature. The third purpose of program evaluation is to provide
information for replicating the program at other sites. Again, although this is not a pri-

mary focus of evaluation related to a student's education program, few parents, students, or educators would dispute that when something has been shown to be effective for one student, it would be wasteful not to take what has been learned in that situation and apply it to other similar and potentially beneficial circumstances.

Traditional program evaluation has, by and large, been a top-down affair conducted by experts in evaluation design, data collection, analysis, and reporting. Agencies engaged in a wide array of programmatic activities, from drug treatment to youth sports, have often had to hire an expert external evaluator to evaluate their program. Moreover, traditional program evaluation usually has identified a single person as the evaluator. Discussions in the evaluation literature address questions such as whether the evaluator should be a staff person for the agency or project or an external party. The gist of these discussions deals with issues related to the objectivity of the evaluator and, because most agencies don't have the luxury of having an expert in program evaluation on staff, the competence of the evaluator.

Although there is often some benefit to having someone who is, at least theoretically, external to the agency to evaluate the program's efficacy, there is also a cost to relying on external experts. First, with regard to the issue of objectivity, although an external evaluator may be more objective than someone internal to the agency, simply bringing in an external evaluator does not ensure complete objectivity. Program evaluators, for example, may hesitate to be too tough on an agency if doing so might jeopardize future contracts (Yin & Schiller, 1990). Beyond simply the question of evaluator objectivity, however, there is a growing concern in the field of mental retardation, particularly within the realm of adult services, that the emphasis on objectivity and measurability in program evaluation and accountability systems has not, in fact, resulted in benefits in the lives of the people served by these programs. In sum, the question is whether the field has employed measurement processes and focused on *measurable* outcomes at the cost of being able to say something meaningful about the quality of the lives led by the people being served by such efforts. The education enterprise must deal with these same issues: Has our procedural, student-focused evaluation process missed the forest for the trees by measuring compliance with legal processes (e.g., IEP forms) or measurable outcomes (e.g., achievement test scores, job placement) but ignoring what really happens to students when they exit the system? The following section examines some of the issues involved in efforts to identify **personal outcomes** that provide meaningful indicators of the quality of life of people with mental retardation served through adult programs. The subsequent section introduces a program evaluation framework, called **empowerment evaluation,** that embodies the personal-outcomes approach to program evaluation. The final section examines the implementation of an empowerment evaluation framework as a means to guide IEP team evaluation decisions.

FROM PROCESS-BASED TO PERSONAL OUTCOMES-BASED EVALUATION

The accountability mechanism in place to ensure an *appropriate* education for students with disabilities is, fundamentally, a process-based mechanism. As long as schools conform to the procedures and processes outlined in the law, the courts have deemed their education system to be *appropriate*. The presumption—not altogether unfounded—is that compliance with such procedural requirements, in essence, lays the foundation for a quality education program. Similar presumptions and procedural accountability mechanisms have been used in other service delivery areas, including deeming service agencies eligible to receive government funds to provide residential or vocational programs serving adults with mental retardation. For example, any residential facility receiving Medicaid funds to pay for services for people with mental retardation must conform with some baseline procedural requirements or they will be placed on "vendor hold" and not receive funding until deficiencies are corrected.

In the early 1990s, an organization called the Council on Quality and Leadership in Supports for People with Disabilities (formerly the Accreditation Council on Services for People with Developmental Disabilities) responded to growing concerns in the field of adult services for people with mental retardation about the disconnection between agency licensure and accreditation and the outcomes of and for people with mental retardation by proposing to focus on personal outcomes, not compliance with procedures or processes. The Council was formed by several national advocacy and professional associations in the field of mental retardation and developmental disabilities, including The Arc (formerly the Association for Retarded Citizens of the United States), the American Association on Mental Retardation, United Cerebral Palsy Associations, Inc., the National Easter Seal Society, and the Autism Society of America. The intent of the Council was to provide an accreditation process for service agencies that addressed issues of quality in such services. Compliance with minimum federal or state processes or procedural requirements to gain Medicaid funding was seen as insufficient to ensure quality, and the purpose of the Council was to create a process by which providers who wanted to go beyond meeting *minimum* requirements could do so and, in turn, receive accreditation as having met more rigorous requirements. For the advocacy and policy associations that formed the Council, this was a means to correct the deficiencies in service provision brought about by a focus only on minimum criteria. For the agency undergoing the accreditation process, it was a way to show that the services it provided went beyond the minimum and were deemed to be high quality. Like licensure, funding, and accreditation accountability processes before them, initial efforts by the Council focused on process and procedural requirements, albeit more rigorous and exacting ones than the minimal criteria set by the U.S. Department of Health and Human Services Health Care Financing Administration (HCFA) to receive Medicaid funds. However, by the late 1980s, it was evident that despite the Council's focus on more stringent processes designed to improve services, the lives of many people with mental retardation and developmental disabilities had not improved.

In 1991, as a result of this dissatisfaction, the Council launched an effort to develop an accreditation system for agencies that formed decisions on service quality on the basis of personal outcomes. The Council defined *personal outcomes* as "what people expect from the services and supports they receive" and the "major expectations that people have in their lives" (1997, p. 3). A more detailed discussion of personal outcomes follows, along with examples of how the Council operationalized these personal outcomes to engage in accreditation activities.

The Council's emphasis on personal outcomes as a component of program evaluation is different from and often in contrast to traditional program evaluation activities:

> Traditional program evaluation is limited because the program goals are set by management or the funding source, and not by the people receiving services. Therefore, program evalu-

ation determines whether the program meets its own goals rather than the outcomes of the people receiving the services and supports. (1997, p. 4)

According to the Council (1997), traditional measures of quality in programs involve input, process, and program outcomes. Input measures refer to those resources such as the physical environment, finances, personnel, and other resources available to the program. Compliance indicators related to input measures usually examine things such as minimal square feet of living space per bedroom or minimal number of staff per person served (Council, 1997). Process measures focus on the arrangement and use of those inputs and usually focus on the degree to which the agency conformed to planning requirements and reporting processes. Program outcomes measures focus on the results of the service or program. This usually involves countable outcomes, such as number of job placements, medication reductions, and so forth.

The Council's approach, however, centered around the importance of measuring personal outcomes if the quality of a given service or program was to be truly determined. As mentioned previously, personal outcomes are, quite simply, those life outcomes that matter most to the person being supported. The Council (1997) suggested the following with regard to personal outcomes:

- The actions and behaviors of agency staff members change when they know and understand people with disabilities as people with priority outcomes similar to their own instead of as disabled people who need certain programs.

- Organizational strategic planning, resource allocation, and evaluation also change when personal outcomes become prioritized, and the organization's role moves from providing programs and services to supporting people in achieving the life outcomes they value. When organizations recognize that the programs and services are not an end in themselves, they are better able to direct resources to provide supports. Personnel and other resources are allocated around such outcomes. There is an emphasis on supports.

- Focusing on personal outcomes places listening to and learning from the person at the center of the organizational life.

- Focusing on personal outcomes focuses attention on the whole person. Most evaluation processes focus only on one segment of a person's life, and the person's existence is divided among agencies and programs. Personal outcomes measures focus on the whole person across all services and settings.

These points have obvious and recognizable overlap with issues discussed in the opening chapter with relation to the definition and conceptualization of mental retardation. The development of personal outcomes illustrates that "services and supports are not ends unto themselves, but make outcomes possible" (Council, 1997, p. 7). The movement to a focus on personal outcomes is, however, not necessarily an easy route. The Council noted several principles of personal outcomes measurement:

- There is no standard definition of any outcome that applies to a group of people.
- It is unlikely that any two people will define an outcome in the same manner.
- People define their own outcomes based on their own experiences.
- Personal outcomes are defined from the person's perspective. (p. 7)

The Council balances these principles with the need to quantify adherence to certain standards of performance that relate to high-quality supports by emphasizing the role of choice and decision making as well as rights and responsibilities in outcome areas. Table 6.1 lists the personal outcomes measured by the Council. The Council's guidelines for surveyors (i.e., those people who conduct the evaluation) contain detailed instructions about how to gather information to come to a judgment about each indicator. For example, under the category of "Identity" and the personal outcome "People choose personal goals," surveyors are instructed to engage in a conversation with the person receiving supports and ask a series of questions, ranging from "How do you want your life to be in the future?" to "What are your hopes and dreams for yourself?" Surveyors then question people who know that person best and ask questions pertaining to the person's goals, how they know what those goals are, and what supports are in place to enable the person to attain those goals. Once information is gathered from these interviews as well as through document checks or other interviews as needed, surveyors answer three questions:

- Have the person's priorities regarding goals been solicited?
- Does the person choose personal goals?
- Are these the goals the person is working toward?

Table 6.1. Personal outcomes measures

Category	Personal outcome
Identity	People choose personal goals.
	People choose where and with whom they live.
	People choose where they work.
	People have intimate relationships.
	People are satisfied with services.
	People are satisfied with their personal life situations.
Autonomy	People choose their daily routine.
	People have time, space, and opportunity for privacy.
	People decide when to share personal information.
	People use their environments.
Affiliation	People live in integrated environments.
	People participate in the life of the community.
	People interact with other members of the community.
	People perform different social roles.
	People have friends.
	People are respected.
Attainment	People choose services.
	People realize personal goals.
Safeguards	People are connected to natural support networks.
	People are safe.
Rights	People exercise rights.
	People are treated fairly.
Health and wellness	People have the best possible health.
	People are free from abuse and neglect.
	People experience continuity and security.

From the Council on Quality and Leadership in Supports for People with Disabilities. (1997). *Personal outcomes measures.* Towson, MD: Author; reprinted by permission.

If the surveyor can respond positively to all three of these questions, the outcome is considered present. For each of the personal outcomes listed in Table 6.1, the surveyor goes through a similar process. The accreditation process also includes indications of organizational performance measures that capture some of the components of more traditional program evaluation, although within a total quality management framework. These two sections, personal outcomes and organizational performance measures, form the basis for accreditation of high-quality services, an accreditation that is based on outcomes, not compliance with specific processes or procedures.

FROM INDIVIDUALIZED TO PERSONALIZED

Although most of us in the special education field place a great deal of stock in the importance of *individualization,* it should be evident from the previous example that the way in which the education programs of students are designed and evaluated is not truly individualized. Perhaps a better way to consider the process is to leave behind the language of individualization with its connotations of curriculum decisions outside the general curriculum and instead look at *personalized educational supports.* The root of the word *individualize* is *individual:* "of or pertaining to a single human being; by or for one person" (Urdang, 1984, p. 678). *Individualize* means to "consider or deal with individually, alone" (Urdang, 1984, p. 678). Conversely, the word *personalize* refers to the process of taking something and modifying it to make it one's own. Whereas *individualization* evokes a sense of separateness from everything else, *personalization* retains a focus on the person while leaving behind any sense of separateness. The processes of person-centered planning and the determination of personal outcomes imbedded into an IEP team decision-making process that begins with the general curriculum, as described in Chapter 4, can lead to the development of a student's educational program, both curriculum and supports, that is truly personalized.

EMPOWERMENT EVALUATION

The focus on personal outcomes described previously takes one step closer to a program evaluation framework that enables IEP teams to make decisions about a student's education program. However, the purpose of the accreditation process used by the Council is sufficiently different from the purpose of designing an evaluation of a student's education program that it cannot simply be replicated within the educational context. For one thing, the Council's process still involves an external evaluator who is responsible for coming into the agency and performing the accreditation survey. The purpose of the Council's program evaluation process is to evaluate the efficacy and quality of an agency's supports and services by taking into account the personal outcomes discussed. One might very well design a program evaluation intended to evaluate the services and supports provided by an entire school under a similar process. However, it is not the school's program that the IEP team is charged with evaluating; it is the program designed for one student. Although the development of personal outcomes is an important part of such a process, there is a better way to approach such an evaluation, referred to as an *empowerment evaluation process,* which is

[T]he use of evaluation concepts, techniques, and findings to foster improvement and self-determination. It employs both qualitative and quantitative methodologies. Although it can be applied to individuals, organizations, communities, and societies or cultures, the focus is on programs. It is attentive to empowering processes and outcomes. (Fetterman, 1996, p. 4)

The empowerment evaluation framework has been used widely to evaluate program and policy spectrums, including programs in substance abuse prevention, welfare reform, HIV prevention, school reform, and crime prevention (Fetterman, 1996). Moreover, the empowerment evaluation approach is well grounded in evaluation theory and practice, having been "institutionalized within the American Evaluation Association" (Fetterman, 1996, p. 3) and embodying the spirit of standards developed by the Joint Committee on Standards for Educational Evaluation. The empowerment evaluation process is described subsequently. Before describing the process, however, it is important to describe how empowerment evaluation differs from typical program evaluation.

First, as has been discussed, traditional program evaluation is objective. The evaluator distances him- or herself from the program being evaluated to provide an unbiased, factual, objective picture of the program. When traditional program evaluation is applied to the education programs of students with disabilities, one is left with the uncomfortably familiar scenario in which students with mental retardation are subjected to standardized intelligence testing. In such testing situations, the tester is instructed, indeed required, to retain some distance from the student (albeit after having established some rapport), to implement the test items in a sequential and specified manner, and then to tally the results for use in making decisions about eligibility and placement. There is rarely any meaningful role for students in this process; if anything, students and family members have test scores interpreted for them so that they might understand the reason for a given decision.

Because previous discussions have emphasized the need for person-centered and student-directed planning, it goes without saying that a top-down, expert-driven program evaluation model does not meet this criteria. However, unlike traditional program evaluation, the empowerment evaluation process has "an unambiguous value orientation—it is designed to help people help themselves and improve their programs using a form of self-evaluation and reflection. Program participants conduct their own evaluations and typically act as facilitators; an outside evaluator often serves as a coach or additional facilitator depending on the internal program capabilities" (Fetterman, 1996, p. 5).

Fetterman continued, stating that empowerment evaluation is, by necessity, "a collaborative group activity, not an individual pursuit," and noting that "an evaluator does not and cannot empower anyone; people empower themselves, often with assistance and coaching" (1996, p 5). Fetterman further contended that because of the democratic nature of the empowerment evaluation process, the intent or purpose of the process changes. Traditional program evaluation emphasizes and results in an evaluation of the program's value and utility. That judgment is the endpoint of the program evaluation process. In empowerment evaluation, however, the determination of a program's utility becomes an indicator by which to improve the program. Fetterman stated, "Program participants learn to continually assess their progress toward self-determined goals and to reshape their plans and strategies according to this assessment. In the process, self-determination is fostered, illumination generated, and liberation actualized" (p. 6).

IMPLEMENTING AN EMPOWERMENT EVALUATION PROCESS

Fetterman and colleagues (1996) identified several steps of the empowerment evaluation process. In combination with the person-centered and student-directed planning context described in Chapter 5, the following steps could provide a framework for IEP teams to make evaluation decisions and improve a student's educational program.

Step 1: Taking Stock

The first step in the empowerment evaluation process involves having program participants, in this case all members of the IEP team, rate the student's education program on a scale of 1 to 10, with 10 indicating the highest level of quality and satisfaction. Because it is often more useful to compartmentalize programs, team members may identify several specific activities or portions of the education program and rate them separately. Program participants also are asked to document their ratings. The importance of this step is tied not specifically to the ratings themselves but to the establishment of baseline information and the opportunity that is provided to allow each participant to express his or her perception of the quality of the program. Fetterman (1996) also noted that this process often illustrates or reinforces the necessity of collecting data to either support or refute some of the perceptions.

Step 2: Setting Goals

The second step of the process is to have program participants indicate how highly they would like to rate their program in the future and to set goals that would lead them to that rating. This goal-setting activity is aimed at the level of improving the program and not specifically related to setting educational goals for the student's IEP. That is, the goal setting is intended to identify ways that the program might be improved overall. Returning to the potential use of this process in an IEP team setting, the team might decide that one component of improving the quality of the student's overall educational program might involve securing some specialized training for the student's teacher; consequently, the team might set a goal to make that happen. It might be that a particular assistive device or physical accommodation is necessary to improve the educational program; as such, the team would put in place goals and an action plan to achieve that. The IEP team might determine that the general curriculum is too narrowly defined for their particular district and set a goal to address issues of universal design in that curriculum. These are IEP team goals, not student goals.

Step 3: Developing Strategies

As a third step, program participants are responsible for developing strategies to achieve overall program objectives. At the level of the educational planning process, this is the determination of the appropriate curriculum and the design of relevant educational supports, including the determination of instructional goals for students.

Step 4: Documenting Progress

In this step, program participants are asked what types of documentation are needed to provide evidence of progress at two levels: progress on the IEP or system goals identified in Step 2 and progress on the specific content or programmatic goals and strategies identified in Step 3.

Figure 6.1 provides the configuration of the generic empowerment evaluation process. It is worth noting that although an empowerment evaluation process is stakeholder-driven, there is still a role for an external evaluator. However, that role changes from one of expert in a top-down model to one in which the evaluator's role is to train program participants to self-evaluate, to facilitate the process, and, when necessary, to advocate on behalf of the program.

SUMMARY

A focus on a functional definition of mental retardation requires a change in the way the success of services and supports is determined. Traditional models of evaluation in education have been student-focused, with goals and objectives set that measure student progress on educational tasks. Although this is an important and necessary component of the educational process, it is too easy to look at a student's lack of progress on such goals as reflective of a problem with the student. For example, among students with mental retardation, the lack of progress on student-focused goals is attributed to the student and his or her disability. The functional model, however, requires that the IEP team attend at least as much, if not more, to the context in which the person is functioning. As such, program evaluation, the process of measuring an agency's success, becomes an important component of the educational process. Not only does program evaluation become important, but it becomes necessary in order to depart from traditional program evaluation processes that incorporate top-down and expert-driven procedures.

It is important to clarify the use of the word *program* in this sense and, indeed, as used throughout this text. We suggested in Chapter 1 that the functional model of mental retardation should move the field from designing programs that attempt to meet student needs to, instead, identifying **individualized (or personalized) supports.** There is a tendency to respond to innovation in education by creating a program. Thus, a school may become inclusive as a response to the demand to include students with disabilities

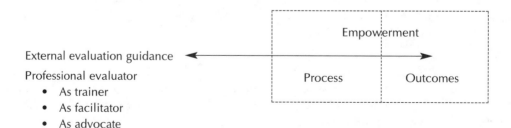

Figure 6.1. Generic empowerment evaluation process. (Adapted from Yin, Kaftarian, & Jacobs, 1996.)

in typical classrooms. Such programs are usually conceptualized as an option outside or in addition to the typical option. In this sense of the term, *program* comes to mean an option. The availability of such options is often limited, either by resources or other factors. Thus, the inclusion program is available only to some students and not to others. IDEA uses *program* (e.g., individualized education program) in a broader sense, not as an option but as an agenda or a plan to be implemented. Such a program, then, is implemented by truly individualized (or personalized) supports, not by a limited set of options (e.g., programs). The use of *program* in reference to program evaluation is broader even than the sense of the term as an agenda or plan. *Program evaluation* refers to the agency's efforts to evaluate its success in implementing that agenda or plan.

Instead of these traditional processes, an empowerment evaluation process with a focus on personal outcomes indicators is recommended. Empowerment evaluation is a process designed to empower the individual through systematic evaluation of the services or supports provided to him or her. Unlike other evaluation mechanisms that emphasize external, objective evaluation, the empowerment evaluation process seeks involvement by key stakeholders in the process. This framework, in turn, provides the mechanism by which to focus on personalized supports and personal outcomes in the lives of students.

ADDITIONAL READINGS

Program Evaluation

Sanders, J.R. (1994). *The program evaluation standards: How to assess evaluations of educational programs* (2nd ed.). Thousand Oaks, CA: Sage Publications.
Shadish, W.R., Cook, T.D., & Leviton, L.C. (1993). *Foundations of program evaluation: Theories of practice*. Thousand Oaks, CA: Sage Publications.

Personal Outcomes

Council on Quality and Leadership in Supports for People with Disabilities. (1997). *Personal outcomes measures*. Towson, MD: Author.
National Center on Outcomes Research. (1999). *The Council on Quality and Leadership in Supports for People with Disabilities: Personal outcomes chart book*. Towson, MD: Author. (Available http://www.ncor.org/frame3.htm)

Empowerment Evaluation

Fetterman, D.M. (1997). Empowerment evaluation and accreditation in higher education. In E. Chelimsky & W.R. Shadish (Eds.), *Evaluation for the 21st century: A resource book* (pp. 381–395). Thousand Oaks, CA: Sage Publications.
Fetterman, D.M. (2000). *Foundations of empowerment evaluation*. Thousand Oaks, CA: Sage Publications.
Fetterman, D.M., Kaftarian, S., & Wandersman, A. (1996). *Empowerment evaluation: Knowledge and tools for self-assessment and accountability*. Thousand Oaks, CA: Sage Publications.
Patton, M. (1997). Toward distinguishing empowerment evaluation and placing it in a larger context. *Evaluation Practice, 18*(2), 147–163.
Scriven, M. (1997). Empowerment evaluation examined. *Evaluation Practice, 18*(2), 165–175.

CHAPTER OBJECTIVES

1. Define *learning communities*, and contrast them with traditional classrooms.
2. Discuss the reasons for establishing learning communities and the importance of creating learning communities that allow access to the general curriculum.
3. Describe how to create a learning community.
4. Discuss how students can participate in learning communities and how this process supports self-determination.

KEY TERMS

Learning community
Multicultural teaching
Intelligence
Task management skills
With-it-ness
Overlapping
Smoothness
Surface management

7

Creating Learning
Communities
for All Students

AFTER HAVING SUCCESSFULLY TAUGHT
STUDENTS WITH A WIDE RANGE OF
CHARACTERISTICS, MS. MILLER DECIDED
TO ADJUST HER WARDROBE TO MATCH
HER TEACHING CONFIDENCE.

A critical feature in achieving access to the general curriculum for students with mental retardation is creating **learning communities** in which students understand their roles and responsibilities, have a voice in the establishment of classroom rules and activities, and respect and value one another. In typical classroom cultures, students often do what someone else wants them to do and conform to someone else's rules. *Learning communities,* however, support diversity and provide the foundation for students' active involvement in their own educational planning and decision making. This chapter introduces issues related to the establishment of learning communities, the importance of collaborative learning to achieve access to the general curriculum, and the role of peer- and student-mediated learning.

WHAT IS A LEARNING COMMUNITY?

In Mr. Guiterrez's fifth-grade classroom, the room is abuzz. Groups of students are scattered about the classroom, working together. Some students are sitting in front of computers, another group of students are huddled in the back of the room on the floor with paper and pencils. Another group of students are working in front of the class aquarium, apparently observing activity in the tank. Mr. Guiterrez is sitting with one group, listening to them read from a paper. Mr. Guiterrez stands up and shakes a tambourine. The class quiets down, and Mr. Guiterrez turns toward the group in the rear of the room. "Mellie," he says, "will your team be finished with the story by 10:30?" Mellie casts her eyes around her group, looking for some sign from them. Answering based on their affirmative nods, she replies, "No problem, Mr. G. We've got you covered."

As part of a school identified by the U.S. Department of Education as a Blue Ribbon School, Mr. Guiterrez's students earn some of the highest achievement scores in their building. This day, students of differing abilities and ethnicities are working together on a series of literacy activities that are tied to the science and social studies standards for the fifth grade. Mr. Guiterrez has two students with disabilities in his classroom. One of them, Ruben, has been identified as having mental retardation and is working on alternative reading standards; however, he continues to work with his classmates during the reading-to-learn block in the morning. In this block, Ruben is responsible for listening and summarizing the work of the group so that he develops the ability to sequence and organize information to tell a logical story or describe a series of events. During the course of the morning, Mr. Guiterrez makes the rounds of his teams, exhorting, quieting, encouraging, and redirecting.

Every classroom is, in fact, a complex culture, comprising the backgrounds and experiences that students bring in a unique mix of ritual, expectation, and values (Ballenger, 1992). This mix is led but not dominated by the teacher, who is responsible for ensuring that specific learning linked to specific standards occurs in that time and place. Like any leader who is responsible for the collective work of a group or a team of people, teachers have the exciting responsibility of creating a classroom community that brings out the best that each individual and the group together can accomplish. In truth, classrooms have always been learning communities (Cochran-Smith, 1995). The degree to which teachers are conscious of creating a feeling of community among the individual members of a class is dependent on the individual nature of teachers and their ability to reflect, describe, and purposely shape that community.

In 1998, cognitive psychologists Brown and Campione named this phenomenon and described effective and ineffective classroom communities. This chapter explores how researchers have come to understand community and its effect on learning in classrooms. To explore the topic fully, many different perspectives of cognitive psychologists, educational anthropologists, critical theorists, and practitioners are offered. It is through these varied lenses that the multifaceted community that comprises a classroom can be explored.

WHY ESTABLISH A LEARNING COMMUNITY?

There is no doubt that affect and cognition are inextricably linked (Colvin & Sugai, 1988). Attention, focus, sustained effort, practice, and mastery occur when learners are engaged in tasks that they describe as meaningful and attainable. Learners are able to use their cognitive skills to the greatest effect when the social milieu in which they are learning provides emotional support. Opportunities for feedback, recognition, and encouragement for effort as well as frequent acknowledgments of progress are essential. Learning requires effort, and effort is expended in environments in which success and recognition are possible. This is true for all kinds of learners, from students who excel at abstract learning tasks in math, science, and the social sciences to those who interpret and use words, the canvas, or the stage to express and define human experience. It is true for those who learn from experience, repetition, and practice and for those who navigate unfamiliar languages, customs, and cultural expectations while trying to grapple with the academic rigor of our nation's classrooms. It is equally true for students with mental retardation. Learning communities are simply the most practicable way to create multicultural, multiability classrooms.

Practicality

In most public schools in the United States, the ratio of students to adults is high. Many public school classrooms have student–teacher ratios of up to 45:1. If students must rely on teachers to provide the emotional, academic, and social feedback that they need in order to learn, then it is likely that many students fail to receive the kind of support that they need to learn to their fullest potential. This is particularly true in today's classrooms, in which the social, economic, ability, linguistic, religious, and cultural experiences and backgrounds of students are so varied. Teachers will not be able to meet the individual emotional, social, and academic needs of every student if they conceive of classroom activities as linear interactions that occur solely between themselves and their students. Anyone who observes or works in a classroom understands that the reciprocal interactions between teachers and their students are only a part of the interactive classroom environment in which learning occurs.

One argument for establishing a classroom learning community is practical. Students need specific, direct, and immediate feedback to support their learning. Teachers must distribute their attention and feedback among so many learners with such different needs that it is impossible for them to support learning by themselves; they need allies. The students in the classroom can become those allies. By teaching students the skills to provide effective and frequent feedback to each other, teachers can increase the support for learning that all students, including students with mental retardation, need.

Multicultural Teaching

Another important rationale for building a learning community is that learning communities nurture and celebrate the existence of diverse cultures through **multicultural teaching.** Whenever people congregate repeatedly, over time, they build a culture of that time and space. Beliefs and attitudes shape what is valued and produced in any community. In many communities in the United States, there is a dominant culture that has sociohistorical roots in Western Europe. The prevailing or dominant Western European–influenced culture is predicated on many ideas and values, including those of individual achievement, personal freedom, survival of the fittest, and economic self-sufficiency. Because these values and others play out in classrooms that are themselves led by teachers who were brought up within the dominant culture or whose family encouraged them to aspire to those values, public schools often reflect the dominant culture of the local community. The United States, however, is also host to a number of other cultures indigenous to North America or from Asia, Africa, Central and South America, and Eastern Europe that have historically been silenced or devalued by the dominant culture. Members of some of these cultures value and celebrate attributes that conflict with those of the dominant culture: interdependence, economic communalism, and family and tribe membership. To an ever-increasing extent, classrooms in this country are filled with students from minority cultures. Consequently, teachers must navigate the boundaries among the various cultures and help students and themselves to understand the cultural expectations and interpretations they bring to classroom events (Ballenger, 1992).

Building a learning community means that conscious attention needs to be paid to the values behind rule making and the degree to which rules and expectations silence or enhance learning opportunities for each and every student. Consider the concept of being "ready to learn." To members of the dominant U.S. culture, this concept encompasses a variety of characteristics, some of which are listed in Table 7.1. These characteristics, however, do not necessarily indicate readiness to learn as much as they indicate the ability of the child to navigate the typical classroom culture in which the teacher is the leader whose authority is unquestioned and in which the classroom is the place where children are expected to display particular sets of skills (Delpit, 1995). Although children of various cultures and backgrounds come to school with developmentally appropriate cognitive skills, many of them are unable to perform the skills expected by the dominant culture (Heath, 1983). As recently as the early 1990s, the response to this

Table 7.1.   Characteristics of kindergarteners who are ready to learn

Children who enter kindergarten ready to learn are able to
1. Listen to and follow directions, even when they may not want to do so or may be more engrossed in something else
2. Respond to their teachers' questions, even if the answer is obvious or the children know that the teacher knows the answer
3. Sort and categorize objects by color, shape, and size

finding was to spend time teaching children to conform to the dominant culture. In doing so, the diversity of expression, creativity, and synergy that comes from identifying, understanding, and valuing difference was lost. With the move from cultural assimilation to true, mulitcultural universal design in the 21st century, classrooms can become much more nurturing and students can experience much greater success.

Learning Abilities

A third critical reason to build learning communities is predicated on an understanding of learning ability and the variance in that ability. The work of psychologists such as Gardner (1991) and Sternberg (1994) moved the discussion about the human potential to learn well beyond concepts such as intelligence and IQ scores. As researchers began to predict human performance in particular situations at the beginning of the 20th century, they made many errors in conceptualizing constructs such as **intelligence.** Unfortunately, although the science behind these constructs has been criticized, the constructs themselves have remained a fundamental element of Western European thought.

Intelligence is popularly thought to be a unitary trait that comes in doses that range widely from a little intelligence to a lot of intelligence. This popular conception has been reinforced by the work of psychologists who have used the normal bell curve to describe human performance and the intelligence or learning potential of individuals. Most people cluster around a particular point, with a few people having extreme intelligence and a few others having limited intelligence. The problem with the notion of intelligence as a predictor of learning is that it is only measured by culturally bound assessments that value certain ways of knowing and processing information. Some measures of intelligence assess the ability of individuals to recognize analogies between two words and then select other words that describe a similar kind of relationship. An example of this type of analogy is that an Arabian is to a horse as a Bic is to a pen. The construct of linguistic analogies coupled with the kind of vocabulary that is used for each analogy place nonnative English speakers, nonnatives of the United States, and individuals whose life experiences are not linguistically based, such as craftspeople, at a disadvantage. Unfortunately, these kinds of assessments are used to predict performance in school. As a result, students from varied cultural backgrounds may be identified as having learning disabilities when their learning abilities and talents are not exposed by such assessments.

Unfortunately, teaching students who are gifted and talented is often seen as preferable to working with students whose learning abilities are inadequately measured by current assessment tools, including students with mental retardation. So, cultural values infuse the way that teachers interpret and use learning assessments and the way that they define the status of the work they do (Eisenhart & Graue, 1993). By doing so, teachers and other educators may inadvertently place at a disadvantage or discount the learning potential of many students, not just students with cognitive impairments.

How and what students are able to learn varies widely. Knowledge grounded in specific practices and honed over multiple experiences can be highly skilled and difficult to attain, even for the most powerful processors of information. Therefore, a baker who may understand the nuances of humidity, temperature, and elasticity may be as skilled as a technical expert in his or her own area as a CEO of a technology company. Situation-specific social skills, the ability to predict, the understanding of markets, and the use of subtle environmental cues that signal changes in performance choices may characterize each individual's expertise in his or her milieu (Bandura & Wood, 1989). However, neither the butcher nor the CEO may be able to acquire or approach the skills of the other individual in his or her chosen arena. Yet, tests of intelligence of both individuals may yield very different results based on the number of years of formal schooling, their linguistic skills, and their knowledge of popular culture.

A growing number of scholars in the disability studies arena believe that ability differences, particularly those that are based on intellectual differences, are cultural constructs rather than absolute performance characteristics of individuals. Consider the following situation: A child who learns through motor or visual experiences rather than through language is disadvantaged in cultures that are linguistically based (Grossman, 1995). Therefore, whenever groups, families, or tribes convene and talk together, this child is at a disadvantage. Over time, perhaps because visual or experiential learning opportunities become less frequent, the child has fewer opportunities to learn new information or skills. The information and skill gap between this child and his or her peers grows larger over time because access to information is so limited. Unfortunately, the child is said to be disadvantaged and, eventually, to have developmental delays because access to opportunities to learn were not available. By the time this child is chronologically old enough to enter kindergarten, he or she appears to have a disability. Does this child have a disability, or did the environment place him or her at a disadvantage?

Exploring disability through this social lens helps us to think more broadly about the skills and abilities that students bring with them to the classroom. It also helps teachers to begin to think about how the learning environments that they construct can support or disable students.

THE SOCIAL NATURE OF LEARNING

In learning communities, students of many different abilities learn together. The work of a variety of researchers helps us to understand how and why such classrooms provide so many opportunities for learning. Bandura (1986, 1989, 1991) and other social learning theorists (i.e., Schunk, 1996) have shown us how students can learn from the examples provided by others. Social learning theory opened a window, for example, on how watching another person practice newly acquired skills and receive feedback on the task could help a learner avoid mistakes, produce a more skilled initial performance, and choose tasks on which he or she might have a higher probability of achieving successful results. The constructivist perspective, discussed in Chapter 4, demonstrates how students build individual and unique conceptual schemas and how they are able to constantly assimilate new information and adjust their mental schemas to describe more precisely the relationships among concepts. Social constructivists take this notion even further and suggest that mental schemas and processes are built and strengthened through interactions with others. Finally, the work of Lave and Wenger (1994) suggests that the content, processes, and tools of learning are specific to particular learning situations. A classroom in the United States has a particular set of expectations and rituals about how knowledge is passed along that requires particular kinds of learning tools, language, and processes. These same tools, language usage, and processes may be woefully inadequate for a novice monk in a Tibetan monastery or an elementary student in Botswana.

These theories help to explain how learning occurs as a result of the opportunity to co-construct meaning through tasks that create opportunities for more than one student to interact together to solve a problem, research texts and the World Wide Web for additional information, construct a model, learn a new skill, or practice an emerging one. The greater the diversity of learners, the more varied the approaches to problem solving, researching, constructing, learning, and practicing are. A richer and deeper understanding of the details and a wider lens to view the issue or content area emerge from the interaction.

HOW CAN TEACHERS CREATE LEARNING COMMUNITIES?

Learning communities that meet the needs of all their members are constructed on a set of principles that must be addressed throughout an academic year.

Principle 1: Knowing Your Students

Teachers should learn as much as they can about the cognitive, social, and affective needs of each of their students. Assuming that students have different understandings of themselves and their abilities, teachers should get to know their students by interviewing each student individually or, if the students are older, using surveys to collect information about the students' interests, avocations, and life experiences. Teachers can ask students to discuss how effective and successful they are as learners, as friends, and as classroom citizens and can use observation and questioning to find out what kinds of recognition and feedback the students most appreciate. Teachers should create connections between themselves and their students by sitting with their students at lunch, conducting home visits, hanging around while the students are using the computer, or finding other times outside of the ordinary classroom interactions to connect with each student (Hollingsworth, 1994).

In addition, teachers should engage other class members in the same sorts of tasks at the beginning of each year or term to create opportunities for students to get to know one another. Creating a biography newsletter or 5-minute video biographies are two ways to do this. If the technology is available, digital photographs can be taken of each student in the class, and classmates can be paired up to write each other's biography for a class web site.

It is important to recognize that students will need different kinds of support to meet their needs for recognition, self-direction, social justice, and self-advocacy. Teachers can purposefully create situations to observe student-to-student interactions as well as interactions between the students and the teacher him- or herself. In the elementary grades, this may be as simple as having students create and perform simple skits for one another. Teachers can work with students at the beginning of the year to pick a theme for creating skits, perhaps one that focuses on issues of social justice and creating friendships. A teacher might, for example, pose a problem around an ostracized child, a child from a different culture or country, or a situation in which a student did not tell the truth to protect another child. Students can then act out a skit that shows how they might solve the problem. In these activities, teachers can look for evidence that each skit team involved all its team members and observe which students assume large speaking roles. These kinds of activities begin the process of creating a sense of community in the classroom and help the teacher to form a more complete understanding of the needs of individual students and what teams to form to ensure success in learning activities.

Principle 2: Maintaining a Student Information System

Teachers should develop, maintain, and use a consistent and sustainable system of collecting information about individual and group performance to help them make informed grouping decisions throughout the year. Setting up situations in which teachers can observe and learn about individual students means that there is a need for a system to record observations about individual students. Teachers can really only be successful in tracking student progress over time if they create a system and a process that they use on a daily basis to enter information. *Daily* is the operative word because teachers observe and preside over so many complex interactions every day.

Computers are important tools and can facilitate such data collection and coding. However, because many teachers in less affluent school systems across the country still do not have access to up-to-date, working computers, the process that is described here can be adapted to notebooks. Basically, teachers should store information by calendar date. For example, in Table 7.2 the teacher has entered journal notes by date and day of the week. Often, commercially available calendar software programs contain a journal feature in which daily notes can be entered. An alternative organizational system for anecdotal notes is to create a word processing or notebook file for each student in which the teacher can make journal entries.

Teachers also need to keep numerical information, such as grades on quizzes, homework, and exams. Several software packages for tracking and compiling grades are available that can be used to enter data and to display trend data so that teachers can begin to look for patterns in student performance. Trend data should be examined at

Table 7.2.   A teacher's journal entries by date

Monday November 5	Jim N. stayed with his science period throughout the period.
	The cricket team is having a hard time sharing materials.
	I spoke with the social worker and discovered that Hannah has been moved to a foster home.
	The class completed 5 of 6 skit performances today.
Tuesday November 6	I am worried about the worm farm activity. Only Sara and Jamal seem invested.
	Teams are spending too much time remembering what they did the day before and cannot move quickly to the next step. I need to teach them how to finish their teams by taking minutes and planning what they will do the next day.
Wednesday November 7	Hannah cried all through math today. I asked her to go see the social worker, but she did not want to leave the classroom.
	I have to ask Jamal and Sara to head up a team of researchers on the worm farm work—one member from each science team. Energy seems to be picking up.
Thursday November 8	I had to remove Jim N. from assembly this morning but took the opportunity to bring Hannah along, too, and read them both a story while my teammate supervised the class. Hannah spent the rest of the day next to me but did not cry today.
	We finished up the last of the skits.
	I took spelling grades. No surprises there. I will give group grades next week.
Friday November 9	I need a break this weekend!
	I will visit Hannah's foster care mom on Tuesday of next week.
	I am going to regroup the literacy teams for *The Snowy Day*.
	I am going to try to put Jim N. in with Jamal.

least once a month so as not to miss subtle changes in student performance that warrant observation, individual student conferencing, family involvement, or support from a student assistance team.

Principle 3: Coaching Collaborative Learning

Teach students how to work together for multiple outcomes. This principle encompasses some complex ideas. First, teachers must teach specific skills to students so that they can collaborate successfully. Students need to learn how to listen to each other and paraphrase what they hear. They need to understand how to take turns and make sure that each of their peers has a chance to voice his or her opinion or ideas. Both of these skills require teaching, modeling, and practicing specific subskills and then holding each student accountable for using these skills in his or her group. Students who work in learning teams need verbal and written feedback about how they work together. The teacher's responsibility is to teach the skills, create learning tasks that are sufficiently engaging to motivate students to participate, and evaluate student performance against task and process standards.

Listening, turn taking, and adjusting the group's process to ensure participation by all group members are important process skills to teach and revisit as groups are formed and reformed throughout the year. Students also need task management skills, including those discussed in detail in Chapter 15. They need to learn and use processes that lead to successful task completion. These **task management skills** include asking and answering the following questions:

- What is the task?
- What are we expected to have or be able to do when we finish this task?
- What knowledge and skills do we need to complete the task?
- What do we know, and what do we need to learn?
- Are there parts of this task that we can assign to individual group members?
- Are there parts of this task that we must do together?
- How long do we have to complete the task?
- In what order will we complete the steps for this task?
- Who will keep track of our progress through the steps?
- Who will keep track of the quality of our work?
- How often do we need to meet?
- How will we provide feedback to each other about our contributions to the task?
- Who wants to provide task status information to our teacher?

The Self-Determined Learning Model of Instruction, described in detail in Chapter 15, provides a process for teaching students with mental retardation how to approach tasks by answering these questions. The words that are used here to identify the questions, nevertheless, need to be adjusted to the age group of the students and for varying levels of support needs. Looking at the questions themselves and practicing them first with relatively familiar tasks help students to rely on a learning process to work in teams. It should be noted that these questions lead to a linear and analytical problem-solving model that is particularly prevalent and valued in the Western European academic tradition. They also happen to be the kinds of problem-solving procedures that are most researched and familiar to the Western orthodoxy. Students who have not been exposed to this sort of problem solving may find it foreign and constricting. As teachers become more familiar with creating learning communities and learning teams, they may help their students to create nonlinear personalized processes that anchor teams to a specific approach that is familiar and comfortable for all members of a team.

Principle 4: Supporting Student Learning Through Redefining the Role of the Teacher

Teachers need to understand and perform their role as a coach with learning groups. Coaches understand the abilities and the limitations of each of their athletes. They help their athletes to capitalize on their strengths and find ways to avoid their limitations and motivate each athlete to put forth maximum effort to accomplish a goal. Great coaches provide feedback on what can be done better, develop an individual relationship with each athlete, and support their athletes when they fail. Team coaching requires emphasis on the group and the individual's responsibility to the group.

Teaching in a learning community is much like coaching. Although content mastery rather than athletic performance may be the goal, teachers still need to attend to the aspects of teaching that motivate teams of learners toward their goals, support the team in learning how to benefit from the abilities of each member of the team, help the team to learn how to support one another, and provide sufficient feedback so that the team can assess its own progress and work more efficiently to master its goals.

Principle 5: Celebrating Learning

Make achievements and successes a public and explicit conversation in the classroom on a daily basis. Chapter 5 emphasized personal outcomes indicators, and teachers applying this perspective can ensure that every student, regardless of age or ability level, receives and talks about success and progress each day.

The benefits of learning communities are many, but without thoughtful planning and evaluating, there are some drawbacks that teachers need to guard against. As groups are being constructed, the needs of students who are more proficient at learning and improving must be considered. Although these students often have the information or skills to lead the work of a group, they also need opportunities to participate in groups in which they can apprentice as well as teach. Students who tend to dominate groups need opportunities to be in groups in which their linguistic skills are matched or challenged by other learners. Students who are shy or reflective need opportunities to work in teams where there is patience or consideration for their style of interaction. Students who have great difficulty with attending to specific tasks or participating in all aspects of a task can partially participate.

Team members need to know what they can and cannot expect from the students. Over time, as a learning community gels, these differences can be accommodated without much intercession from the teacher; however, without guidance and social skill support, the accommodations and modifications that students create around their team members can be dysfunctional and stigmatizing. Investing in building a learning community means that teachers spend time in designing and planning their teams; teaching team interaction skills; mixing and matching team members; and differentiating on the basis of student skill and need, task complexity, and learning outcomes.

WHAT ROLES AND RESPONSIBILITIES
DO STUDENTS HAVE IN A LEARNING COMMUNITY?

In a learning community, students assume a variety of roles that support their own affective and social development while helping to propel the work of the community itself. Students learn how to support, not judge, their team members. In Mr. Guiterrez's classroom, described at the beginning of this chapter, students are asked on a daily basis to evaluate their contributions to their team. Mr. Guiterrez collects these evaluations and uses them to identify teams that he needs to facilitate more closely. As students become more comfortable in their roles, daily evaluations fade into weekly and then biweekly self-evaluations.

As supporters, students are taught to look for and orally comment on the strengths and assets that their fellow team members bring to a task. Much like doubles partners on the tennis court learn to encourage rather than criticize each other's performance, teams are encouraged to comment frequently and positively on group participation, listening skills, creative problem solving, self-advocacy, and sharing of roles and responsibilities. Performing these skills requires specific, direct instructions complete with modeling skilled performance, practicing the elements of the skills, and receiving formal feedback and evaluation from the classroom teacher. Students can be taught such skills as time management, problem solving, strategic learning skills, goal setting, and task management even in the elementary grades.

WHAT DO TEACHERS NEED TO TEACH
TO ACHIEVE AN ACTIVE LEARNING COMMUNITY?

Facilitating learning communities requires skills that are not necessarily emphasized in many teacher preparation programs. For instance, an important tactic for teaching leadership is to model it. Leadership is a complex set of skills and dispositions that can be tapped in each individual. It requires confidence in one's own ability to provide direction and in the members of the group to rise to the task; clarity in the initial direction to be taken; and an ability to adjust levels of encouragement and feedback to nuances in group members' attitudes, receptivity, actions, and skills. Teachers can model these skills for their students, and they also can talk about the approaches to leadership they use so that students become conscious and reflective about their own skills in this arena. Teachers also need excellent collaboration skills—not only with their colleagues but also with their students—so that successful completion of tasks and activities is as important to the students as it is to the teacher.

A critical component of any learning community is the use of data and other evidence to make, refine, and transform instructional and classroom management decisions. Findings from research about teaching demonstrate that teachers who are adept at collecting and reviewing evidence to examine the success of their learning approaches are more likely to improve their teaching processes and tactics. Fine-grained analyses of student performance lead to improved teaching approaches and, ultimately, to greater student accomplishment. Hence, teachers must develop their skills in organizing, collecting, analyzing, and interpreting and using data and other evidences to guide instructional decisions.

In classrooms designed as learning communities, this means that teachers collect observational and anecdotal information about the students' strengths and weakness in working as teams and use this information to teach and reinforce process skills. In addition, teachers use brief assessments to look at individual skill development and respond to those data by intensive direct teaching segments that scaffold the students' ability to master particular content or tasks.

HOW CAN STUDENTS HELP DESIGN AND SUSTAIN A LEARNING COMMUNITY?

If assessment is to become a cornerstone of successful learning communities, the collection and management of information systems need to be thought out and implemented in a way that engages students and teachers in using information to improve performance. In other words, assessment is a part of the work of the entire learning community. To manage the task of collecting and organizing information, teachers can have students correct their own work and enter the results in a paper or digital database. By focusing attention on different sets of evidences each day—spot-checking work or focusing only on particular groups of students whose performance varies from day to day—ongoing data can be collected. Students can engage in critical inquiry by working in pairs to review and assess each other's work. The key here is to enlist students in self- and other-evaluation so that data that gauge student learning are continually collected and reviewed. The empowerment evaluation process described in the previous chapter provides a framework through which to engage in these classroom-level evaluations.

CLASSROOM MANAGEMENT IN A LEARNING COMMUNITY

Managing a classroom as a learning community means that teachers facilitate the work of large numbers of students through attention to the flow of a given activity period. The primary function of attending to flow is to ensure that students spend as much time as possible engaged in learning. The work of Kounin in the 1970s has great relevancy to the concept of *flow*. Kounin (1970) suggested that teachers who achieve instructional fluency or flow share several skills: 1) with-it-ness, 2) overlapping, 3) smoothness, 4) momentum, and 5) coherence (see Table 7.3).

With-it-ness

With-it-ness is the teacher's ability to be aware of all activity occurring in the classroom (Kounin, 1970). Teachers should consciously scan the classroom, check on each of the groups, provide feedback, and react to incidences that may be interfering with opportunities to learn. Initially, teachers may need to prompt themselves to scan the environment by using a cue that occurs on a regular and frequent basis in the classroom,

Table 7.3.	Elements of classroom management
With-it-ness	
Overlapping	
Smoothness	
Momentum	
Coherence	
Routines and procedures	
Transitions	
Group focus	
Surface management	

Source: Kounin (1970).

such as each time the door opens or each time the teacher picks up a pencil. Scanning is something teachers must teach themselves to do.

Overlapping

Teachers in learning communities need to be able to attend to both the curriculum activity and students' behaviors simultaneously, which is called **overlapping.** So, while one group may be struggling with identifying the big idea in a reading passage, the teacher may also be attending to how the group is engaging in joint problem solving. By moving back and forth between the content and the process, the teacher can keep the group engaged in learning both skills.

Smoothness

Teachers lead students from one activity to the next, planning transitions and making verbal connections between activities so that students are led logically from one activity to the next. **Smoothness** helps to reduce the number of redirections that are used in the classroom and increases task engagement. Smoothness maintains an evenly distributed flow of instruction from the beginning to the end of an activity or lesson. When handling distractions, the interaction should be brief and direct. The task at hand is to keep everyone's attention on the learning target. For example, if there is a need to debrief with a student, it should be done when it is not taking up the time of the other learners. Or when class members need reminders about the materials they need to complete a task, teachers should have samples nearby to remind students of the supplies they need rather than using up time to discuss the materials. Smoothness is broken when explanations or directions are too long. Teachers should try to keep directions to three-step procedures and provide a visual list of directions. Teachers can then check for understanding; for example, a teacher might say, "Are we going upstairs before we expose our film?" Finally, students always have more questions than teachers have time to answer. Evaluate how to answer a question that will help the whole group get started, stay engaged, or finish a task. If the answer to the question keeps the class from becoming engaged, teachers should try to answer it individually, at a later time. The notion is that large groups need to focus on the topic so that all learners can become engaged. When comparing the performance of novice and expert teachers, Good and Brophy (1994) noted that expert teachers spent more time than their novice colleagues in developing, teaching, and ensuring that routines and procedures were learned so that everyday tasks were automatic and required little attention on the part of either the teacher or the students. Expert teachers plan how classrooms will be used for learning and teach students how and for what purposes the classroom is laid out. Managing surface behaviors adeptly means that the momentum of a lesson or activity can be maintained.

Surface Management

Surface management techniques (Wood & Long, 1991) help to ensure smoothness and prevent potentially distracting behavior. Using a few techniques—showing genuine interest in student work as a student seems to be losing interest, moving closer to students who seem restless, surprising students who may not be aware of your presence, and reminding students about steps in a routine—are all techniques teachers can use to prevent serious disruption of the class flow. Time spent in developing, nurturing, and extending the concept of learning communities means that teachers spend more time in promoting and supporting prosocial behavior, citizenship, and learning and less time managing and disciplining.

Active Teaching

In addition to surface management techniques that can prevent behavior problems, teachers in learning communities use features of active teaching to engage the entire class. These features include alerting the group, connecting new information to prior knowledge, presenting information in engaging ways to pique student interest, maintaining coherence in the sequence of information that is offered, and ensuring that students have multiple opportunities to practice skills and receive feedback before expecting that they will be able to perform a skill without support.

DO LEARNING COMMUNITY STRUCTURES CHANGE FROM ELEMENTARY TO MIDDLE TO HIGH SCHOOL?

There are unique challenges for learning communities at the elementary, middle, and high school levels that require careful planning and teaching. In general, the developmental differences among students are greatest in the early elementary levels and, therefore, great care in planning lessons that are accessible to all students is required. In middle school, students are constantly working on shaping and defining their identities. Yet, as personal differences emerge, they may reject or deny those differences because of their simultaneous need to fit in with the group. This tension between self and group can lead to self-imposed isolation, lack of participation, and disruption in group activities. To help students continue to learn despite these developmental struggles, teachers should consider the size of groups that are formed, the length of tasks that students are asked to accomplish together, and the degree of skill proficiency that particular activities require. Because sexual identity is also a significant developmental issue for students in middle school, teachers should consider using same-sex groupings at times as well as attending to the social-developmental abilities of individuals who work in teams. At the high school level, learning communities are affected by students' multiple responsibilities and competing interests. For example, some students are responsible for helping to support their families by holding outside jobs for pay; some students may be focused on achieving high grades to enter highly selective colleges and universities; and some students may be balancing these ambitions with participation in sports and other extracurricular activities. Understanding the competing interests that students have and their difficulties in managing and choosing among these priorities affects the expectations and groupings used in learning communities.

SUMMARY

This chapter has highlighted the purposes and features of creating learning communities. We do so in advance of discussions about specific classroom instructional decision making, unit design, and lesson planning (see Chapter 8) and instructional strategies in inclusive environments (see Chapter 9) because establishing a learning community is a prerequisite to success at these subsequent levels. Creating learning communities in which students learn important skills of citizenship, mutual support, and self-advocacy is a vital component of ensuring that each and every student is able to gain access to and progress in the general curriculum. This is particularly important for students with mental retardation.

ADDITIONAL READINGS

Learning Communities

Good, T., & Brophy, J. (1994). *Looking in classrooms* (6th ed.). New York: HarperCollins.

Jorgensen, C.M. (1998). *Restructuring high schools for all students: Taking inclusion to the next level.* Baltimore: Paul H. Brookes Publishing Co.

Lipsky, D.K., & Gartner, A. (1999). *Inclusion and school reform: Transforming America's classrooms.* Baltimore: Paul H. Brookes Publishing Co.

Peterson, R. (1992). *Life in a crowded place: Making a learning community.* Portsmouth, NH: Heinemann.

Putnam, J.W. (2000). *Cooperative learning and strategies for inclusion: Celebrating diversity in the classroom* (2nd ed.). Baltimore: Paul H. Brookes Publishing Co.

CHAPTER OBJECTIVES

1. Define *instructional decision making,* and explore the relationship among assessment, curriculum, and instruction in gaining access to the general curriculum.
2. Describe building-level curriculum and instructional decisions and discuss elements that can serve as the basis for such decisions.
3. Discuss differentiated instruction and its implications for providing access to the general curriculum for students with mental retardation.
4. Define *classroom-level curriculum* and *instructional decision making,* and identify steps to implementing such decisions.

KEY TERMS

Building-level curriculum
Curriculum mapping
Vertical alignment
Open- and close-ended curriculum targets
Differentiated instruction
Classroom-level decisions
Class map
Units of study
Unit planning models

Summative assessment
Performance-based assessments
Lesson plans
Task analysis
Multilevel curriculum planning
Curriculum overlap
Cognitive taxonomies
Learning taxonomies

8

Designing
Educational Supports

Instructional Decision Making

RAISING THE BAR
HAS A CHANCE ONLY WHEN
CURRICULUM, ASSESSMENT, AND
INSTRUCTION ARE ALIGNED.

The preceding chapters provided an overview of the curriculum decision-making process, which can lead to an appropriate formal curriculum for students with mental retardation that is derived from both the general curriculum and the student's unique learning needs. In this chapter, the discussion about curriculum moves from the national, state, and district level (curriculum design and planning) and the IEP team level (curriculum decision making) to the building and classroom levels (instructional decision making). This chapter begins with an examination of the relationship among curriculum, assessment, and instruction and then presents a framework for understanding important building-level structures that facilitate the design, implementation, and evaluation of classroom-level curriculum and instructional decisions. Although instructional decision making is emphasized, in reality this building- and classroom-level discussion continues to involve curriculum design and curriculum decision-making activities. In the final section of this chapter, ways that school professionals can make classroom-level instructional decisions to support inclusive school communities and ensure access to the curriculum for all students are discussed.

ASSESSMENT, CURRICULUM, AND INSTRUCTION

Instructional decision making requires the synthesis of assessment, curriculum, and instruction. Each of these individual processes is dependent on and contributes to the design of the others. Because it is not possible, in one chapter, to address the complexities of the iterative, cyclical process of designing, implementing, and evaluating assessment, curriculum, and instruction, we have separated and dealt with each of these topics in chapters throughout the text. Although Chapter 2 draws a distinction between curriculum (the *what*) and instruction (the *how* of the educational process), it is often the case that at the classroom level, curriculum and instruction become inextricably linked and tied to assessment activities. Assessment at this juncture must be ongoing, purposeful, and performed within the contexts of both curriculum and instruction and must address both student and teacher outcomes (Sands, Kozleski, & French, 2000).

BUILDING-LEVEL CURRICULUM AND INSTRUCTIONAL DECISIONS

Although this chapter focuses on classroom curriculum and instructional decision making, it is important to note that this process is affected by decisions at many other levels. For example, national and state standards, such as those discussed in Chapter 3, may influence district-, building-, and classroom-level curriculum and instructional decisions. District-level school boards often set directions and policies affecting curriculum and instruction at the building and classroom levels. It is critical to note, however, that to provide the types of curriculum experiences noted previously, it is important to transfer curriculum decision making from the district level to the IEP, building, and classroom levels (Sage, 1996; Sailor, 1991; Sapon-Shevin, 2000/2001). "It is only when the personal needs, goals, and interests of students are understood that school experiences that are responsive to the students can be formulated and important school outcomes can be ensured" (Sands et al., 2000, p. 293).

Kniep and Martin-Kniep (1995) described seven elements that can serve as the basis of building-based curriculum and instruction discussions: 1) shared vision, 2) goals, 3) outcomes, 4) standards, 5) curriculum and assessment frameworks, 6) standards for professional practices, and 7) organizational structures. Building-level discussions should include representative school professionals, support personnel, student body representatives, family members, and community members. The elements should not be approached in a linear manner but must build on and reinforce one another; that is, decisions made about one element should inform and guide decisions about the others. For example, if collaborative problem solving is a key value identified through the process of defining the vision and outcomes for the school, then principles of collaborative problem solving should guide all of the decisions that are made about instruction, curriculum, and assessment, and organizational structures should be built to support those efforts. These same values then should guide the manner in which teachers work collaboratively with their students to plan for, implement, and evaluate the curricula in their classrooms. Attention to all of these building-level elements is critical if school organizations are going to create an environment that supports professional practices necessary for designing curriculum and instruction that provides access to the general curriculum for all students (Ferguson & Kozleski, 2000). Moreover, because implementing schoolwide curriculum adaptations and instructional strategies is critical in providing greater access, these **building-level curriculum** and instruction discussions become even more important.

Defining building-wide visions, goals, and outcomes requires in-depth analysis and agreement on what is important for students to learn and how they can best learn it. These discussions generally lead to the definition of a school mission, a set of operating principles, and broadly stated student outcomes. For example, in one school district, curriculum-level decision makers formulated outcomes that each student would be 1) a complex thinker, 2) an effective communicator, 3) an ethical person, 4) a quality worker, 5) a responsible citizen, and 6) a self-directed learner (Jefferson County Schools, 1995). In another school community, members adopted the same student outcomes as their district but personalized the formal curriculum using the following belief statement:

We Believe:
All children can learn.
Children learn best by doing.
When children have choices, they take responsibility for their learning.
Children deserve to be surrounded by good books.
After successes, children are ready to take challenges and risk occasional failure.
Children learn best through trial and error.
Children enlarge their vocabularies when they learn new words in context.
Children need a variety of kinds of experiences. (Perez, 1991, p. 5)

A belief statement such as this serves as an important guide for school professionals about how to make key decisions when designing, implementing, and evaluating curriculum and instruction. It is critical that school professionals who are responsible for supporting the educational programs of students with mental retardation are involved in these and similar building-wide efforts.

Delineating student standards, curriculum, instruction, and assessment frameworks helps define the key outcomes, topics, subjects, skills, and processes that are important for all students to master and is the overall way of assessing whether students have met these key elements. As stated previously, national-, state-, or district-level standards often inform and drive the definition of student standards (Jorgensen, 1997). However, building personnel often have some latitude to include a recommended sequence in which the standards will be covered and to denote which instructional strategies will be most effective for meeting those standards. This is referred to as **curriculum mapping** (Association for Supervision and Curriculum Development [ASCD], 1999) or **vertical alignment** and is done to address the developmental needs of children and to prevent unnecessary overlap or redundancy in students' curriculum experiences.

One of the most critical attributes that building-level decision makers can address in their curriculum and assessment frameworks is the degree to which these frameworks remain **open-ended** or **close-ended.** These terms are used to describe the amount of specificity and direction provided by curriculum standards, benchmarks, goals, or objectives at both the building and classroom levels. Close-ended standards, benchmarks, or goals and objectives are specific and often narrowly defined. Examples of close-ended standards include expecting all students to recite their multiplication tables using numbers 0–10, write and correctly spell 300 of the most commonly used vocabulary words, diagram and illustrate the grammatical structure of 50 compound sentences, or write a five-page paper on the history of the United States. Conversely, examples of open-ended standards include the following: All students have knowledge about themselves as learners; all students demonstrate skills to both regulate themselves and interact with others across multiple, changing environments; all students ask questions, manipulate materials, make observations, and analyze data; all students have a system for communicating their needs, interests, and goals; and all students have basic tools of literacy and numeracy. Research suggests that open-ended standards allow for greater flexibility as to what, when, and how topics are addressed in the classroom (Stainback, Stainback, Stefanich, & Alper, 1996) and are more consistent with universally designed curriculums, ensuring that a wide range of students, including students with mental retardation, can show progress in the curriculum. It is clear that open-ended curriculum frameworks and assignments facilitate the ability of school professionals to respond to and support diverse, individual student needs within whole-group instruction (Bingham, 1995).

The final step of building-level curriculum and instructional decision making is to create the organizational structures that allow desired outcomes to occur for all students. Organizational structures facilitate and support effective and efficient use of human, fiscal, and material resources; operational structures; role definitions and expectations; communication and decision-making systems; and human resource development. Organizational structures set forth teacher schedules, the roles assigned to all personnel, the structures created for how decisions get made, and budgetary tasks. For example, if the staff of a building identifies collaboration as an important value, then building-level supports must be in place for school professionals to respond collectively to the individual needs of students (Sage, 1996; Stainback, Stainback, & Jackson, 1992). This could include creating a daily block schedule for planning and professional development that permits shared time for general and special education teachers and related services personnel. Schools committed to diverse communities of learners and principles of democratic teaching and learning must build organizational structures to reflect their principles and beliefs. In other words, they practice what they preach; their organizational structures reflect the values and beliefs that serve as the foundation to their decisions about their vision, goals, outcomes, standards, curriculum frameworks, and standards for professional practices (Sands et al., 2000).

CLASSROOM-LEVEL INSTRUCTIONAL DECISIONS

Classroom-level instructional decision making begins by extending the curriculum decisions made at the building level and by the student's IEP team. All teachers and school professionals should have a clear understanding of the directions and standards set forth at the building level. These then are applied to each of the steps of making classroom-based instructional decisions. At the classroom level, two additional philosophical frameworks offer support to teachers as they begin to solidify their classroom-based curriculum goals and plans: universal design for learning and differentiated instruction. The importance of applying principles of universal design to education and learning was emphasized in Chapters 2 and 3, and the use of technology to ensure that instructional materials are designed with principles of universal design in mind is addressed in Chapter 16.

Differentiated instruction emerged from the field of gifted education (Tomlinson, 1995, 1999) and provides a framework for discriminating content, process, and products based on students' readiness, interests, and learning profiles. When teachers apply the principles of differentiated instruction they approach learning with students' needs first and then plan their curriculum. Differentiated instruction is based on the premise that students must be engaged in instruction "through different learning modalities, by appealing to their different interests, and by using varying rates of instruction along with varied degrees of complexity" (Tomlinson, 1999, p. 2). The basis of both universal design and differentiated instruction is that instructional and curriculum designs must be accessible to the widest spectrum of students possible, including students with mental retardation. This means that school professionals must develop, implement, and evaluate assessment, curriculum, and instruction through multiple paths that allow students with different backgrounds, learning styles, interests, and abilities to gain access to information, practice new skills, and demonstrate their learning in a personalized manner. Flexibility and alternatives are key to designing instruction when applying the principles of universal design and differentiated instruction.

Several fundamental assumptions about teaching and learning serve as the foundation of universal design and differentiated instruction. First, within this framework, all students are accepted for who they are and where they are in terms of their learning strengths and needs. There is an underlying belief that all students, not excluding students with mental retardation, vary in their readiness, interests, and learning profiles (Tomlinson, 1999). Second, teachers should approach the classroom-level design of curriculum, instruction, and assessment by making adjustments for all learners and not just for students with identified disabilities. Thus, changes should be made in the content, process (e.g., instructional strategies, materials, grouping), and products expected of students, and such adaptations should be implemented schoolwide. Third, curriculum and instructional materials should be greatly expanded, including the use of digital and online resources, as discussed in detail in Chapter 16. Fourth and finally, universal design and differentiated instruction assume that students are an integral part of the education process and, therefore, should work collaboratively with teachers in the design, implementation, and evaluation of curriculum and instruction.

Applying the assumptions and principles of differentiated instruction requires ongoing, thoughtful reflection about and targeting of teaching goals and student needs. A comprehensive text (see Tomlinson, 1999) on the steps to differentiating instruction is provided in the *Additional Readings* section at the end of this chapter. Overall, it is best to start small, grow slowly, involve students along the way, establish supportive routines, and strive for organization. For example, one fifth-grade teacher began by establishing a center in which students could develop their editing and proofreading skills. Students were at very different levels of readiness in their proficiencies in spelling, punctuation, and sentence structure. In addition, they had varied interests. The teacher created a variety of materials that reflected all of their needs. For example, the teacher would write notes from book characters, sports heroes, and so forth to pique and maintain student interest and motivation (Tomlinson, 1999). Students were then matched to materials that reflected both their interests and their individual proficiencies in editing and proofreading.

CLASSROOM CURRICULUM AND INSTRUCTIONAL DECISIONS

Classroom curriculum and instructional decision making typically entail three levels of planning: 1) assessing students to get to know them; 2) designing **units of study,** including culminating assessment activities and daily learning experiences and instruction; and 3) creating individualized modifications. This process occurs in the context of curriculum decisions made by the IEP team (see Chapter 4) but extends and operationalizes these IEP curriculum decisions. It is not the purpose of the IEP meeting to make every curriculum and instructional decision; instead, its purpose is to lay a framework on which teachers can build with building- and classroom-level curricular and instructional decisions. In the next section, we review the basic purpose of and overall steps required for each of these stages.

Assessing Students to Get to Know Them

Assessment has multiple functions. Educators use assessment for determining achievement; understanding basic student needs in areas such as cognitive, affective, communicative, and physical/health needs; verifying eligibility for special services or supports; monitoring student progress; and making instructional decisions. In designing classroom curriculum, assessment is inseparable from instruction. Teachers need to assess first for the purposes of learning about their students. What do they know? What do they want to know? What is important for them to know? How do they learn best? What are their cognitive, affective, communicative, and physical/health needs and strengths? What are the cultural expectations and values that this group of students and their families bring to the classroom? What are their strengths and preferences? This information is used for both IEP curriculum decision making and classroom curriculum and instructional decision making.

Collaboration can be key in gathering this data. It is important to build reliable partnerships with families and to support meaningful involvement of students and family members in assessment and decision making driven by assessment (see Chapter 10). Synthesizing this data provides a **class map** of students' strengths, preferences, and needs, which is invaluable for making instructional decisions, such as how to differentiate instruction, which particular instructional strategy to use, or which curriculum adaptations might be beneficial.

Designing Units of Study

Units of study are the maps that teachers create to organize and plan for how they are going to support students to help them learn and demonstrate their understanding of the content, skills, processes, and knowledge required to achieve grade-level and broader school outcomes. The first step in designing units is to have a clear understanding of what needs to be accomplished by the end of the school year. Teachers rely on various sources of information during this step. First, they rely on the grade-level standards and benchmarks that have been articulated at the district and building levels. Second, teachers must assess what students already know about stated grade-level expectations. Some students may already have the skills that are expected of them at a certain grade, whereas others may not have mastered previous grade-level outcomes on which to build to achieve current grade-level expectations. Without this knowledge, teachers cannot plan personalized instruction that responds to students' readiness levels. Third, teachers must understand the cognitive, affective, communicative, and physical/health domains that are developmentally appropriate for the students. For example, the cognitive domain includes components such as attention, perception, working memory, long-term memory, organization structures, and self-regulatory functions. The general curriculum can be augmented to teach students needed strategies and skills such as note-taking, outlining, use of mnemonics, chunking information, generating questions, research skills, self-monitoring, and comparing and contrasting, which enable them to make progress in content areas. Finally, teachers must continually refer to their class maps of students' learning preferences, styles, and so forth to match or add the students' other curriculum needs to the overall grade-level plans.

Once teachers understand the big picture for the school year, they must *backward-map* to determine what students will need to know and do by the middle of the year and then plan for more manageable instructional units (usually by quarters). When a teacher has an overall idea of what needs to be accomplished by the end of the school year and has divided that content, skills, and knowledge into mid-year and quarterly components, he or she is ready to plan units of instruction. Teachers can turn to several models to guide unit planning. Broadly, **unit planning models** tend to be organized by subject area, discipline structure, integrated designs, learner-centered designs, experience-centered designs, problem-centered designs, or life-situations designs (Armstrong, 1989; Morrison, 1993; Ornstein & Hunkins, 1988). Comprehensive discussions of these models are available through a variety of resources (see *Additional Readings* at the end of this chapter). Generally, models for unit planning vary in the scope and nature of the content introduced; the manner that information is organized; and the inherent flexibility allowed for students to interact, proceed through the unit, and then demonstrate their learning.

More often, teachers are applying integrated unit designs in school environments that support students with diverse ethnic, cultural, linguistic, socioeconomic, and ability needs (e.g., see Educational Leadership, 1994/1995; Kucer, Silva, & Delgado-Larocco, 1995; Sapon-Shevin, 2000/2001). Integrated curricula are characterized by a focus on information that is generated by students, is relevant to their lives, and helps them develop the skills that are necessary to be successful in school as well as in the future. Furthermore, integrated curricula are designed to respond to the multiple ways in which students learn, to focus learning on concepts, and to increase opportunities for students to explore, discover, and apply information across many content areas (Kovalik, 1993). These characteristics are consistent with the principles and values of universal design and differentiated learning that were discussed previously. A backward design process typically is applied to integrated unit planning. This process involves three steps: 1) identify desired results, 2) determine acceptable evidence, and 3) plan learning experiences and instruction (Wiggins & McTighe, 1998).

Identify Desired Results   As a teacher chooses and defines learning targets for a unit, it is important to remember to apply the previously discussed principles regarding defining open-ended versus close-ended learning targets or outcomes. The unit planning form depicted in Figure 8.1 promotes consideration about the content experiences that all students share, those that most students share, and finally, those that some students share (Joint Committee on Teacher Planning for Students with Disabilities, 1995). For example, a target that all fifth graders will write a five-page research paper that references 10 articles on the topic of tectonic plates is narrow. Not every student will be equivalently challenged by this assignment. Some students will be able to complete it with minimal effort. Others may struggle and achieve average success, whereas still others may find the assignment completely out of reach.

Teachers must continually reevaluate and reformulate their stated learning outcomes to ensure that they are focusing on targets that are of benefit to all students, including students with mental retardation. In the case of the fifth-grade research paper, the learning target could be adapted in a variety of ways to increase the access and learning potential for a broader range of students. For example, extending or shortening the length of the paper and the number of required references would allow a broader range of students to complete the assignment successfully. The students could use a variety of formats, including oral or visual presentations, a web site, or expressive art formats or video formats, to transmit the research report. Finally, by allowing students to choose different topics for the paper, more students will be able to address issues that are personally relevant and functional.

Teachers of students with mental retardation requiring extensive or pervasive support should work collaboratively with their colleagues (either general or special education, depending on the teacher's role) in determining unit level and, later, learning experience level outcomes and targets. Once teachers are clear on the differentiated content elements of the unit, they are more prepared to match the appropriate instruction, materials, resources, strategies, adaptations, products, and evaluations to individualize instruction and support the greatest number of students.

Determine Acceptable Evidence   The next step in the backward design process of creating units is to determine the evidence that will indicate that students have achieved the desired results. This introduces another level and type of assessment, often referred to as **summative assessment.** Summative assessments are designed to reveal what students have learned at the end of a unit, grading period, or school year. In keeping with achieving access to the general curriculum through curriculum adaptations, which include modifications to students' responses to the curriculum, teachers should plan culminating unit assessments that offer students a variety of methods and mediums for demonstrating their achievements. The use of performance-based assess-

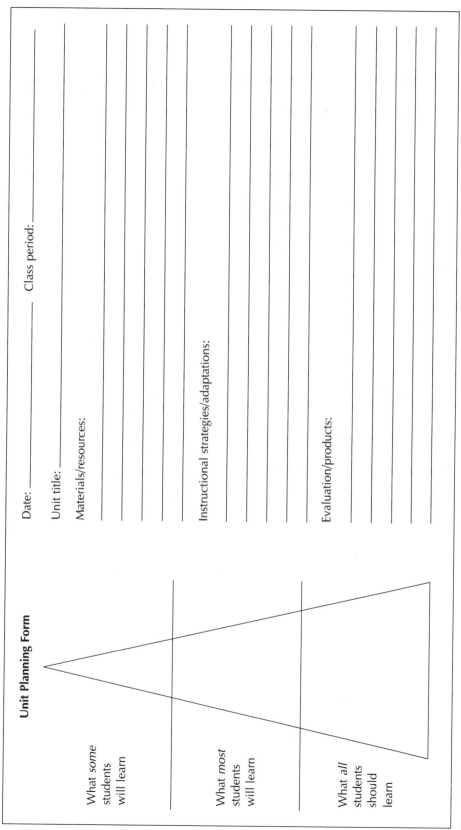

Unit Planning Form

Date: _____ Class period: _____

Unit title: _____

Materials/resources:
_____
_____
_____

Instructional strategies/adaptations:
_____
_____
_____

Evaluation/products:
_____
_____
_____

What *some* students will learn

What *most* students will learn

What *all* students should learn

Figure 8.1. Sample unit planning form. (From Schumm, J.S., Vaughn, S., and Leavell, A. [1994]. Planning pyramid: A framework for planning for diverse student needs during content area instruction. *The Reading Teacher,* 47[8], 608–615; reprinted by permission.)

ment is increasingly recognized as a way to meet these demands (Silver, Strong, & Perini, 2000) and may be of particular benefit to students with mental retardation.

Performance-based assessment allows students to express themselves and demonstrate their understanding and skills through authentic activities and tasks. Performance-based assessment moves beyond typical paper-and-pencil tasks, which often only tap students' factual knowledge and not their ability to apply knowledge. For example, a student with mental retardation requiring extensive or pervasive supports who is learning to use an augmentative communication device is being taught how to locate and activate certain buttons that emit different types of expressive communicative messages. Observations (as measurement) to determine whether the student selects a specific response to a given target cue can occur in a tightly controlled environment; however, in order to determine whether the student can use the system in a meaningful and authentic manner, it would be necessary to observe how the student uses the system in his or her interactions with peers and adults across school, home, or community environments. This is the essence of performance-based assessments.

A key to supporting students to succeed on the culminating activities and assessments is to be clear about the criteria by which student performance will be judged and to communicate these criteria in advance to the students. These criteria should extend from teachers' learning targets, and teachers must determine in advance what constitutes acceptable performance in order for students to achieve unit goals and objectives. What are the required components? What criteria will be applied to decide if a student is proficient, partially proficient, or below expectations? Communicating these criteria to students is essential. In doing so, teachers provide students with a means of establishing plans for completing their work, monitoring their progress, and evaluating the quality of their work. This process serves to advance self-directed learning and the skills and attitudes necessary for self-determination (see Chapter 15).

Plan Learning Experiences and Instruction   Once the learning targets and culminating activities have been identified, the information needed to plan the day-to-day activities that will support students to achieve unit outcomes is available. Generally, this planning leads to **lesson plans,** which serve as a tool for breaking large units of study into smaller, manageable increments. Lesson plans can be written to cover small portions of time, for example, a 10-minute mini lesson, or larger blocks of time over many days. The amount of time needed for a particular lesson will vary according to the complexity of the learning targets and the number of tasks needed to scaffold students' readiness levels to meet those targets. For example, a teacher may emphasize the use of mnemonics as a means of helping students to organize and remember information. If students already have been taught various mnemonic strategies, the classroom teacher may start each day with a mini lesson during which students quickly model or demonstrate the various steps. Conversely, if this is the first time a group of students have been exposed to mnemonic strategies, the classroom teacher, perhaps in collaboration with a special education colleague, may prepare a lesson that spans multiple days and allows for modeling, demonstrations, student practice, and teacher feedback on the steps that are necessary in order to apply mnemonic strategies.

Generally, lesson plans set forth the topic or theme of the lesson as well as clear expectations regarding the purpose of the lesson (rationale), how the lesson will be conducted (activities), what students are expected to accomplish (objective), and how those accomplishments will be measured (evaluation). Thus, the essence of synthesizing curriculum, instruction, and assessment is documented through the lesson plan. Although there are many forms that can be used to plan lessons, Figure 8.2 illustrates a lesson planning form (Bulgren & Lenz, 1996) that is an extension of the unit planning form presented in Figure 8.1. Again, this form provides an opportunity for school professionals to plan how they will support student diversity within curriculum activities.

As with planning a unit, teachers should create lesson plans that work for the greatest number of students possible. Following the logic that directed curriculum and instructional decision making at the building level and units of study, teachers should write lesson plans that do the following:

- Support a progression of skills or knowledge that leads to the intended outcomes of the unit (and therefore school outcomes)
- Reflect objectives that can be met and demonstrated in many ways
- Connect new information to previous knowledge or skills
- Engage students through multiple forms of learning
- Incorporate physical, cognitive, and affective skills and knowledge in objectives
- Match instruction, content, and assessment (Sands et al., 2000, p. 312)

Teachers must clearly understand exactly what their learning targets are; the cognitive, affective, communicative, and physical/health demands required of these targets; and the sequence necessary to reach these targets in order know where each student will be able to enter the learning sequence and what he or she will need in order to succeed. Teachers can incorporate three tools in their lesson design—task analysis, cognitive taxonomies, and learning taxonomies—to assist students in addressing these needs.

Task Analysis The use of **task analysis** enables teachers to break down the component parts of skills or a knowledge set to understand the demands that will be made on students and match those demands with the class map. Task analysis is a process that can be applied to help make decisions about the requisite skills that need to be taught as well as, in some cases, the order in which skills or knowledge should be taught. The steps in task analysis (Wolery, Bailey, & Sugai, 1988) include the following:

- Define the instructional objective: What should learners be able to do?
- Break the desired outcome into its component parts.
- Write down each separate skill or knowledge base.
- Put the steps into sequence—either sequentially or for increasing levels of difficulty—for teaching.
- Specify necessary prerequisite skills.

Whereas the steps in task analysis appear simple, deciding on a learning target is complex. Deciding on a learning target involves the classroom curriculum decisions presented previously in this chapter, the needs of the learners, and then, consideration of the content to be taught. In particular, teachers have to be concerned with what they want students to be able to do with the information or skills they are taught. A cognitive taxonomy helps categorize the learning targets.

Cognitive Taxonomies **Cognitive taxonomies** are used to classify the cognitive demands of learning targets (Biehler & Snowman, 1993). Perhaps the most familiar cognitive taxonomy is the one developed by Bloom and colleagues (1956). Bloom's

Date: _____ Class period: _____ Unit: _____

Lesson objective(s): _____

_____

_____

Materials   Evaluation

In-class assignments   Homework assignments

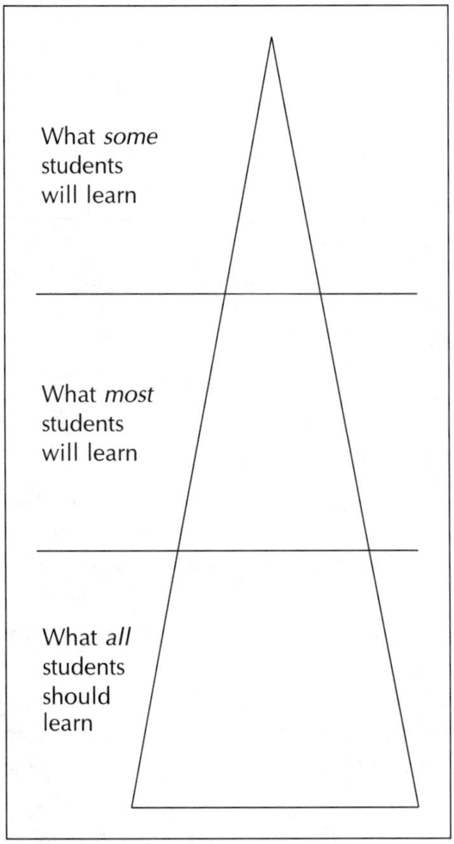

                                                      Agenda

                                        1 _____

What *some*
students   _____
will learn
                                        2 _____

                                                        _____

                                        3 _____

                                                        _____

What *most*
students   4 _____
will learn
                                                        _____

                                        5 _____

What *all*
students   _____
should
learn   6 _____

                                                        _____

                                        7 _____

                                                        _____

Figure 8.2. Sample lesson form. (From J. Bulgren and B.K. Lenz [1996]. Strategic instruction in the content areas. In D.D. Deshler, E.S. Ellis, and B.K. Lenz [Eds.], *Teaching adolescents with learning disabilities* [2nd ed., p. 430]. Denver, CO: Love; Reproduced by permission of Love Publishing Company.)

taxonomy is a means of categorizing the cognitive skills that students call into action when involved in learning and achieving learning targets. The categories of Bloom's taxonomy are listed and defined in Table 8.1. As one ascends Bloom's taxonomy, the cognitive demands on students are more complex. Wiggins and McTighe (1998) proposed an alternative of what constitutes students' cognitive understandings and skills. They proposed that when student understand, they

1. Can explain: provide thorough, supported, and justifiable accounts of phenomena, facts, and data
2. Can interpret: tell meaningful stories, offer apt translations, provide a personal dimension to ideas and events; make it personally relevant
3. Can apply: effectively use and adapt new information across multiple contexts
4. Have perspective: see and hear points of view through critical eyes and ears; see the big picture
5. Can empathize; find value in what others might find odd, alien, or implausible
6. Have self-knowledge: perceive the personal style, prejudices, projections, and habits of the mind that both shape and impede their own understanding, are aware of what they do not understand and why understanding is so hard (1998, p. 44)

As cognitive taxonomies are applied in unit- and lesson-planning activities, teachers should track whether they are introducing students to increasingly complex skills and content. When learning objectives are set, students are usually expected to demonstrate their competence across all levels of higher ordered thinking skills and content types. For all students to succeed, teachers need to consider at which levels of the taxonomy

Table 8.1. Bloom's taxonomy of educational objectives

Competence	Skills demonstrated
Knowledge	Observe and recall information Know dates, events, places Know major ideas Master subject matter
Comprehension	Understand information Grasp meaning Translate knowledge into new context Interpret facts and compare and contrast Order, group, and infer causes Predict consequences
Application	Use information Use methods, concepts, and theories in new situations Solve problems using required skills or knowledge
Analysis	See patterns Organize parts Recognize hidden meanings Identify components
Synthesis	Use old ideas to create new ones Generalize from given facts Relate knowledge from several areas Predict and draw conclusions
Evaluation	Compare and discriminate between ideas Assess value of theories and presentations Make choices based on reasoned argument Verify value of evidence Recognize subjectivity

Source: Bloom, Englehart, Furst, Hill, and Krathwohl (1956).

students can be expected to achieve. For young children to be successful at employing higher ordered thinking skills, such as analysis, synthesis, and evaluation, they must be provided with information that is developmentally appropriate. For example, this may mean that students are provided with concrete criteria, such as a sample that reflects what the final product should look like, in order to evaluate whether their work has been completed accurately. The same may hold true for students with mental retardation. Teachers should not assume that students with mental retardation can only perform at lower levels of cognitive taxonomies. Instead, teachers must apply what they understand about a student's cognitive abilities and create materials and supports that allow him or her to achieve at all levels. In addition to tracking learning targets according to a cognitive taxonomy such as Bloom's, lesson plans should also reflect consideration of the learner's previous experience with a skill or topic. A **learning taxonomy** can help you with this.

Learning Taxonomies   Once a learning target has been specified, curriculum decision makers also must consider the learner's previous experiences with a skill or topic. Haring, Liberty, and White (1980) drew distinctions among novice to expert learners. They categorized learning into the following five phases:

- Acquisition
- Fluency
- Generalization
- Adaptation
- Maintenance

A learning taxonomy helps teachers to distinguish between those curriculum activities they might use if learners had no prior experience with a task or skill to be learned versus those curriculum activities they might use to make sure that students continue to maintain their accuracy with a well-learned skill. Learning taxonomies provide the basis of differentiation. Learning activities that are used to teach students who are learning a skill for the first time are organized very differently from activities that are used to maintain skills. During acquisition lessons, teachers need to make sure that they present information clearly and in a variety of formats, provide lots of concrete and abstract models and examples, check students' understanding of new information or skill development frequently, and make sure that students can demonstrate basic knowledge before sending students away to practice on their own. When students can perform successfully under guided circumstances, then they are ready to move to a fluency phase.

During the fluency phase of learning, students practice a skill until they are able to perform it with some degree of automaticity. In other words, they no longer have to talk themselves through each step in the sequence to remember what step comes next. Students demonstrate generalization when they apply what they know about one skill to another skill or when they use a skill across multiple environments. For example, generalization has occurred if a student learns a particular strategy for note-taking in social studies and then applies or adapts the strategy in science. Also, applying the principles of writing across multiple genres constitutes generalization. Students with mental retardation have been taught to apply and generalize a visual self-management system for appropriate on-task behaviors while traveling in the hallways and ordering lunch (King-Sears, 1999).

Applying task analysis, a cognitive taxonomy, and a learning taxonomy to the design of lesson plans and units helps to 1) define the point of entry in the learning sequence, 2) track the cognitive demands of each learning unit or task, and 3) sequence the curriculum targets and experiences to take students from the novice to the expert stage. Using this information, teachers can begin to match these targets with the learning needs of students and can make decisions about the materials and instructional strategies they will incorporate to achieve these learning targets. Finally, when this level of detail has been applied to unit and lesson plans, teachers will be able to identify those students who may not benefit from planned instruction and who may require additional adaptations, augmentations, or alternative curricular activities.

Creating Individualized Modifications

Chapter 4 summarized three levels of curriculum modifications (i.e., adaptation, augmentation, and alteration) that can be considered during the curriculum decision-making process and that form the basis for achieving access to the general curriculum. Teachers who have been involved in the IEP planning process already have considered which curriculum modifications can be applied to enable students to progress. The function of the IEP is to document recommendations for 1) instructional strategies or curricular content that may not typically be represented in a student's educational experiences and 2) adaptations and modifications to existing instructional practices and curricular standards. As such, the initial steps in considering adaptations and other modifications are completed in the IEP process. There will likely be a need for **classroom-level decisions** about curriculum modifications and about ensuring that principles of universal design are incorporated into materials and methods. Chapter 16 discusses in greater detail the use of technology to achieve these outcomes.

School professionals should work collaboratively to determine the need for and prescribe the nature and extent of classroom-level adaptations—modifications and devices that support and benefit individual students (Warger & Pugach, 1993, 1996). Recommended processes for collaborative steps to identifying adaptations and modifications (Filbin, 1994; Stainback & Stainback, 1992; Udvari-Solner, 1995) include

1. Identify the learning targets for the whole class.
2. Identify the learning targets for the student in question.
3. Identify the cognitive, affective, communicative, and physical/health strengths and needs of the student (from the IEP if applicable).
4. Evaluate the cognitive, affective, communicative, and physical demands of the lesson or class activities.
5. Analyze discrepancies among student strengths and needs and the demands of the lesson or class activities.
6. Examine the range of choices for adaptations and modifications in content, assessment, or instructional strategies; match those options to student needs; and institute an evaluation plan to ensure that the strategy worked.

Following these steps allows teachers to set different goals and objectives for a student while allowing him or her to participate in similar activities with his or her peers. In some cases, following these steps can lead to students participating in quite different experiences. With the application of both universal design and differentiated instruction, students may be working with the same content but at different levels of cognitive understanding and skills at any given time. Within any given topic, students can develop an understanding of facts, concepts, principles, attitudes, or skills (Tomlinson, 1999). Within the field of special education, this has been referred to as **multilevel curriculum planning** (Villa, Van der Klift, et al., 1995). This type of curriculum planning and implementation should be evident in any classroom devoted to the values of inclusive education and to ensuring that all students progress in the general curriculum.

Subsequent chapters provide further detail about instructional and content areas typically considered as part of an alternative curriculum that may or may not be met within the context of the general curriculum. If a student's unique learning needs cannot be met by adapting or augmenting the general curriculum, it is necessary to describe some alternative curricular areas. At the classroom level, teachers might apply the strategy of curriculum overlap to ensure that the student's unique needs are being met in the context of the typical classroom. **Curriculum overlap** is when teachers and students address more than one content area in a given activity or series of lessons (Villa, Van der Klift, et al., 1995). For example, in a high school biology course, cooperative groups were assigned to conduct experiments on wind flow and weather patterns. One student with mental retardation and limited support needs had IEP goals specified in the affective domain. In addition to contributing to his group's report, he had to turn in a self-evaluation of his collaboration skills.

SUMMARY

Even though the IEP team makes a number of curriculum decisions based on state- or district-level standards or benchmarks, teachers need to be prepared to play a critical role in building- and classroom-level instructional and curriculum decision-making activities. At the building level, decision makers can ensure that state- or district-level standards and benchmarks are open-ended, thus allowing greater access to the curriculum by students with mental retardation, are similarly open-ended when adopted at the campus level, and can work to make close-ended curriculum targets more open-ended. At the classroom level, teachers can use various strategies to ensure that principles of universal design are incorporated into unit-planning and lesson-planning design and can ensure that **differentiated instruction** is used to meet the diverse needs of students. Lesson plans should be designed using task analysis and should take into account cognitive and learning taxonomies. Only when these steps have been completed would it be necessary to consider an alternative curriculum for students with mental retardation.

ADDITIONAL READINGS

Unit Planning Models

Beane, J.A. (1995). Introduction: What is a coherent curriculum? In J.A. Beane (Ed.), *Toward a coherent curriculum: 1995 Yearbook of the Association for Supervision and Curriculum Development* (pp. 1–15). Alexandria, VA: Association for Supervision and Curriculum Development.

Burns, R. (1995). *Dissolving the boundaries: Planning for curriculum integration in middle and secondary school.* Charleston, WV: Appalachian Educational Laboratory.

Doll, R.C. (1992). *Curriculum improvement: Decision making and process* (9th ed.). Needham Heights, MA: Allyn & Bacon.

Drake, S. (1993). *Planning integrated curriculum: The call to adventure.* Alexandria, VA: Association for Supervision and Curriculum Development.

Jacobs, H.H. (1989). *Interdisciplinary curriculum: Design and implementation.* Alexandria, VA: Association for Supervision and Curriculum Development.

Perrone, V. (1991). *Expanding student assessment.* Alexandria, VA: Association for Supervision and Curriculum Development.

Silver, H.F., Strong, R.W., & Perini, M.J. (2000). *So each may learn: Integrating learning styles and multiple intelligences.* Alexandria, VA: Association for Supervision and Curriculum Development.

Tomlinson, C.A. (1995). *How to differentiate instruction in mixed-ability classrooms.* Alexandria, VA: Association for Supervision and Curriculum Development.

Tomlinson, C.A. (1999). *The differentiated classroom: Responding to the needs of all learners.* Alexandria, VA: Association for Supervision and Curriculum Development.

Wiggins, G., & McTighe, J. (1998). *Understanding by design.* Alexandria, VA: Association for Supervision and Curriculum Development.

CHAPTER OBJECTIVES

1. Discuss how to plan instruction in inclusive environments, including addressing unique learner needs and curriculum targets.
2. Define and describe four types of instruction, including teacher-mediated, peer-mediated, technology-mediated, and activity-anchored strategies.
3. Identify the elements of direct instruction, and discuss their importance to the education of students with mental retardation.
4. Discuss how to incorporate peer-mediated instruction in inclusive classrooms.
5. Identify how to assess instruction and ask questions used to monitor teaching effectiveness.

KEY TERMS

Direct instruction
Teacher-mediated instruction
Peer-mediated instruction
Technology-mediated instruction
Activity-anchored instruction
Mastery learning
Error correction and practice

Discrimination training
Cumulative review
Advance organizers
Co-teaching
Peer tutoring
Classwide peer tutoring
Reciprocal teaching
Cooperative learning
Role play and simulation

9

Teaching Strategies that Work in Inclusive Classrooms

ATTEMPTS AT AIRLIFTING CERTAIN
SPECIAL CLASS APPROACHES INTO
REGULAR CLASS ARE UNSUCCESSFUL,
THEY JUST DON'T FIT.

T here is no mistaking an inclusive classroom. Diversity flourishes: Thoughtful teachers ensure that no student is left behind or shunted aside by the classroom community, and students speak a variety of languages; represent a variety of ethnicities, cultures, and religions; and exhibit a range of abilities. Yet, within this diversity there is a sense of common purpose and caring among the students and teachers. Mindful that their students' backgrounds and experiences are uniquely informed by their culture, race, ethnicity, ability, economic background, and gender as well as the students' individual cognitive and affective development (Banks & McGee-Banks, 2001), teachers in inclusive classrooms plan carefully to create successful learning opportunities for each and every student. Teachers consider how the learning preferences, interests, and abilities of each student can be supported through a variety of instructional strategies, grouping structures, and materials. They make reflective choices among available materials and instructional approaches to address individual as well as collective student needs and to determine whether instruction is leading to important school and curriculum outcomes for all students. Teachers in inclusive classrooms expect to work with school professionals, students, related services personnel, families, and community members to support the types of instruction that meet the needs of students. Because the primary instructional goal is to make the curriculum accessible and meaningful for all students, teachers work collaboratively to design and carry out instruction.

This chapter provides a description of the stages of instructional planning, implementation, and evaluation that lead to effective instruction for a broad range of students, including students with mental retardation. The chapter begins with a review of the assumptions that should guide instruction in inclusive classrooms. Then, specific approaches to instructional planning, implementation, and evaluation are discussed and described. The chapter ends with an overview of instructional adaptation and a framework that teachers can use to choose sound instructional approaches where adaptations are needed.

ASSUMPTIONS ABOUT INSTRUCTION IN INCLUSIVE CLASSROOMS

Any serious analysis of *what* to teach (the curriculum) is always linked to the choices that are made in *how* to teach (instruction). Often, curriculum and instruction are decoupled and introduced in separate chapters. However, it is critical for teachers to understand that, as we emphasized in the discussion about educational decision making, content is a critical factor in making choices about how to teach a particular concept or skill.

In Chapter 8, the principles, values, and characteristics of classroom-level curriculum decision making that promote access to the general curriculum are described. Those same principles, values, and characteristics provide the framework that guides planning, implementation, and evaluation of instruction. Instruction in inclusive classrooms is flexible and varied in order to meet students' individual and collective needs. This means that a variety of strategies, materials, environmental supports, and groupings are used daily in the classroom because, although all children can learn and succeed, they may not be able to do so in the same way or on the same day (Udvari-Solner & Thousand, 1995). To create this varied instructional environment, teachers draw from a variety of teacher- and student-led strategies. At any point in time, instruction in an inclusive classroom may involve the whole class, small groups of students, individuals working alone, or one-to-one tutorials. One or more of these approaches can operate concurrently. In addition, a variety of instructional materials need to be on hand to support not only these instructional groupings but also the varied curriculum targets that are necessary to meet students' needs.

Students are an integral part of what goes on in an inclusive classroom; they learn from each other in intentional and unexpected ways. Therefore, instructional choices need to emerge from a student-centered perspective and create and support positive peer relationships, just as IEP planning and program evaluation need to come from the same perspective. Inclusive classrooms are based on several learning theories that assume that 1) learning evolves from the particular context in which novel ideas, skills, and activities are experienced (Lave & Wenger, 1991); 2) the community in which learning occurs affects the degree to which learning may be said to have occurred (Delpit, 1995); and 3) learning requires both the affective and intellectual involvement of the learner (Brown & Campione, 1986).

PLANNING INSTRUCTION

Planning instruction hinges on a teacher's ability to assess what students already know, determine what students need to know, understand how each student best learns, and consider students' interests and motivations (the same steps to curriculum decision making described in Chapter 8). Using this information, teachers then can select and match the instructional strategies that best meet the intended curriculum outcomes and respond to student needs. Given the wide range of instructional strategies from which to choose and the multiple curriculum goals that need to be met within an inclusive classroom, there is no single correct strategy or model to teach the curriculum (Falvey & Grenot-Scheyer, 1995; Joyce, Weil, & Showers, 1992). Successful instruction requires that teachers apply multiple strategies to meet student needs. Teachers should attend to two key elements in their planning: learner needs and curriculum targets.

Matching Instruction to Learner Needs

Foremost for every teacher is the need to understand thoroughly the cognitive, affective, communicative, and physical/health needs of his or her students. Each of these domains are complex. For example, cognition involves components such as attention, perception, memory, and executive function. The affective domain involves internal factors such as self-concept, self-regard, self-awareness, self-control, and motivation as well as external factors such as social cognition and social skills. The communication domain involves aspects of both receptive and expressive communication across three components: form, content, and use. The physical/health domain is comprised of several physical systems and subsystems, including the sensory, musculoskeletal, central nervous, cardiovascular, immunological/metabolic, and respiratory systems. The complexity of each domain is intensified when one considers the interdependent relationships among the domains. For instance, our affective state of mind is interdependent with our cognitive capacity. If a student is under great stress, his or her ability to focus and maintain attention to cognitive tasks may be compromised. Understanding students' individual styles, preferences, and approaches to learning based on their cognitive, affective, communicative, and physical/health needs greatly assists the process of matching instruction to students' needs. For example, some students really need to be able to get up and move around at various intervals throughout the day. Standing stations, where students can stand to do independent work (often referred to as *seatwork*), provide students with an alternative matched to their needs.

Each of these domain areas may call for different instructional strategies. For example, from a cognitive standpoint, some learners need support in order to attend to specific features of the lesson, others need assistance with interpreting and using information, whereas still others need support to help them efficiently store and organize information for future use. Table 9.1 provides an overview of a broad range of strategies that support learning across all of the components of cognition. The table also provides a range of instructional strategies that support students' affective, communicative, and physical needs. For example, peer-mediated strategies can offer students the opportunity to practice affective skills such as turn taking or perspective taking. Peer-mediated methods also can provide opportunities for students to expand their vocabulary or apply augmentative communication systems in a meaningful context. The use of strategies that incorporate movement, such as experiential learning (e.g., creating plays, problem-based learning), can provide necessary supports for students who have specific physical needs.

Matching Instruction to Curriculum Goals

Given the complexity of inclusive classrooms, teachers must choose instructional strategies that match the curriculum intent of their lesson while meeting the multiple learner needs of their students. As discussed in Chapter 8, teachers find themselves teaching to a variety of knowledge schemas, cognitive taxonomies, and learning taxonomies. The acquisition of different types of knowledge schemas or stages of learning requires the use of different instructional strategies. For example, modeling is an effective strategy for teaching concepts. Through teacher demonstration and modeling of exemplars and nonexemplars, students can begin to formulate their understanding of the features and critical attributes of a concept. Sands, Kozleski, and French (2000) provided an example of how teaching a concept through demonstration and modeling can address multiple learners' needs:

> During a lesson on photosynthesis, the teacher chooses to demonstrate the effect of light on the production of food in plants. By choosing to demonstrate at the beginning of the lesson the teacher creates a concrete example of the results of photosynthesis. The demonstration supports the needs of a variety of learners who range from concrete to abstract problem-solvers. The demonstration becomes the focal point of discourse and problem solving. Some students engage in describing what they saw. Other students engage in predicting possible reasons for the effects they observed. Other students attempt to represent symbolically the relationships between light and plant food production. The use of demonstration meets multiple students' needs. (p. 345)

Other types of knowledge schemas may best be supported by the use of alternative instructional strategies. For example, when students are first being introduced (acquisition) to a procedure (e.g., how to set up the headings on assignment papers), **direct instruction** may be the best choice. By varying the complexity of his or her language, including visual as well as oral information (e.g., picture cues) and by sequencing instruction in small steps, a teacher can help most of his or her students gather and

Table 9.1. Possible instructional strategies for supporting learning in the cognitive domain

Cognitive component	Instructional strategies
Attention	Using tape recorders Writing down what you say Using lots of visuals with auditory information Using auditory cueing systems Checking for understanding frequently Providing models Providing systematic, direct instruction
Perception	Putting no more than five items on an overhead Giving no more than three steps in any set of directions before you check for understanding Using at least two modalities to present information Providing frequent opportunities for student participation Checking for experience base with content Repeating yourself Giving clear examples Increasing the size of salient information Underlining, boldfacing, and italicizing critical information Pointing to key information Circling key information
Working memory	Giving no more than three steps in any set of directions before you check for understanding Using at least two modalities (e.g., visual, auditory, smell, taste, touch) to present information Providing frequent opportunities for student participation Using systematic, direct-instruction approaches
Long-term memory: Procedural	Scaffolding Making strategies clear and specific Building new strategies on old strategies Applying strategies directly to tasks Emphasizing transfer and generalization Emphasizing self-regulation
Long-term memory: Declarative	Anchoring instruction—tying it to learners' previous experiences Using media and computer databases Facilitating reading of sources Assigning interviewing tasks Using journal for writing down students' understandings and questions Using activity-based experiments Employing application-level testing in which students have to use information to do something Holding students accountable for information shared through testing and portfolio assessment
Long-term memory: Organizational structures	Starting cooperative learning groups Emphasizing concept attainment—using exemplars and nonexemplars to list attributes of categories Sequencing order of assignments to parallel problem-solving steps Using discovery learning Posing problems and interventions with paradoxes, dilemmas, and discrepancies
Long-term memory: Conditional	Giving long-term assignments that require problem solving and the use of other critical thinking skills Using jigsaw approaches—building from one form of understanding to another Using debating formats Giving essay exams Doing performance assessment Assigning readings from competing points of view Posing novel problems to cooperative learning teams Holding tournaments
Self as learner	Using cognitive behavior modification Modeling Using self-questioning—What did I do? Did it work? Why or why not? What could I do differently? How do I like to get information? Give information?
Self-reinforcement	Using cueing, self-monitoring
Self-regulation	Using self-instructional strategies Using self-questioning—Do I understand what is happening? What am I supposed to be paying attention to? Does this make sense? How can I do it differently?

retain information through direct instruction (Sands et al., 2000). With students who have a difficult time sustaining attention, teachers may want to write down what is said, use lots of visuals to accompany oral information, check for student understanding frequently, and provide models. When curriculum targets involve synthesis or evaluation levels of knowledge, problem-based strategies, the use of debate or cooperative learning may be the best strategies to choose. Knowing the knowledge schemas, cognitive taxonomy, and learning stages that are demanded by curriculum goals and objectives is critical to a teacher's ability to select and match appropriate instructional strategies.

IMPLEMENTING INSTRUCTION

Implementing instruction involves both initiating the specific strategy or set of strategies chosen as well as managing the overall operation of the classroom. Depending on the grouping and instructional strategies that are employed, teachers engage in various behaviors to orchestrate and modulate the instructional environment. This chapter introduces the most frequently used and researched instructional strategies that can support learning successes for all students. To assist teachers in choosing among many instructional approaches, instructional strategies are presented in four major categories. The first category, **teacher-mediated strategies,** encompasses strategies that are mediated or led by a teacher or group of teachers. The second set of strategies, facilitated and supported by students working with each other, are called **peer-mediated strategies** because they require the presence of more than one student to be accomplished. A third set of instructional approaches are **technology mediated** and rely on the use of computers, computer networks, the Internet, and other kinds of software and hardware that support instruction. The fourth set of instructional strategies are **activity-anchored** and require careful planning of experiences that will happen inside as well as outside of the classroom in community environments.

Teacher–Mediated Strategies

Teacher-mediated strategies require the leadership of a teacher to introduce, pace, and coach student performances. These strategies can be used to teach subject matter content such as history, calculus, or geology; foundational skills such as reading, math, and the use of technology; process skills such as problem solving, research, and inquiry; and personal skills such as time management, note-taking, and organization. Teacher-mediated strategies can be used with large groups, or whole-classroom instruction, and small groups, or one-to-one instruction. The use of these strategies is predicated on content knowledge, the assessment of learner knowledge and skills, and the selection of strategies that match both learner skills and the desired outcomes of the lesson. Ultimately, the student is the central player in any learning that goes on, but teacher-mediated strategies are focused on the interaction between the teacher and the student. The following sections introduce the reader to direct instruction and a variety of direct-instruction strategies that may be useful in teaching. For teachers who work with students with mental retardation, these strategies are fundamental teaching tools because they do not rely on the learner's skill in generalizing, building patterns for learning new information, or problem solving in unfamiliar situations with unfamiliar tasks (Mortweet et al., 1999).

Direct Instruction   Direct instruction has been demonstrated to result in successful learning outcomes in math, reading, strategy skills, and academic learning (Carnine, Silbert, & Kameenui, 1990; Deschler, Ellis, & Lenz, 1995; Gersten, Woodward, & Carnine, 1987; Gersten, Woodward, & Darch, 1986; Harris & Graham, 1996; Kameenui & Simmons, 1990; Lovitt, 1995). For many students who face challenges in learning, behavior, and/or social and emotional development, structured, explicit, direct instruction helps to develop skills, processes, strategies, and understanding. Not only does direct instruction research demonstrate success in academic content areas, but it also produces similar effects for teaching daily living (e.g., bathing, brushing teeth), oral communication (e.g., greeting others, requesting help), and transportation in the community (e.g., bus riding) (Snell, 1994).

Direct instruction typically is conceptualized as having five elements: 1) focused instruction, 2) mastery learning, 3) error correction and practice, 4) discrimination training, and 5) cumulative review (Gersten et al., 1986). Direct-instruction approaches to teaching and learning focus on the activities of the teacher in assuring that learning occurs. For example, teachers can vary antecedents and consequences for behavior. Providing a model of the learning target, providing verbal prompts or physical assistance to the learner to help him or her perform the target, or modifying the materials used to achieve the learning target are examples of how teachers can vary antecedents (Wolery et al., 1988). Direct-instruction approaches prescribe what teachers should do before, during, and after instruction occurs. This part-to-whole instructional approach is most helpful when students are learning a new, foundational skill rather than practicing a relatively intact skill in a novel or unfamiliar environment or content area (Rivera & Smith, 1997). Table 9.2 identifies the sequence of a direct-instruction lesson.

Focused Instruction   One of the hallmarks of direct instruction is its targeted nature. Teachers using direct instruction state the goals of instruction so that students are able to narrow their focus on the targets of learning. Once the teacher has set broad targets for the entire class, students should be encouraged to adapt these goals to their individual needs and interests. Contracts for learning are a variation of the goal-setting component. Students can personalize their learning goals in collaboration with their teachers, identifying the evaluation criteria and benchmarks for success.

Mastery Learning   In mastery learning, *time,* not individual ability, is the key variable in assuring that students achieve mastery. **Mastery learning** is based on the

Table 9.2.   Sequence of events in a direct-instruction lesson

Step	Events
1	Encourage student effort by linking lesson objectives to at least one of these rationales:
	Goal attainment: Learn this skill to reach a personal goal.
	Pleasure: Learn this skill because it is fun to do (e.g., skiing, playing tennis, baking).
	Utility: Learn this skill because it is necessary to achieve a future goal.
	Model the desired performance or product
	Isolate and teach the steps to successful performance
	Check student understanding at the end of each step
2	Ensure that students can perform each step
3	Provide opportunities to practice in which the teacher can coach and offer corrective feedback and reinforcement
	Assign independent practice
4	Assess student competence and re-teach (if necessary)

premise that given enough time, almost all learners can achieve competent performance or mastery of a task or concept (Bloom, Madaus, & Hastings, 1981). Thus, a teacher using direct-instruction techniques will plan on spending more time coaching and supporting some students and providing more opportunities for independent practice for others. Sometimes, these steps in direct instruction are referred to as *scaffolding.* This term refers to forms of temporary and adjustable supports that teachers give students to help them move from their current abilities to the intended goal (Monda-Amaya & Pearson, 1996; Rosenshine & Meister, 1992). Forms of supports can include the provision of prompts, cues, questions, error analyses, metaphors, elaboration, or cognitive modeling (i.e., as a teacher models the task, he or she talks out loud sharing his or her own thinking).

Using prompts and cues means that teachers purposefully and carefully insert verbal or physical prompts into a teaching cycle to cue students to perform a new skill in the appropriate sequence. For example, suppose that a second-grade teacher has just instructed her students to listen to each sentence that they read to make sure that what they read makes sense. She has modeled the behavior with several kinds of text, has used specific verbal models that she wants her students to adopt, and is now asking a small reading group to read aloud as a group, inserting the "does it make sense" question at the end of each sentence. Initially, the teacher uses an overhead projector with text to guide her students to read aloud as a group, one sentence at a time. When they reach the period, the teacher uses her index finger to point to the period at the end of the sentence and prompts her students to say aloud, "Did that just make sense?" When the students are able to do this in a group that is reading aloud, they return to holding their own texts and reading in turn. The teacher then cues students to remember to repeat their end-of-sentence questions. Rather than saying, "What do you say now?" the teacher's use of her index finger on her page with a quick double drum is sufficient to prompt students to ask the question. This is one example of how purposefully inserting cues in instruction can help students make the transition from the unfamiliar to the familiar. Cueing enables teachers to manage the amount of time students spend thinking about their forthcoming response (Rowe, 1986), thus combating impulsivity and improving the quality of responses. Cueing also assists students in knowing how to think about a particular topic. For example, the teacher may cue students to reach consensus, engage in problem solving, or assume the role of devil's advocate. Moreover, without much effort, the teacher can continue to use a cue only with those students who are not advancing through the skill more quickly.

To choose effective scaffolding techniques, teachers must assess their students' success on a frequent, if not daily, activity in the direct-instruction classroom. Assessments may consist of observations, quizzes, and student performances. Whatever choices teachers make about assessment, they must judge student performance against a standard and analyze individual performance and make adjustments in the kinds of initial instruction, practice, and feedback being given so that every student can be successful.

Helping students learn to improve their reading comprehension might involve summarizing the main ideas, reminding them to use strategies for developing and monitoring their comprehension (identifying key ideas, summarizing, taking notes, questioning themselves), or providing them with an advance organizer (Good & Brophy, 1994). Scaffolding allows students to engage in complex tasks that they might not otherwise be able to manage on their own until they can understand how to perform the task and in which situations to apply it (Monda-Amaya & Pearson, 1996). Performance tasks such as handwriting, reading out loud with youngsters and pausing while they say one of the words in a sentence, and physical tasks such as skipping rope often are taught by successive approximations. Students are reinforced over time for performance or behavior that more closely approximates a desired performance or outcome.

Error Correction and Practice   Systematic, consistent feedback is a hallmark of direct instruction; therefore, teachers using this model are encouraged to provide specific and frequent verbal comments that describe and affirm student effort, practice, and correct performance. Further, correcting errors is a critical component of teaching. By correcting an error in a performance, students get better at identifying the elements of successful performance and learn to self-assess as they perform with more and more skill. Like scaffolding, **error correction** requires thought and attention on the part of the teacher. Good correction rewards effort, encourages more practice, and helps the student to identify the part of a task that was performed in error. For example, proving a theorem in geometry requires a certain set of procedures, completed in a particular sequence. Students need to know where an error occurred in their proof, why what they did was not accurate or correct, and what an accomplished or satisfactory performance might look like. Teachers need to identify the error, pinpoint the nature of the error, and provide an accurate model.

Generally, practice is guided first and then is performed independently. The rationale for guided practice initially is to make sure that students do not inadvertently teach themselves an inaccurate process or response. Relearning is more difficult and requires more intervention from a teacher than learning the correct process or skill initially. When students are able to perform a task or skill accurately with guidance, teachers need to offer opportunities to complete the same task without guidance. Finally, students should be asked to complete successfully variations of a task or procedure.

Discrimination Training   **Discrimination training** is a crucial element of direct instruction because it creates the opportunity for students to recognize exemplars and nonexemplars of the performances and tasks that they have been learning to accomplish. The ability to apply newly acquired rules to unfamiliar examples and nonexamples is a way of assessing the depth and stability of learning. When learners can approach a problem and apply their knowledge base to understanding and acting on a new situation, they are said to be in the fluency stage of learning. To achieve this level of competence, students need practice in distinguishing among models. The teacher as coach/model is particularly effective in this stage of direct instruction because the teacher's role is most often to coach and remind students of their complete repertoire so that they can produce an accomplished performance. Discrimination training can become more complex and tap into higher order thinking skills when teachers begin to challenge their students to find similarities and differences in problems, tasks, and events. According to Marzano, Pickering, and Pollock (2001), a variety of researchers have found that asking students to compare, classify, and create metaphors and analogies results in understanding and retaining content knowledge. At their most fundamental levels, these processes of comparing and contrasting are excellent examples of higher order discrimination training.

Cumulative Review   Finally, in **cumulative review,** a student is asked to put together all the steps of a particular skill and produce a competent performance or product. Consider the task of writing a newspaper article. Depending on a student's initial skills prior to learning to accomplish the task, the student may have learned to outline an article based on the five questions of who, when, where, what, and why. Initially, a teacher using direct instruction may ask students to practice writing several responses to a *who* question. After achieving accuracy on that task, the instructor may ask the students to hone their ability to answer *when* questions, practicing that skill until they reach a particular level of competence.

Modifying Cognitive Processes

Since the 1970s, cognitive psychology has explored the ways that individuals learn to process information and regulate their learning processes. Using principles of direct instruction, in which target behaviors or content expertise are identified and analyzed by component parts, cognitive psychologists helped educators to understand that learning processes may need to be taught and that there are effective approaches to teaching these skills. For students with mental retardation, teaching these skills is critical because they may not be able to develop these skills and strategies through experience alone. The content of these processes can be summarized into three major areas. The first area encompasses skills for *learning how to learn*. Some students need to be taught how to focus their attention and how to monitor the length of sustained attention they give to any learning task. Through learning how to learn, students are taught to direct and manage their own learning. This means that students not only learn to set goals for their own learning, they also are taught to regulate their own learning processes such as attention to task, concentration, memory retrieval and storage, and checking for understanding. *Self-regulation* refers to the degree that individuals are metacognitively, motivationally, and behaviorally active participants in their own learning process (Zimmerman, 1986).

A second set of cognitive skills that can be taught are *strategic skills* such as thinking critically about issues, performances, and theories and predicting events across content or disciplines. An individual's approach to a task is called a *strategy* when it includes how that person thinks and acts when planning, performing, and evaluating task performance (Lenz, Ellis, & Scanlon, 1996). Strategic skills may be either global or task specific. For instance, problem solving may be thought of as a global skill that requires identifying the core or target problem, identifying potential solutions, analyzing the efficacy of each solution, choosing a solution that meets the efficacy criteria, and then completing the steps of the solution in a logical sequence. Cognitive strategies are deliberate, planned processes learners use to process information. Learners employ global strategies in order to sequence approaches to tasks and activities. Global strategies assist students in automatizing problem solving. In that way, they can allocate more of their mental processes to higher ordered thinking and less to procedural demands.

Although global strategies might describe the general steps for problem solving, content areas and specific topics may require students to know particular repertoires to learn a specific sequence of steps. Task-specific strategies also capitalize on benefits of automaticity. Examples of task-specific strategies are procedures that students learn to employ when reading new material. Most of the research in teaching students to think critically suggests that these skills are progressive. That is, students need practice in content-specific areas to develop generalized skills in concept formation, comparison and contrast, pattern recognition, and the other higher ordered thinking skills mentioned previously (Hyde & Bizar, 1989; Joyce et al., 1992). Research in the area of reading instruction has shown that the application of critical thinking skills to the process of reading has resulted in increased reading comprehension for many groups of students from elementary through college levels (Cook & Mayer, 1988; Paris & Newman, 1990; Pressley et al., 1992). To apply critical thinking skills to the reading process, competent readers get ready to read text by anticipating what information or ideas they will encounter. Furthermore, they constantly monitor their own thinking throughout their reading by analyzing and synthesizing what they read and comparing it to what they know. To teach students how to think and be more strategic in their learning, teachers must structure, direct, model, and facilitate overt opportunities for students to develop, use, and evaluate critical thinking and learning strategies. Because learning involves making associations between new and previous understandings and experiences, instruction must develop students' thinking and self-regulation skills.

A broad research base also supports the benefits of strategy instruction, particularly in areas such as reading, writing, test taking, study skills, self-monitoring, and self-reinforcement (Schunk & Zimmerman, 1994). In particular, researchers have noted that many low achievers, students at risk, and students with disabilities fail to activate strategic approaches to learning (Swanson, 1991), but when these students learn to use these processes, improved academic and social gains are noted (Palincsar, David, Winn, & Stevens, 1991; Schunk & Cox, 1986; Schunk & Swartz, 1993; Wong, 1991). For example, teaching poor readers to adopt specific, prereading techniques helps them to set a purpose, heighten motivation, and activate thinking (Kameenui & Simmons, 1990). These prediction activities are based on the presumption that reading and thinking are related and that reading comprehension is enhanced when critical thinking skills, such as prediction, are activated prior to the act of reading.

A third set of skills are called *process skills* and are specific to particular kinds of tasks. For instance, proficient readers know how to summarize what they have read and often perform this task without consciously choosing to do so. Skilled learners also know how and when to take notes and how to represent their learning visually. The work of Deshler and his colleagues in Kansas and similar work at the University of Oregon has demonstrated that students can learn skills to support their learning processes and that many students need to be taught these skills explicitly to succeed in school.

The recommended teaching strategies in all three areas are remarkably similar. That is, the teacher, as in other forms of direct instruction, explicitly identifies the skill to be learned, provides exemplars or models of an accomplished performance, and helps students to learn the component skills needed to become proficient. Students learn to identify good and poor examples of the strategy in use, polish their own performance while being coached, practice their skills in low-stakes situations, and then, finally, produce an accomplished performance as an evaluation.

Advance Organizers   The use of **advance organizers** (also discussed in Chapter 4) is an instructional strategy that supports the presentation of new information to students. Think of advance organizers as cognitive maps. Advance organizers help learners to incorporate new information into their existing cognitive schemas and help them to anticipate relationships between prior and new knowledge. Advance organizers signal the learner that he or she may need to change his or her internal maps to accommodate new information. According to Ausubel (1963), advance organizers aid students in their organization and processing of new material information. Furthermore, Ausubel maintained that advance organizers activate student participation in traditionally passive instructional activities, such as lectures and reading. Other forms of organizing information and activating student participation include the use of lesson organizers, chapter survey routines, unit organizers, and course organizers (Lenz,

Bulgren, Schumaker, Deshler, & Boudah, 1994; Lenz, Marrs, Schumaker, & Deshler, 1993; Schumaker, Deshler, & McKnight, 1989).

Co-Teaching **Co-teaching** is a collaborative arrangement between school professionals in which they create solutions to challenges and plan, teach, and modify lessons together. School professionals may choose to co-teach because it fosters the inclusion of students with disabilities in general education classes (Bawrens, Hourcade, & Friend, 1987) and makes it possible to provide students with a more individualized and diversified learning experience (Cook & Firend, 1995). Through co-teaching, school professionals jointly create units, plan lessons, modify lessons for individual needs, and carry out classroom instruction (Warger & Pugach, 1993). The intent is to create a class-room community in which all students are valued members and to develop innovative teaching strategies that would not be possible if only one teacher were present. Moreover, each of the participants in the co-teaching process benefits from the back-ground knowledge and experience of the other. The participants have equal standing, with neither party taking a back seat to the other.

Peer-Mediated Instruction

Whereas teacher-mediated instructional approaches focus on the relationship between the learner and the teacher, peer-mediated instructional strategies capitalize on the rela-tionships between peers. Of course, teachers create the context in which these peer-learning interactions occur, but the teaching and learning focus on what students together construct and extract from experiences, tasks, and events.

Like teacher-mediated strategies, peer-mediated strategies are useful for teaching in the content areas as well as teaching the basic tools for learning: literacy, numeracy, and technology. Although peer-mediated strategies can be used with large groups, they require organizing the whole into smaller groups to engage in purposeful reflection, inquiry, and experimentation. Peer-mediated instruction is typically done in dyads or small groups. Grouping can and should be flexible, alternating between the use of het-erogeneous and homogeneous groupings to meet different curriculum targets. There are a variety of different approaches to peer-mediated strategies, including peer tutoring, reciprocal teaching, cooperative learning, role playing, and center-based learning. As Marzano and colleagues (2001) pointed out, these strategies have stood up under rigor-ous research conditions and have demonstrated success in helping students to achieve in the academic curriculum. In the following sections, a few of many different approaches to peer-mediated instruction—peer tutoring, reciprocal teaching, coopera-tive learning, and role playing and simulations—are reviewed.

Peer Tutoring There are a variety of approaches to **peer tutoring,** some of which are successful with young children in preschool programs and others that are used successfully in elementary and secondary classrooms (Kohler & Strain, 1999; Utley, Mortweet, & Greenwood, 1997). Whereas some teachers use mixtures of peer strategies both to suit their instructional styles and to address the context and the needs of their students, many other teachers find that peer activities are difficult to manage and often elect not to use these strategies in spite of the data that demonstrate their effectiveness (Kohler, Ezell, & Paluselli, 1999). Researchers have found that when teachers plan for differentiation of materials, content, and student outcomes, peer activities result in suc-cessful academic learning (Kohler et al., 1999).

A simple, yet effective peer-tutoring strategy involves organizing students into pairs for brief periods of time to discuss their reactions or connections to content presented in class. Telling one another about what has just been taught seems to enhance memory and learning (Weaver & Cotrell, 1986). In another version of peer tutoring, students work together to solve problems. One student acts as the problem solver while the other student acts as a monitor for the problem-solving process. The problem solver talks aloud while completing a task, giving a running monologue of thoughts, strategies, ideas, and notions for solving the problem. The monitor cues the problem solver with appropriate questions: What is your purpose? What are you expecting? Does that make sense? Why? What are you thinking? Did you skip a step? The focus of this method is on helping students make their thinking visible so they can track their thought patterns and correct faulty reasoning and strategies for doing tasks. To be effective, this method requires intense, guided practice, but it is worthwhile because of its power to adapt to many subjects and to emphasize the self-reflective aspects of cognition, affect, and communication (Mortweet et al., 1999).

In Think/Pair/Share (Lyman & McTighe, 1988), students are first exposed to new information by listening to a lecture or presentation, watching a video, or reading a passage. They then take time to think, talk with each other in pairs, and finally share responses with the larger group. The teacher signals students to switch to think, pair, and share modes by using cues. Longwill and Kleinert (1999) reported that even in high school, models of peer tutoring enhance student performance for both members of the tutoring pair.

Classwide peer tutoring pairs students for brief, but frequent, periods of drill and practice of factual material (Delquadri, Greenwood, Whorton, Carta, & Hall, 1986). This method has been positively related to improved student achievement on weekly quizzes (Maheady, Sacca, & Harper, 1988). It helps focus the student's attention for an intense practice period. Although there is great variation in how pairs of students work together to support and coach each others' learning, research seems to demonstrate that peer-tutoring outcomes are positive in multiple environments with many different kinds of students.

Reciprocal Teaching   **Reciprocal teaching** is another form of peer tutoring that was developed to support the teaching of reading comprehension (Brown & Palincsar, 1984). Palincsar (1986) described reciprocal teaching as ongoing interaction between two students about a particular reading passage that they are working on. Pairs of students read a text passage either silently or orally, depending on their ability to read fluently. After the passage is read, one member of the pair is designated as the dialogue leader and asks questions about the content to the other member of the pair. The other member of the pair discusses these questions, raises additional questions, and in the case of disagreements rereads the text to find evidence to support his or her perspective. Once the pair has reached agreement about the basic elements of the passage, the discussion leader attempts to summarize and synthesize the passage. The pair clarifies and defines vocabulary as needed. Finally, the pair predicts what will happen next in the text. According to Lederer (2000), reciprocal teaching has been demonstrated to improve reading comprehension ability in students because it helps students to use cognitive processes to think critically about what they read and evaluate its meaning.

Cooperative Learning   **Cooperative learning** groups are distinguished by five components: positive interdependence, face-to-face interaction, individual accountability, interpersonal and small-group skills, and group processing (Johnson & Johnson,

1991). Plans for cooperative lessons must attend to each of these five elements as well as to specific academic and social objectives. There are many variations and approaches to cooperative learning, such as informal and formal cooperative-learning techniques. Informal cooperative groups are temporary, ad hoc groups that last from a few minutes to an entire class period. In contrast, formal cooperative learning groups last longer— from one class period to several weeks of instruction that are focused on one specific task or project.

Role Play and Simulations **Role play** involves students dramatizing a situation. The purpose of role play and simulations vary. They can be used to evaluate students' conceptual understandings of events, phenomena, and problem-solving strategies in a variety of subject areas. They also can be used to teach routines and procedures. For example, teachers can use role play to provide guided practice to students so that they can be coached to perform accurate classroom attendance procedures. Finally, role play also frequently is used to develop and practice interpersonal skills (Goldstein, 1988).

Technology–Mediated Instruction

A thorough review of the uses of technology for students with mental retardation is provided in Chapter 16. This section provides an overview of the use of technology-mediated instruction as it relates to supporting different curriculum content areas and learning outcomes. Technology-mediated instruction can be supported through a variety of *low-tech* and *high-tech systems.* Low-tech systems would include the use of tools such as calculators, audio recorders/players, and low-tech (e.g., battery-operated) switching systems that allow students with significant physical needs and/or mental retardation to operate electrical equipment or toys. High-tech systems are represented by computers, networks, digital-based systems, or complex communication systems such as those using voice-activated technology. Technology-mediated instruction can be used for a variety of purposes and across all grouping formats—whole-group, small group, independent, and one-to-one. Technology-mediated instruction can be used for anything from introducing models and concepts and supporting the development of problem-solving skills to providing drills, practice, and feedback as students develop automaticity of basic procedural skills (e.g., math computation, sentence development, and basic writing skills) or lower-level cognitive-based skills (e.g., spelling words, basic math facts). Technology-mediated instruction provides the critical flexibility needed for student access to and demonstration of their achievement of the curriculum. Information can be communicated, translated (e.g., text to speech), and received through text-based, auditory-based, and graphically based mediums. This allows teachers and students to use a variety of materials ranging from auditory prompts and cues, graphics, organizers, outlines, video demonstrations, digitally recorded readings, and audio recordings to scaffold instruction and assess curriculum outcomes.

Activity–Based Strategies

Activity-based or **activity-anchored instructional strategies** require students to be actively engaged in learning experiences that require them to solve problems and think critically. Activity-anchored instruction most likely occurs in small-group or independent formats. Activity-based instruction can involve research-based projects, field trips, experiments, teamwork, or internships. Often, students learn best in environments where the skills that they are expected to acquire are actually used in the authentic and daily conduct of work in a particular environment. Increasingly, schools are using instructional methods such as expeditionary learning, service learning, problem-based learning, and apprenticeships. All of these approaches to teaching have great merit in tying the general education curriculum to the typical special education curricular approach called *functional skills* (see Chapter 12). The linkage among these approaches is the belief in the value of teaching in authentic, real-life environments (as in expeditionary and service learning) or of working on real-life problems (as in problem-based learning). See *Additional Readings* at the end of this chapter for a list of resources on these instructional approaches.

ASSESSING INSTRUCTION

Assessing instruction is closely linked to assessing curriculum. Teachers need to constantly monitor whether students are making adequate progress toward their goals and objectives and their stated outcomes. Through instruction, teachers gain valuable insight regarding how well students are progressing toward curriculum outcomes. Assessing instruction itself, however, has less to do with assessing students' progress than it has to do with assessing the management and effectiveness of specific instructional strategies and the instructional environment.

As teachers implement instructional strategies and manage the classroom environment, they should reflect on the following questions to monitor their effectiveness:

- Am I using a tone of voice that communicates high expectations yet confidence in students' abilities?
- Did I have an accurate understanding of what students already knew and need to know, and therefore, does this strategy appear to be a good match for my curriculum targets?
- Am I implementing the strategy in a correct manner?
- Have I selected materials that truly anchor and support my instruction?
- Is the physical setup of the room supporting or serving as a barrier to instruction?
- Are students able to engage in the curriculum given the grouping strategies and instructional strategies I have selected?
- Is the climate of the classroom supporting or detracting from the instructional strategies I am using?
- Are transitions from one activity to another smooth?
- Have I provided students with sufficient support so that they can practice or work on their own?
- Am I making efficient use of the human resources available to me, including students, paraprofessionals, my special education colleagues, volunteers, and related services personnel?

Assessing instruction is based on subtle variables that are not as easily observed as curriculum outcomes. Teachers who use a simple system of rotating observations so that every student is observed at least once during the week can assess student performance at multiple and various times during the day. One informal assessment tool is the use of observation notes that are written quickly as activities unfold in the classroom. These notes as well as samples of student work can then be used to analyze student understanding, skill fluency, and error patterns. These informal assessments form the basis of the data that are used to answer the questions. As a result, teachers can quickly make adjustments that improve student learning.

ADAPTING INSTRUCTION FOR INDIVIDUAL NEEDS

Adjustments that are made to content are labeled *curriculum modifications*. Adjustments that are made to instruction are labeled *instructional adaptations*. The goal of instructional adaptations is to more closely align the learning preferences and needs of a student with the teacher's teaching style. If curriculum and instructional planning have been approached by applying the principles of universal design and differentiated instruction, the need for instructional adaptation should be minimal. As with curriculum modification, teachers should rely on collaborating with colleagues, especially their special education peers, to help design and implement instructional adaptations. Chapter 4 reviewed the decisions that must be made that form the basis for curriculum and instructional modifications to achieve access to the general curriculum. Teachers who have been involved in the IEP planning process, described in Chapter 4, will have already considered what instructional adaptations can be applied to enable students to progress. As discussed previously, the function of the IEP is to document recommendations for 1) instructional strategies or curricular content that may not typically be represented in a student's educational experiences and 2) adaptations and modifications to existing instructional practices and curricular standards. As such, the initial steps in considering adaptations and modifications are completed in the IEP process.

Several components of instruction should be considered when adapting instruction. These include grouping strategies, location of instruction, physical arrangements of the environment, materials, presentation format, and student response formats. As we have mentioned before, grouping can include whole-group, small group, one-to-one, and independent formats. The location of instruction can involve different areas in the class or other school environments such as the cafeteria, the office, hallways, the library, and the gym. There are many factors that can be adapted within the physical environment, including lighting, sound, temperature, height of furniture, type of furniture, location of furniture, and location of materials. The types of materials that can be used to scaffold instruction are endless, especially with the expanded availability of technology. Presentation formats can include visual, graphic, auditory input, symbols, text-based, signing systems, and so forth. Finally, student response formats can be picture-based, typed, audiotaped, performance-based, written, and oral as well as include the range of technology-mediated formats discussed previously.

For students with more extensive or pervasive support needs, more individualized approaches to instruction may need to be used to teach a specific skill. Providing specific prompts, such as full physical prompts by the teacher to assist a student to perform the learning target, is one example of a highly individualized approach (Snell, 1994). Sands and colleagues provided the following example for a student with mental retardation:

Let's suppose that a second grade teacher is creating a routine in her classroom that all children will simply leave the classroom whenever they need to use the bathroom. The teacher establishes a routine for leaving the classroom that involves students finding their own magnet-backed photograph and placing it on the "out-of-class" board before leaving to go to the bathroom. They must go directly to the bathroom and return directly to the classroom. When students re-renter the classroom, they find their photos again and place them on the attendance board. When the classroom teacher originally taught this routine, she taught it to the whole class and provided small group practice time. For the first week that she instituted this procedure, she provided group rewards to each team in her class that was able to successfully complete the procedure each morning and afternoon. The second week that she used the procedure, she used a daily acknowledgment procedure. By the third week, she was randomly giving students feedback who used the system correctly. By the end of the third week, only the student with mental retardation still had trouble with the routine because her working memory requires more practice than most learners in order for her to produce a new skill without prompts and cues. The classroom teacher decided to set aside some individual instructional time with Annie. She used an instructional procedure called the "discrete trial" to teach Annie this routine. Like other forms of direct instruction, discrete trial begins by breaking tasks down into small components and then, helping students to practice routines by carefully inserting only the necessary prompts that help a student successfully complete a step in the process. (2000, pp. 360–361)

Discrete trial is an example of a direct-instruction process that is designed to meet the unique needs of one learner and requires completing the instructional process with one student responding to one teacher. Because most teachers are rarely in the situation to provide this type of intensive instruction, discrete-trial procedures can also be thought of as an instructional adaptation. This process, like other forms of tutoring, requires the full attention of a teacher. If school professionals can anticipate that they or a support person may need to provide this level of assistance, they may choose to free some time to provide this level of assistance by planning the instructional schedule so that all students are working in small groups or teams. There are other, intensive, procedurally based instructional models that require very small teacher to student ratios, such as graduated guidance, differential reinforcement schedules, cueing, and time delay (e.g., Snell, 1994; Wolery et al., 1988). When students need these intensive levels of instruction to master skills, school professionals and support personnel must work collaboratively to plan and carry out instruction.

A FRAMEWORK FOR GUIDING INSTRUCTIONAL DECISIONS

Udvari-Solner (1995) designed a framework for thinking about adjustments to instruction that also can assist teachers—in conjunction with their colleagues, students, and family members—to make sufficient changes in the way that lessons are designed, structured, and delivered. One such framework has six components to investigate: 1) the structure of the instructions, 2) the demands and evaluation criteria of the task, 3) the learning environment, 4) the materials used for learning, 5) the support structure, and 6) participatory activities. According to Udvari-Solner, teachers who organize their instructional delivery by thinking about each of these components can create an instructional process that responds to the needs of all their learners. Of course, the trick in answering these questions is to do it with the needs of your students in mind. That means that when your classroom has widely divergent students, in terms of their interests, backgrounds, abilities, and communication and language preferences, you need to think broadly and creatively about how to approach any given lesson or curriculum unit.

For instance, in considering the structure of instructions, a teacher might ask the questions, "What can my students do well and to what extent can they actively participate in this lesson?" and, "Are there ways that I can increase student participation by changing the lesson format?" Perhaps, the teacher will consider the demands and evaluation criteria of a particular task or lesson by identifying the needs of students that could be integrated into a particular lesson. In considering the learning environment, teachers may reflect on how all students can contribute meaningfully to the work of their team or group. In planning for participation and contribution, teachers will also weigh the kinds of materials that will be needed and select materials that reduce the level of abstraction.

SUMMARY

Instructional strategies are closely linked to the curriculum. Teaching a diverse group of students requires knowledge of each learner and his or her learning needs, an understanding of multiple ways to introduce and sequence content, and skill in selecting instructional approaches that will accommodate the diversity of student needs and abilities. For students with mental retardation, the instructional focus must include learning how to learn as well as learning core concepts and skills. Both teacher- and peer-mediated instructional strategies can be effective if teachers are able to differentiate the curriculum, materials, and instructional approaches, understanding that no single approach can meet the needs of all learners. Teaching in an inclusive classroom requires consistent and constant assessment of student learning so that adjustments can be made to the curriculum and instructional choices to improve outcomes for students.

ADDITIONAL READINGS

Cooperative Learning

Bellanca, J., & Fogarty, R. (1990). *Blueprints for thinking in the cooperative classroom.* Palatine, IL: Skylight Publishing, Inc.

Holt, L. (1993). *Cooperative learning in action.* Columbus, OH: National Middle School Association.

Johnson, D.W., Johnson, R.T., & Holubec, E.J. (1991). *Cooperation in the classroom* (Rev. ed.). Edina, MN: Interaction Books.

Kagan, S. (1989). *Cooperative learning resources for teachers.* San Juan Capistrano, CA: Resources for Teachers.

Slavin, R.E. (1990). *Cooperative learning: Theory, research, and practice.* Upper Saddle River, NJ: Prentice Hall.

Instructional Strategies

Deshler, D.D., Ellis, E.S., & Lenz, B.K. (Eds.). (1996) *Teaching adolescents with learning disabilities: Strategies and methods* (2nd ed.). Denver, CO: Love.

Harris, K.R., Graham, S., Deshler, D., & Pressley, M. (1997). *Teaching every child every day: Learning in diverse schools and classrooms.* Cambridge, MA: Brookline Books.

Hogan, K., & Pressley, M. (1997). *Scaffolding student learning: Instructional approaches and issues.* Cambridge, MA: Brookline Books.

Kameenui, E.J., & Simmons, D.C. (1990). *Designing instructional strategies: The prevention of academic learning problems.* Columbus, OH: Merrill.

Pressley, M.J., & Woloshyn, V. (1995). *Cognitive strategy instruction that really improves children's academic performance.* Reston, VA: Council for Exceptional Children.

CHAPTER OBJECTIVES

1. Discuss the historical role of the family in education, contrast that role with current understandings of the role of family, and identify why parental and family involvement is critical to educational success.
2. Identify barriers to effective family involvement and discuss myths about families and professionals that contribute to such barriers.
3. Critically examine reasons why parents and family members of students with mental retardation might be hesitant to address future-oriented issues.
4. Describe practices that empower families.

KEY TERMS

Family and parent involvement
Partnerships
Life cycle transitions
Reliable alliances
Group Action Planning

10

Establishing Equal School–Home Partnerships

Parental and Family Involvement in Education

DECISIONS ABOUT A CHILD'S LIFE: SOMEONE IN THE *FAMILY* SHOULD BE WEARING THE PANTS.

Family and parent involvement throughout a student's educational career is critical to successful educational experiences for all students but perhaps particularly so for students with mental retardation. The Education for All Handicapped Children Act (PL 94-142), passed in 1975, was written to emphasize parents' and families' involvement in the educational planning and decision-making process for their family members, and procedural safeguards have been established to help ensure such involvement. Cutler (1993), describing the special education process to parents, summarized the Individuals with Disabilities Education Act (IDEA) of 1990 (PL 101-476) as "a declaration of your child's educational rights and of your rights as a parent to *participate in the educational process*" (p. 3, italics added). The language in IDEA appoints parents and professionals as equal partners in the educational process.

Moreover, the framework proposed in this text essentially requires the establishment of an equal school–home partnership. During the planning and program evaluation process, the design of educational supports, the establishment of community-based supports and ongoing friendships, and the promotion of self-determination, the active involvement of family members from preschool through secondary education is critical. This chapter outlines methods and strategies to establish equal **partnerships** between school and home across various ages. It emphasizes a shift from parents as simply partners to parents as allies and provides strategies and methods to achieve this outcome.

IMPORTANCE OF FAMILY INVOLVEMENT IN EDUCATION

For much of the first half of the 20th century, schools were responsible only for academic instruction, whereas families were responsible for emotional and social development and instruction (Flaxman & Inger, 1991). Changes in the structure of the family and society since the 1960s and changing demographics in the United States have significantly altered the role of schools in society and the role of parents regarding school responsibilities (Flaxman & Inger, 1991). The contemporary notion of parental involvement dates back to the early 1960s when the passage of federal legislation designed to address societal problems mandated parental involvement in planning and decision-making about curriculum, instruction, and school improvement. The Head Start program was among the first to employ such a model, bringing educators and parents of young children together to address both child and family-related issues (Flaxman & Inger, 1991). The Education for All Handicapped Children Act of 1975 (PL 94-142) also mandated such collaboration.

Many reasons exist for family involvement and parent–professional collaboration in the educational process. Sinclair and Christenson (1992), noting that school–home collaboration is integral to the success of students, suggested the following general reasons to support parental involvement:

- Only through collaboration can real change occur. Schools and professionals alone cannot meet the complex, multiple needs of children in America today.
- Child development and learning does not occur in a single environment and without influence from multiple sources. "Children learn, grow, and develop both at home and at school. There is no clear cut boundary between home and school expe-

riences for children and youth. Rather, there is a mutually influencing quality between experiences in these two settings" (Sinclair & Christenson, 1992, p. 12).

- The definition of education has expanded with advances in research about human learning and cognition.

According to Sinclair and Christenson,

> A learning environment is educative when it enables the individual to learn and develop specialized skills; it is miseducative when it fails to encourage positive human development. The educative community is produced when learning environments of the home and school are linked together and carefully coordinated to serve the developmental needs of the individuals. (1992, p. 12)

If professionals are to achieve positive educational outcomes, they must actively involve families and collaborate with parents to ensure learning opportunities throughout the student's day. This stance has been substantiated by research that documents that parental participation in the educational process results in more positive educational outcomes for students, including better school attendance, reduced dropout rates, enhanced student self-esteem and confidence, and improved educational achievement scores (Flaxman & Inger, 1991). Sinclair and Christenson summarized the primary effects of family involvement as follows:

- All forms of parent involvement strategies seem to be useful; however, those that are meaningful, well-planned, comprehensive, and long-lasting offer more opportunities for parents to be involved and appear to be more effective. Student achievement is greater with high levels of meaningful involvement.
- Parent involvement affects noncognitive behavior; student attendance, attitudes about school, maturation, self-concept, and behavior improve when parents are involved.
- Parents, teachers, communities, and schools benefit when parents are involved. In general, there are more successful educational programs and effective schools.
- Student achievement gains are most significant and long lasting when parent involvement begins early in students' school careers. (1992, p. 13)

BARRIERS TO EFFECTIVE FAMILY INVOLVEMENT

Sonnenschein (1981) characterized the parent–professional partnership as an uneasy relationship. A partnership is a two-way street; to understand breakdowns in collaborations between home and school, one needs to examine the actions and beliefs of both parties.

Professional Mishandling of Parents

The educational process, historically, has been one in which families are not equal partners, and their participation has often been marginalized (Turnbull & Turnbull, 2001). One factor that contributes to this unequal role is the inaccurate or unfair conceptualizations of parents that professionals too often hold. Sonnenschein (1981) identified several such conceptualizations.

For example, many professionals perceive parents as vulnerable clients and view their role in the school–home interaction as one of a helper. Relationships built on these assumptions typically position the professional as the expert, someone who has the answers and, essentially, the power and control to change outcomes for the family. Such relationships do not lend themselves to equal partnerships or collaborative efforts. A related perception, according to Sonnenschein (1981), is that of parents as patients. Historically, the birth of a child with a disability has been viewed as an event precipitating a grieving and acceptance process, described as being similar to the process of coping with the death of a loved one. Parents are labeled as being at one point or another in this acceptance continuum and often are seen as not coping well or are seen as experiencing stress or anxiety as a result of their inability to come to terms with their child's disability. This leads to perceptions that the family members themselves need remediation and attention. Once again, a relationship based on these assumptions does not lend itself to effective collaboration. The truth of the matter is that coping with the birth of a child with a disability varies widely from family to family and is best described by the individual family's coping strategies and abilities than by some global strategy.

Singer and Powers (1993) summarized the problems with these first two types of relationships when describing the tenets of traditional models of caring for families. One such tenet has been that family support is oriented toward professional control and the fitting of families into programs. The assumption is that special expertise is required to assist troubled families and that families should turn over decision making to professionals and program administrators. A second tenet is that "families are necessarily pathological because of the 'burden' imposed by raising a child with a disability" (Singer & Powers, 1993, p. 4). Accordingly,

> This orientation stresses family problems and uses language derived from medicine in which pathology, treatment, cure and prescription are common terms. It is assumed that parents require training, need assistance to learn how to raise their children and, invariably, are distressed. (Singer & Powers, 1993, p. 5)

Yet another common misperception about families is that they are responsible for their child's disabling condition. Turnbull and Turnbull experienced this, stating that professionals they were dealing with never "came right out and said, 'You caused it,' but everything they did was based on that premise" (1978, p. 42). Early theories regarding the etiology of certain disabilities, most noticeably autism, explicitly blamed parents (usually mothers) for their child's condition. Professionals often assume that the parent is somehow to blame for the disability. Whether this perception is grounded in fact or is simply part of the mythology of disability, its impact on creating partnerships is devastating.

Part of the reason that the perception of the parent as responsible for the child's disability exists is that many parents harbor guilt and questions about their own culpability in their child's developmental outcomes. It is a short distance from parental feelings of guilt to professionals' assumptions of responsibility. In a similar manner, professionals frequently perceive parents as less observant, intelligent, and perceptive. Part of this emerges from inappropriate assumptions that because the child has these characteristics, then, so too does the family. Again, views of the parent as responsible or less able stigmatizes parents and builds barriers to collaboration and partnership. Myths about the family's capacity to contribute to planning and decision making are too widely accepted and often used to prevent effective collaboration and partnerships. Cutler (1993) listed several such myths, including:

- Parents are naive laypeople who cannot and should not teach.
- Parents are too emotionally involved to evaluate their children.
- Parents are still obedient school pupils who should be seen and not heard.

The roots of the first myth lie in the stereotype of the school's role in society. Many educators, indeed many people in general society, continue to hold the view that schools should only teach academic skills (i.e., the three R's) and that teaching should be done by experts. This belief, however, contradicts what is known about learning. As described previously, learning and development occur every minute of every day, and for education to be most effective, educators must capitalize on this fact. Parents spend the most time with their children, and in the long run, they are their children's only constant teacher. Teachers who can effectively involve parents as teachers (*not* as expert educators who replicate what occurs in the classroom) are effective and successful.

The second myth pertains to perceptions about parents as victims, clients, or patients. The assumption is that until parents work through their grief and accept the child's disability (acceptance is implicitly defined as viewing the child as the professional does), then they cannot move past the emotional and mental barriers they have erected to contribute in a meaningful manner. This belief is inaccurate, yet pervasive.

The final myth springs as much from the system as from any particular bias individual educators may hold. School systems are complex bureaucracies that often require insider knowledge to navigate. Educators themselves come to accept this as fact in a very short time, but because they are in the system, they can at least somewhat work their way through the maze. Parents are viewed as outside the system, and many educators portray parents as naive about the way things really work and, as such, believe that parents need to let them (e.g., the educator, administrator) work the system for them. Add to this the belief that professionals hold a key to teaching and learning, and it is obvious that the parent who tries to become active and demands equal treatment is seen as naive and in some ways incapable.

When a parent or family member comes in and attempts to overcome the various barriers to equal partnership, he or she is sometimes seen as a problem and labeled as aggressive or unrealistic, creating yet another perception and barrier to partnerships. Some parents find that this occurs very early on in their interactions with schools and may adopt an equally strident position, digging in for trench warfare instead of trying to work with schools. The cycle repeats itself and the school–home relationship becomes confrontational and is ultimately destroyed. Although families may eventually obtain at least some of what they want, it is at great cost to the family, educators, and the student. There are no winners in this situation. Many parents come to the conclusion that this process is more harmful for their son or daughter than helpful and decide not to fight the system. As a result, they are apt not to press for what they want because of fear that the resulting environment will be more difficult for their child.

Parent Mishandling of Professionals

An equal number of barriers to collaboration are raised by parents or family members. Like educators, parents bring inaccurate perceptions and beliefs to the school–home relationship. Cutler (1993) identified three such false beliefs held by many parents:

- Educators are super experts in their field.
- Educators are totally objective.
- Educators are free agents.

As Cutler noted, these myths are the mirror images of the myths about parents. They are, in many ways, as damaging to family involvement as beliefs about parents. Educators have skills and training that enable them to work with students with disabilities and to provide answers to difficult problems and situations. They also have a large number of students, limited time, and high demands on their time. Educators are as constrained by the system as parents are and often equally frustrated. However, the stereotype of the professional as the expert, perpetuated by schools and readily accepted by many parents, places undue burden on teachers and creates unrealistic expectations among parents. These unrealistic expectations are often played out in unreasonable demands on the teacher's time and unfair criticism if the teacher is unable to deliver.

If parents are viewed as too emotional or unobjective to be useful to the process, educators are viewed as too objective. Some feel the need to maintain this image. This has been reinforced by the concept of professional distance, a concept almost all educators become familiar with during their training. Some professions, such as counseling, emphasize distancing and the maintenance of absolute objectivity as necessary for success. Objectivity is often emphasized to prevent professional burn-out or overinvolvement and internalization of the family's problems. In either case, it is unfair to characterize teachers as totally objective, just as it is to characterize parents as completely subjective. Educators may strive to maintain credibility by distancing themselves from the family at least partially because it is expected of them. Needless to say, partnerships cannot be formed under these circumstances.

The final false belief about educators held by many parents is described by Cutler as the belief that educators are free agents. According to Cutler, "Many parents ask why, if the school personnel know a program is needed, they don't just set it up. Since it is the school's job to educate all children, parents expect that school people will do what is necessary" (1993, pp. 35–36). What these parents fail to take into account is that far from being free agents, teachers and educators are bound to a system that is often slow and unresponsive and that has limited time, money, and personnel. Teachers are often caught between their empathy and agreement with the family member and the reality that advocating on behalf of the parent may be perceived as disloyal and, in some circumstances, may lead to ostracism, limited career options, and job loss. In addition, educators may find themselves with conflicts between what they see as their responsibility to the student and their responsibility to the family. When these various responsibilities clash, it is little wonder teachers distance themselves from the process!

Parents and families contribute to barriers to effective collaboration in other ways as well. Many professionals feel thwarted in their attempts to work with families because the family is searching for a professional who will tell them what they want to hear. Typically referred to as *shopping around* and associated with the diagnosis process, it is not unusual for family members (for both good and bad reasons) to disregard one professional's advice or efforts to collaborate because they do not coincide with the family's expectations. If professionals are guilty of bringing biases and expectations to the table, so too are parents and family members.

The experience of having a child with a disability is one that is frequently associated with perceptions and beliefs that are not conducive to effective partnerships. Although we eschew the traditional perceptions of parents as detailed previously, we do not wish to dismiss as invalid the range of emotions and feelings that accompany the birth of a child with a disability and the impact of this experience on family stress and coping. The truth is that many children with disabilities require more time and energy on the part of parents than do many children without disabilities. There are truths embedded in the older notions of the cycle of acceptance of disability. Parents feel disillusioned, disappointed, frightened, frustrated, alone, vulnerable, and guilty and as if they have been treated unfairly. They also feel committed, joyful, excited, hopeful, confident, and proud. It is unfair to represent one without the other.

For some parents, however, the experience of raising a child with a disability can become too stressful. Likewise, some parents may cope with their child's disability by creating unrealistic expectations (both too positive or too negative) or denying certain limitations. Frankly, these scenarios are not uncommon to parents of children without disabilities! These circumstances may lead to situations in which parents are not honest with themselves or professionals about their feelings and expectations. Parents who are overwhelmed at home may find it difficult to admit to a professional that they do not want or are not, at that time, capable of taking on additional responsibilities such as working with their son or daughter at home or participating in multidisciplinary team meetings (Cutler, 1993). Parents may feel that their authority or integrity is threatened by professional advice and adopt a "no one is going to tell me what to do" attitude. Finally, parents who experience a great deal of stress may become overreliant on professionals and make unreasonable demands for attention and time.

Yet another barrier to family involvement is that, too often, parents and educators approach a problem or an issue from differing temporal orientations. Educators tend to be future-oriented, looking at what may happen 1, 5, or 10 years from now. Parents, often by necessity, must take life one day at a time and are not able or willing to look at what is in store for their son or daughter. Many people procrastinate when having to consider what may be negative outcomes. In far too many cases, medical professionals, and sometimes educational personnel as well, have painted negative outcomes as the only possibilities for children with disabilities. Even today, parents are too often told at the time of the birth of their child with mental retardation that institutionalization is the only option they can reasonably consider. This disturbing opinion understandably contributes to parental unwillingness to focus on future outcomes.

A quick consideration of the types of issues that parents and family members face is enough to begin to understand why some families are hesitant to address future-oriented issues. Turnbull and Turnbull (1996) identified a number of issues encountered by parents during **life cycle transitions,** including the transition from secondary education to adulthood. These include

1. Adjusting emotionally to the possible chronicity of their son's or daughter's disabling condition
2. Identifying issues associated with the emerging sexuality of their son or daughter

3. Addressing possible peer isolation and rejection at a time in development when peers play an increasingly important role

4. Planning for career and vocational options

5. Arranging for leisure activities

6. Dealing with the physical and emotional changes associated with puberty

7. Planning for postsecondary education

8. Planning for the possible need for guardianship

9. Addressing the need for impending living and work environments

Other barriers that contribute to ineffective family involvement do not rest on the side of educators or families but instead are legitimate differences. Parents and educators alike may feel a certain competitiveness in the collaborative process. Parents feel that because they know the child best, they can be the most effective teachers. Professionals feel that their background and expertise make them the best teacher. There are legitimate claims on both sides, and this just illustrates that there is little use in placing blame in the breakdown of the school–home collaboration process. It should be evident that all parties contribute to the situation and that it requires efforts from all parties to remedy the situation.

ESTABLISHING EFFECTIVE PARENT–PROFESSIONAL PARTNERSHIPS

To overcome barriers to family involvement, professionals need to recognize that the role of the family in education has changed and will continue to change. As such, the role of the educator must change to accommodate and take advantage of these shifts. McFadden and Burke identified a new paradigm for human services that "envisions a social order wherein most important decisions are made at the local level.... and people are empowered to develop their own solutions to issues affecting their lives" (1991, p. iii). Themes that are repeated in this paradigm are empowerment, leadership, choice, and flexibility. Within this paradigm, it becomes the responsibility of the professional to increase the participation of family members in the decision-making process. McFadden and Burke stated, "It is our belief that decisions that affect the quality of life experienced by people with developmental disabilities and their families are best made in consultation with and participation by the consumers themselves [people with disabilities and their families]" (1991, p. iv).

Educators rarely see students and their families as customers. The terms *teacher* and *student* in and of themselves connote a relationship far removed from that of a customer who dictates by his or her actions what services are provided. To move toward a truly collaborative relationship, educators need to incorporate into their multiple identities the role of enabler and to view as their responsibility the empowerment of families and students to assume greater control in educational planning and decision making. By so doing, they set the stage for more positive adult outcomes for youth with disabilities and for greater success on their part.

Singer and Powers (1993) identified several basic principles of family support that can be applied to empower families to be involved in educational planning, decision making, and program implementation. Empowering practices seek to enhance a sense of community for families. Special education has and continues to be a process by which students and families become separated from the mainstream of the school community. For example, instead of becoming active with other parents through the Parent–Teacher Associations, families of students with disabilities join the Special Education Parent–Teacher Associations. To enhance a sense of community for families of youth with disabilities, educators need to emphasize the common needs of all families and work to improve the family's link with the broader community and wider ranges of support. Clearly such initiatives are necessary for inclusive school communities.

A second tenet of family support is to focus more broadly on the family's needs, not just on child-focused concerns. This recognizes that student success is linked directly to family success. Schools are, more and more, becoming the location for community-based family services (Martin, 1992). Even if such services do not exist, schools can provide a referral service. Third, educators must encourage shared responsibility and collaboration. Parents are equal partners by law and must be viewed as such by professionals. As Singer and Powers elaborated, all families have strengths, and when problems are identified in a family, members can learn to solve these problems if given the opportunity and resources. Practitioners must put aside assumptions and biases and enable family members to experience meaningful control and choice.

Singer and Powers (1993) also pointed out that professionals must respect family boundaries and privacy to the greatest degree possible. What is at least implied by many special educators is that the home environment should replicate the school environment. For example, a teacher may have families give their son or daughter a worksheet. Instead, activities in the home must be configured within the flow of the natural routine. There are many developmentally and educationally valuable opportunities in the home that families can be guided to use as learning experiences.

If educators act on the premise that their efforts are to empower families and place value on students with disabilities as people first, it is likely that the battle is won. Such attitudes manifest themselves in changes in behavior and action. Flaxman and Inger (1991) provided some pragmatic suggestions for school practices that encourage family involvement and reflect the orientation described previously:

- Increase the awareness and sensitivity of school staff to parents' time constraints: announce meetings long enough in advance to allow parents to arrange to attend.
- Give parents blanket permission to visit the school at all times—to visit the classroom, use the library, or talk to the teachers or administrators.
- Establish or support family learning centers in schools, storefronts, and churches, and offer help to parents who want to help their children learn.
- Make the school facilities available to a variety of community activities.
- Facilitate teen-, single-, working-, and custodial-parent peer support groups.
- Provide before-school child care so that working parents can see teachers before going to work.
- Conduct evening meetings, with child care, so that working parents can attend.
- Conduct evening assemblies to recognize students and parents for their contributions to the school.
- Establish bilingual hotlines for parents.
- Send messages in the family's language not only on routine notices but also on things parents can do at home to help educate their children.

- Do not make last-minute school cancellations.
- Print all signs in the languages spoken by school families (Flaxman & Inger, 1991, p. 6).

Sonnenschein (1981) pointed out that if educators assume that all parents have strengths and view parents as partners, they can quickly build a relationship based on mutual trust and respect. She identified the following visible indicators of such a relationship:

- Information, impressions, and evaluations are promptly and openly shared.
- Collaborators are able to communicate their feelings, needs, and priorities without worrying about being labeled in a derogatory way.
- Collaborators can ask each other for help without being made to feel weak or incompetent and are able to say "I don't know" or "I don't understand" without fearing the loss of respect or credibility.
- Efforts are made to avoid the use of jargon or any practice that tends to make the other feel like an outsider. Careful attention is given to the implementation of procedures that encourage dialogue and equal sense of control.

Sinclair and Christenson (1992) echoed these indicators in identifying five key elements of effective and respectful parent–professional interactions: 1) mutual respect for skills and knowledge, 2) honest and clear communication, 3) two-way sharing of information, 4) a consensus on goals, and 5) shared planning and decision making. Like many others, these authors emphasized communication as the first step in collaboration.

Partnerships to Reliable Alliances

Turnbull and Turnbull (2001) recommended that the objective toward which educators working with students with disabilities should strive is to create an environment in which they can form **reliable alliances** with parents and family members. The image of a reliable ally is a person who is a partner in a process and works to achieve a shared or common goal. Table 10.1 lists opportunities that exist that enable the formation of school–home partnerships, and obligations that exist for professionals if they are to use the opportunities for partnerships to create reliable alliances. Table 10.2 expands on

Table 10.1. Opportunities for partnerships and obligations for reliable alliances

Opportunities for partnerships	Obligations for reliable alliances
Communicating among reliable allies	Knowing yourself
Meeting families' basic needs	Knowing families
Referring and evaluating for special education	Honoring cultural diversity
Individualizing for appropriate education	Affirming and building on family strengths
Extending learning in home and community	Promoting family choices
Attending and volunteering at school	Encouraging great expectations
Advocating for systems improvement	Practicing positive communication skills
	Warranting trust and respect

From Turnbull, A.P., & Turnbull, H.R. (2001). *Families, professionals, and exceptionality: A special partnership collaborating for empowerment* (4th ed., p. 34). Upper Saddle River, NJ: Prentice Hall; adapted by permission.

Table 10.2. Creating a reliable alliance

Obligation	Issue	Disempowering actions	Empowering actions
Knowing yourself	You feel frustrated when you talk with parents who concentrate on barriers rather than solutions.	Tell parents that you wish they would not be so negative.	Listen to the barriers, empathize, and then break their and your actions down into small, manageable steps.
Knowing families			
Family characteristics	Parents tell you that they are going to be busy on the night of the school open house, but you sense that they are not comfortable in coming to the school.	Tell parents that they will be letting their child down if they don't come.	Invite the parents to come to the school at another time, such as when their child is performing in a music program or otherwise demonstrating a strength of which everyone can be proud.
Family interaction	A parent asks you to visit the family's apartment for a conference at a housing project (where there was a recent shooting) rather than coming to school for a meeting.	Tell the parent you don't feel safe in coming into the neighborhood.	Talk with the school social worker and get advice on alternatives for home visits in this particular housing project.
Family functions	Parents of a student who is failing every subject are not showing any concern about school failure.	Tell the parents that you object to their family priorities and that they are only hurting their son.	Meet with the family and find out their priorities for their son, both this year and in the future.
Family life cycle	The family has just moved to a new community and neither the student nor parents know anyone at the child's new middle school.	Assume that the parents may be interested in coming to the school open house next year; leave them on their own to make connections in the new community and school.	Call the parents, issue a special invitation to come to the school open house, and arrange with another family to meet the new parents and students and introduce them to others.
Honoring cultural diversity	The school handbook is only available in English, yet the parents speak Mandarin.	Tell the parents that maybe their child or some friends can translate parts of the handbook to them.	Talk with your administrator about getting the handbook translated into Mandarin or securing someone to explain it to them.
Affirming and building on family strengths	A father is an accomplished photographer and particularly enjoys using his home video camera to record family activities.	Tell the father that it is impractical for him to videotape his child at school, especially when he or she is interacting with other children.	Ask the father if he would be willing to get other families' consent to tape classroom activities and make the tape available to families.
Promoting family choices	A parent asks if a conference can be arranged before school to accommodate her work schedule.	Tell the parent it is against the teacher-union policy.	Ask the parent if it would be possible to talk on the telephone early in the school day rather than to meet at school.
Envisioning great expectations	A group of parents ask you to explore the use of e-mail in communicating with families.	Dismiss their request as too far-fetched because of limited computer access.	Form a committee of families and educators to contact computer companies about the possibility of being a model site for technology demonstrations.
Using interpersonal communication skills	You are participating in a conference with parents who are extremely angry that their gifted child is making poor grades and who believe that it is your fault.	Tell the parents that they have not provided proper supervision for homework and that the poor grades are their fault.	Listen empathetically and ask if they would be willing to brainstorm options that would involve them and you collaborating to promote their child's program.
Warranting trust and respect	The school administration asks parents to contribute to a fund to pay for the classroom newspaper, but the parents do not have the money to contribute.	Tell them they'll not be able to get the newspaper because they have to pay their own way.	Identify a nonmonetary way for them to contribute to the class; tell them their classroom contribution represents their donation; keep everything confidential.

From Turnbull, A.P., & Turnbull, H.R. (2001). *Families, professionals, and exceptionality: A special partnership collaborating for empowerment* (4th ed., pp. 200–201). Upper Saddle River, NJ: Prentice Hall; reprinted by permission.

171

these obligations and illustrates how responses to opportunities to form partnerships can lead to reliable alliances.

Chapter 5 discussed the importance of a person-centered, student-directed planning process in the design of a student's educational program. Turnbull and Turnbull (2001) described a process called **Group Action Planning** that embodies both the characteristics of person-centered and student-directed planning. They identified the characteristics of Group Action Planning as

- The group contains an approximately equal proportion of participants from the groups of friends, community citizens, family members, and professionals.
- The student with disabilities is present and has been provided opportunities to learn more about the planning process and his or her role in that process.
- Planning proceeds within a reflective, creative process that focuses on divergent problem solving.
- The process is facilitated by an individual skilled in collaborative communication.
- The meeting is held in an informal setting, most often the home of the family or friends.
- The atmosphere is relational, fun, and affirming and focuses on strengths, capabilities, contributions, and dreams.
- Planning is not a one-shot deal but ongoing as needed.
- Visions and relationships guide the process.
- Group members form reliable alliances with every member, assuming responsibility for transforming visions to reality.

Table 10.3 lists the steps to implementing the Group Action Planning process. Whether educators working with students with disabilities implement the Group Action Planning process or adopt some other person-centered process, it is important to ensure that the planning process leads to the creation of reliable alliances. It should also be noted that the Group Action Planning process is, at its heart, a problem-solving process and that educators can prepare students to participate in a meeting such as this by using the self-regulated problem-solving process described in Chapter 15 to ensure that the planning process is both family friendly and student-directed.

SUMMARY

Research in education is clear that active family involvement in the educational process is critical to student success. For students with disabilities, this may be even more important. Family members often provide lifelong supports for their son or daughter with mental retardation, become their job coaches and vocational placement specialists, ensure safety and quality in living and work environments, and provide the means for supporting the person to live a life of high quality. Cecelia Pauley, a young woman with Down syndrome who speaks frequently at conferences about the importance of inclusion, illustrated the importance of family to successful outcomes:

> In the seventh grade, my mom and dad asked me the questions on the McGill Action Planning Survey (MAPS). They asked me at home. Before they had talked to me about

Table 10.3. Steps in the Group Action Planning process

Step	Objectives
1. Invite support	Find a place to meet that is casual, accessible, and comfortable. Find convenient times to meet. Invite stakeholders Explain what the intent and purpose of the process is. Choose a facilitator.
2. Create connections	Leave ample time prior to and after meetings for visiting and networking. Offer food. Be alert to and recognize each others' special days (e.g., birthdays).
3. Share great expectations	Encourage participants to think big. Think of ideal jobs, homes, friends, recreations, and so forth. Think "what if" and "why not."
4. Solve problems	Treat problems as questions. Brainstorm to answer questions and solve problems. Address one problem at a time. Seek quantity, not quality, of ideas. Encourage input from all. Discourage negative or critical remarks. Decide on the best ideas and discard others. Pick the best solution. Develop an action plan.
5. Celebrate success	Get together once in a while for pure enjoyment. Have food and drink available, and let members know they are appreciated and valued.

From Turnbull, A.P., & Turnbull, H.R. (2001). *Families, professionals, and exceptionality: A special partnership collaborating for empowerment* (4th ed., p. 300). Upper Saddle River, NJ: Prentice Hall; reprinted by permission.

what I wanted, but I did not know what choices I had. This was the first time I felt like I had a choice in what I wanted to do. These were my answers to the questions.

1. Who is Cecelia? "I am a good person."
2. What are Cecelia's strengths? "I like to have fun. I like to sing and dance and act in plays. I like people."
3. What are Cecelia's needs. "I need to listen to my teachers more. I need to study more."
4. What is Cecelia's vision for herself. "I want to have a job. I want to get married. I want to have kids. I want to have a house. I want to be able to travel. I want to visit my sister Cathy."
5. What is Cecelia's nightmare for herself. "If all of my family went away."

I felt happy when my dad asked me these questions. I wanted people to know how I felt. But I did not know anyone cared except my family. Sometimes I felt good about being me. Sometimes I didn't. I felt upset that I could not tell people how I felt. This was the first time I felt like what I wanted mattered. It changed my whole life.

My dad talked to me about inclusion. I did not know what inclusion meant. He told me I could go to school with my friends near my house and be in class with them. I thought that was neat. I wanted to be with my friends and go to school with them. My dad then had the teachers at Cabin John Middle School hold a special IEP [individualized education program] meeting. He told them I wanted to be included in regular classes in the eighth grade. I was mainstreamed for the first time in English, science, and math. I liked that. I think my friends liked having me in their class, too.

In high school, I was not invited to the 60-day review meeting the first year. The teachers made all the decisions without me. I began to attend IEP meetings in the tenth grade, but the teachers did not ask me what I wanted. My dad asked me at home. He and my mom spoke for me in the meetings. At the end of the tenth grade, my guidance counselor, Mrs. Suter, asked me what courses I wanted to take the next year. I picked my classes. Some of the classes got changed in the IEP meeting, but they asked me first. I liked that. At the end of the eleventh grade, Mrs. Suter asked me what classes I wanted to take in the twelfth grade. I picked my classes. I got to take all of them that time. I felt great. (1998, p. 124)

Cecilia Pauley is a self-determined young person at least partially (and one could argue primarily) because her parents held high expectations for her, advocated for her on her behalf, and were actively involved in her life and her school activities. Innumerable other stories like Cecilia's illustrate the importance of active family involvement, yet many families feel that the school does not want them to participate, and the school–home relationship becomes, at best, an uneasy partnership. By emphasizing the person-centered planning process discussed in Chapter 5 and by recognizing the importance of families in the process, however, schools can create reliable alliances with families to the benefit of all, especially the student.

ADDITIONAL READINGS

Family Involvement and Empowerment

Beckman, P.J. (Ed.). (1996). *Strategies for working with families of young children.* Baltimore: Paul H. Brookes Publishing Co.

Harry, B. (1992). *Cultural diversity, families, and the special education system.* New York: Teachers College Press.

Morningstar, M.E., Turnbull, A.P., & Turnbull, H.R. (1995). What do students with disabilities tell us about the importance of family involvement in the transition from school to adult life? *Exceptional Children, 62,* 249–260.

Naseef, R.A. (2001). *Special children, challenged parents: The struggles and rewards of raising a child with a disability* (Rev. ed.). Baltimore: Paul H. Brookes Publishing Co.

Powell, T.H., & Gallagher, P.A. (1993). *Brothers and sisters: A special part of exceptional families* (2nd ed.). Baltimore: Paul H. Brookes Publishing Co.

Pueschel, S.M. (2001). *A parent's guide to Down syndrome: Toward a brighter future* (Rev. ed.). Baltimore: Paul H. Brookes Publishing Co.

Roberts, R.N., Rule, S., & Innocenti, M.S. (1998). *Strengthening the family–professional partnership in services for young children.* Baltimore: Paul H. Brookes Publishing Co.

Santelli, B., Poyadue, F.S., & Young, J.L. (2001). *The parent to parent handbook: Connecting families of children with special needs.* Baltimore: Paul H. Brookes Publishing Co.

Turnbull, A.P., & Turnbull, H.R. (1978). *Parents speak out: Views from the other side of the two-way mirror.* Columbus, OH: Charles E. Merrill.

Turnbull, A.P., & Turnbull, H.R. (2001). *Families, professionals, and exceptionality: A special partnership collaborating for empowerment* (4th ed.). Upper Saddle River, NJ: Prentice Hall.

Wehmeyer, M.L., Morningstar, M., & Husted, D. (1998). *Family involvement in transition planning and program implementation.* Austin, TX: PRO-ED.

Group Action Planning

Blue-Banning, M.J., Turnbull, A.P., & Pereira, L. (2000). Group Action Planning as a support strategy for Hispanic families: Parent and professional perspectives. *Mental Retardation, 38,* 262–275.

Turnbull, A.P., Blue-Banning, M.J., Anderson, E.L., Turnbull, H.R., Seaton, K.A., & Dinas, P.A. (1996). Enhancing self-determination through Group Action Planning: A holistic emphasis. In D.J. Sands & M.L. Wehmeyer (Eds.), *Self-determination across the life span: Independence and choice for people with disabilities* (pp. 237–256). Baltimore: Paul H. Brookes Publishing Co.

Turnbull, A.P., Turbiville, V., Schaffer, R., & Schaffer, V. (1996). Getting a shot at life through Group Action Planning. *Zero to Three, 16*(6), 33–40.

Turnbull, A.P., & Turnbull, H.R. (1996). Group Action Planning as a strategy for providing comprehensive family support. In L.K. Koegel, R.L. Koegel, & G. Dunlap (Eds.), *Positive behavioral support: Including people with difficult behavior in the community* (pp. 99–114). Baltimore: Paul H. Brookes Publishing Co.

CHAPTER OBJECTIVES

1. Define *positive behavioral support,* and compare and contrast positive behavioral supports with other applied behavior analysis models.
2. Discuss the impact of positive behavioral supports at multiple levels, and discuss characteristics of positive behavioral supports.
3. Summarize the knowledge concerning the efficacy of positive behavioral supports.
4. Define *functional behavioral assessment* and describe its implementation.

KEY TERMS

Positive behavioral supports
Primary interventions
Secondary interventions
Tertiary interventions
Functional behavior analysis
Wraparound services

11

Positive Behavioral
Supports and
Classroom Management

TERRORLESS LEARNING

An ongoing concern for many teachers of students with mental retardation is how to manage the classroom to ensure a nondisruptive learning environment for all students and how to deal with challenging behaviors exhibited by a few students. Many teachers report that they feel unprepared to respond to challenging behaviors; this insecurity is often more pronounced among teachers working in inclusive settings. Students with mental retardation who exhibit challenging behaviors are decidedly a minority, but teachers should be comfortable with supporting these students. The context in which such efforts must be approached has been emphasized in previous chapters; teachers need to create learning communities for all students (Chapter 7) and approach the design of interventions to support students with challenging and problematic behavior within the context of the curriculum decision-making process described in Chapter 4. Figure 3.1 suggests that gaining access to and promoting progress in the general curriculum require multiple levels of interventions (whole school, partial school, individualized) with similarly differentiated curricular and instructional design efforts (adaptation, augmentation, alteration) and individualized supports (intermittent, limited, extensive/pervasive). This multilevel approach is essential for addressing challenging behavior as well.

POSITIVE BEHAVIORAL SUPPORTS

Carr and colleagues (1999) reviewed the literature pertaining to positive behavioral interventions and supports. These authors, noting that challenging behaviors (e.g., aggression, self-injury, tantrums) have at times been barriers to successful inclusion, stated that the "goal of positive behavior support is to apply behavioral principles in the community in order to reduce problem behaviors and build appropriate behaviors that result in durable change and a rich lifestyle" (p. 3). The foundations of positive behavioral supports, these authors noted, were in early efforts to apply behavioral principles to improve the lives of children with severe behavior problems, with particular focus on the role of the functional assessment process to guide the development of behavioral interventions.

The difference between positive behavioral supports and other applied behavioral analytic approaches is a focus on the environment. Carr and colleagues defined **positive behavioral supports** as "an approach for dealing with problem behavior that focuses on the remediation of deficient contexts (i.e., environmental conditions and/or behavioral repertoires) that by functional assessment are documented to be the source of the problem" (1999, p. 1).

The field of positive behavioral support reflects yet another area of intervention and treatment that has moved from emphasizing the person with a disability as a problem to be fixed to recognizing that intervention must focus on the interaction between the social and environmental context and an individual's limitations. Positive behavioral supports strive to change the environment so that the behaviors become irrelevant or counterproductive for the person. Positive behavioral supports focus on two primary modes of intervention: 1) altering the environment before a problem behavior occurs and 2) teaching appropriate behaviors as a strategy for eliminating the need for problem behaviors to be exhibited (Carr et al., 1999). Consistent with the discussion in Chapter 1, these interventions should be viewed as supports, not as services or programs.

Significantly for educators, positive behavioral supports have focused considerable attention on addressing challenging behaviors in school settings and on school violence (Horner, Albin, Sprague, & Todd, 2000; Sugai & Horner, 1994; Sugai, Sprague, Horner, & Walker, 2000; Turnbull & Turnbull, 2001; Warren et al., 2000) by providing interventions at an individual, classroom, or whole-school level. Positive behavioral supports have been demonstrated to reduce principal's office referrals, create classroom environments more conducive to learning, and assist students with ongoing behavior problems to improve their behavior. Positive behavioral support involves the application of behaviorally based approaches to enhance the capacity of schools, families, and communities to design effective environments that improve the fit or link among the students and the environments in which teaching and learning occur. Attention is focused on creating and sustaining school environments that improve lifestyle results (e.g., personal, health, social, family, work, recreation) for all children and youth by making problem behavior less effective, efficient, and relevant, and desired behavior more functional (Wehmeyer, Wickham, & Sailor, 2000).

In addition, the use of culturally appropriate interventions is emphasized. Haring and De Vault indicated that positive behavioral supports are

Comprised of (a) interventions that consider the contexts within which the behavior occurs, (b) interventions that address the functionality of the problem behavior, (c) interventions that can be justified by the outcomes, and (d) outcomes that are acceptable to the individual, the family, and the supportive community. (1996, p. 116)

Positive behavioral supports also involve families and other community services, forming a collaborative effort among parents, teachers, and school personnel such as that emphasized in Chapter 8.

Turnbull and Turnbull (2000) discussed the impact of positive behavioral supports at four levels of activity. First, the approach recognizes that "a student's behavior is affected by the philosophies, policies, procedures, practices, personnel, organization, and funding of education agencies and other human services agencies involved in the student's education" (p. 185). As such, the first level of intervention necessarily focuses on systems change, the process of changing features of the agency or agencies. Included in such systemic efforts are service inclusion efforts that bring together a wide array of supports in a unified and easily accessible manner.

Second, positive behavioral supports emphasize altering the environment. Turnbull and Turnbull noted that such environments are usually altered by

1. Making different life arrangements by building on student strengths and preferences, identifying student and family priorities, building social and friendship networks and promoting health and wellness;
2. Improving the quality of the student's physical environment, including increasing the predictability and stability of events in school building, minimizing noise and other irritants;
3. Making personal accommodations for students;
4. Making instructional accommodations for students. (2000, p. 185)

In addition, Turnbull and Turnbull emphasized that such interventions cannot be limited to the school alone. If students live in unsafe homes, experience physical pain or poor health, or do not receive adequate rest or nutrition, interventions need to extend beyond the school.

A third level of action for positive behavioral supports is a focus on skill instruction to enhance the possibility that students will act appropriately. Such activities can extend from teaching specific behavior patterns or routines (how to behave in school hallways between classes) to instruction to promote general problem-solving and self-management skills, such as those skills discussed in Chapter 15.

The final level of intervention is a focus on behavioral consequences. Positive behavioral supports seek to make problem behaviors ineffective and to provide students with ways to achieve their goals and wants without resorting to inappropriate behavior. Turnbull and Turnbull identified the following characteristics of positive behavioral support:

1. Rather than viewing the student and his or her behavior as the problem to be addressed, positive behavioral support views the systems and environments in which the student receives his or her education or related services and the student's and other's skill impairments as the focus of intervention.
2. Rather than trying to "fix" only one student, positive behavioral support makes adjustments to and accommodations in the systems and environments and promotes appropriate skills in the student and others.
3. Rather than just trying to eliminate or extinguish problem behavior, positive behavioral support creates new contacts, experiences, relationships, and skills for the student.
4. Rather than being a short-term intervention, positive behavioral support recognizes that significant effort and time may be required to achieve systemic changes, alter environments, develop skill repertoires, and establish positive behavioral consequences.
5. Rather than being implemented only by a behavior specialist, positive behavioral support efforts are developed, implemented, and evaluated by stakeholder teams through person-centered planning.
6. Rather than being used in systems that are inflexible, positive behavioral support is implemented by systems that are flexible and person-centered or that become so through the use of PBS [positive behavioral support].
7. Rather than being used as a technology to shape a student's behavior according to acceptability criteria established only by professionals, positive behavioral support focuses on creating lifestyles desired by students and family members.
8. Rather than being technologies that are so specialized they can only be designed and implemented by highly trained specialists, positive behavioral support focuses on enabling a wide array of stakeholders, including the student him- or herself, to implement the strategies. (2000, pp. 187–188)

In addition, the Individuals with Disabilities Education Act (IDEA) Amendments of 1997 (PL 105-17) require a student's IEP team to consider special factors when developing the IEP, including the use of positive behavioral interventions, strategies, and supports to address problem behaviors.

Efficacy of Positive Behavioral Supports

The efficacy of positive behavioral support with individual students is well-documented. Carr and colleagues (1999) reviewed more than 100 research articles published over the course of more than 10 years in multiple refereed journals. Key findings included

- Positive behavioral supports were successful in achieving at least an 80% reduction in challenging behavior for approximately two thirds of the behavioral outcomes studied.

- Successful behavior change is substantially enhanced when a functional assessment is conducted as the basis for planning the intervention(s).

- Positive behavioral supports are more effective when significant people (e.g., educators, families) change their behavior as contrasted to designing changes only for the individual with challenging behavior.

- Positive behavioral supports are more effective when the environment is reorganized as contrasted to when the environment is not reorganized.

- Positive behavioral supports are more effective when carried out by significant people in the individual's life (e.g., educators, families) than by people who do not have ongoing relationships with the individual (e.g., researchers, clinicians).

- Positive behavioral supports are just as effective with individuals who have multiple disabilities as with individuals who have a single disability.

Sugai and colleagues (1999) proposed a model for schoolwide discipline and intervention implementation of positive behavioral supports based on work conducted in schools in Oregon (e.g., Colvin, Sugai, Good, & Lee, 1996) and Kansas (Turnbull & Turnbull, 2001; Warren et al., 2000). The model, depicted in Figure 11.1, employs the same multilevel support emphasis depicted in Figure 3.1.

This model suggests that up to 90% of students in schools do not have any difficulties with adhering to school rules. These students do not need any individual behavioral assessment or interventions beyond those already in place in schools and classrooms and benefit from well-articulated and practiced schoolwide expectations of behavior. They often do not get into trouble and have no obvious difficulties at home or outside of the school. The key for this level of supports is that behavioral expectations are clearly communicated and that they have a role in determining the rules governing that behavior.

Approximately 5%–15% of students in a school may have difficulties that result in disciplinary actions. They may interfere with the learning of others, disrupt instruction, or threaten the safety or authority of the school. It has been suggested that this group generates approximately 60% of office referrals. This is a group for whom regular schoolwide rules and expectations are not enough. They require a more systematic and individualized approach, often a functional behavioral assessment. These students may qualify for special education services that are addressed with an IEP, they may be referred for needs assessment, or they may not qualify for services. Regardless, they need individual supports and interventions that the schoolwide level of supports does not address.

Finally, the third level of supports addresses the approximately 1%–7% of students who have difficulty in school as well as other environments. They may have previous relationships with mental health, juvenile justice, or special education service systems. These students require highly individualized supports, which often require coordination with other agencies outside of the school.

IMPLEMENTING POSITIVE BEHAVIORAL SUPPORTS

The model pictured in Figure 11.1 identifies three levels of interventions that constitute steps to implementing positive behavioral interventions and supports.

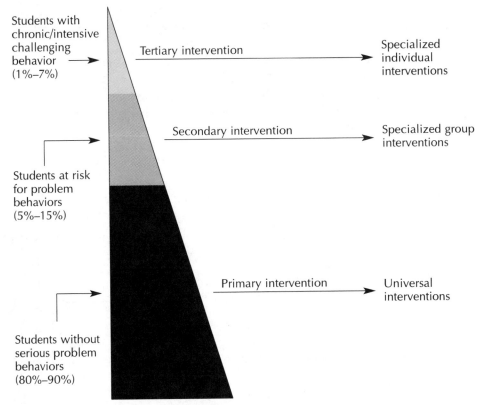

Figure 11.1. Continuum of behavioral support model. (From Sugai, G., Horner, R., Dunlap, G., Lewis, Nelson, C., Scott, T., Liaupsin, C., Ruef, M., Sailor, W., Turnbull, A., Turnbull, H., Wickham, D., & Wilcox, B. [1999]. *Applying positive behavior support and functional behavioral assessment in schools* [p. 11]. Washington DC: OSEP Center on Positive Behavioral Intervention and Support; reprinted by permission.)

Support Level 1: Primary Interventions **Primary interventions** provide clear expectations and positive feedback for all students throughout all educational settings (e.g., halls, cafeteria, playgrounds, buses). The following procedures have been documented to be successful in whole-school models (Horner, 2000; Lewis & Sugai, 1999; Lewis, Sugai, & Colvin, 1998; Todd, Horner, Sugai, & Sprague, 1999):

- Behavioral expectations are clearly defined: These expectations are stated simply and positively and are few in number.

- Behavioral expectations are taught: Each expectation is explicitly taught in multiple school settings so that students will know exactly what is expected of them in all settings.

- Appropriate behaviors are acknowledged: Schools build a positive incentive program in which students are affirmed at least four times as often as they are negatively sanctioned.

- Program evaluations and adaptations are made by a positive behavioral support team: A school team has as a priority monitoring and improving the whole-school approach.

As an example of setting schoolwide expectations for behavior, a middle school in Oregon established High Five Expectations: 1) Be respectful, 2) be responsible, 3) follow directions, 4) keep hands and feet to oneself, and 5) be there and be ready (Sugai et al., 1999). All students were taught the skills they needed to achieve these expectations at the beginning of the school year and were provided frequent reinforcement (through a schoolwide token reinforcement system that focused on catching students who were adhering to the High Five Expectations). The U.S. Department of Education's Office of Special Education Programs (OSEP) Technical Assistance Center on Positive Behavioral Intervention and Support recommended the steps in Table 11.1 in establishing an effective schoolwide system (Sugai et al., 1999).

Support Level 2: Secondary Interventions Secondary interventions recognize that some students may benefit from additional instruction to practice the expectations of whole-school positive behavioral support or may need more specialized interventions. Using the program evaluation collected by a school team, specific groups may be targeted for additional instruction. For example, one class may experience trouble waiting in line in the lunchroom. At this level of intervention, procedures are put in place to identify which expectations are difficult to meet, and lesson plans are written to directly teach small groups of students. Students receiving this level of supports may also benefit from a more systematic functional analysis of behavior, as described subsequently, but that is not a given as the targeted support may be as straightforward as simply providing additional instructions to students about how to meet certain behavioral expectations.

Support Level 3: Tertiary Interventions Tertiary interventions are directed to students who have a need for personalized interventions and support. In this component a school-based team conducts a functional assessment for the student in the school. When students have a disability, typically the multidisciplinary evaluation team and/or the IEP team conduct the functional assessment. Thus, the functional assessment becomes an integral part of ensuring that students with disabilities receive an appropriate education. When a student does not have a disability but requires individualized supports, a behavioral support team is constituted (often called a *needs assessment team*) in order to conduct the functional assessment. The functional assessment process is critical to the success of intervention design at this phase.

Table 11.1. Steps to establishing effective schoolwide behavioral support expectations

Step	Process
1	Establish a schoolwide leadership or behavioral support team, composed of administrators, grade-level representatives, support staff, and parents to direct the process.
2	Secure administrator agreement of active support and participation.
3	Assess the status of schoolwide discipline or positive behavioral supports and define short- and long-term goals for improving the schoolwide system.
4	Secure a commitment and agreement from at least 80% of the staff for active support and participation.
5	Establish an implementation action plan that is based on the status assessment and emphasizes the adoption of research validated practices.
6	Establish a data system that permits the regular and efficient monitoring and evaluation of the effectiveness of the implementation of the schoolwide system of discipline.

Functional Behavioral Assessment The federally funded OSEP Technical Assistance Center on Positive Behavioral Intervention and Support defined **functional behavioral support** as "a systematic process of identifying problem behaviors and the events that (a) reliably predict occurrences and nonoccurrence of those behaviors and (b) maintain the behaviors across time" (Sugai et al., 1999, p. 12). The purpose of the functional behavioral assessment, according to the OSEP Technical Assistance Center, is 1) to operationally define the problem behavior, 2) to generate hypotheses that describe the antecedent events that predict occurrence and nonoccurrence of the behavior and that describe the consequences of the behavior that serve to maintain (or reinforce) the problem behavior, 3) to collect data testing these hypotheses, and, finally, 4) to use that information to create a behavioral support plan. Behavioral support plans, accordingly, employ knowledge gained through the functional assessment process to intervene in changing setting events; implementing antecedent strategies; teaching behaviors, skills, and strategies; and changing consequences for appropriate and inappropriate behavior (Sugai et al., 1999).

Table 11.2 presents the basic steps to conducting a functional behavioral assessment and designing a behavioral support plan. Although there is insufficient space to provide a detailed discussion of these steps, several of the steps warrant discussion. (Readers are referred to the *Additional Readings* section for resources providing greater levels of detail.) One purpose of the functional assessment is to operationally define the problem behavior. Operational definitions define the problem behavior not in terms of general descriptors (e.g., aggression), but using specific taxonomies of behavior (e.g., hitting, biting, kicking). The functional assessment is also intended to generate hypotheses about what predicts or reinforces the occurrence or nonoccurrence of the problem

Table 11.2. Conducting functional assessments and designing positive behavioral support plans

Activity	Process and participants	Desired outcome
Collect information concerning conditions where problem behavior is observed and not observed	Review records, interviews with stakeholders, observations	Describe the setting events, triggering events, the ways in which the problem behavior is exhibited, and the consequences associated with the behavior
Operationally define problem behavior	Review of records, interviews with stakeholders, observations	Problem behavior is operationally defined
Conduct observations to collect data testing hypotheses of behavior definition, antecedent, and setting events, and consequences	Direct observations, primarily by teacher, school psychologist, or behavior specialist	Finalize problem definition, antecedent, and consequence hypotheses
Design positive behavioral support plan	Team of stakeholders	Specify desired or alternative behavior, antecedent strategies, consequence strategies, needed instructional activities, indicators of success
Develop implementation scripts	Team of stakeholders	Develop scripts that provide directions for when, where, and how of implementing behavior plan
Plan implementation and monitoring	Team of stakeholders	Implement plan and monitor efficacy
Plan evaluation	Team of stakeholders	Evaluate efficacy of plan and revise as necessary

Adapted from U.S. Department of Education, Office of Special Education Programs, Positive Behavioral Support Center. (2000); reprinted by permission.

behavior. Setting events are those events or circumstances, both antecedent to the behavior (i.e., occurring prior to the behavior) or concurrent with (i.e., occurring at the same time), that increase the likelihood of the behavior occurring. Such setting events often include medical or other conditions (e.g., illness, pain, exhaustion) that affect the student's health and physical well being, social conditions (e.g., interpersonal conflicts, isolation) that affect the student's psychological or emotional well being, and environmental conditions (e.g., homelessness, poverty, overcrowded living conditions) that affect both. Setting events tend to be recurring and consistent over time. Antecedent events are those events or circumstances that are not as long term or pervasive as setting events but still reliably trigger problem behaviors such as task demands, requests from specific adults, or peer interactions. Consequent events are those that follow problem behavior and through either positive reinforcement (i.e., introduction of a positive reinforcer) or negative reinforcement (i.e., removal of a punisher) maintain the problem behavior. If a task demand is regularly removed when a student responds to the task request with a problem behavior (e.g., tantrums), the removal of the task demand serves as a negative reinforcer to maintain the behavior.

Many intervention strategies have been used successfully with students who need individual positive behavioral supports, including some of the following:

- Alter the environment: Accommodate students' environmental needs and consider room and seating arrangements.

- Increase predictability and scheduling: Use visual or written schedules to provide structure and prepare students in advance for changes and transitions.

- Increase choice making: Encourage students to express preferences and take them into account in planning instruction and environment supports and teach students specific skills in decision making.

- Make curricular adaptations: Adjust tasks and activities so that they are presented in formats that are consistent with students' strengths, needs, and preferences.

- Appreciate positive behaviors: Catch the student being good and provide affirmation to students and families; maintain a four-to-one ratio of positive to negative statements. Also teach students to use self-monitoring as a way to track their own success and embed rewards within difficult activities.

- Teach replacement skills: Teach students a different way to accomplish their purpose without needing to engage in the impeding behavior as well as problem-solving skills so that they will know how to generate appropriate alternatives when they encounter problems.

- Change systems: Work with other educators and families to develop state-of-art services and supports and within your community to create inclusive opportunities in which students with impeding behaviors can participate in a successful way.

Support Level 4: School–Family–Community Supports

School–family–community supports recognize that some students need supports and interventions that extend beyond school settings. Other models that are compatible with this component are typical of school-linked services (Adelman & Taylor, 1997; Kagan, Goffin, Golub, & Pritchard, 1995; Sailor, 2002; Schorr, 1997) and community schools (Benson & Harkavy, 1996; Lawson & Briar-Lawson, 1997).

This level of supports is characterized as relying on the same processes and interventions described in tertiary interventions but conducting them across multiple environments, including home, neighborhood, and community settings. This approach, borrowed from the mental health field, is described as **wraparound.** This model is a process—driven by the needs of children, youth, and families—for providing services to meet priority needs (Burns & Goldman, 1999; Clark, Lee, Prange, & McDonald, 1996; Eber, Nelson, & Miles, 1997; VanDenBerg & Grealish, 1998).

A unique feature of the wraparound approach is that it brings together families, professionals, and other interested stakeholders to think outside of the box in seeking to integrate and transform services in a way that has typically not been available. Wraparound team members generally consider needs and a broad variety of life domains, including residence, social, emotional/psychological, educational/vocational, safety, legal, medical, spiritual, cultural, behavioral, and financial issues (VanDenBerg & Grealish, 1998). Thus, wraparound can address each area to consider child and family needs and to put together an array of services and supports that are responsive to those needs. A critical dimension of wraparound is that people from various service sectors agree to blend their otherwise separate resources to create a single fund that in turn pays for a comprehensive service and support plan (Eber et al., 1997; VanDenBerg & Grealish, 1998). Areas included in this level of supports include

- Student services: Develop behavior change programs, transition plans for high school, medication management, peer support, after-school training, develop school–home homework plans.

- School services: Provide support in school settings to prevent out-of-school suspensions and provide technical assistance in the changing roles of school-based staff and inclusion of students with emotional and behavior disorders.

- Home services: Assist with psychiatric evaluations, support families in crisis, provide transportation to needed appointments, secure before-school child care, develop home behavior plans.

- Community services: Provide recreational coaching, develop business partnerships, and create community service liaisons for rent waivers and utility payments.

SUMMARY

The positive behavioral supports model introduces a mechanism by which teachers and school professionals can address problem behaviors in a systematic way and in a manner consistent with the tenets of this text: by focusing on the environment and social context and not on the student as the problem. When teachers use strategies such as those identified in Chapter 7 to create classrooms as learning communities that support all students, they create a climate that minimizes disruptive and problem behaviors. Creating such learning communities is, in reality, one way to engage in primary prevention activities that make problem behavior less effective and minimize disruptions. These whole school interventions focus on communicating expectations clearly to all students, catching students being good, and involving students in rule setting and decision making. Some students may need slightly more intensive supports (secondary prevention) that might include opportunities to learn specific skills needed to succeed.

Only a small proportion of students need the most intensive supports. For students with mental retardation who need this level of intervention, the IEP team should be involved in the multidisciplinary process to conduct a functional behavioral assessment and to determine intervention strategies that go all out to address the environmental and social contexts that predict occurrence of the problem behavior and to teach students skills they need to succeed. Although there is a need for experts in psychology and behavior analysis to contribute to the process, the functional assessment should include a wide array of perspectives and involve key stakeholders in a meaningful manner. It is particularly important to recognize that in a great many situations, what needs to change most is not the student but the circumstances in which he or she lives, learns, or plays.

ADDITIONAL READINGS

Positive Behavioral Supports

Carr, E.G., Horner, R.H., Turnbull, A.P., Marquis, J.G., McLaughlin, D.M., McAtee, M.L., Smith, C.E., Ryan, K.A., Ruef, M.B., & Doolabh, A. (2000). *Positive behavior support for people with developmental disabilities: A research synthesis.* Washington, DC: American Association on Mental Retardation.
Koegel, L.K., Koegel, R.L., & Dunlap, G. (Eds.). (1996). *Positive behavioral support: Including people with difficult behavior in the community.* Baltimore: Paul H. Brookes Publishing Co.
Lewis, T.J., & Sugai, G. (1999). Effective behavior support: A systems approach to proactive school-wide management. *Focus on Exceptional Children, 31*(6), 1–24.
Lovett, H. (1996). *Learning to listen: Positive approaches to people with difficult behaviors.* Baltimore: Paul H. Brookes Publishing Co.

Functional Assessment

Fitzsimmons, M.K. (1998). *Function behavior assessment and behavior intervention plans.* Reston, VA: Council for Exceptional Children. (Available: http://ericec.org/digests/e571.htm).
O'Neill, R.E., Horner, R.H., Albin, R.W., Sprague, J.R., Storey, K., & Newton, J.S. (1997). *Functional assessment and program development for problem behavior: A practical handbook* (2nd ed.). Pacific Grove, CA: Brooks/Cole.
Sugai, G., & Horner, R. (2000). *Functional behavioral assessment.* Mahwah, NJ: Lawrence Erlbaum Associates.

School-Linked and Wraparound Services

Adelman, H.S. (1996). Restructuring education support services and integrating community resources: Beyond the full service model. *School Psychology Review, 25,* 431–445.
Behrman, R.E. (1992). School-linked services. *The Future of Children, 2*(1).
Eber, L., Nelson, C.M., & Miles, P. (1997). School-based wraparound for students with emotional and behavioral challenges. *Exceptional Children, 63*(4), 539–555.
Office of Educational Research and Innovation. (1994). *School-linked comprehensive services for children and families: What we know and what we need to know.* Washington, DC: U.S. Department of Education. (Available: http://eric-web.tc.columbia.edu/families/School_Linked/).
VanDenBerg, J., & Grealish, E.M. (1998). *The wraparound process.* Pittsburgh, PA: The Community Partnerships Group.

CHAPTER OBJECTIVES

1. Define *functional academic content.*
2. Identify a framework for functional academic content, and discuss instruction in key domains within that framework.
3. Discuss the role and importance of ecological analyses in determining functional content.
4. Identify guidelines to use in determining what functional content to include in a student's individualized education program (IEP).

KEY TERMS

Functional academic content
Personal finances
Applied money concepts
Applied time concepts
Community mobility and access
Household management
Career and job preparation
Ecological analysis

12

Teaching Functional Academic Content

IT'S A BALANCING ACT!

Throughout this text, we emphasize the importance of considering both the general curriculum and students' unique learning needs in determining the curricular content of IEPs for students with mental retardation. When such decisions are made using the decision-making model described in Chapter 4, it seems likely that the students' education program will be determined by the general curriculum "to the maximum extent appropriate," as required by IDEA. Implementing whole-school interventions, providing curriculum adaptations and augmentations, and implementing innovative instructional strategies decrease the need for an alternative curriculum for students with mental retardation. It is obvious, however, that students with mental retardation have unique learning needs, particularly in relation to core academic areas, and that the academic differences between students with mental retardation and their same-age peers without disabilities increase as students age.

This, however, does not necessarily require that students with mental retardation receive an alternative curriculum—they do only to the extent that the standards or benchmarks that drive the curriculum are close-ended as opposed to open-ended. As is discussed in Chapter 8, close-ended standards are those that embody narrowly defined performance requirements (e.g., eighth-grade students will write a five-page essay on world geography), while open-ended standards are written to allow for multiple means of expression and student response (e.g., eighth-grade students will show evidence of knowledge about world geography). When standards and benchmarks are open-ended, students with mental retardation can work on functional content within the context of the general curriculum. It is important to note that we do not suppose, *a priori*, that such a focus constitutes an alternative curriculum but instead suggest that curriculum planning and design be done in such a manner that these activities can be situated within the general curriculum even when they are not age- or grade-normed (see Chapter 2). (One can easily locate state academic standards and benchmarks that are open-ended and provide logical ways to infuse functional academic content into the general curriculum context.)

WHAT IS FUNCTIONAL ACADEMIC CONTENT?

Edwin Delattre (1997), currently Dean of Education at Boston University, pointed out a tendency in the field of education to use and repeat terms with a disregard for their precise meanings. Though the criticism was aimed for the most part at general education, those of us in special education and related disability fields are not without certain culpability in this regard. The terminology can be elusive: We work with *IEP* kids; we advocate for *positive behavioral supports;* some of our more lofty colleagues are *postmodernists*. Getting a handle, for example, on what precisely and reliably **functional academics** are can be most vexing. Consider the following questions taken from a final mathematics examination for eighth graders in Salina, Kansas, circa 1895 ("Feeling Smug?," 2001):

- A wagon box is 2 feet deep, 10 feet long, and 3 feet wide. How many bushels of wheat will it hold?
- If a load of wheat weighs 3,942 pounds, what is it worth at 50 cents per bushel, deducting 1,050 pounds for tare?
- Find the interest on $512.60 for 8 months and 18 days at 7%.

- District No. 33 has a valuation of $35,000. What is the necessary levy to carry on a school 7 months at $50 per month and have $104 for incidentals?

Most readers know that the applied contexts of questions contained in today's tests of mathematical knowledge and skills differ from those reflected in these questions. These exam questions require skills in addition, subtraction, multiplication, and division, using multiple-digit numbers with decimals, and regrouping. Considerable knowledge is required, including basic number concepts, place value, decimals, and their relationship to percentage. Modern academic curricula generally cover more content, and higher levels of content complexity are reached in earlier grades than in the past. Today, an eighth-grade mathematics curriculum typically assumes students' knowledge of prealgebraic concepts and related problem-solving skills. However, one cannot discount the utilitarian rigor of the mathematics curriculum of 1895. These questions were relevant to that era and applicable to the agricultural context in which the examinees lived and labored. Most of Salina, Kansas, was (and still is) steeped in the farm economy. For most late 19th-century rural citizens, achieving an acceptable degree of independence and a satisfactory quality of life required one to know how to perform and apply these calculations. Indeed, each year, most of the youth who took this exam did not return to school thereafter, opting instead to live and work in the agricultural economy.

The end goals of formal education for *all* students should be the achievement of maximum independence and the best possible quality of life (Knowlton, 1998). It could successfully be argued that, if these questions are representative of what was taught in mathematics to Salina, Kansas, eighth graders in 1895, the curriculum was indeed *functional* to these students' ultimate independence and quality of life because, assuming their mastery of target skills, the students would be able to apply knowledge and skills relevant to meeting the demands of their environments. Accordingly, relevance and applicability are key components of **functional academic content** because independence and lifestyle quality, and for that matter sheer survival, hinge on our appropriate responses and adaptations to the demands of our environments.

Each of these four mathematics exam questions is relevant to the environmental demands of the late 19th-century U.S. rural plains. Kansas in particular was, and continues to be, a significant producer of wheat. Whether one worked directly or indirectly in farming, using multiplication knowledge and skills to determine a maximum wagonload of wheat would meet a variety of environmental demands related to cutting, hauling, storing, and selling wheat as one's primary manner of livelihood. Moreover, banks loaned money to citizens who fed it back to the local and regional farm economies; it therefore behooved farmers, merchants, and certainly bank employees, as well as the spouses and children of all, to compute and comprehend the effects of interest rates. Finally, rural America in 1895 was still learning how to school itself. The advent of common schools in rural areas had occurred during this era, and a particularly important demand on a literate citizenry in a rural farm community was the effective and frugal operation of its school.

Are the applications of the four basic arithmetic operations to the storage and sale of wheat and the determination of mill levies relevant and applicable to achieving for today's students maximum independence and the highest possible quality of life? Probably not, although there will always be an objection to any attempt at a universal, iron-clad definition of what is or isn't functional. Defining what is functional is highly contextual; what is functional for one student in one setting may not be functional for another student in another setting (Wolfe & Harriot, 1997). In this instance, the relevant objection has to do with students who one day will become a part of the agricultural economies of small rural communities, as in Kansas, a state that has successfully resisted large-scale school consolidation to this day. Consequently, Kansas has many tiny towns, with exceedingly small schools, where citizens do indeed need to know these things (Hodgkinson, 1997).

One could argue that such applications of mathematics perhaps are not functional in relation to the attainment of satisfactory independence and quality of life in the rest of the United States in this day and age. However, by applying the operations of addition and subtraction of multiple-digit numbers to the maintenance of a checking account, one would probably conclude that these applications indeed are functional because they enable students to successfully meet a critical environmental demand that is predictive of a certain level of independence and lifestyle quality. Similarly, by applying relevant knowledge and skills to nearest-dollar cost estimation and thus enabling a student to recognize whether she or he received a reasonable amount of change, the teacher would have taught the student how to meet one environmental demand of shopping, which is crucial to independence.

Note that we have not yet described any particular kind or category of students, including students with mental retardation. At one level, it is not necessary to differentiate students with mental retardation in any more of a specific way than by the fact that they are students who are learning to live and work with some degree of personal satisfaction in today's world. In this light, keep in mind that just as the beauty of universal design in curriculum is its relevance and applicability to knowledge and skills for all students, so too is the relevance and applicability of a truly functional curriculum to maximum independence and the best possible lifestyle quality for *any* student.

In this chapter, we describe the means for determining functional academic knowledge and skills for students with mental retardation. We begin with a framework of domains, or areas of eventual adult life and work in the community, within which more specific academic curricular goals can be identified. We then describe and exemplify some tools with which specific knowledge and functional skills can be identified and taught. Finally, we examine ways in which appropriate decisions concerning the selection of functional academic skills can be made.

A FRAMEWORK FOR FUNCTIONAL ACADEMIC CONTENT

Since the 1980s, a host of curriculum guides have emerged for people with mental retardation and extensive or pervasive support needs. Among them is the Syracuse Community-Referenced Curriculum model (Ford et al., 1989), used to identify the 10 adaptive skill areas cited in the American Association on Mental Retardation's definition of mental retardation (Luckasson et al., 1992). Some of these curriculum guides are very well researched and validated, while others are merely armchair lists of skills. Despite the discrepancies in the research bases that underlie such curriculum guides, the fact is that the teacher of students with mental retardation, knowing the necessity of teaching skills that are functional, needs a starting point—that is, a framework with which to begin determining what needs to be taught and why.

A review of curriculum guides designed specifically for individuals with mental retardation reveals two things. First, research-based or not, similar configurations of knowledge and skill domains appear in all of them. Different terms are used, and of course the order of domains varies; nonetheless, there is general agreement as to the main areas of necessary knowledge and skills. Second, our bias is to consider social and communication skills as pervasive, cutting across the following domains of knowledge and skills, forming a framework for functional academic content areas that can enhance independence and quality of life: 1) personal finances, 2) applied money concepts, 3) applied time concepts, 4) community mobility and access, 5) household management, 6) interacting with local government and community agencies, 7) grooming and self-care, 8) engagement in leisure activities, 9) health and safety, and 10) career and job preparation. In the following sections, we briefly describe each domain and the general sets of demands for each.

Personal Finances

Most people use a bank to keep funds earned through employment as savings and/or expenditures for living and leisure costs. Thus, when one attempts to manage these **personal finances,** demands emerge related to budgeting, keeping a checkbook, endorsing and depositing paychecks, using ATM machines, and communicating with tellers.

Teachers should begin focusing on functional academic content for this domain as early as possible (certainly within the context of the general curriculum during the elementary years) by emphasizing the operations of addition and subtraction; using concrete manipulatives; and, when necessary, providing the accommodation of a hand-held calculator. Literacy instruction would include reading and writing numbers and dates and students' comprehension of the importance of the personal signature. Most of us successfully manage our finances with the help of resource people (i.e., supports) from banking institutions. Thus, students should know bank tellers' and managers' roles and be able to initiate interactions with them.

Applied Money Concepts

Independence and a good quality of life mean not only that one manages money but also that one can use it appropriately. These are **applied money concepts.** We must respond to demands to select an appropriate denomination of currency when making a purchase; recognizing an appropriate amount of change; using a vending machine; ordering and paying for meals; buying food, clothing, and supplies; and interacting with clerks.

Teachers should eschew the use of play money, opting instead for the real thing. As instruction in this area progresses through the years, teachers and families need to make decisions concerning which denominations should be targeted for mastery, and whether it is even necessary any more for the student to recognize and use coins. Few items cost less than a dollar, and most vending machines now receive dollar bills. Considerable thought also should be given to the possibility of circumventing the use of cash altogether with the use of checks and debit cards. How decisions are made concerning whether a teacher should teach a given skill in the first place is discussed in subsequent sections.

Applied Time Concepts

Successful people know what time it is and arrive at a destination at or before an appointed time. With skills related to **applied time concepts,** adults meet demands of daily sequences of events, the attachment of specific times to such sequences, and punctuality. Also included are reading clock faces (hands and digital), as well as calendars (weekly, monthly, and yearly).

Generally speaking, of all of the skills related to meeting environmental demands forced by the passage of time, comprehending and following a planned, daily sequence of events is perhaps of utmost importance. Thus, as early as preschool, teachers should establish a sequential structure with minimal variance. Daily schedules, digital and/or clock hand times, and corresponding events can be posted and referred to repeatedly. Students should wear watches and be cued to refer to them as eventual self-prompts of the need to make activity transitions. The earlier such habits are established, the higher the odds that they will "generalize" to secondary school, job, and community environments that produce even more crucial demands in this regard.

Community Mobility and Access

Many people with mental retardation live and work in the community in which they attended school (Beck, Broers, Hogue, Shipstead, & Knowlton, 1994). Therefore, the community takes on significant importance as a dependable referent for instruction in **community mobility and access.** Particularly in more urban areas, mobility demands are met with the use of busses, cabs, and trains. In less urban areas, independence in regard to mobility is more difficult, and teachers, transition specialists, and others must help arrange for the proper mobility supports.

All students need instruction regarding their community and how to gain access to its many varied environments. Integration of instructional objectives for students without disabilities and students with mental retardation can readily be achieved using a variety of community referents. Beck and colleagues (1994) have termed this approach *community-based instructional integration* (CBII). Classroom teachers and special educators who employ CBII focus on the same general academic curriculum objective, but use community settings rather than classrooms as the instructional venues. It's the contextual *applicability* of the objectives, not the objectives per se, that may be altered in relation to the students' relative intellectual levels. Intermediate-level elementary school students, working on decimals, make a purchase at a convenience store and calculate the sales tax, arriving at the exact price of purchase; students with mental retardation, each assigned to a team of students without disabilities, learn that items will always cost more than the price marked because there will be a tax on each item. It could be argued that, despite the relevance and applicability of this skill, no student, regardless of ability, would, on his or her own, apply decimal multiplication to the calculation of sales tax and total cost. CBII involves inclusive practices that are implemented to facilitate this applicability on the part of all students.

Household Management

Most successful people keep house on a part-time basis, though most will agree **household management** could be a full-time job. Even self-cleaning ovens must be cleaned, dishwashers must be emptied, and smoke alarm batteries tested and changed. Perishable foods must be stored in the refrigerator and discarded when they spoil.

Failure to respond to household management demands can have consequences that range from inconvenient (e.g., bad odor) to dire (e.g., fire). Most schools have components of a full household, albeit they may be spread around the school's campus. There are kitchens, laundry centers, and family and consumer studies areas wherein other home management skills can be taught. Moreover, community transition programs serve older students with disabilities, often renting fully equipped apartments or duplexes for instructional purposes.

Interacting with Local Government and Community Agencies

Sooner or later, almost everyone must confer with the government concerning Social Security, Medicare, taxes, utilities, and so forth—the list can be endless. Moreover, local communities tend to have a variety of public and not-for-profit agencies that require a certain way of interacting that will elicit their services. In many cases, support people (e.g., advocates, sponsors) can accompany and support the person with mental retardation in such interactions or perhaps interact on behalf of the person. Early on, however, as the general social studies curriculum covers local community governance, students can begin to learn about agencies and resources in their community. As they grow older, as part of their instruction in community mobility and access for example, students can be introduced to support people in various local government and community agencies and learn about the roles these people perform.

Grooming and Self-Care

Grooming and self-care demands include bathing, dressing, managing hair, treating minor ailments, and so forth. Weather and color coordination must be taken into account in the selection of clothing. It is important to introduce as early as possible a functional sight-word vocabulary that would include common self-care items and pertinent information on the labels of such items.

Engagement in Leisure Activities

Regarding leisure activities, demands of access must be met. These would include exchanges of fees for access as well as actual behavioral responses, ranging from watching a movie to rollerblading. Most leisure access demands call for appropriate social interaction, communication skills, and comprehension of selected community-referenced words and applied money skills.

Health and Safety

Maintaining one's health and safety presents a variety of demands (see also Chapter 13). These requirements include habits such as wearing one's seat belt, using health services, appropriately using cross-walks, and so forth.

Career and Job Preparation

Though many have advocated for a life-span approach to career education, special education practices seem to relegate career education to secondary and postsecondary vocational preparation. Yet, career education should begin **career and job preparation** in the elementary grades, providing for *all* children an awareness of career possibilities and the attitudes and work habits that they will eventually need. Career education for older students typically includes instruction in job identification, work habits, and work attitudes. Specific demands that relate to job preparation include searching newspaper advertisements and job announcements, making an application, and interviewing for jobs. Demands also include adapting to changes or promotions in jobs as well as to the more standard aspects of daily work such as equipment malfunctions and the like. As is the case with all of these domains, social/interpersonal and communication demands are pervasive.

IDENTIFYING ENVIRONMENTS AND THEIR DEMANDS

The curriculum must be *relevant* to activities in home and community environments and directly *applicable* to the demands they produce in order for the student to function effectively. How well any person meets life's demands dictates the degree of independence and the goodness of lifestyle quality that he or she will experience. This is the essence of functional academic content's utility (Wolfe & Harriot, 1997).

During the era of self-contained instructional services for students with mental retardation, teachers employed a host of methodologies, most of which contain explicit or implicit assumptions of necessary developmental prerequisites (e.g., Katims, 2000). Through the years, strict adherence to these assumptions has led to a myth about adults with mental retardation who, for example, can repeatedly sort and neatly stack denominations of play money without error yet cannot insert a real dollar bill into a modern vending machine. Since the mid-1970s, in the midst of the deinstitutionalization movement and the advent of the federal mandate for a free, appropriate public education, practitioners have been reminded to reflect on how functional their teaching objectives really are (Brown et al., 1979; Brown, Nietupski, & Hamre-Nietupski, 1976). Beck and colleagues (1994) reduced this consideration to its most basic question: "Will the student need it when he or she is 21?" The schematic in Figure 12.1 shows the proper relationship between the functional and developmental emphases in curriculum for students with mental retardation.

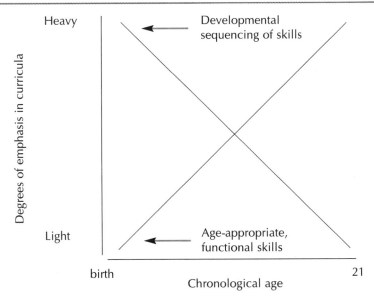

Figure 12.1. Ideal relationship between functional and developmental emphases in a curriculum for students with mental retardation.

Early childhood special education interventions tend necessarily to be developmental in design. Interventionists focus on prelinguistic skills or motor development, for example. There is even room in early childhood programs for preacademic interventions. The guiding light in this design is a walking-before-running premise. Developmentally based interventions do not necessarily lead to bad practices; rather, bad practices stem from a lack of consideration, on the part of professionals in concert with parents or guardians, of when to emphasize functional academics instead of developmental prerequisites to traditional academics (Beck et al., 1994).

Thus, Figure 12.1 depicts an interrelationship between developmental and functional emphases rather than pitting one against the other. The intent of the graphic is not to direct practitioners as to when the developmental emphasis should change to a functional emphasis. Such a shift in curricular emphasis is part of a curriculum planning process (Knowlton, 1998) in which curricular personalization for any single student is the result of collaborative, longitudinal planning among professionals and family members.

Ecological Analysis

America seems to excel in testing (Gould, 1981; Kaufman, 1994). The education profession, with its reform-based, high-stakes testing, and the special education field, with its rich and not altogether benign history of formal assessment, are clearly the line leaders in this regard. Most special educators would agree that the procedural and paperwork burdens accompanying unbiased assessment methods are necessary civil rights protections rather than enablers of best professional practices.

Educators are often more adept at testing students with mental retardation than they are at teaching them. Explicitly or implicitly, the AAMR definition committee realized this as they constructed the 1992 model of mental retardation (Luckasson et al., 1992). IQ score ranges and related severity levels are irrelevant to the definition. The focus is more on the level and nature of supports *in situ* rather than on assessment data *in vitro*. Accordingly, the most productive approach to identifying and teaching functional academic skills that a student will need as an adult minimizes testing and emphasizes **ecological analysis** as well as trial teaching with rational, data-based reflection in natural environments.

Using Ecological Analysis to Identify Environments and Demands

Ecological analysis involves the identification of environments, their subenvironments, and the specific demands entailed therein. We describe the process again in Chapter 14, but it is worth reviewing it in the context of functional academic content as well. It is useful to employ the previously mentioned 10 domains as contexts within which specific environments, subenvironments, and their demands for knowledge and skill application are identified. Langone (1990) advanced the concept of the community-based needs assessment (CNA) in which relevant environments in the home, community, and workplace are identified, delineated into subenvironments, then tagged with target skills on which instruction will focus. This represents the first major step of the ecological analysis: identifying environments and subenvironments within which the student will interact.

It is often desirable to identify a few same-age students without disabilities and count the environments and subenvironments they use regularly. This can provide a useful standard. If, for example, a student is in two environments daily (home and school) and eats at Mr. Gatti's restaurant once a week, he or she interacts in only three major environments per week. If that student is a 19-year-old high school senior, her or his same-age peers in high school or college average nearly 50 discrete environments each week (Knowlton, 2000). For students without disabilities, time rather than intellectual limitations imposes a ceiling on the total number of environments accessed. The task becomes obvious: Increase the number of environments the student can gain access to as well as the demands within new and current environments that she or he can meet.

Table 12.1 lists specific home, school, and community subenvironments and environmental demands for a student with mental retardation. Whereas Langone's (1990)

Table 12.1. Environments, subenvironments, and examples of demands

Environments	Subenvironments	Examples of demands
Home	Living area	Many compact discs on floor out of cases
	Kitchen area	Salad needs preparation
	Bathroom	Razor blade is dull
	Bedroom	Clothing colors need coordination
School	Bus to school	Most seats are taken
	First- and second-hour classrooms	Small-group projects
	Third-hour classroom	Time-keeper needed for cooperative group
	Music room	Asked to sing bass harmony part
	Job sampling	Need four chairs per table at food court
	Bus to home	Must excuse self (to aisle seatmate) to exit bus
Mr. Gatti's restaurant	Cashier area	Need proper bills for $5.95 charge
	Buffet	Pizza slices need to be selected
	Game room	Video game needs to be selected

CNA moves on to identify skills presumed to be necessary in identified environments, the ecological analysis focuses on further delineation of subenvironments into specific demands that have a high probability of emerging within them. The subenvironments shown in Table 12.1 can actually produce an untold number of specific demands, most of which are novel and unanticipated. In fact, one wonders if anyone would be capable of responding in appropriately adaptive ways to *all* possible demands a particular environment and subenvironment might place before us. The fact that humans are adept at responding well to most novel demands speaks volumes about human adaptability. As teachers, we should anticipate the more likely demands and teach students how to respond to them productively.

At this point, current environments, subenvironments, and demands have been identified, with the realization that, for the student, 1) more than three environments need to be identified and 2) for each subenvironment, there will be a host of specific demands. Our work as teachers involves anticipating the more likely demands produced with the most frequency in that subenvironment, and then making decisions about what skills should be taught in light of those demands. In this manner, independence operationally refers to one's capability to respond adaptively and productively to all demands of a specific subenvironment.

Making all such responses competently, one is deemed independent. People with mental retardation can function with complete independence in some environments and with virtually complete dependence on other people in other environments. Whereas a typical person might easily navigate a bookstore to purchase a book but is helpless in an airplane cockpit, so too might a person with mental retardation be independent in her or his home yet (at least initially) dependent on other people in the bookstore. If the local bookstore is an environment identified as desirable for a student to gain access to, then the teacher should take the student to the bookstore, observe the environmental demands and her or his responses to them, and engage in *trial teaching.*

DETERMINING WHAT FUNCTIONAL CONTENT TO TEACH

Functional academic content involves those skills that are relevant and applicable to environments for which access maximizes the student's independence and enhances her or his lifestyle quality. Lou Brown and his colleagues (Brown et al., 1985), with reference to students with extensive and pervasive support needs, provided highly useful guidelines for curriculum decisions. Here, we adapt those guidelines for functional academic decisions in regard to students with mental retardation. If all eight questions below can be answered in the affirmative, the teacher should focus on the skill; if all of the questions are answered in the negative, the teacher should not teach the skill. More often than not, however, there will be a mix of yes/no responses, and thus the teacher should make such decisions collaboratively with the student, her or his family members, and other professionals in a manner described in Chapters 4 and 5.

1. *Can we increase the number of environments?* All things being equal, the number of environments most people can gain access to and, within these, the number of subenvironments in which they can respond productively to demands define a major dimension of their lifestyle quality. People tend to perceive their quality of life as satisfactory when they are competent at performing activities that meet envi-

ronmental demands at home, on the job, and in the community (Knowlton, 1998). There are very few (if any) home, job, or community environments that the majority of people are unable to gain access to. For people with mental retardation, academic skills should function as tools that ultimately can help the student gain access to a new environment or to new subenvironments within an already accessible environment. The guideline of increasing environments arguably has high priority. In many cases, if the teacher cannot answer this question affirmatively, then he or she should probably not be teaching the academic skill in question.

2. *Will the skill maximize independence?* Most people rarely are called on to be independent in the absolute sense (Knowlton, 1998). Instead, people tend to be interdependent with one another: We often act in ways affected by the actions of others, which, in turn, affect the actions of others. Moreover, we usually seek the input of others before we act. Although people infrequently find themselves completely dependent on one or more other people, it is generally the case that most of us behave in ways that are interdependent in relation to one another. Thus, this guideline of maximizing independence is not quite as simple as it may seem. Dever's (1989) definition is helpful in providing a useful perspective on independence, defining it as exhibiting patterns of behavior, appropriate to settings frequented by others of the person's age, in a manner that requires the least assistance from others. Accordingly, the standard is not complete independence in the absolute sense, but rather maximum independence in the contextually relevant sense. That is, can the academic skill, when taught, result in the student needing less assistance in meeting the demands of a particular environment?

It should be noted that a teacher may choose not to teach a particular academic skill even though it reduces the student's need for assistance if he or she discovers that the need for assistance may itself be normalizing and may enhance the student's social interactions with peers without disabilities. For example, Table 12.1 includes the demands of the school environment during third hour when the student serves as a time keeper for a cooperative group project. This demands knowledge of digital clocks to the nearest second but not knowledge of face clocks with second hands. To meet the latter demand, one student without disabilities may work with the student with mental retardation to alert the group as to when third hour is about to conclude. This partnership results in a social relationship between the two students that does not necessarily justify not teaching clock-face reading but it is nonetheless a consideration in the decision of what applied time skills need to be taught.

3. *Is the skill chronologically age appropriate?* This guideline refers directly to the concept depicted in Figure 12.1. As one's chronological age increases, the question of chronological age-appropriateness becomes more salient. As such, one is not likely to question the decision to teach selected picture-word pairs taken from the Dolch sight vocabulary list to an 8-year-old child with mental retardation. The words would be useful to him or her in third-grade literacy/language arts curricula. A 15-year-old tenth-grade student with mental retardation no doubt should also be taught key picture-word pairs but not from the Dolch list. A more appropriate list would be leisure-oriented words (e.g., the name of a favorite pop singer) or job-related words (e.g., *application* or *wages*).

4. *Are there sufficient opportunities for practice in relevant environments and subenvironments?* There is no question that natural environments should serve as teaching settings and

as places in which repeated practice should occur. Beck and colleagues (1994), among others, addressed a common dilemma: Community- or job-based instruction is needed but the general education curriculum must be used in inclusive settings. Their CBII model teaches academic skills in community settings with a curriculum that is just as relevant and applicable for students without disabilities as it is for students with mental retardation. Thus, when students with mental retardation are taught to estimate costs and match these with appropriate cash denomination combinations, students without disabilities apply this skill to the computation of the exact amount of sales tax and the exact purchase price. True relevance and application of academic skills are produced in natural environments, without regard to the cognitive level of the student being taught.

5. *Do parents and family members consider the skill appropriate?* Chapter 10 emphasizes the importance of establishing school–home partnerships and Chapters 4 and 5 discuss the role of families as IEP team members and decision makers. It is important that family and parental preferences be addressed in conjunction with student preferences.

6. *Will the skill enhance physical well-being?* This guideline is easily disregarded but probably should not be. Leisure and food-related contexts provide many applied opportunities for relevant academic instruction. And yet it seems that nutrition and fitness are often de-emphasized in favor of easy relevant applications. For example, it's easier to apply math to a cake recipe than to a tossed salad. It's easier to apply literacy skills to a video game than to a treadmill. Nonetheless, a criterion of physical fitness and good nutrition should be applied to instruction in natural environments. Moreover, with increasing concern for the fitness and nutrition of students without disabilities and the normalcy of the fitness center as an accessible natural environment, we suspect that this guideline's importance will only increase.

7. *Will the skill enhance social status?* This guideline refers to any aspect of the academic skill and its instruction that increases social interaction and with it the odds of a greater social acceptance for the student with mental retardation. Use of a fitness center as an applied context for academic skills, for example, clearly could enhance the social status of a student with mental retardation, as could, of course, more participation in physical education classes or intramural and interscholastic sports.

8. *Is there a sufficient probability that the skill can be acquired?* This guideline competes with the first two in terms of relative importance. What cannot be taught to a student needs to be performed by someone else for that student (Brown et al., 1979), or the student simply will not be able to gain access to the particular environment in question. Teachers sometimes determine, ideally through collaborative, longitudinal planning, that they will not attempt to teach a particular skill to a student. Considering the mindless repetition of attempts in the past to teach developmental prerequisites to students with mental retardation, he or she may view some targets of instruction as simply too time-consuming or too complex to be useful to the student in meeting environmental demands. As just mentioned, the consequence for the student is that she or he either will not gain access to that environment or will need support from someone else.

A teacher might also decide to teach the student to circumvent the demand for a skill. Given the increasing popularity of debit cards, one result of collaborative, longitudinal planning for a student might be to stop teaching the selection of proper currency denominations and other cash-related skills and to teach debit card usage instead.

Finally, a teacher can make the effort to teach a particular skill over time and devote the supports necessary to facilitate knowledge and skill acquisition on the student's part. These decisions again are a function of collaborative, longitudinal planning involving professionals, families, and students, in which the eight questions listed receive careful consideration.

SUMMARY

In this chapter, our intent is to encourage readers to think first about the meaning of *functional* in the context of a functional academic content for all students, not just for students with mental retardation. Too often, a *functional curriculum* has simply meant a curriculum other than that which typical students receive. Our belief is that all students benefit when functional aspects of the curriculum are stressed. Second, when standards and benchmarks are open-ended, there is often no conflict between functional activities and the general curriculum. Issues of ecological validity and community-referenced learning are important to consider in identifying functional academic content.

ADDITIONAL READINGS

Functional Life Skills Approaches

Baker, B.L., & Brightman, A.J. (with Blacher, J.B., Heifitz, L.J. Hinshaw, S.P., & Murphy, D.M.). (1997). *Steps to independence: Teaching everyday skills to children with special needs.* (3rd ed.). Baltimore: Paul H. Brookes Publishing Co.

Brolin, D.E. (1995). *Career education: A functional life skills approach.* Upper Saddle River, NJ: Prentice-Hall.

Cronin, M.E., & Patton, J.R. (1993). *Life skills instruction for all students with special needs: A practical guide for integrating real-life content into the curriculum.* Austin, TX: PRO-ED.

Ford, A., Schnorr, R., Meyer, L., Davern, L., Black, J., & Dempsey, P. (Eds.). (1989). *Syracuse community-referenced curriculum guide for students with moderate and severe disabilities.* Baltimore: Paul H. Brookes Publishing Co.

Mannix, D. (1991). *Life skills activities for special children.* Center for Applied Research in Education.

Wehman, P. (2001). *Life beyond the classroom: Transition strategies for young people with disabilities* (3rd ed.). Baltimore: Paul H. Brookes Publishing Co.

Functional Content Areas

Agran, M., Marchand-Martella, N.E., & Martella, R.C. (1994). *Promoting health and safety: Skills for independent living.* Baltimore: Paul H. Brookes Publishing Co.

Knapczyk, D.R., & Rodes, P.G. (1996). *Teaching social competence: A practical approach for improving social skills for students at-risk.* Pacific Grove, CA: Brooks/Cole.

Schleien, S.J., Meyer, L.H., Heyne, L.A., & Brandt, B.B. (1995). *Lifelong leisure skills and lifestyles for persons with developmental disabilities.* Baltimore: Paul H. Brookes Publishing Co.

CHAPTER OBJECTIVES

1. Discuss the importance of healthy sexuality for all people, and describe how to achieve this for students, including those with mental retardation.
2. Identify the components of a curricular approach to sex education, and discuss the role of school–home–community partnerships in sex education.
3. Discuss the importance of social relationships, and define key terms in social inclusion.
4. Identify key strategies in facilitating friendships.

KEY TERMS

Friendships
Adolescent development
Individuation
Sex education
Human immunodeficiency virus/acquired immunodeficiency syndrome (HIV/AIDS) awareness
Social inclusion
Social relationships

13

The Emergent Self

Sexuality and Social Inclusion

MYSTERIES OF FRIENDSHIP.

As students with mental retardation mature into adolescence and adulthood, they face many challenges pertaining to their emerging self: sexuality, the establishment and maintenance of **friendships** with peers, changing relationships with parents and members of the opposite gender, their self-image and self-awareness in the context of experiencing mental retardation, and their attempts to become included into their community. In this, they are not unlike all other adolescents, and their struggles with these issues should be considered within the context of similar struggles and issues experienced by adolescents without disabilities. Unfortunately, it is too often the case that many of these issues are only addressed if and when they become difficult for the student with mental retardation and others in his or her life. This chapter examines issues pertaining to adolescence, such as promoting healthy sexuality in students with mental retardation; assisting students in developing friendships, relationships, and social networks; and enabling students to become socially included in school, work, recreation and leisure, and postsecondary education settings.

ADOLESCENT DEVELOPMENT

To be consistent with the parameters for discussing mental retardation in this book, any consideration of sexuality, peer relationships, friendships, and social inclusion for young people with mental retardation must be framed within the context of typical **adolescent development,** experiences, and challenges. Although a comprehensive survey of adolescent development is beyond the scope of this chapter (see *Additional Readings* for resources), information about adolescent development must guide efforts to assist young people with mental retardation in these areas. First and foremost, preadolescence and adolescence are periods of significant biological, physical, social, and psychological changes. The complex mixture of physical maturation, changing peer relationships, emerging sexuality, changing family relationships, increased responsibility and expectations, and other variables leads to difficult circumstances. Research suggests that, for several reasons, individuals with mental retardation have less knowledge about issues such as sexuality or social expectations. The educational process is one vehicle for helping young people with mental retardation gain the knowledge that can see them through these sometimes confusing and difficult times.

Second, many developmental psychologists believe that the primary task of adolescence is to achieve **individuation,** or decreasing dependence on others for care (Damon, 1986). This involves addressing issues of self-concept (i.e., how the adolescent views himself or herself), self-esteem (i.e., what the adolescent feels about himself or herself), sex-role socialization, sexuality, peer groups and friendships, and career exploration and development. It is important to consider individuation when supporting young people with mental retardation during preadolescence and adolescence.

Adolescence is a time of experimentation for young people. Dusek noted that

One may decide to be a leader or a follower, an active athlete or passive observer, and experiment with a host of other roles that relate to how one views oneself. Because adolescents do not have to accept the degree of responsibility that adults do when they take on various roles, the long-term consequences of trying out a role and having it fail are not as great as they are for adults. Adolescents can determine the degree to which various social roles and situations are comfortable. It is a time when one may ask the question "Who am I?" and begin to answer it meaningfully. (1996, p. 11)

Perhaps young people with mental retardation are infrequently allowed to experiment with the variety and diversity of roles that their peers evaluate. Thus, they may not have enough experience to answer the question "Who am I?"

Finally, the young person's relationship with his or her family changes during adolescence. As suggested in Chapter 10, as the school–home partnership is often an uneasy relationship, adding the adolescent struggle with individuation, independence, and autonomy can further erode it. As such, it is critical that educators strive to form alliances with the family so that family members can address difficult transition issues with the knowledge that all parties in the planning process have a shared agenda.

HEALTHY SEXUALITY

Education's promotion of healthy sexuality and sexual development acknowledges the fact that humans are sexual and that issues pertaining to that sexuality play a key role in the lives of adults. As previously mentioned, these issues are often addressed in the education of students with mental retardation only when they become a problem for the student or the people with whom the student interacts, such as circumstances of inappropriate personal contact, unwanted sexual expression, or in situations in which exploitation or sexual abuse might exist. People with mental retardation are frequently seen as sexual beings only in the negative roles of sexual predators or victims of sexual abuse and violence.

Nonetheless, changes in the conceptions of disability and mental retardation also lead to the understanding that people with mental retardation are sexual beings. This is illustrated by the position statement on sexuality that was adopted by The Arc, the largest U.S. association that focuses exclusively on mental retardation (see Figure 13.1).

The field of education has made progress in recognizing the importance of **sex education** as a means to ensure protection from sexual exploitation and abuse or to prevent the spread of sexually transmitted diseases. Yet, few people in society and, thus, in the education field perceive people with mental retardation as spouses and parents. May and Kundert (1996) surveyed special education personnel preparation programs and found that 41% do not provide any course work related to sex education. Nonetheless, many people with mental retardation want a loving, long-term relationship that is emotionally and sexually fulfilling and includes the possibility of parenting children.

Schwier (1994) interviewed couples with mental retardation about their relationships and their thoughts about marriage, parenting, and sexuality. Schwier noted that the residential and vocational supports that are available to most people with mental retardation limit the quality and types of relationships that can develop, citing the following as an example:

> A recognized couple have been seeing each other, mostly at the sheltered workshop where they both work, for years. John and Carol are in their mid-30s. An alarmed staff person "catches" them kissing and holding hands, so the two are separated and told if they are seen holding hands again at work at any time, they will be punished. Staff express concern that productivity will drop and say "if we let them do it, then everybody will want to do it." (p. 7)

The truth is that when it comes to expressing one's sexuality, it is likely the case that everybody does want to do it, independent of what others (e.g., workshop staff) do

ISSUE

Sexuality is a natural part of every person's life. Sexuality includes gender identity, friendships, self-esteem, body image and awareness, emotional development and social behavior, as well as involvement in physical expressions of love, affection and desires. This issue requires respect and understanding.

The commitment to full inclusion into the community has given people with mental retardation new experiences, different risks, and more opportunities to make choices. Currently, many people with mental retardation are not receiving education and support to protect them from abuse, exploitation, unwanted pregnancy, and sexually transmitted diseases, while safeguarding their dignity and rights.

POSITION

The Arc recognizes and affirms that individuals with mental retardation are people with sexual feelings, needs and identities, and believes that sexuality should always be seen in the total context of human relationships.

The Arc believes that people with mental retardation have fundamental rights as individuals to:

- have privacy;
- love and be loved;
- develop friendships and emotional relationships;
- learn about sex, sexual exploitation, sexual abuse, safe sex and other issues regarding sexuality;
- exercise their rights and responsibilities in regard to privacy and sexual expression and the rights of others;
- marry and make informed decisions concerning having children; and
- develop expressions of sexuality reflective of age, social development, cultural values and social responsibility.

The Arc further advocates that on an individual basis people with mental retardation who have children receive proper supports to assist them in rearing their children.
The Arc also believes that the presence of mental retardation regardless of severity must not, in itself, justify either involuntary sterilization or denial of sterilization to those who choose it for themselves.

Figure 13.1.   The Arc's position statement on sexuality. (From Arc, The. [1996]. *Sexuality: Position statement #9*. Silver Spring, MD: Author. [Available: http://www.thearch.org/posits/sex.html]; reprinted by permission.)

or do not want. The previous scenario illustrates legitimate questions about how one expresses love and emotion in settings such as work. Yet, it is likely that John's and Carol's lives are so circumscribed by the systems that control where they live and work and so devoid of meaningful opportunities to share personal private time that to address the appropriateness of their kissing and holding hands at work misses the forest for the trees. Contrast that scenario with the following one, also from Schwier:

Allen: We are newlyweds. The weddin' was okay. Everybody said they really enjoy it. My brother came. I met Nadine back in '77 cause I move here. In 1960, I was in institute for ten years in Oregon. A girl I know there induced me to Nadine. I thought she was really nice. Couple year before we get married, we know each other.

Nadine: I think he cute when I see him. I don wanna tell nobody how old I am. I was a baby when my family just drop me off at intitution. My dress was all white and had a belt on it. I had white flowers. My bridesmaid was my friend.

Allen: We talk about our own baby, but we don't have enough money. We need to talk to a doctor and see if we would be possible to do operation so Nadine could have a baby. It's a big responsibility. I like lots of things about Nadine. We can do things together when we're married. We don't hold hands very much like some people. Sometimes if I go somewhere, she want to go with me and if she go somewhere, she want me to go with her. (1994, pp. 77–81)

The couples whom Schwier interviewed (some married, some dating, some with children, some without children) spoke about the same concerns, joys, benefits, and challenges that all people face in starting and maintaining a relationship. In many ways, however, they are pioneers, charting territory uncovered by other people with mental retardation, and they often travel that territory without having had the opportunity to learn more about healthy sexuality in school.

Most states' general curricula address healthy sexuality and social development. Therefore, this is another area in which providing students with mental retardation access to the general curriculum can fill a need for educational and instructional experiences. In some states, the standards specify teaching about topics such as **HIV/AIDS awareness,** other sexually transmitted diseases, self-concept, and healthy peer relationships. The California Department of Education's health education standards for high school address many of these issues, as shown by the following example:

Standard 8: The student will understand his or her developing sexuality, the benefits of abstinence from sexual activity, and how to be respectful of the sexuality of others. Students in high school who meet this standard will be able to:

- Recognize that abstinence is the only totally effective method of contraception
- Analyze other methods of contraception
- Explain human sexuality and analyze the effects of social and cultural influences
- Identify influences and pressures to become sexually active
- Apply communication/refusal skills as they relate to responsible decision making
- Understand how to be respectful of the sexuality of others, including personal and social characteristics of sexual harassment

The following tasks and assignments might be used to determine whether the student is meeting the standard:

- Students will list the advantages and disadvantages of each type of birth control, recognizing that abstinence is the only totally effective method of contraception.
- Students will role-play assertive refusal skills.
- Students will analyze unhealthy relationships/situations as they relate to sexual activity, abuse, harassment, and violence.
- Students will research community agencies and hotlines that can be utilized in case of need.

- Students will evaluate situations involving sexual harassment and recognize the broad interpretations of actions. (California Department of Education, 1998)

In other states, health education standards do not specify outcomes related to healthy sexuality but, instead, emphasize the acquisition of skills that enable students to set goals and make decisions that lead to better health outcomes. For example, the Wisconsin Department of Education suggested that promoting self-determination for students with mental retardation plays a critical role in achieving outcomes such as healthy sexuality and peer relationships (see Table 13.1).

Similarly, many states' general education curricula contain learning standards for direct instruction in parenting skills. Such instruction is important for students with mental retardation. Although there is no comprehensive estimate of the number of people with mental retardation who are parents, the Oregon Developmental Disabilities Council Family Support Initiative (1989) identified 358 families in Oregon alone with parents considered to have cognitive impairments. The Nebraska Family and Consumer Sciences Essential Learning Elements provided an example of including parenting skills instruction in the general curriculum:

4.0   Analyze roles and responsibilities of parenting.
4.0.1 Determine effects of parenting practices on the individual, family and society.
4.0.2 Determine societal conditions that impact parenting across the life span.
4.1   Evaluate parenting practices that maximize growth and development.
4.1.1 Identify communication strategies that promote positive self-esteem in family members.
4.1.2 Analyze nurturing practices.
4.1.3 Evaluate practices of interaction that encourage appropriate behavior.
4.1.4 Determine criteria for selecting care and services for children. (Nebraska Department of Education, 1995)

SEXUALITY AND INDIVIDUALS WITH MENTAL RETARDATION

We have highlighted two reasons to focus on sexuality education for students with mental retardation: 1) People with mental retardation are people first and, like all humans, are sexual beings, and 2) healthy sexuality and parenting are important parts of the general curriculum in many states. There are other reasons to focus both instructional and research attention on issues of healthy sexuality for students with mental retardation. Among the most frequently reported concerns by parents of young people with severe developmental disabilities are issues pertaining to their son's or daughter's sexuality in relation to the transition to adulthood (Thorin & Irvin, 1992). Therefore, schools need to work with families to address these issues within the context of families' values and needs, emphasizing the need for person-centered processes to be adopted in educational planning and decision making. Very little information is known about the sexual experiences and behavior of individuals with mental retardation living in the community (McCabe, 1993). The little that is known about the sexual experiences of individuals with mental retardation and their opportunities to express sexuality comes from old studies in institutional settings (Mulhern, 1975).

Some information exists regarding the knowledge of and attitudes toward sexuality by individuals with mental retardation. Adults with mild intellectual disabilities in Australia (ranging from 16 to 40 years of age) had significantly lower levels of knowl-

Table 13.1. Sample Wisconsin standard on health education

C. GOAL SETTING AND DECISION MAKING

Content Standard

Students in Wisconsin will demonstrate the ability to use goal-setting and decision-making skills to enhance health

Rationale:

  Decision making and goal setting are essential lifelong skills needed to implement and sustain health-enhancing behaviors. These skills make it possible for students to apply health knowledge to healthy lifestyle development. Decision-making and goal-setting skills enable individuals to work collaboratively to improve the quality of life in their families, schools, and communities.

PERFORMANCE STANDARDS

By the end of grade 4 students will:

  C.4.1   Demonstrate the ability to apply a decision-making process to health issues
  C.4.2   Explain when to ask for assistance in making health-related decisions and setting health goals
  C.4.3   Predict outcomes of positive health decisions for themselves
  C.4.4   Set a personal health goal and track progress toward achievement
  C.4.5   Analyze how behaviors may have both good and bad consequences

By the end of grade 8 students will:

  C.8.1   Demonstrate the ability to individually and collaboratively apply a decision-making process to health issues
  C.8.2   Analyze how health-related decisions are influenced by individuals, family, and community values
  C.8.3   Analyze how decisions regarding health behaviors have consequences for themselves and others
  C.8.4   Develop and implement a personal health plan addressing personal strengths, needs, and health risks.

By the end of grade 12 students will:

  C.12.1   Demonstrate the ability to use various decision-making strategies related to health needs and risks
  C.12.2   Apply knowledge of individual, family, and community influences to decision-making processes
  C.12.3   Predict immediate and long-term impacts of health decisions on the individual, family, and community
  C.12.4   Develop, implement, and evaluate an effective plan for a healthy and productive life.

From Nikolay, P., Grady, S., & Stefonek, T. (1997). *Wisconsin's model academic standards for health education* (p. 12). Madison, WI: Wisconsin Department of Public Instruction; reprinted by permission.

edge about sexual issues than a comparison group of university students across virtually every area of sexuality except for menstruation and body part identification (McCabe & Cummins, 1996). Lunsky and Konstantareas (1998) found that adults with mental retardation held significantly less accepting attitudes about sociosexual situations (e.g., menstruating, consensual hand holding, kissing, petting, masturbation, having sex, using birth control) than did typical adults and adults with autism, a finding that supports similar findings by McCabe and Cummins (1996). Lunsky and Konstantareas identified a number of possible reasons to explain their results, including

- Limited resources for providing up-to-date information about healthy approaches to sexuality for individuals with mental retardation

- A lack of interactions with typically developing peers who provide information about sexuality and role models

- Limited training for special educators in teaching about sexuality

- Parents' and family members' hesitancy to address sexuality because of fears about vulnerability and abuse

- The highly structured settings in which many people with mental retardation live or work

McCabe and Cummins (1996) found that even though people with intellectual disabilities were less likely to have experienced sexual intercourse or other sexual interactions than their peers who developed typically, they were more likely to have been pregnant or to have a sexually transmitted disease. The devastating consequences of contracting HIV/AIDS have resulted in a greater awareness of sexually transmitted diseases. The epidemiology of HIV infection in adults with mental retardation or developmental disabilities is poorly understood. In 1989, Kastner, Nathanson, Marchetti, and Pincus reported that adults with mental retardation have been diagnosed with HIV in at least 11 states and with AIDS in 7 states. More recent statistics are unavailable, but one can only surmise that those numbers have increased. Interventions to increase knowledge about HIV/AIDS and other sexually transmitted diseases, including AIDS awareness training, have been shown to be beneficial for people with mental retardation (Jacobs, Samowitz, Levy, & Levy, 1989; Scotti, Speaks, Masia, Boggess, & Drabman, 1996).

Promoting Healthy Sexuality for Students with Mental Retardation

Given these issues and the fact that healthy sexuality and effective parenting skills are an important component of the general curriculum, it is important to ensure that students with mental retardation receive instruction about sexuality and parenting. However, implementing a sexuality or sexual awareness curriculum as a stand-alone or alternative curriculum is not sufficient. Similar to all other curricular matters, students with mental retardation need curriculum adaptations for gaining access to materials about sexuality and healthy development. Instruction about sexuality, sexual activity, and relationships must occur in conjunction with a strong focus on promoting self-determination (see Chapter 15). All students need knowledge about sexuality and healthy development, but they also need the capacity to solve problems and make decisions concerning their own sexuality and sexual activity.

What methods, materials, and strategies exist to enable teachers to teach students with mental retardation about sexuality? Whitehouse and McCabe (1997) reviewed the available programs and noted that the programs widely vary from focusing exclusively on AIDS prevention to a broader spectrum of issues. The topics that are covered in the broader programs vary according to gender and populations. Whitehouse and McCabe identified the following as key curricular components that need to be addressed as part of a broader focus on sexuality:

- Distinguishing body parts and reproductive organs
- Family life skills
- Self-care skills
- Social manners and social interactions
- Interpersonal relationships
- Nutrition
- Puberty
- Attitudes about sexuality
- Physical and emotional components of sexual relationships
- Sexual and relationship vocabulary

- Masturbation and sexual intercourse
- Reproductive health
- Menstrual management
- Breast self-examinations and other physical examinations
- Sexual abuse avoidance
- Birth control and abstinence
- Prevention of sexually transmitted diseases

These content areas mirror those needed for all students. In addition, as is the case for addressing these issues with all students, addressing them for students with mental retardation must be done within a school–home context that creates partnerships and allows significant input from families and parents. Walcott illustrated the ways in which focusing on these issues for students with mental retardation can be even more sensitive:

> The curriculum accommodates the cognitive limitations of these young people and provides methods that include visual and tactile cues. For example, teaching sexuality education to this population requires teaching such facts as actual positions in coitus through the use of pictures, displays, and films. Pictures? Displays? Films? How to choose them? How to acknowledge the inhibitions of parents—and teachers—regarding pictures of sexual behavior? (1997, p. 73)

Walcott (1997) developed a process for addressing these issues, which can be applied to the education of all students. First, a needs analysis is conducted that includes education professionals, parents and family members, and adults with mental retardation in the process of documenting local needs and concerns. Second, a stakeholder committee is formed to evaluate materials, suggest directions, and so forth. Third, all stakeholders in the education process, from professionals to family members, are informed of the intent to develop a sexuality curriculum and offered the opportunity to provide input and direction. Finally, the selected materials are tested out before being fully implemented.

Chapter 14 discussed the importance of locally referenced planning in relation to community-based instruction. The importance of locally referenced planning can be applied to sexuality education as well. The social context in which the public schools operate precludes teachers in some communities from addressing the full range of sexuality education issues and topics. Religious and cultural factors and prohibitions must be taken into consideration during planning, and this must occur as a function of the individualized education program (IEP) decision-making process. The ways in which some of these factors are addressed vary. Some sexuality education programs have trained parents to be the trainer, whereas others have consulted parents about the attitudes they wish to have communicated to their children.

SOCIAL INCLUSION

The terms *friend, peer,* and *relationship* refer to components of the broader term **social inclusion** (or **social relationships**). It is easy to say that friends are important, but it is more difficult to actually define what is meant by the term *friend* and to identify how one goes about making a friend. Snell and Janney (2000) defined some components of social relationships, which are presented in Table 13.2. Friendships are critical, as they serve a variety of roles for students with mental retardation, including enhancing communicative, cognitive, and social skills; providing nurturance, support, and a sense of well being; and becoming the basis for more intimate relationships in adulthood (Grenot-Scheyer, 1994). Since the late 1980s, there has been increased emphasis on the importance of relationships among students with intense support needs and their typically developing peers (Strully & Strully, 1989).

Promoting Friendships

Bishop, Jubala, Stainback, and Stainback (1996) identified a number of strategies for facilitating friendships among students with disabilities and their peers. These steps begin with the prerequisite of proximity and opportunities for interaction. Students with mental retardation do not develop friendships with their peers unless they are physically sharing classrooms, buses, gymnasiums, and other school environments. Physical proximity is a necessary component of facilitating friendships. Teachers need to go beyond just physical proximity, however, to create learning climates in which all students are valued, class members establish and enforce rules pertaining to social interactions among classmates, and teachers arrange for interactions that can lead to the growth of friendships. Bishop and colleagues emphasized the importance of ensuring that students with disabilities contribute in meaningful ways to classroom activities across all content and curricular areas. Providing accommodations and curriculum adaptations can lead to such contributions.

Bishop and colleagues (1996) also suggested going beyond just creating opportunities for friendship to creating an awareness of friendships and the importance of them for all students. They noted that some high schools have even established friendship clubs that focus on providing opportunities for meeting different people and identifying common interests. For example, if two students share a love of baseball, this shared interest may provide a basis for a friendship. Stainback and Stainback (1990) emphasized the importance of skill building in friendship development. They listed the following behavior categories as warranting instructional focus:

- Positive interaction style: Teach students to be active listeners, give positive feedback, ask questions, and respond to the needs of others.

- Areas of compatibility: Introduce students to peers who have common interests and experiences and teach a student how to ask questions of peers about hobbies, interests, talents, experiences, and beliefs, as well as how to acknowledge and share their common interests.

- The perspective of others: Teach students to consider the needs, feelings, and interests of others; to compromise on activity choices; to listen to ideas and needs of others; and to interact with tact and sensitivity.

- Trustworthiness and loyalty: Teach students the importance of keeping a friend's secrets, keeping promises, standing up for friends, and supporting the rights of friends.

Table 13.2. Components of social relationships

Component	Definition
Friend	Someone socially important to an individual; someone whom a person particularly likes (Fryxell & Kennedy, 1995)
Social interaction skills	Includes an array of interpersonal behaviors, such as greeting others, approaching an individual or a group, listening to others, commenting/acting on others' requests or remarks, initiating an exchange, asking others to respond to or engage in an activity, entering into an ongoing social dyad or group, taking turns, taking actions, intended to maintain an exchange or social activity, and terminating an interaction.
Social competence	Encompasses both an individual's effectiveness in influencing the behavior of a peer and the appropriateness of the behavior (given the setting, culture and context) (Odom, McConnell, & McEvoy, 1992).
Social networks	The individuals identified as being socially important to a person; the patterns of interaction, acquaintance, and friendship an individual has with others, usually peers.
Social reciprocity	The interdependent exchange of interactions between two individuals that reflects balanced turn-taking.
Development of friendships	A growth process that leads to close human relationships between two individuals and reflects several ongoing processes such as creating opportunities for interaction; learning social skills that facilitate interactions; and generating organizational, emotional and social supports to maintain relationships.
Peer support	Actions taken by individuals of the same age that involve lending emotional and social sustenance and assistance to each other in a reciprocal unidirectional manner.

From Snell, M.E., & Janney, R. (2000). *Teacher's guides to inclusive practices: Social relationships and peer support* (p. 8). Baltimore: Paul H. Brookes Publishing Co; reprinted by permission.

- Conflict resolution: Teach students how to resolve their own conflicts and support peers in doing so.
- Friendship skills: Provide specific examples of relationships and behavior to teach students how to act with friends.

A number of resources emphasize the importance of circles of friends strategies in building social relationships for individuals with intensive support needs. Snell and Janney defined the *circles of friends exercise* as "a friendship awareness activity used to introduce students and adults to the universal need for social relationships and peer support" (2000, p. 59). The exercise creates a chart consisting of four concentric circles, with the innermost circle labeled "intimacy," the next circle labeled "friendship," the third circle labeled "participation," and the fourth circle labeled as "exchange." Students and family members fill the circles with names of people with whom they are closest (intimate) or good friends (friendship), then they fill in the people with whom the student interacts regularly (participation) and who are paid to provide supports (exchange). Next, participants engage in a discussion about these names, which gets students and family members to consider why people were placed as they were and how the student might prefer the people to be organized.

Whether teaching social skills, creating friendship clubs, or designing learning environments that respect diversity and lead to opportunities for meaningful contributions and interactions, it is critical for activities that promote social inclusion, strengthen and build social relationships, and nurture and facilitate friendships for students with mental retardation to be conducted within the context of the general classroom and as driven by the general curriculum. Similar to healthy sexuality, all children and youth have these needs, not just students with mental retardation.

SUMMARY

The importance of social relationships, friendships, intimacy, and sexuality to a person's quality of life cannot be overemphasized. To deny people with mental retardation these essential components is, in essence, to deny them the opportunity to live a rich, full life. It is critical that teachers working with students with mental retardation address these issues within the general curriculum and the general classroom. It is particularly important that educators focusing on sexuality education build meaningful, collaborative relationships with parents, families, and community members in implementing sexuality training and education.

Returning to the story of Allen and Nadine (Schwier, 1994), Nadine suffered a brain aneurysm and died a year after her marriage to Allen. They met in 1977 but were not married until 1991, and one wonders whether they would have married earlier and enjoyed more time together if they had not had to battle societal prohibitions about relationships and sexuality for people with mental retardation. Mainly, however, one is reminded that every moment with loved ones and friends is precious, and that to deny any person an opportunity to have moments such as those is, perhaps, the cruelest outcome of not addressing issues of sexuality and friendship.

ADDITIONAL READINGS

Adolescent Development

Dusek, J.B. (1996). *Adolescent development and behavior* (3rd ed.). Upper Saddle River, NJ: Prentice Hall.

Kimmel, D.C., & Weiner, I.B. (1995). *Adolescence: A developmental transition* (2nd ed.). New York: John Wiley & Sons.

Pueschel, S.M., & Suštrová, M. (Eds.). (1997). *Adolescents with Down syndrome: Toward a more fulfilling life*. Baltimore: Paul H. Brookes Publishing Co.

Sexuality and HIV/AIDS Prevention

Edwards, J.P. (1997). Growing into a social-sexual being. In S.M. Pueschel & M. Suštrová (Eds.), *Adolescents with Down syndrome: Toward a more fulfilling life* (pp. 59–69). Baltimore: Paul H. Brookes Publishing Co.

Mason, C.Y., & Jaskulski, T. (1994). HIV/AIDS prevention and education. In M. Agran, N. Marchand-Martella, & R. Martella (Eds.), *Promoting health and safety: Skills for independent living* (pp. 161–191). Baltimore: Paul H. Brookes Publishing Co.

Schwier, K.M. (1994). *Couples with intellectual disabilities talk about living and loving*. Rockville, MD: Woodbine House.

Schwier, K.M., & Hingsburger, D. (2000). *Sexuality: Your sons and daughters with intellectual disabilities*. Baltimore: Paul H. Brookes Publishing Co.

Social Relationships and Social Inclusion

Odom, S.L., McConnell, S.R., & McEvoy, M.A. (1992). *Social competence of young children with disabilities.* Baltimore: Paul H. Brookes Publishing Co.

Snell, M.E., & Janney, R. (2000). *Social relationships and peer support.* Baltimore: Paul H. Brookes Publishing Co.

CHAPTER OBJECTIVES

1. Define *community*, and discuss its importance in the lives of people with mental retardation.
2. Discuss the normalization principle and its influence in the field of mental retardation.
3. Define *community-referenced planning* and *community-based instruction*, and discuss characteristics of these approaches.
4. Discuss the potential conflict between community-based instruction and inclusion, and identify ways to address those issues.

KEY TERMS

Community
The Community Imperative
Normalization
Community-referenced planning
Community-based instruction
Ecological inventory

14

Community-Based Instruction

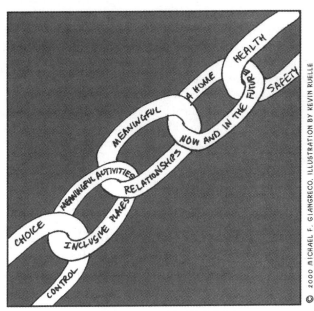

VALUED LIFE OUTCOMES:
SEEKING TO MAKE EVERY LINK STRONG.

Perhaps the most significant change in the lives of people with mental retardation in the last century was the shift in focus—which emerged in the post–World War II era—from congregate working and living settings as preferred options to the **community** as the optimal living and working environment. For example, Braddock (1998) documented that in 1960, there were only 336 community residential settings for people with developmental disabilities in the United States but that by 1996, there were 70,635. Concurrently, in 1967 there were 194,650 institutionalized Americans; by 1996, this figure had dropped to 59,726. Only the most philosophically entrenched argue today against the notion people with mental retardation should live within their communities, and, as such, much of the focus in the educational programs of students with mental retardation has, similarly, been on the community.

Best practice in the education of students with mental retardation has been that as students grow older, they receive proportionally more of their instruction in ecologically valid community settings. By the time they reach high school, students should be receiving instruction in the community for much of their school day. Since the 1990s, however, there has been a growing conflict among the best practices established in community-based instruction for youth with more intense support needs and the widely held value for the inclusion of students with mental retardation in typical classrooms. This may seem to be an either/or situation, and many educators are confused and hesitant to address what seem to be equally valid, though incompatible, perspectives. It is the perspective of this text that the community instruction/inclusion conundrum must be addressed within the context of decisions about the student's curriculum. This conflict is more than just one of *where* a student receives his or her education (e.g., in the typical classroom versus in the community) but is as closely tied to the *what* question (e.g., the content of a student's education program). This chapter begins with a brief overview of what is meant by *community* and examines community-based instruction and its importance in the education of students with mental retardation. It also reviews educational supports for youth with mental retardation between the ages of 18 and 21, a time during which there is no comparable general curriculum and during which community-based instruction is the dominant means of providing educational services and supports. The chapter closes with a discussion of how to address the community inclusion problem and an exploration of the role of community-based learning for all students.

COMMUNITY: WHAT IS IT? WHY IS IT IMPORTANT?

The importance of the community to the field of mental retardation is illustrated by **The Community Imperative,** a declaration supporting the rights of all people with disabilities to community living. The original version of *The Community Imperative* was issued by the Center on Human Policy at Syracuse University in 1979 in response to specific testimony submitted in the Wyatt v. Stickney case (1974) focusing on conditions at the Partlow State School and Hospital in Alabama. The purpose of *The Community Imperative* was to serve as a vehicle for people in the field to communicate their belief to the court and to the nation that all people, regardless of the nature or severity of their disability, have the right to community inclusion. The document was drafted by the Center on Human Policy under the leadership of Dr. Burton Blatt (author of *Christmas in Purgatory,* the 1964 exposé on institutions that prompted significant action by the Kennedy Administration) and was endorsed by more than 300 parents, people with disabilities, researchers, and professionals, including leaders such as Gunnar and Rosemary Dybwad, Seymour Sarason, Marc Gold, Bengt Nirje, and other pioneers in the field of mental retardation. *The Community Imperative* stated

In the domain of Human Rights

- All people have fundamental moral and constitutional rights.
- These right must not be abrogated merely because a person has a mental or physical disability.
- Among these fundamental rights is the right to community living.

In the domain of Educational Programming and Human Services:

- All people, as human beings, are inherently valuable.
- All people can grow and develop.
- All people are entitled to conditions that foster their development.
- Such conditions are optimally provided in community settings.

Therefore, in the fulfillment of fundamental human rights and in securing optimum development opportunities, all people, regardless of the severity of their disabilities, are entitled to community living. (Center on Human Policy, 2000)

In 2000, the Center on Human Policy reissued *The Community Imperative*, seeking endorsement from organizations and individuals as a means to focus attention on the principles underlying community inclusion. A question-and-answer sheet on the Center's web site states that

The time to debate the place of people with disabilities in the society and the community has long since passed. It is time to shift attention to assuring that community living is accomplished in a manner consistent with the values and beliefs expressed in *The Community Imperative*. (Available: http://soeweb.syr.edu/thechp/community_imperative.html)

Burton Blatt's writings heavily influenced the predisposition in the field toward community. In his final book, titled *The Conquest of Mental Retardation*, he noted,

It is difficult to discuss institutions without engaging in controversy. After all, the Willowbrooks and Pennhursts of the world are famous for being infamous. On the other hand, one of the persistent criticisms of the deinstitutionalization movement has been the assertion that the effectiveness of community living has not been well documented. Nevertheless, the ineffectiveness of the institution has been more than adequately documented. I see no reason why vigorous examinations of community placement cannot be achieved in order to settle the question. (1987, p. 159)

Later in the same text, Blatt noted the seeming futility of trying to prove the efficacy of the community:

Has there been a conclusive demonstration of the effectiveness of living in one's natural home? Some may think this is a silly question. After all, the overwhelming majority of people in our society live in ordinary homes. What does it mean to document the effectiveness of one's home? To the degree that mentally retarded people live in ordinary homes and in ordinary neighborhoods, it becomes less and less possible to document the effectiveness of those environments. Simply stated, the controversy is between those who believe that all children should live in ordinary communities and attend ordinary schools in ordinary classes, and those who contend that children with special needs are best served in specialized programs. (p. 160)

The idea that people with mental retardation should be in the community was planted with the introduction of the **normalization** principle to the North American audience (Wolfensberger, 1972). Robert Scheerenberger (1987), in his two-volume chronicle of the history of mental retardation, suggested that no single categorical principle has ever had a greater impact on services for people with mental retardation than that of normalization. Nirje (1969) explained that the normalization principle had its basis in "Scandinavian experiences from the field" (p. 228) and emerged, in essence, from a Swedish law on mental retardation that was passed July 1, 1968. In its original conceptualization, the normalization principle provided guidance for creating services that "let the mentally retarded obtain an existence as close to the normal as possible" (p. 229). Nirje stated, "As I see it, the normalization principle means making available to the mentally retarded patterns and conditions of everyday life which are as close as possible to the norms and patterns of the mainstream of society" (p. 228).

Nirje (1969) identified eight facets and implications of the normalization principle:

1. Normalization means a normal rhythm of day.

2. Normalization implies a normal routine of life.

3. Normalization means to experience the normal rhythm of the year.

4. Normalization means the opportunity to undergo normal developmental experiences of the life cycle.

5. Normalization means that the choices, wishes, and desires [of the mentally retarded themselves] have to be taken into consideration as nearly as possible and respected.

6. Normalization also means living in a bisexual world.

7. Normalization means normal economic standards [for the mentally retarded].

8. Normalization means that the standards of the physical facility should be the same as those regularly applied in society to the same kind of facilities for ordinary citizens.

Scheerenberger noted that "at this stage in its development, the normalization principle basically reflected a lifestyle, one diametrically opposed to many prevailing institutional practices" (1987, p. 117), as was aptly illustrated by Blatt and Kaplan (1966). In fact, the ideas forwarded by Nirje in 1969 remain, to a significant extent, the philosophical basis on which exemplary services are based more than 30 years after their original presentation.

A "normal rhythm of the day" means that people with disabilities should go about their day in much the same way that most people do: getting out of bed, getting dressed, eating under normal circumstances within typical settings (e.g., families), going to bed at times comparable with peers, and having opportunities for personal time and relaxation. A "normal routine of life" means that people with disabilities should live in one place, work or attend school in another, and have leisure activities in various places. A "normal rhythm of the year" means that people with disabilities should experience holidays and family days of personal significance, including vacations.

Much of the emphasis in the normalization principle relates to the importance of people with disabilities experiencing the rich stimulation of being involved in one's community, living with family members, and experiencing friendships. The normalization principle stresses that contact with people without disabilities, and people from both genders, is critically important across all age ranges. The importance of economic self-sufficiency is also highlighted. Finally, it is evident that self-determination is critical to the normalization principle, as Nirje went on to describe in subsequent writings (Nirje, 1972). At a time when most services for people with disabilities viewed them as patients, when public education was not available, and when public opinion viewed them as charity cases and eternal children, Nirje stressed the importance of choice and the need to respect the preferences and dreams of people with mental retardation. In a later paper on the normalization principle, Nirje stated, "Normalization also means that normal understanding and respect should be given to the silent wishes or expressed self-determination of persons [with mental retardation]" (p. 174).

Stating that community is important to the field of mental retardation does not, however, explain the term itself. What is the community, and is it a panacea to solve all of life's problems? Defining *community* is both difficult and, in some ways, unnecessary. Most people know community when they see it, even if they can't define it. Lakin, Hayden, and Abery (1994) noted that in its simplistic sense, the concept of community implies shared space. In its most complex sense, it implies aspects of mutuality, reciprocity, shared interests, interpersonal relationships, interdependent roles and involvement, and common expectations and standards. Lakin and colleagues defined being part of a community as "to share space with people who have mutual interests, enjoy relationships, develop interdependencies, and share common expectations" (p. 4).

The second question—is community the panacea for all ills?—is, unfortunately, easier to answer: No, of course the community is not the solution to all problems, nor does a community focus ensure quality. Kendrick noted that there are "diverse interpretations for specific community hopes and expectations, ranging from near utopian expectations of rapid social inclusion to continued existence in punitive segregation" and that "there are many realities of community life for all citizens that are problematic" as "community living may routinely subject people with disabilities to continued social devaluation, rejection, exploitation, disregard and neglect, abuse, segregation, abandonment, poverty, powerlessness, and so forth" (1994, p. 365).

So why is there the overwhelming preference, indeed value, for community, such as that expressed in *The Community Imperative,* in reference to supports and services for people with mental retardation? Ruth Sienkiewicz-Mercer, a woman who lived in a state institution for people with mental retardation, noted in her autobiography titled *I Raise My Eyes to Say Yes,*

> I had never had a place of my own. As a result, I had never worried about buying groceries and planning meals, paying the rent and the phone bill, balancing a checkbook, making appointments, figuring out how to keep the appointments I made—all of the things adults just do. But starting out in society at the age of 28, after living at a state institution for the mentally retarded for sixteen years, I found these everyday tasks confusing and wonderful and frightening. (1989, p. 202)

Sienkiewicz-Mercer's observation illustrates that living life to its fullest is, fundamentally, about addressing problems and solving them, about accepting challenges and taking risks. Robert Perske's classic call for allowing people to assume risks illustrates this further. In Wolfensberger's text, *Normalization,* Perske wrote,

The world in which we live is not always safe, secure and predictable.... Every day that we wake up and live in the hours of that day, there is a possibility of being thrown up against a situation where we may have to risk everything, even our lives. This is the way the real world is. We must work to develop every human resource within us in order to prepare for these days. To deny any person their fair share of risk experiences is to further limit them for healthy living. (1972, p. 199)

Robert Perske, Ruth Sienkiewicz-Mercer, Bengt Nirje, and Burton Blatt all emphasized that life is only worth living in the context of relationships and experiences that enable one to take risks, pursue goals, meet challenges, and make things happen, or to paraphrase another author who wrote on similar themes, to engage in the pursuit of life, liberty, and happiness. A century of experience has taught us that the place where such pursuit occurs is one's community.

Community-Based Instruction

The educational programs of students with mental retardation have always been, to some degree, prescribed by the outcomes expected of and programs available to people with mental retardation. To the degree that these expectations have changed and that programs have been replaced by a supports paradigm, so, too, has educational programming changed. The education of students with mental retardation has always been at least community-referenced. For example, a 1927 "curriculum for the special class" was titled *Making Citizens of the Mentally Limited* (Whipple, 1927) and is surprisingly contemporary with its emphasis on teaching youth with mental retardation skills to hold jobs and to become productive citizens. Noticeably, however, the early emphasis on community was applied only to individuals with limited support needs, and people with more intense support needs were not considered as candidates for community inclusion. Throughout most of the 20th century, the curriculum of students with mental retardation continued to be community-referenced and what changed was the expectations for and outcomes available to people with mental retardation, including people with more intense support needs. In the late 1970s and early 1980s, the focus for educational programs for most students with mental retardation, though perhaps more for students with extensive or pervasive support needs, switched to being both community-referenced and community-based.

The focus on community-based instruction for students with mental retardation was generated by researchers engaged in the development of educational programs for students with extensive and pervasive support needs, largely through the efforts of Lou Brown and his colleagues at the University of Wisconsin–Madison (see *Additional Readings*). These authors often referred to the students who would benefit from this community-based focus as the lowest intellectually functioning 1% of the school population of a particular age, a grouping that would have included students who were then referred to as having moderate, severe, or profound mental retardation (as well as other subpopulations, including students who were deafblind and students with multiple physical, as well as cognitive, disabilities).

A number of factors contributed to the emergence of community-based instruction as important to students with mental retardation, some that related to student learning characteristics, and some that related to societal changes and changes in expectations for students with mental retardation. Proponents noted that students with cognitive disabilities experienced considerable difficulty with generalizing learning from one environment to another, and, as such, learning needed to occur in ecologically valid settings; that is, learning should occur in settings in which the student might use the particular skill. Similarly, students with mental retardation, by definition, learned fewer skills over the same time period than their peers, making it more important that those skills be functional and that students learn them in environments in which they will be able to successfully use them.

At the same time, the number and type of outcomes that were seen as available for people with more significant disabilities were changing. Among the most visible of such changes was the shift in vocational outcomes that were possible for people with mental retardation from sheltered and congregate options, such as sheltered workshops or vocational activity centers, to community-based competitive employment options made feasible by the advent of supported employment strategies (Wehman, 1981). With the group-home model, by then the preferred living arrangement, the community was becoming more and more the norm for adults with mental retardation, and education needed to reflect that changing norm.

CHARACTERISTICS OF COMMUNITY-REFERENCED PLANNING AND COMMUNITY-BASED INSTRUCTION

Community-referenced planning and **community-based instruction** incorporate several basic characteristics. First, community-referenced planning is ecologically valid. Brown and colleagues (1979) introduced an **ecological inventory** approach to curriculum development that has five basic steps:

1. Select the instructional domain (e.g., vocation, recreation/leisure, independent living, and so forth).

2. Identify current and future environments in this domain in which the student needs to learn skills and knowledge to better enable him or her to succeed.

3. Prioritize the need for instruction in specific subenvironments in each environment.

4. Identify activities within each subenvironment.

5. Task analyze the priority activities into their component skills (Ryndak & Alper, 1996).

So, for example, a student's instructional domain might be vocational, and a student may have expressed a preference to work with animals. The ecological inventory might, then, identify a specific environment (e.g., pet store) and subenvironments within that environment (e.g., stock room, checkout counter, animal cages), prioritize the subenvironments in which the student will most likely function, identify tasks within prioritized subenvironments (e.g., cleaning cages, feeding animals, cleaning windows), and, finally, provide a task analysis for use in teaching each task.

Ryndak and Alper (1996) also pointed out that community-referenced planning is locally referenced. By using an ecological inventory approach, learning tasks are tied to settings in the student's environment and are based on local standards and performance demands. Take, for example, McDonald's restaurants. They are, of course, present in many communities across the United States and, indeed, internationally, but it would be incorrect to assume that one could write a standardized curriculum to teach students skills at McDonald's restaurants because of the variability among even these seemingly homogeneous settings. Franchises vary according to numerous menu items and item size availability, the features of the way that the items are displayed, how condiments are provided, or how the store is set up with regard to restrooms or counters. Some stores fill the drinks behind the counter, others give the customer an empty cup to fill with ice and drinks at a separate drink station. Some stores use wrapped straws available with other condiments, some use straw dispensers, and others have straws distributed by personnel. Some use prepackaged salt or ketchup, others use ketchup dispensers and have salt shakers on the tables. Suffice it to say that just because a student receives instruction in a McDonald's restaurant, there is no guarantee that he or she will be able to function independently in another McDonald's. As such, the specific environment in which the student will function should be the basis for instruction, and planning should be locally referenced.

Other key features of community-referenced planning and community-based instruction are that such activities are chronologically age-appropriate (discussed in Chapter 5) and planning and instructional activities are socially validated. This means that instructional content areas are meaningful to students and family members and that prioritization of environments, subenvironments, and tasks occurs based on stakeholder preferences, values, and interests.

QUALITY EDUCATIONAL SUPPORTS FOR STUDENTS AGES 18–21

Before turning attention to issues raised by perceived conflicts between community-based learning and inclusion and to examining how community-based learning can be implemented within the context of the general curriculum and school reform, it is important to note a unique circumstance in educational services and supports for students with mental retardation that is related to community-based learning: the education of students with mental retardation between the ages of 18 and 21.

The Education for All Handicapped Children Act of 1975 (PL 94-142) required that the state provide a free, appropriate public education (FAPE) to students with disabilities between the ages of 3 and 21 residing within the United States, except when its application to those people would be inconsistent with state law or practice. In most states, students with mental retardation are eligible for services from the public school system after their same-age peers have graduated. High-quality educational services and supports for students in this age group (in the absence of a general curriculum) have characteristics similar to community-based learning characteristics. Wehmeyer, Bolding, Yeager, and Davis (2001) identified seven quality indicators that should form the core of any educational services and supports for students with mental retardation ages 18–21.

Appropriate educational services for students with mental retardation ages 18–21 are provided in an age-appropriate environment allowing for social interaction and promoting community inclusion. Because the typical high school is no longer an age-appropriate environment for students between the ages of 18 and 21, such educational supports need to be provided in environments that are age-appropriate and promote interaction with same-age peers. A number of settings meet these requirements, and the most prevalent is community or junior college. This setting is normative for students in this age range, and community colleges frequently offer unique learning opportunities. Other settings in which quality services have been provided include university and 4-year college campuses, community-based businesses and agencies, or even storefronts in shopping malls or other areas of high public concentration.

However, moving educational services to an age-appropriate setting is only the first step. It is very easy to set up fundamentally segregated programs within age-appropriate settings. This problem is partially offset by another indicator of quality education services, that the majority of students' education by ages 18–21 should be community-based. However, for those times during which the student is on the campus or in a facility, quality services should provide opportunities for inclusive education. Innovative schools have found that one way to ensure inclusion is to make the facility home to a wide array of activities (e.g., neighborhood or school group meetings, blood drives, polling). The emphasis in high-quality programs is to get students into their community and to make the point of service delivery a place in which the community can congregate as well.

High-quality educational services are ecologically valid and community-based. One tenet of community-based instruction was that as students with mental retardation got older, they would receive progressively and proportionally more of their instruction in community-based settings that approximated the environment in which they might live, work, learn, or play as adults. Students ages 18–21 should spend most if not all of their time learning employment-related skills in work settings, living skills in homes, and recreation and leisure skills in the community.

High-quality services are outcomes-oriented. Transition services for students with disabilities need to be outcomes-oriented and include a wide array of outcomes, such as employment, living, postsecondary education, and leisure outcomes. Most such transition-related efforts primarily emphasize employment and residential outcomes. However, high-quality services also need to focus on recreation and leisure outcomes and postsecondary education opportunities. Moreover, personal outcomes are the best indicators of program quality.

Academic instruction in high-quality programs is functional and focused on outcomes. Students at this age continue to have many academic and content-oriented learning needs, and many parents continue to request instruction in academic and content areas. As such, educators must provide this instruction in ways that promote functional skills in inclusive settings. Providing services in a college setting, particularly in community and junior colleges, equals opportunities to gain access to more basic and sometimes remedial classes with same-age peers.

High-quality services emphasize person-centered planning and active family involvement. The educational process for students must be individualized and have active participation from a range of key stakeholders.

High-quality services involve active participation of adult service providers in planning and implementation. Another component of high-quality services involves interagency collaboration in planning, particularly those agencies serving the student. This partnership is often difficult to form because of issues regarding financial liability. High-quality supports for students ages 18–21 with mental retardation have active involvement from service agencies and community businesses in which students may someday work or become customers.

High-quality services implement best practices in transition. This rather catch-all indicator simply communicates that educational services for students ages 18–21 with mental retardation are, at their core, transition-oriented, and the wealth of best practice strategies associated with effective transition services (e.g., job shadowing, job sampling, leisure training) should be present in services for students ages 18–21 as well.

Community-Based Instruction and Inclusion

In 1991, Brown and colleagues wrote about the 0% Club and the 100% Club as representing two diverse opinions about how much time students with severe intellectual disabilities should spend in the general education classroom. The 0% Club included those people who believed that students with severe intellectual disabilities should not spend any time in the general education classroom, whereas the 100% Club represented those people who believed that students should spend every moment of their school day in the general classroom.

Neither the 0% Club nor the 100% Club probably have many, if any, members. The contrast is useful, however, to illustrate the potential conflict between the value of inclusive classrooms and the need to address functional life-skills instructional needs. In practice, however, most teachers working with students with mental retardation seem to value both inclusion and community-based instruction as confirmed by Agran, Snow, and Swaner (1999). However, some researchers have called for an end to community-based instruction because of the need for inclusion (Tashie, Jorgensen, Shapiro-Barnard, Martin, & Schuh, 1996), and in many districts, the result of implementing an inclusion program was the dismantling or demise of any community-based instruction.

Community-based instruction did not seem any more resilient for a variety of reasons. At a programming level, the two approaches seem mutually incompatible. When schools began to implement inclusive practices, it was natural to focus on staying in the general classroom at the expense of community-based instruction, even though school practitioners were not opposed to community-based instruction. In addition, community-based instruction can be difficult to implement because it requires more intensive personnel allocations, complex transportation arrangements, and consideration of liability and other legal issues related to moving instruction from the classroom to the community. This complexity undoubtedly contributed to its abandonment in the name of inclusion.

A third factor is that community-based instruction strategies were developed to meet the needs of students with the most intense support needs and remained best practice only within that population. Inclusion, although it emerged as an issue first for students with more extensive and pervasive support needs, was applied as a principle and value to a wider array of students. Although there is really no way to determine, community-based instruction was probably never widely implemented with students requiring less intense support. The cost, liability, and difficulty of providing community-based instruction has ensured that it didn't extend to the education of many students.

Is community-based instruction relevant only for youth with mental retardation who have extensive and pervasive support needs? If students can generalize from a simulated learning situation, it is more efficient to provide instruction in simulated, school-based settings, even for instruction in life skills. If this is the case, how can schools resolve the impasse between the value of (and the relative ease of delivery associated with) inclusion and the need of some students for community-based learning?

The answer to this conundrum is to move the discussion from the emphasis on where a student receives his or her education to an emphasis on what the education program of all students contains. In so doing, the educational needs of students with mental retardation can be considered within the context of school reform efforts that emphasize community-based instruction. The degree to which students with mental retardation learn in the community can then be determined through the general curriculum, which outlines the degree to which *all* students learn in the community.

SCHOOL REFORM, ACCESS TO THE GENERAL CURRICULUM, AND COMMUNITY-BASED LEARNING

A number of school reform models emphasize the importance of community-based instruction in the education of all students. Newmann and Wehlage (1995) described standards for *authentic pedagogy*, identified in Table 14.1. These standards describe high-quality instruction to promote authentic learning. Although this model has been applied primarily to learning in social sciences and mathematics, one of the criteria for authentic pedagogy is its value beyond school. When assessing value beyond school, Newmann and Wehlage looked for evidence that the instructional task asks students to address a concept, problem, or issue that is similar to one that they have encountered or are likely to encounter in life beyond the classroom. They also looked for evidence that the task asks students to communicate their knowledge, present a product or performance, or take some action for an audience beyond the teacher, classroom, or school building. Ecological validity and community-referenced instruction are clear values in such assessment standards.

Other school reform efforts emphasize community-based learning. School reform efforts based on Howard Gardner's (1993) multiple intelligences (MI) theory emphasized, for example, a need for a "school–community broker" role, a person who searches for educational opportunities for students within the wider community. In one school in which the school day had been designed with the MI theory in mind, students spent half of their school day studying traditional subjects through project-oriented learning activities and then spent the second half of the day in the community for future contextual

Table 14.1. Standards for instruction in authentic pedagogy

Domain	Standard
Construction of knowledge	Instruction involves students in manipulating information and ideas by synthesizing, generalizing, explaining, hypothesizing, or arriving at conclusions that produce new meaning and understanding for them.
Disciplined inquiry	Instruction addresses central ideas of a topic or discipline with enough thoroughness to explore connections and relationships and to produce relatively complex understandings.
	Students engage in extended conversational exchanges with the teacher and/or their peers about subject matter in a way that builds an improved and shared understanding of ideas or topics.
Value beyond school	Students make connections between substantive knowledge and either public problems or personal experiences.

From Newmann, F.M., & Wehlage, G.G. (1995). *Successful school restructuring* (p. 4). Madison: Wisconsin Center for Education Research; adapted by permission.

exploration and learning. These learning experiences are different from the typical field trip because students return to the same location many times over the course of a school year to complete projects (e.g., work on sculpture at a local art museum, study the life cycle of butterflies at the zoological park) (Gardner, 1993). Gardner's emphasis on community-referenced planning and community-based learning is based on his theory of how knowledge about cognitive development and learning must drive instructional activities.

When schools commit to community-referenced and community-based learning, a larger number of resources are available for students with mental retardation to learn in the community, and that experience becomes the normative experience, not the exception. The typical classroom is changed to include the community, not just the school classroom. Decisions about the amount of time that students spend receiving instruction in the community are then made based on student proximity to graduation or school departure and future plans for education or employment, as well as the issue of generalization. A senior without a disability whose career objective relates to a specific vocational area may spend much of his or her school day in the community learning the knowledge and skills that he or she needs to become gainfully employed after graduation. A student who is entering college the following year may spend more learning time in library settings that not only provide resources for completing high school courses but also enable him or her to learn important study and writing skills. In such a circumstance, a student with mental retardation receiving his or her education in the community would not encounter an inclusion–community dichotomy.

The decision, then, to provide community-based instruction becomes a function of different circumstances and variables and, like all decisions about instruction, is a function of the student's curricular content and unique learning needs. Eligibility for most community-based instruction programs is often based on a student's diagnosis, and decisions about content are made outside of the general curriculum and, essentially, constitute an alternative curriculum. However, these school reform models place emphasis on community-referenced planning and community-based instruction as necessary to meet the unique learning needs of most, if not all, students, regardless of disability.

SUMMARY

Considerable progress has been made in educating students with mental retardation in the community. The 1992 AAMR definition of mental retardation defined *supports* as leading toward community inclusion and participation (Luckasson et al., 1992). There is a continuing need to ensure that the education programs of students with mental retardation are planned with the community in mind (community-referenced) and that instruction occurs in that community so as to ensure generalization. Community-based instruction should not, however, be adopted at the expense of students being included, nor should the drive for inclusion preclude community-based instruction. Numerous school reform models emphasize community-referenced planning and community-based learning for all students. When students turn 18 and are still receiving educational supports, such supports need to continue to be community based, focused on personal outcomes, and designed to provide optimal opportunities for social and community inclusion.

ADDITIONAL READINGS

Normalization

Wolfensberger, W. (1972). *The principle of normalization.* Toronto: National Institute on Mental Retardation.

Community-Based Instruction

Baumgart, D., Brown, L., Pumpian, I., Nisbet, J., Ford, A., Sweet, M., Messina, R., & Schroeder, J. (1982). Principle of partial participation and individualized adaptations in educational programs for severely handicapped students. *Journal of The Association for Persons with Severe Handicaps, 7,* 17–27.

Brown, L., Branston-McClean, M.B., Baumgart, D., Vincent, L., Falvey, M., & Schroeder, J. (1979). Using the characteristics of current and subsequent least restrictive environments in the development of curricular content for severely handicapped students. *AAESPH Review, 4,* 407–424.

Brown, L., Nisbet, J., Ford, A., Sweet, M., Shiraga, B., York, J., & Loomis, R. (1983). The critical need for nonschool instruction in educational programs for severely handicapped students. *Journal of The Association for Persons with Severe Handicaps, 8,* 71–77.

Brown, L., Schwarz, P., Udvari-Solner, A., Kampschroer, E.F., Johnson, F., Jorgensen, J., & Gruenewald, L. (1991). How much time should students with severe intellectual disabilities spend in regular education classrooms and elsewhere? *Journal of The Association for Persons with Severe Handicaps, 16,* 39–47.

Falvey, M.A. (1989). *Community-based curriculum: Instructional strategies for students with severe handicaps* (2nd ed.). Baltimore: Paul H. Brookes Publishing Co.

Ferguson, D.L., & Baumgart, D. (1991). Partial participation revisited. *Journal of The Association for Persons with Severe Handicaps, 16,* 218–227.

CHAPTER OBJECTIVES

1. Define *self-determination*, and summarize its historical underpinnings.
2. Describe a functional theory of self-determination, including component elements of self-determined behavior on which to base instruction and describe development.
3. Discuss the importance of self-determination in the education of students with mental retardation and summarize research on self-determination and mental retardation.
4. Describe a model of teaching to enable students with mental retardation to become self-regulated problem solvers.
5. Identify instructional methods and strategies to promote student progress in the general curriculum.

KEY TERMS

Self-determination
Self-governance
Determinism
Causal agency
Interdependence
Quality of life
Component elements
Choice making

Problem solving
Decision making
Goal setting and
  attainment
Self-advocacy
Self-awareness and
  self-knowledge

15

Self-Determination

Curriculum Augmentation and Student Involvement

RODNEY LEARNS NOT TO MAKE
A MOVE UNTIL HE IS TOLD.

During the 1990s, promoting **self-determination** became recommended practice in the education of youth with disabilities, particularly as it pertains to the delivery of transition services. Although learning discrete skills related to goal setting or problem solving is still important, there is a need to broaden the efforts to promote and enhance self-determination for all students with (and without) disabilities. It is a lifelong focus that shifts from choice, self-awareness, and exploration to autonomy and self-sufficiency. More than just enabling students to become more self-sufficient adults, promoting self-determination is one way to augment the curriculum to provide students with specific strategies (e.g., self-monitoring skills, self-evaluation skills) that enable them to better succeed within the general curriculum. Moreover, the acquisition of skills and knowledge related to becoming more self-determined (e.g., goal-setting skills, problem-solving skills, decision-making skills, leadership skills) is already embedded in the general curriculum and thus provides logical entry points for students with mental retardation to gain access to the general curriculum. This chapter describes the self-determination construct, discusses the emergence of the construct within the field of education and its importance to students with mental retardation, and examines ways in which self-determination provides a point of entry for gaining access to the general curriculum as well as promoting self-regulation and student-directed learning skills that can augment the general curriculum.

SELF-DETERMINATION

The self-determination construct has it historical roots in political science and philosophy dating from the 17th century. The most common use of the term is as a political/sociocultural term referring to the rights of peoples to self-governance. The 20th-century value for national self-determination as a principle of international justice emerged from twin 18th-century notions that the people are sovereign and are to be thought of as a nation. Through the 19th century, the belief that a people should have the right to determine their own government gained wide acceptance. This political meaning of the construct has been carried over into sociocultural contexts in which the right to self-governance is used in reference to people or peoples who are not citizens of a country but who share a common characteristic or circumstance that, for whatever reason, has resulted in unequal treatment or access. There are numerous examples of this use. One day, for example, during the African American holiday Kwanzaa is devoted to self-determination.

Historically, then, self-determination refers to **self-governance.** *Self-governing* means 1) exercising control or rule over oneself or 2) having the right or power of self-government (Urdang, 1984). This theme of self-governance can be applied to individuals. Theories of personal self-determination are theories of how or why people become self-governing and exert control or rule over their lives.

Self-Determination in Psychology

The construct of self-determination first emerged within psychology in the 1930s and 1940s when personality psychology emerged as a discipline distinct from general psychology and philosophy. For example, Angyal (1941) proposed that an essential feature of a living organism is its autonomy, in which *autonomous* means self-governing or governed from inside. According to Angyal, an organism "lives in a world in which things happen according to laws which are heteronomous (e.g., governed from outside) from the point of view of the organism" (p. 33). Angyal argued that the science of personality is, in essence, the study of two essential components or determinants to behavior, autonomous determination (or self-determination) and heteronomous determination ("other" determination).

Later use of the construct in psychology focused on the field of motivation. Deci and colleagues (Deci, 1992; Deci & Chandler, 1986; Deci & Ryan, 1985) proposed a theory of intrinsic motivation that incorporates a central role for self-determination. Deci summarized self-determination theory as

> [D]istinguish[ing] between the motivational dynamics underlying activities that people do freely and those that they feel coerced or pressured to do. To be self-determining means to engage in an activity with a full sense of wanting, choosing, and personal endorsement. When self-determined, people are acting in accord with, or expressing, themselves. (1992, p. 44)

Within self-determination theory, Deci and Ryan defined *self-determination* as the following:

> The capacity to choose and to have those choices, rather than reinforcement contingencies, drives, or any other forces or pressures, to be the determinants of one's actions. But self-determination is *more than a capacity, it is also a need.* We have posited a basic, innate propensity to be self-determining that leads organisms to engage in interesting behaviors. (1985, p. 38, italics added)

Self-Determination and Determinism

The meaning of the word *determination* in *self-determination* is synonymous with *determinant,* defined as "an event or antecedent condition that in some way *causes* an event" (Wolman, 1973, p. 97, emphasis added). The psychological inquiry into self-determination looks at determinants of human behavior (e.g., causes of human behavior), including physiological, structural, environmental, and/or organismic factors. This is derived from the philosophical doctrine of *determinism,* the "doctrine that all phenomena, including behavior, are effects of preceding causes" (Wolman, 1973, p. 97). Although an absolute form of determinism suggests that the future of the world (or an organism) is fixed in one unavoidable pattern or direction (Weatherford, 1991), Bandura noted that in discussions of human agency and personal causation, references to the term *determinism* imply the "production of effects by events, rather than the doctrinal sense meaning that actions are completely determined by a prior sequence of causes independent of the individual" (1997, p. 7).

Whether discussing self-determination as a personal construct related to determinism or as a national or political construct pertaining to self-governance, one thing is consistent. Self-determination is always opposed to "other" determination. Mithaug noted that self-determination always has a social context and stated that "this focus on the social nature of the concept directs our attention to the interaction between a person's capacity to choose and act and the social environment that mediates opportunities for those choices and actions" (1998, p. 42). Understanding that both self-determination and mental retardation exist within the context of social interaction has vital consequences for students with mental retardation. Promoting self-determination is about, in essence, making an impact on the individual's capacity (and opportunity) to act within his or her environment.

Self-Determination as Empowerment

Inherent in the initial attention to the topic of self-determination within the field of special education was its association, primarily by disability advocates and policy makers, with *empowerment*. In a speech at the 1989 National Conference on Self-Determination, an event organized by the U.S. Department of Education's Office of Special Education Programs (OSEP), Robert Williams effectively captured this link between self-determination and empowerment, stating,

> Without being afforded the right and opportunity to make choices in our lives, we will never obtain full, first class American citizenship. So we do not have to be told what self-determination means. We already know that it is just another word for freedom. We already know that self-determination is just another word for describing a life filled with rising expectations, dignity, responsibility, and opportunity. That it is just another word for having the chance to live the American Dream. (Williams, 1989, p. 16)

It is evident from Williams's remarks that for many people in the disability community, the use of the term *self-determination* attests to their legitimate demand for the right to personal self-governance, not just in the internal, psychological sense but in the social, political sense as well.

Self-Determination in Education

In the early 1990s, OSEP funded research and model development activities to enhance the self-determination of children and youth with disabilities through the education system (Ward & Kohler, 1996) and to promote active student involvement in educational planning and decision making (Wehmeyer & Sands, 1998). This initiative emerged as a response to studies showing that important adult outcomes, such as employment, independent living, and community inclusion, were not being achieved by young people with disabilities (Chadsey-Rusch, Rusch, & O'Reilly, 1991), despite 15 years of special education law and practice. Policy makers suggested that one of the reasons that students with disabilities were not succeeding once they left school was that the educational process had not adequately prepared them to become self-determined young people. Martin, Marshall, Maxson, and Jerman put it this way:

> If students floated in life jackets for 12 years, would they be expected to swim if the jackets were suddenly jerked away? Probably not. The situation is similar for students receiving special education. All too often these students are not taught how to self-manage their own lives before they are thrust into the cold water of postschool reality. (1993, p. 3)

As a result of this federal focus, numerous instructional and assessment methods, materials, and strategies are available that enable teachers to promote student self-determination (Field, Martin, Miller, Ward, & Wehmeyer, 1998; Wehmeyer, Agran, & Hughes, 1998), and research indicates that teachers working with students with disabilities acknowledge the importance of promoting self-determination for students with disabilities (Wehmeyer, Agran, & Hughes, 2000). Efforts in this area, focused across the range of the disability categories in the IDEA Amendments of 1997 (PL 105-17), have focused on identifying education's role in promoting self-determination (Field et al., 1998), including efforts focused on mental retardation (Wehmeyer, 2001).

A FUNCTIONAL MODEL OF SELF-DETERMINATION

Most definitions of self-determination in the educational literature focus on the specific behaviors or actions in which people engage that, in turn, enable them to exert control over their lives. Sands and Wehmeyer suggested, however, that one cannot define self-determination as a set of skills or behaviors but instead must look at the function of that behavior in the person's life (Sands & Wehmeyer, 1996; Wehmeyer 1996a, 1998). People who are self-determined act in ways that enable them to achieve desired goals and enhance their quality of life. Virtually any action or behavior can be applied to achieve that end. Reflecting this emphasis, Wehmeyer defined *self-determination* as "acting as the primary causal agent in one's life and making choices and decisions regarding one's quality of life free from undue external influence or interference" (1996a, p. 24). Broadly defined, *causal agency* implies that it is the individual who makes or causes things to happen in his or her life. Self-determined people act as the agent in their lives. They act with intent to shape their futures and their destiny.

We have framed causal agency and self-determination within the concept of quality of life. Quality of life is a complex construct that has gained increasing importance as a principle in human services. Schalock (1996) suggested that quality of life is best viewed as an organizing concept to guide policy and practice in order to improve the life conditions of all people and proposed that quality of life is composed of a number of core principles and dimensions. One of those core dimensions of quality of life is self-determination.

Self-determination emerges across the life span as children and adolescents learn skills and develop attitudes that enable them to become causal agents in their own lives. These attitudes and abilities are the component elements of self-determination, and this level of the theoretical framework drives instructional activities. As they acquire these component elements, individuals become increasingly self-determined. Table 15.1 lists these elements.

A complete discussion of each of these component elements is not feasible within the context of this chapter (see Wehmeyer, Agran, & Hughes, 1998); however, describ-

Table 15.1. Elements of self-determined behavior

Choice-making skills
Decision-making skills
Problem-solving skills
Goal-setting and attainment skills
Self-management and self-regulation skills
Self-advocacy and leadership skills
Perceptions of control and efficacy
Self-awareness
Self-knowledge

ing the component elements is important for two reasons. First, instruction occurs at this level. That is, instructional strategies, methods, materials, and supports enable educators to teach self-determination by enhancing students' capacity in each of these areas. Wehmeyer and colleagues (1998) identified numerous methods, materials, and supports to promote these component elements. Second, each of these component elements has a unique developmental course or is acquired through specific learning experiences. By describing the development of each of these component elements, we can describe the development of self-determination (Doll, Sands, Wehmeyer, & Palmer, 1996; Wehmeyer, Sands, Doll, & Palmer, 1997). The development and acquisition of these component elements is lifelong and begins when children are very young. Some elements have greater applicability for secondary education and transition, whereas others focus more on elementary years. Promoting self-determination as an educational outcome requires not only a purposeful instructional program but also one that coordinates learning experiences across the span of a student's educational experience.

RESEARCH IN SELF-DETERMINATION AND MENTAL RETARDATION

Until the early 1990s, there was, literally, no research on self-determination and people with mental retardation, primarily because most people assumed people with mental retardation could not become self-determined. Since then, a body of research has emerged, which is summarized in this section.

How Self-Determined Are People with Mental Retardation?

Wehmeyer and Metzler (1995) examined the self-determination of more than 4,500 adults with mental retardation by analyzing data from a national survey of the independence, productivity, and inclusion of Americans with developmental disabilities. From this sample, only 33% of respondents indicated that they had a choice regarding where they currently lived; 12% had a voice in hiring the staff or attendant who worked with them; 21% chose, either with or without assistance, their roommate; 44% chose their job or day activity; 26% indicated they had the opportunity to pay their own bills; and 42% indicated they did some banking on their own. The overall picture provided by this study suggested that too many people with mental retardation lack opportunities to control their lives and their destinies. Wehmeyer, Kelchner, and Richards (1995, 1996) examined the self-determination of 408 adults with mental retardation using an expansion of the survey analyzed by Wehmeyer and Metzler. They confirmed the findings from the previous study, indicating that people with mental retardation experience limited self-determination.

Impact of Environment on Self-Determination

Knowing whether people with mental retardation are self-determined may be less important than knowing how the environments in which they live, learn, work, and play have an impact on self-determination. Research to explore the role of environment in self-determination is only now emerging, particularly as it pertains to people with intellectual disability. Wehmeyer and colleagues (1995) examined the degree to which individuals had control over and choice in major domains in their lives (e.g., home/family living, employment, recreation and leisure, money management). Respondents who lived independently or with family members were more self-determined than respondents who lived in group homes and those who lived in large, congregate settings were the least self-determined.

Tossebro (1995) studied the relationship between self-determination and environment for 591 people with intellectual disability using staff ratings of the degree of freedom a person had to make decisions and to influence day-to-day activities in his or her life and then correlated these ratings with living unit size. Self-determination was significantly positively related to unit size for residences with 1–5 residents and was negatively related to unit size for residences with 6–16 residents. Thus, as with the Wehmeyer et al. (1995) study, self-determination was fostered by smaller, more homelike residences. Other studies have examined the impact of environment on component elements of self-determination, particularly choice making. Stancliffe (1997) and colleagues (Stancliffe & Abery, 1997; Stancliffe & Wehmeyer, 1995) have shown that environmental factors influence the amount of choice available to people with intellectual disability, in each case with more restrictive settings that minimize choice-making opportunities.

Stancliffe, Abery, and Smith (2000) reported findings from a study that examined the personal control exercised by 74 adults with mental retardation who lived in community-based settings. These authors found that personal characteristics (e.g., adaptive behavior, challenging behaviors), self-determination skills, and environmental factors (e.g., residential size, type of funding stream, community living situation) all contributed to personal control. Trends from this study supported previous research, emphasizing that living environments are more likely to support self-determination when they have fewer residents and employ flexible practices and funding mechanisms.

Wehmeyer and Bolding (1999) conducted a matched-samples study to examine the role of environment on self-determination independent of the contribution of level of intelligence, which has often been confounded with living environments (e.g., people with more significant disabilities are more likely to live or work in more restrictive environments). For the sample, 273 individuals with mental retardation were recruited on the basis of whether they worked or lived in one of three environments hypothesized to limit or promote self-determination: 1) a noncongregate, community-based (e.g., independent living, competitive employment) environment; 2) a congregate, community-based (e.g., group home, sheltered employment) environment; or 3) a congregate, non–community-based (e.g., institution, work activity program) environment. Participants in each environmental group were matched with one other person in each other group on the basis of IQ score (within 5 points), and, when possible, by age and gender. This resulted in 91 matched triplets, in which individuals differed only according to the environment in which they lived or worked. Data analysis indicated that there were significant differences in level of self-determination, autonomy, life satisfaction, and opportunities to make choices based on environment, with people who lived or worked in noncongregate, community-based settings having significantly more adaptive levels on each measure.

In a follow-up to that 1999 study, Wehmeyer and Bolding (2001) measured the self-determination of individuals with mental retardation both before and after they moved from a more restrictive to less restrictive working or living environment. There were significant changes in scores on measures of self-determination, goal setting, and choice making as a function of this move, further supporting the fact that it is, in many cases, the environment that limits self-determination, and that the limitation is not a function of the individual's level of support needs.

Given these findings, it is important to determine whether self-determination is important to people with mental retardation. Wehmeyer and Schwartz (1998) measured the self-determination of 50 adults with mental retardation residing in group homes and also collected data on individual quality of life. Higher self-determination scores were predictive of more positive quality-of-life scores. Wehmeyer and Schwartz (1997) measured the self-determination of adolescents with mental retardation (in addition to adolescents with learning disabilities) and found that 1 year after graduation from high school, students who were more self-determined had achieved more favorable adult outcomes, particularly in securing paid employment. In addition, Sands, Spencer, Gliner, and Swaim (1999) found that student self-determination was one predictor of active student involvement in educational planning and decision making.

The existing research related to self-determination and mental retardation suggests that greater self-determination contributes to more active involvement in educational planning and decision making for youth with mental retardation, is predictive of more positive adult outcomes when these young people exit school, and results in a higher quality of life for adults with mental retardation. Yet, despite these benefits, it appears that most adults with mental retardation are not self-determined and have limited opportunities to assume greater control over their lives, and that although teachers value self-determination, most students with mental retardation are not receiving targeted instruction to enhance this outcome.

PROMOTING SELF-DETERMINATION AND ACCESS TO THE GENERAL CURRICULUM

Efforts to promote or enhance self-determination involve activities across three domains: capacity enhancement, the provision of opportunities to exert control, and the design and implementation of accommodations and supports. The latter, which has been emphasized throughout the text, involves the design of environmental and other accommodations that enable people with mental retardation to exert greater control over their lives and the use of technological and nontechnological supports to maximize control. For example, in the early elementary years, it is important to build into the school day frequent opportunities for students to express preferences and make choices and to allow students to self-manage some aspects of their learning. One means of achieving this would be to make learning materials (e.g., glue, crayons) available for students to obtain (and return) independently. In a circumstance in which a student may not be able to reach the trays or holding bins because he or she cannot reach them or physically control his or her movement from one place to another, an accommodation might be to lower the trays for easier access for a student using a wheelchair or to make them more portable (in a rolling tray) for a student with a motor disorder such as cerebral palsy.

Technology plays an increasingly important role in providing such accommodations. For example, a student with mental retardation may never learn math skills sufficient to allow him to maintain his own checkbook but may be able to learn a simple computer software program that balances a checkbook and develops a budget when check amounts are entered. Also, friends and family can provide needed accommodations that enable a student to maximize his or her involvement. A student may not be able to make independent medical decisions but could learn some of the steps involved, including identifying some options for consideration and choosing the option that he or she prefers. Key people in the person's life could accommodate for limited decision making by selecting the steps the person can assume independently, those in which the student needs some assistance, and those that might need to be completed by the family member or friend.

Providing opportunities for students to exert control, make choices, participate in decisions, and self-advocate is as important as teaching specific skills, and teachers should seek such opportunities. Active involvement in educational planning and decision making, as discussed in Chapter 5, is an excellent context in which to practice and learn skills related to self-determination and to build beliefs about oneself and one's capacity to succeed. Promoting self-determination provides access to the general curriculum in two ways. First, state and local standards frequently include goals and objectives that pertain to component elements of self-determined behavior. For example, the Texas Essential Knowledge and Skills standards require students to learn effective problem-solving, decision-making, or goal-setting skills. The sixth-grade social studies standards state:

> (6.23) *Social studies skills.* The student uses problem-solving and decision-making skills, working independently and with others, in a variety of settings. The student is expected to:
>
> A) use a problem-solving process to identify a problem, gather information, list and consider options, consider advantages and disadvantages, choose and implement a solution, and evaluate the effectiveness of the solution; and
>
> B) use a decision-making process to identify a situation that requires a decision, gather information, identify options, predict consequences, and take action to implement a decision. (Texas Education Agency, 1996)

These performance goals represent just a few across numerous core areas in virtually every set of state-adopted standards in which students are expected to learn and apply effective problem-solving and decision-making processes. By identifying areas in the general curriculum in which all students are expected to learn skills and knowledge related to the component elements of self-determined behavior, teachers can promote self-determination and progress in the general curriculum. The following sections summarize instruction in the component elements across a student's educational experience, from preschool and elementary school through secondary education.

Choice Making

Making a choice is, quite simply, the communication of a preference, and instruction in choice making focuses on one or both of these elements, either the identification of a preference or the communication of that preference. Except in unique circumstances, there is usually no need to teach choice making, although there may be a need to enable or teach children who have limitations in communication new, alternative, or more appropriate ways to indicate their preferences. By and large, educational efforts should be aimed at using choice-making opportunities to provide experiences of control and to teach students that not all options are available to them and that options are constrained for all people. Brown, Appel, Corsi, and Wenig (1993) suggested seven types of choices that can be infused in instructional activities: 1) choosing within an activity, 2) choosing among two or more activities, 3) deciding when to do an activity, 4) selecting the person with whom to participate in an activity, 5) deciding where to do an activity, 6) refusing to participate in a planned activity, and 7) choosing to end an activity at a self-selected time.

Problem Solving

A *problem* is "a task whose solution is not immediately perceived" (Beyth-Marom, Fischhoff, Jacobs Quadrel, & Furby, 1991, p. 21). Instruction in problem solving typically includes three focal points: 1) problem identification, 2) problem explication and analysis, and 3) problem resolution. Instruction should occur within environments that emphasize the student's capability to solve problems, promote open inquiry and exploration, and encourage generalization. Teachers should serve as role models by verbalizing the problem-solving steps used on a day-to-day basis and should make sure that students are provided with adequate support to successfully solve problems.

Decision Making

Making a decision is a process of selecting or coming to a judgment about which solution is best given one's circumstances, values, priorities, and needs. Beyth-Marom and colleagues (1991) suggested that most models of decision making incorporate the following steps: 1) listing relevant action alternatives; 2) identifying consequences of those actions; 3) assessing the probability of each consequence occurring (if the action were undertaken); 4) establishing the relative importance (value or utility) of each consequence; and 5) integrating these values and probabilities to identify the most attractive course of action. Baron and Brown proposed that "deficient decision-making is a serious problem throughout society at large and a problem that needs addressing in childhood or adolescence" (1991, p. 6). Students need to learn how to define the issue or problem about which a specific decision is to be made, collect information about their specific situation, and use this information to identify options for consideration. Once these options are clarified, students need to learn to identify and evaluate the consequences and outcomes of actions based on the various options. When those consequences have been detailed, choice-making skills can be applied to select a specific alternative. Finally, students must implement this plan of action. Although emphasis on choice making should occur early in a student's educational career, decision-making skills are probably better addressed at the secondary level.

Goal Setting and Attainment

To become the causal agent in his or her life, a person needs to learn the skills necessary to plan, set, and achieve goals. Educational efforts to promote goal-setting and attainment skills should focus on the identification and enunciation of specific goals, the development of objectives and tasks to achieve these goals, and the actions necessary to achieve a desired outcome. The educational planning and decision-making process is an enterprise that revolves around goal setting, implementation, and evaluation. The involvement of students in this process, across all grades, is a good way to promote goal-setting and attainment skills. Teachers and parents can model effective skills such as identifying short- and long-term goals, describing objectives, implementing plans based on these goals and objectives, and reevaluating and refining the plans.

Self-Management and Self-Regulation Skills

The definitional framework of self-determined behavior identified such actions as self-regulated. Self-regulated behaviors include self-monitoring, self-evaluation, self-instruction, and self-reinforcement. These strategies are discussed in Chapter 4 as illustrations of augmenting the curriculum.

Self-Advocacy and Leadership Skills

Self-advocacy skills are those skills individuals need to advocate on their own behalf. To advocate means to speak up or defend a cause or person. By definition, instruction to promote self-advocacy focuses on two common threads—how to advocate and what to advocate. Elementary-age students can begin to learn basic self-advocacy skills, but most instructional emphasis in this area will apply during secondary education. One particularly important area in which students with disabilities should receive instruction involves the education and transition process itself and rights (and responsibilities) within that system. For many students with disabilities, school is a place they are forced to go to do things that someone else decides for them. It is little wonder that motivation is a problem!

Students who are approaching transition-age can be taught about their rights under the IDEA Amendments of 1997 and about the purpose and process involved in transition decision making. Other topics that could become the cause for which students need to advocate on their own behalf include the adult services system (disability and general), basic civil and legal rights of citizenship, and specific civil and legal protections available to people with disabilities (e.g., the Americans with Disabilities Act of 1990 [PL 101-336]). Such instructional efforts necessarily deal with both rights and responsibilities.

The curricular strategies for teaching how to advocate include instructional emphasis on how to be assertive but not aggressive; how to communicate effectively in one-to-one and small- and large-group situations; how to negotiate, compromise, and use persuasion; how to be an effective listener; and how to navigate systems and bureaucracies. It is evident that each of these is closely tied to the acquisition and emergence of other self-determination skills. For example, a reliable understanding of one's strengths and weaknesses is an important component if one is to actually use strategies such as negotiation and compromise to achieve an outcome. Likewise, students need to be able to link such advocacy to specific goals and incorporate it into the problem-solving or decision-making process.

Perceptions of Control and Efficacy

The final component elements (perceptions of control and efficacy, self-awareness, and self-knowledge) of self-determined behavior focus not on skill development but on the attitudes, perceptions, and beliefs that enable individuals to act in a psychologically empowered or self-realizing manner. If a person is to act in or on a given situation, it is important for that person to believe that he or she has control over outcomes that are important to his or her life. The role of educators in promoting internal perceptions of control, as well as adaptive efficacy and outcome expectations, positive self-awareness, and realistic self-knowledge, is more complex than just providing adequate instructional experiences. Positive perceptions of control and efficacy emerge as children make choices about things that they do every day (e.g., selecting clothing) and as these choices are honored and supported. In addition, an educational program that emphasizes problem solving, choice and decision making, goal setting, and attainment skills using student-directed learning activities provides ample opportunities for students to learn that they have control over reinforcers and outcomes that are important to them.

It is particularly important to consider the learning environment and to evaluate its effect on student perceptions of control. Teachers who use an overly controlling style or whose classrooms are rigidly structured limit the development of positive perceptions of control. This does not mean that classrooms must become chaotic; allowing greater control is not the same as relinquishing all control and abolishing rules and regulations (Deci & Chandler, 1986). Instead, classrooms can be structured such that students can perform more actions for themselves, such as obtaining their own instructional materials.

Self-Awareness and Self-Knowledge

For one to act in a self-realizing manner, one must possess a basic understanding of one's strengths, weaknesses, abilities, and limitations as well as knowledge about how to utilize these unique attributions to improve one's quality of life. Students learn this, as do all people, through their own interpretation of events and experiences. This process is not one of pure introspection, however, and does not focus exclusively or even primarily on an understanding of limitations. In many cases, students with mental retardation are quite able and more willing to identify what they do poorly than what they do well. The specter of having a disability, as pictured in disease or deficit models, hovers over any circumstance, and students dwell more on what they are unable to accomplish than what they can achieve. Because special education has been essentially remediative in nature, this is not surprising. Adopting a functional definition of mental retardation necessitates a switch in focus from deficit and remediation to capacity and efficacy.

SELF-DETERMINATION AS CURRICULUM AUGMENTATION

In addition to addressing the component elements identified in Table 15.1 when they occur in the general curriculum, enabling young people with and without disabilities to become self-regulated problems solvers and goal setters is an effective tool for augmenting the general curriculum. Wehmeyer and colleagues (Mithaug, Wehmeyer, Agran, Martin, & Palmer, 1998; Wehmeyer, Palmer, Agran, Mithaug, & Martin, 2000) developed a model of teaching that enables teachers to, in essence, teach students to teach themselves. Joyce and Weil defined a model of teaching as "a plan or pattern that can be used to shape curriculums (long term courses of study), to design instructional materials, and to guide instruction in the classroom and other settings" (1980, p. 1). Such models are derived from theories about human behavior, learning, or cognition, and effective teachers employ multiple models of teaching, taking into account the unique characteristics of the learner and types of learning. We have proposed a model of teaching, called the *Self-Determined Learning Model of Instruction*, that is derived from an earlier instructional model, the *Adaptability Instruction Model* promoted by Mithaug, Martin, and Agran (1987) and Mithaug, Martin, Agran, and Rusch (1988). It incorporates principles of self-determination and self-regulated learning.

SELF-DETERMINED LEARNING MODEL OF INSTRUCTION

Implementation of the self-determined learning model of instruction consists of a three-phase instructional process depicted in Figures 15.1, 15.2, and 15.3. Each instructional phase presents a problem to be solved by the student. The student solves each problem by posing and answering a series of four *Student Questions* per phase that students learn, modify to make their own, and apply to reach self-selected goals. Each question is linked to a set of *Teacher Objectives*. Each instructional phase includes a list of *Educational Supports* identified that teachers can use to enable students to self-direct learning. In each phase, the student is the primary agent for choices, decisions, and actions, even when actions are teacher-directed.

The *Student Questions* in the model are constructed to direct the student through a problem-solving sequence in each phase. The solutions to the problems in each phase lead to the problem-solving sequence in the next phase. Their construction was based on theory in the problem-solving and self-regulation literature that suggests that any person must follow a means–ends problem-solving sequence for actions to produce results that satisfy that individual's needs and interests. In the model, students are taught to solve a sequence of problems to construct a means–ends chain—a causal sequence—that moves them from where they are (i.e., not having their needs and interests satisfied) to where they want to be (i.e., a goal state of having their needs and interests satisfied) by having students answer the questions that connect their needs and interests to their actions and results via goals and plans.

To answer the four questions in this sequence, students must regulate their own problem solving by setting goals to meet needs, constructing plans to meet goals, and adjusting actions to complete plans. Thus, each instructional phase poses a problem the student must solve (e.g., "What is my goal?" "What is my plan?" "What have I learned?") by, in turn, solving a series of problems posed by the questions in each phase. The four questions differ from phase to phase but represent identical steps in the problem-solving sequence. That is, students answering the questions must: 1) identify the problem, 2) identify potential solutions to the problem, 3) identify barriers to solving the problem, and 4) identify consequences of each solution. These steps are the fundamental steps in any problem-solving process, and they form the means–end problem-solving sequence represented by the *Student Questions* in each phase.

Because the model is designed for teachers to implement, the language of the *Student Questions* are written in such a way that not every student is expected to understand them nor does the model assume that students have life experiences that enable

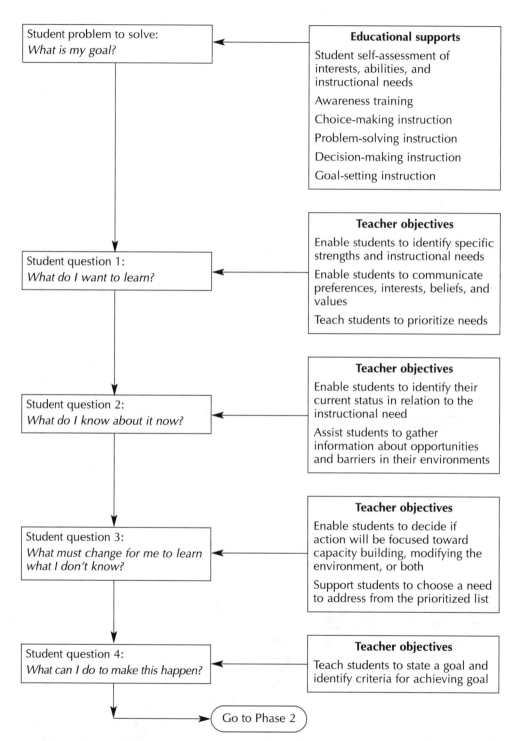

Phase 1: Set a goal

Student problem to solve:
What is my goal?

Educational supports

Student self-assessment of interests, abilities, and instructional needs

Awareness training

Choice-making instruction

Problem-solving instruction

Decision-making instruction

Goal-setting instruction

Student question 1:
What do I want to learn?

Teacher objectives

Enable students to identify specific strengths and instructional needs

Enable students to communicate preferences, interests, beliefs, and values

Teach students to prioritize needs

Student question 2:
What do I know about it now?

Teacher objectives

Enable students to identify their current status in relation to the instructional need

Assist students to gather information about opportunities and barriers in their environments

Student question 3:
What must change for me to learn what I don't know?

Teacher objectives

Enable students to decide if action will be focused toward capacity building, modifying the environment, or both

Support students to choose a need to address from the prioritized list

Student question 4:
What can I do to make this happen?

Teacher objectives

Teach students to state a goal and identify criteria for achieving goal

Go to Phase 2

Figure 15.1.   Instructional Phase 1 of *Self-Determined Learning Model of Instruction.*

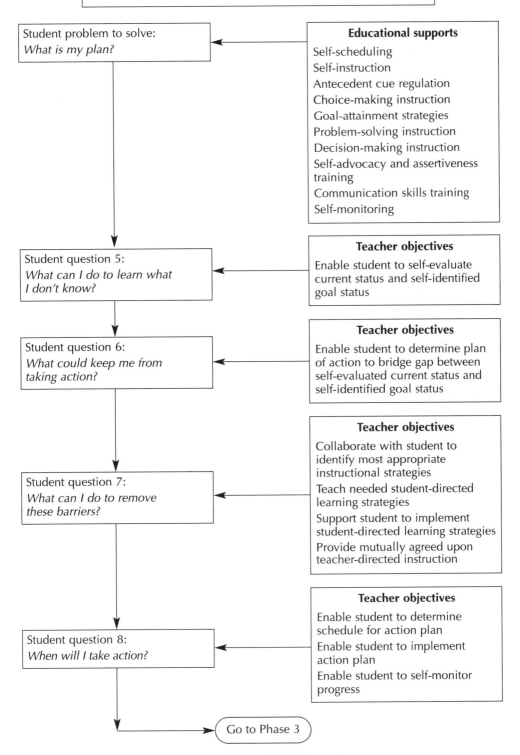

Phase 2: Take action

Student problem to solve:
What is my plan?

Educational supports

Self-scheduling
Self-instruction
Antecedent cue regulation
Choice-making instruction
Goal-attainment strategies
Problem-solving instruction
Decision-making instruction
Self-advocacy and assertiveness training
Communication skills training
Self-monitoring

Student question 5:
What can I do to learn what I don't know?

Teacher objectives

Enable student to self-evaluate current status and self-identified goal status

Student question 6:
What could keep me from taking action?

Teacher objectives

Enable student to determine plan of action to bridge gap between self-evaluated current status and self-identified goal status

Student question 7:
What can I do to remove these barriers?

Teacher objectives

Collaborate with student to identify most appropriate instructional strategies
Teach needed student-directed learning strategies
Support student to implement student-directed learning strategies
Provide mutually agreed upon teacher-directed instruction

Student question 8:
When will I take action?

Teacher objectives

Enable student to determine schedule for action plan
Enable student to implement action plan
Enable student to self-monitor progress

Go to Phase 3

Figure 15.2.   Instructional Phase 2 of *Self-Determined Learning Model of Instruction.*

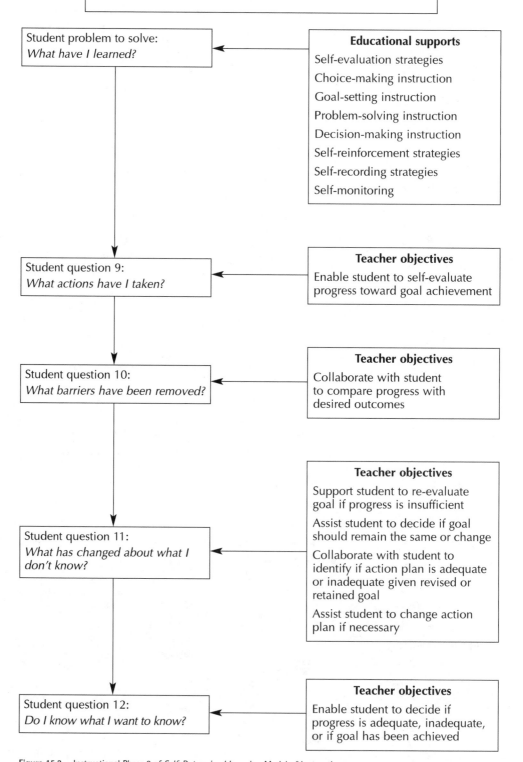

Phase 3: Adjust goal or plan

Student problem to solve:
What have I learned?

Educational supports

Self-evaluation strategies

Choice-making instruction

Goal-setting instruction

Problem-solving instruction

Decision-making instruction

Self-reinforcement strategies

Self-recording strategies

Self-monitoring

Student question 9:
What actions have I taken?

Teacher objectives

Enable student to self-evaluate
progress toward goal achievement

Student question 10:
What barriers have been removed?

Teacher objectives

Collaborate with student
to compare progress with
desired outcomes

Student question 11:
*What has changed about what I
don't know?*

Teacher objectives

Support student to re-evaluate
goal if progress is insufficient

Assist student to decide if goal
should remain the same or change

Collaborate with student to
identify if action plan is adequate
or inadequate given revised or
retained goal

Assist student to change action
plan if necessary

Student question 12:
Do I know what I want to know?

Teacher objectives

Enable student to decide if
progress is adequate, inadequate,
or if goal has been achieved

Figure 15.3. Instructional Phase 3 of *Self-Determined Learning Model of Instruction.*

248

them to fully answer each question. The *Student Questions* are written from a first-person point of view in a relatively simple format with the intention that they function as a starting point for discussion between the teacher and the student. Some students learn and use all 12 questions as they are written. Other students need to have the questions rephrased to be more understandable. Still other students, due to the intensity of their instructional needs, may need to have the teacher paraphrase the questions for them.

The first time a teacher uses the model with a student, the initial steps in the implementation process are to read the question with or to the student; discuss what the question means; and then, if necessary, change the wording to enable that student to better understand the intent of the question. Such wording changes must, however, be made such that the problem-solving intent of the question remains intact. For example, changing *Student Question 1* from "What do I want to learn?" to "What is my goal?" changes the nature of the question. The *Teacher Objectives* associated with each student question provide direction for possible wording changes. It is perhaps less important that actual changes in the words occur than that students take ownership over the process and adopt the question as their own, instead of having questions imposed on them. Going through this process once as a student progresses through the model should result in a set of questions that the student accepts as his or her own.

The *Teacher Objectives* within the model are just that—the objectives a teacher tries to accomplish by implementing the model. In each instructional phase, the objectives are linked directly to the *Student Questions*. These objectives can be met by using strategies provided in the *Educational Supports* section of the model. The *Teacher Objectives* provide a road map to assist the teacher to enable the student to solve the problems stated in the *Student Questions*. For example, regarding the first question, "What do I want to learn?" associated *Teacher Objectives* comprise the activities in which students should be engaged to answer this question. In this case, helping the students answer this question enables students to identify their specific strengths and instructional needs; to identify and communicate preferences, interests, beliefs and values; and to prioritize their instructional needs. As teachers use the model, it is likely that they can generate more objectives that are relevant to the question.

The *Educational Supports* are not actually a part of the model but are what Joyce and Weil (1980) referred to as the model's *syntax*—how the model is implemented. However, because the implementation of this model requires teachers to teach students to self-direct learning, we believe it is important to identify some strategies and supports that could be used to successfully implement the model. The majority of these supports are derived from the self-management literature.

The emphasis in the model on the use of instructional strategies and educational supports that are student-directed provides another means of teaching students to teach themselves. Using the *Student Questions* teaches students a self-regulated problem-solving strategy. Concurrently, teaching students to use various student-directed learning strategies provides students with another layer of skills that enable them to become the causal agents of their lives. As important as it is to use the student-directed learning strategies, however, not every instructional strategy implemented is student-directed. The purpose of any model of teaching is to promote student learning and growth. There are circumstances in which the most effective instructional method or strategy to achieve a particular educational outcome is a teacher-directed strategy. One misinterpretation of self-determination is that it is synonymous with independent performance. That is, people misinterpret self-determination as meaning that one does everything oneself. However, causal agents do not necessarily do everything for themselves but instead are the catalysts in making things happen in their lives. Students who are considering what plan of action to implement to achieve a self-selected goal can recognize that teachers have expertise in instructional strategies and take full advantage of that expertise.

Wehmeyer and colleagues (2000) conducted a field test of the model with teachers serving adolescents who receive special education services. Each teacher was asked to identify at least one but no more than three students with whom to implement the model, resulting in a total of 40 students with mental retardation, learning disabilities, or emotional or behavior disorders. Students identified a total of 43 goals they wanted to address (three students chose two goals). Of the 43 goals, 10 focused on acquiring or modifying social skills or knowledge, 13 focused on behavioral issues (e.g., compliance with school procedures, controlling behavior in specific circumstances, learning more adaptive behavior), and 20 addressed academic needs.

The efficacy of the model to enable students to achieve educationally valued goals was examined using the Goal Attainment Scaling (GAS) process (Carr, 1979). According to Carr, GAS "involves establishing goals and specifying a range of outcomes or behaviors that would indicate progress toward achieving those goals" (1979, p. 89). In addition to this indicator of goal attainment, Wehmeyer and colleagues (2000) also collected pre- and postintervention data regarding student self-determination using The Arc's Self-Determination Scale (Wehmeyer, 1996b), a student self-report measure of self-determination and locus of control, and they administered a questionnaire examining student goal orientation.

The field-test indicated that the model was effective in enabling students to attain educationally valued goals. Twenty-five percent of the total number of goals on which students received instruction were identified as having been achieved as expected, and 30% of the total goals addressed were identified as having exceeded expectations. Of the remainder, slightly more than 25% of the GAS scores indicated that students made progress on their goal but did not fully achieve it, and just less than 20% of the scores were rated as the least favorable outcome, essentially indicating no progress on the goal. In addition, there were significant differences in pre- and postintervention scores on self-determination and locus of control, in both cases with postintervention scores more positive than preintervention scores and with students showing a general trend toward more effective goal-oriented behavior.

SUMMARY

Promoting student self-determination is important at multiple levels. The general curriculum contains, across multiple grade levels, standards and benchmarks that pertain to goal setting, problem solving, and decision making. As such, instructional focus in these areas can enable students to progress in the general curriculum. Moreover, learning to become more self-determined provides students with strategies, such as self-regulated problem-solving strategies, that enable them to learn other content matter in the general curriculum and, thus, form an effective way to augment the general curriculum. Such efforts are important from early childhood through secondary education and are particularly important to students with mental retardation, who often do not have the opportunity to learn and exercise such skills.

ADDITIONAL READINGS

Determinism

Weatherford, R. (1991). *The implications of determinism*. London: Routledge.

Self-Determination in Special Education and Mental Retardation

Field, S., Martin, J.E., Miller, R., Ward, M., & Wehmeyer, M.L. (1998). *A practical guide to teaching self-determination*. Reston, VA: Council for Exceptional Children.

Nirje, B. (1972). The right to self-determination. In W. Wolfensberger & B. Nirje, (Ed.), *Normalization: The principle of normalization in human services* (pp. 176–200). Toronto: National Institute on Mental Retardation.

Sands, D.J., & Wehmeyer, M.L. (1996). *Self-determination across the life span: Independence and choice for people with disabilities*. Baltimore: Paul H. Brookes Publishing Co.

Wehmeyer, M.L. (1998). Self-determination and individuals with significant disabilities: Examining meanings and misinterpretations. *Journal of The Association for Persons with Severe Handicaps, 23*, 5–16.

Wehmeyer, M.L. (2001). Self-determination and mental retardation. In L.M. Glidden (Ed.), *International review of research in mental retardation* (Vol. 24, pp. 1–48). Mahwah, NJ: Lawrence Erlbaum Associates.

Wehmeyer, M.L., Abery, B., Mithaug, D.E., Powers, L.E., & Stancliffe, R. (in press). *Theory in self-determination: Foundations for educational practice*. Springfield, IL: Charles C Thomas.

Wehmeyer, M.L., Agran, M., & Hughes, C. (1998). *Teaching self-determination to students with disabilities: Basic skills for successful transition*. Baltimore: Paul H. Brookes Publishing Co.

Self-Determination in Other Disciplines

Biestek, F.P., & Gehrig, C.C. (1978). *Client self-determination in social work: A fifty-year history*. Chicago: Loyola University Press.

Deci, E.L. (1975). *Intrinsic motivation*. New York: Kluwer Academic/Plenum Publishers.

Deci, E.L., & Ryan, R.M. (1985). *Intrinsic motivation and self-determination in human behavior*. New York: Kluwer Academic/Plenum Publishers.

McDermott, F.E. (Ed.). (1975). *Self-determination in social work: A collection of essays on self-determination and related concepts by philosophers and social work theorists*. London: Routledge and Kegan Paul.

CHAPTER OBJECTIVES

1. Define *assistive technology*, and discuss its potential utility for students with mental retardation.
2. Discuss barriers to access to assistive technology for people with mental retardation.
3. Summarize the application of universal design principles in assistive technology, and compare and contrast the application of this construct with curriculum and instruction.
4. Discuss the potential benefits of the Internet and computer-based technologies for students with mental retardation and identify barriers to these benefits.

KEY TERMS

Assistive technology
Computer use
Principles of universal design
Access to the Internet
Educational Multimedia Fair Use Guidelines

16

Technology and Students with Mental Retardation

SIMPLE ACCOMMODATIONS
IN THE AGE OF LITIGATION

This chapter addresses the use of technology in two primary ways in the education of students with mental retardation. First, it summarizes the use of assistive technology devices to remove limitations to learning introduced by disability. Second, it examines technology use more broadly, including the use of assistive technology devices and the Internet, as a key factor in both curriculum adaptations and in providing supports across the student's life span and circumstances.

ASSISTIVE TECHNOLOGY AND MENTAL RETARDATION

Assistive technology devices have the potential to improve the lives of people with disabilities. This was emphasized by the Congress of the United States in the Findings and Purposes section of the Technology-Related Assistance for Individuals with Disabilities Act of 1988 (Tech Act; PL 100-407). In this legislation, Congress stated that the provision of assistive technology devices and services to individuals with disabilities enables individuals to do the following:

> (A) Have greater control over their own lives, (B) participate in and contribute more fully to activities in their home, school and work environments, and in their communities, (C) interact to a greater extent with non-disabled individuals, and (D) otherwise benefit from opportunities that are taken for granted by individuals who do not have disabilities. (p. 1044)

In short, the use of assistive technology has the potential to increase the independence, productivity, self-reliance, and self-determination of individuals with disabilities.

These benefits are not specific to adults. There is ample evidence that the use of assistive technology benefits students with disabilities as well (Flippo, Inge, & Barcus, 1995). The importance of assistive devices in the education of students with disabilities has been recognized in the Individuals with Disabilities Education Act (IDEA) of 1990 (PL 101-476). The act defined **assistive technology devices** as "any item, piece of equipment or product system, whether acquired or commercially off the shelf, modified or customized, that is used to increase, maintain, or improve the functional capabilities of children with disabilities" (20 U.S.C. 1401 [25], Sec. 300.5).

This act also defined assistive technology services as those that "directly assist a child with a disability in the selection, acquisition or use of an assistive technology device" (20 U.S.C. § 1401 [25], Sec. 300.6), including the evaluation of a child's assistive technology needs; purchase, lease, or other acquisition of devices; and training or technical assistance for the child and professionals working with the child. The act then required that schools ensure that assistive technology devices or services, or both, be made available to a child with a disability if required as a part of the child's special education or related services or as supplementary aids and services. This commitment to providing assistive technology was further strengthened in a policy statement issued by the U.S. Department of Education's Office of Special Education Programs (OSEP). This statement, in essence, specified that the IEP team must, on a case-by-case basis, consider a child's need for assistive technology. If assistive technology is needed within the realm of mandated special education or related services, the IEP must include a statement of the nature and amount of services needed (Inge & Shepherd, 1995).

The 1997 amendments to IDEA (PL 105-17) included as a requirement that the IEP team shall "consider whether [a] child needs assistive technology devices and services"

(Sec. 614[d]). That means that public school agencies must consider the assistive technology needs of every student receiving special education services, not just students for whom the IEP team determines assistive devices or services are necessary. It is likely that this requirement will heighten the attention to and, hopefully, increase access to assistive technology for children and youth with disabilities.

Assistive technology devices can support a student by either removing the barriers imposed by the disabling condition or providing the means to adapt the environment, including the curriculum, so that the student can succeed in spite of the limitation. So, for example, a student who cannot speak clearly may be at a disadvantage when responding to the teacher's questions or when participating in group discussions. However, students can use assistive devices (e.g., augmentative and alternative communication voice-output devices) that, essentially, remove the barrier imposed by the limitation (e.g., unclear speech). The use of assistive technology, in this case, may remove the need to adapt the curriculum.

Assistive Technology Use by People with Mental Retardation

For assistive technology to be useful in the lives of people with mental retardation, it must be accessible. There has been a growing suspicion that assistive technology is underutilized by people with mental retardation, despite evidence of its benefits (e.g., Dattilo, 1987; Realon, Favell, & Dayvault, 1988; Realon, Favell, & Phillips, 1989). Until the mid- to late 1990s, however, there was very limited research to confirm this suspicion. To address the paucity of information in this area, The Arc conducted a national survey of family members of people with mental retardation that examined assistive technology use by people with mental retardation and their families and barriers to this use. The results of this study included a report about the utilization of assistive technology by adults with mental retardation (Wehmeyer, 1998) and a report about the same issues as they pertain to students with mental retardation (Wehmeyer, 1999).

Family members of people with mental retardation responded to a survey asking questions about assistive technology use in five use-specific areas and about the use of computers. Both the adult and the student surveys contained identical questions in each of the five use-specific areas. For example, in the mobility device area, respondents were first asked if their family member used a mobility technology device. If they indicated yes, they were directed to a question asking them to identify which device was used (i.e., crutch, cane, or walking stick; walker; wheelchair; scooter; other) and a follow-up question on funding for the device (i.e., private insurance; personal funds; charitable donation; school/agency program; Supplemental Security Income, Plan for Achieving Self Support, or other government funding; other). In addition, the survey asked if the family member with mental retardation had received adequate assessment or evaluation services before purchasing the device and information about how to appropriately and effectively use the device. Respondents were then asked to rank the family's satisfaction with the device.

If respondents indicated that their family member with mental retardation did not use a mobility technology device, they skipped to a question that asked if their family member could potentially benefit from such a device. If they responded yes to this question, they were asked to identify the beneficial device and to check *all* relevant barriers to their family member using or benefiting from a mobility device:

- Lack of funding and/or high cost of device
- Little information about product
- Unavailable assessment/evaluation
- Unavailable product
- Complexity of the device
- Difficult product upkeep
- Inadequate training for the person to learn to use the device

The other four use-specific areas asked similar questions. In the hearing and vision device section, potential device choices included text reader, adapted computer keyboard, special alarm, braille printer, white cane, hearing aid, and other hearing or vision device. In the communication device section, choices included synthesized speech communicator, picture book, nonspeech, touch or point system, light or switch operated system, or other communication device. Choices in the home adaptations section included ramps, extra-wide doors, stair lift, hand rails, raised toilet, adapted door locks, lowered counters, slip-resistant floors, or other home adaptations. Finally, available choices in the environmental control and independent living section included adaptive eating device; button hooks or other dressing implements; adapted telephone; switches for leisure/play device; rocker knife, spoon/fork grip, or other adapted utensils for eating; switches for independent living; environmental control unit or other environmental control; and independent living devices.

The final survey area examined personal **computer use.** Respondents identified whether there was a computer in their home and, if so, whether it was purchased specifically for the family member with a disability. If they answered yes, respondents were asked to identify how the computer was purchased. The survey then asked whether the family member with mental retardation had access to a computer in any environment, and if so, which environment (i.e., family home, recreational and leisure environment, living residence other than family home, day activity program or school, place of employment, other). If respondents indicated yes, they were asked to identify how their family member used the computer (i.e., educational activities, household finances and budgeting, recreational and leisure activities, work-related activities, communication, other). If respondents indicated that their family member did not have access to a computer in any environment, they were asked if the family member could benefit from such access and then asked to indicate relevant barriers to computer access (e.g., lack of funding, little information).

Table 16.1. Frequency and percentage of respondents indicating an adult family member with mental retardation used technology or did not use technology but would benefit from such use

Device purpose	Device use		Device need	
	Frequency	Percentage	Frequency	Percentage
Mobility	155	12.7	30	2.5
Hearing and vision	107	8.9	57	5.0
Communication	59	4.9	104	9.3
Home adaptations	117	9.7	95	8.4
Environmental control	66	5.5	87	7.6

Table 16.2. Frequency of responses to barriers to assistive technology use by area and total

	Device purpose					
Barriers	Mobility	Hearing/vision	Communication	Home adaptations	Environmental control	All areas
Information	13	18	47	23	53	154
Cost	20	25	33	44	23	145
Assessment	6	7	28	12	16	69
Availability	3	3	11	2	7	26
Complexity	6	7	20	2	8	43
Staff	1	5	13	1	5	25
Training	6	13	23	2	13	57
Upkeep	2	2	2	1	0	7

The results from both reports indicated that assistive technology devices were greatly underutilized by people with mental retardation. Tables 16.1 and 16.2 report data from the results regarding adult family members who have mental retardation. As can be seen in Table 16.1, for most of the device-use areas, the percentage of respondents who indicated that their son or daughter could benefit from assistive devices matched or exceeded the number of people reporting that their son or daughter did use such a device. Table 16.2 lists the barriers identified by family members who reported that their family member with mental retardation could benefit from but did not currently use an assistive device.

Trends in these findings were similar for students with mental retardation, as can be seen in Tables 16.3 and 16.4, although on average, there was greater use of technology by young people with mental retardation as compared with adults. The relationship between use and need remained consistent—in general there were more respondents indicating that their family member needed devices than those indicating that their family member used a device. The exception in both reports was the mobility device area

Table 16.3. Respondents indicating a family member who was a student using technology or not using technology but would benefit from such use by age groups and total sample

Device purpose	Ages (in years)	Frequency use	Percent use	Frequency need	Percent need
Mobility	1–5	16–67	24	1–67	1
	6–15	65–303	8	12–303	4
	16–21	27–146	18	3–146	2
	Total sample	108–516	21	16–516	3
Hearing/vision	1–5	8–67	12	7–67	10
	6–15	34–303	11	47–303	16
	16–21	14–146	10	12–146	10
	Total sample	56–516	11	66–516	13
Communication	1–5	14–67	21	25–67	37
	6–15	62–303	20	75–303	25
	16–21	27–146	18	28–146	19
	Total sample	103–516	20	128–516	25
Home adaptations	1–5	8–67	12	16–67	24
	6–15	46–303	15	56–303	18
	16–21	32–146	22	22–146	15
	Total sample	86–516	17	94–516	18
Environmental control	1–5	14–67	21	21–67	31
	6–15	46–303	15	65–303	21
	16–21	18–146	12	30–146	20
	Total sample	78–516	15	116–516	22

Table 16.4. Barriers to assistive technology use reported by respondents whose student–age family member could benefit from but did not currently use assistive technology

Barrier	Age	Mobility	Hearing–vision	Communication	Home adaptations	Environmental control	Total responses
				Device purpose			
Cost	1–5	0–1	4–7	13–25	12–16	13–21	42
	6–15	7–12	30–47	48–75	42–56	34–65	161
	16–21	1–3	5–12	15–28	12–22	19–30	52
	Total sample	8–16	39–66	76–128	66–94	66–116	255
Information	1–5	0–1	4–7	12–25	5–16	12–21	33
	6–15	6–12	16–47	36–75	15–56	35–65	108
	16–21	1–3	3–12	12–28	11–22	16–30	43
	Total sample	7–16	23–66	60–128	31–94	63–116	184
Assessment	1–5	0–1	1–7	3–25	3–16	2–21	9
	6–15	2–12	9–47	27–75	7–56	12–65	57
	16–21	2–3	1–12	5–28	5–22	4–30	17
	Total sample	4–16	11–66	35–128	15–94	18–116	83
Availability	1–5	0–1	0–7	2–25	0–16	3–21	5
	6–15	2–12	4–47	7–75	5–56	8–65	26
	16–21	0–3	0–12	2–28	2–22	4–30	8
	Total sample	2–16	4–66	11–128	7–94	15–116	39
Complexity	1–5	0–1	3–7	2–25	0–16	1–21	6
	6–15	2–12	9–47	22–75	0–56	4–65	35
	16–21	1–3	1–12	7–28	1–22	5–30	15
	Total sample	3–16	13–66	31–128	1–94	10–116	58
Training	1–5	0–1	1–7	2–25	1–16	1–21	5
	6–15	0–12	9–47	16–75	1–56	3–65	29
	16–21	0–3	1–12	7–28	2–22	3–30	13
	Total sample	0–16	11–66	25–128	4–94	7–116	47
Upkeep	1–5	0–1	0–7	0–25	0–16	0–21	0
	6–15	1–12	0–47	4–75	1–56	0–65	6
	16–21	0–3	0–12	0–28	0–22	0–30	0
	Total sample	1–16	0–66	4–128	1–94	0–116	6

(respondents predominantly indicated their family member used a wheelchair), in which there was limited need compared with use in both samples. The reason for this exception is that insurance companies typically pay for the purchase of a wheelchair. The barriers tables (Tables 16.2 and 16.4) show similar patterns, with cost and information being among the biggest barriers. (Cost was less of a barrier for students because IDEA requires that schools provide assistive technology services.)

These student and adult groups differed quite a bit in the final area, computer use. For the adult sample, 33% of the respondents ($n = 399$) indicated there was a computer in their home. A smaller percentage (23%; $n = 284$) indicated their adult family member used a computer. Of these 284 computer users, 88 indicated they used it in a day activity program, 46 at work, 135 at home, 28 in a living situation other than home, 40 in a recreation or leisure program, and 28 in other situations. (Respondents checked all that applied.) When asked to identify what the person with mental retardation did with the computer, 30 respondents indicated it was used for communication, 130 for educational activities, 10 for household finances or budgeting, 183 for leisure activities, 29 for work-related activities, and 26 for other activities. (Again, respondents checked all that applied.)

Sixty-eight percent of the respondents ($n = 349$) with school-age family members who have mental retardation indicated there was a computer in their home. Eighty-three percent ($n = 421$) of the respondents indicated that the student in their family had access to or used a computer, either at home or in another environment. Of these 421 computer users, 382 indicated they used it in school program, 4 in a work setting, 242 at home, 8 in a living situation other than home, 36 in a recreation or leisure program, and 9 in other situations. (Respondents checked all that applied.) When asked to identify what the student with mental retardation did with the computer, 70 respondents indicated it was used for communication, 362 for educational activities, 1 for household finances or budgeting, 270 for leisure activities, 6 for work-related activities, and 19 for other activities. (Again, respondents checked all that applied.)

Addressing Underutilization

We have described the reports on the survey (Wehmeyer, 1998, 1999) performed by The Arc in detail for several reasons. First, these studies represent, to a large extent, the knowledge about and barriers to assistive technology use among people with mental retardation. Second, providing more detail about survey areas also provides a means of describing the breadth of what is referred to as *assistive technology*. It is not feasible to cover all the types and varieties of assistive devices in this chapter, although readers can gain more information about specific devices from sources listed in the *Additional Readings* section at the end of this chapter. It is important to note that not every assistive technology device is an expensive, technical gadget. Often the most simple devices are overlooked and underutilized, from spoon or pencil grips to easy-to-make switches.

In previous chapters, we have emphasized the importance of applying universal design features to curriculum planning and decision making to ensure that students with mental retardation have access to the general curriculum. The principles of universal design as applied to assistive technology design and development provide many of the keys to addressing the underutilization of assistive technology by students and adults with mental retardation. The Trace Center, a rehabilitation engineering research center at the University of Wisconsin–Madison, identified seven **principles of universal design** to consider when designing assistive technology. These are as follows:

1. Equitable use: A design is useful and marketable to any group of users.
2. Flexibility in use: A design accommodates a wide range of individual preferences and abilities.
3. Simple and intuitive use: Use of the design is easy to understand, regardless of user's experience, knowledge, language, or cognitive skills.
4. Perceptible information: The design communicates the information needed by the user, be it through different modes or by providing adequate contrast.
5. Tolerance for error: The design minimizes adverse consequences or accidental or unintended actions.
6. Low physical effort: The design can be used comfortably with minimum fatigue.
7. Size and space for approach and use appropriate: Design allows for approach, reach, manipulation, and device use independent of user's body size, posture, or mobility. (Trace Center, 1995, p. 1)

An important component in ensuring universal design of assistive technology devices that benefit people with mental retardation is to ensure that cognitive limitations are considered when designing devices for equitable or simple and intuitive use. Too often technology designers have failed to take into account cognitive limitations when considering device design, although that is changing. As more and more Americans live longer, the incidence and prevalence of cognitive impairments in the general population, such as dementia or Alzheimer's disease, increase. Thus, there is a growing market for assistive technology devices that benefit both this population and people with mental retardation. For example, a federally funded rehabilitation engineering center on aging was working on the development of a microwave oven that could be used independently by someone with impaired thought processes. This microwave scanned the Universal Product Code on any product placed in the oven and read this code to obtain heating instructions. The person using the oven simply had to press a start button to heat the product adequately. It is quite simple to see how that same oven might increase the independence of a person with mental retardation.

The focus on community and the value for self-determination and inclusion is also important to addressing assistive technology underutilization. One of the barriers to device use (mainly for adults with mental retardation) identified by The Arc's survey was problems related to device upkeep and availability in more congregate living or working settings. Factors pertaining to the safety of the device (e.g., keeping it from being used inappropriately or by inappropriate others) or ways to keep a device from simply disappearing between shift changes often lead to the device being kept in secure areas in the group home or institution or workshop, resulting in its unavailability on frequent occasions. Also, barriers as simple as state-mandated purchasing policies often render devices unusable if they are, for example, battery-operated. Instead of simply going to the local grocery store to replace the batteries, staff members have to order batteries through purchasing processes that are often cumbersome and lengthy, and the device sits unused in the interim.

These problems are not constricted to adult-service arenas—the same barriers exist in schools. For example, a hearing device was purchased for a young man with Down syndrome by the school district as part of his educational program. He received instruction on how to use the device and did so throughout the day, resulting in marked improvement in his school performance. However, because the device had been purchased by the district, school personnel did not allow this young man to take the device home with him or use it outside of school for fear it would get lost, stolen, or damaged. In a similar way, policies that restrict computer use to only certain times of the day or to certain computer labs may remove the potential benefit of the technology to provide supports for students with mental retardation.

TECHNOLOGY PROVIDING ACCESS AND SUPPORT

In many ways, technology can help students gain access to and progress in the general curriculum. Such efforts are particularly important for curriculum adaptations and augmentations. Specifically, researchers at the Center for Applied Special Technology (CAST; 1998–1999), who operate the federally funded National Center on Access to the General Curriculum (NCAGC), suggested that using computer technology to adapt inaccessible materials and individualizing learning with customized software applications provide promising practices for gaining access through universal design. Figure 16.1 shows the essential qualities of universally designed materials identified by CAST.

Education, Computer Use, and the Internet

The general public has increased their use of computers to enhance autonomy (e.g., using software to budget and balance checking accounts or prepare annual tax filings), to

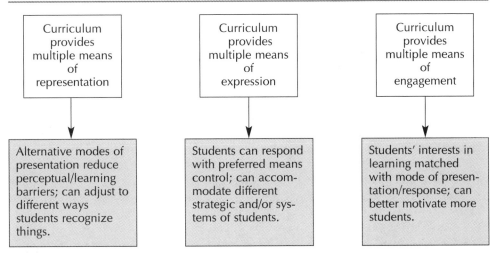

Figure 16.1. Essential qualities of universal design for learning identified by the Center for Applied Special Technology (CAST; 1998–1999).

increase productivity (e.g., using word processors, accounting spreadsheets, or graphics software), or to participate in recreational or leisure activities (e.g., using computer video games or genealogy software). Yet, the reports based on The Arc's survey suggested that too few people with mental retardation similarly benefit (Wehmeyer, 1998, 1999).

There is a growing body of evidence, though, that people with mental retardation can benefit from computer use (Davies, Stock, & Wehmeyer, 2001). For example, computers have been used with these individuals for a great number of things, including teaching communication skills (Iacono & Miller, 1989), teaching vocational tasks (Davies & Stock, 1994; Davies & Stock, 1997b), anti-victimization training (Holzberg, 1994), promoting language acquisition (Holzberg, 1995), budgeting and money management (Davies & Stock, 1995), motivation (Keyes, 1994), recreation and leisure training (Dattilo, Guerin, Cory, & Williams, 2001), menu planning (Davies & Stock, 1997a), classroom instruction (Vockell & Milhail, 1993), and indicating career preferences (Stock, Davies, & Secor, 1996). Davies and colleagues (2001) identified several potential benefits of computer use by individuals with mental retardation including:

- Enhanced self-esteem and self-confidence
- Increased independence
- Opportunities for self-direction and enhanced self-determination
- Increased efficient use of time

Moreover, the use of personal computers as tools to support autonomy and productivity and to provide leisure and recreation opportunities has been greatly enhanced by the rapid growth of **access to the Internet.** Like other aspects of computer and software access, however, access to the Internet is restricted for many people with mental retardation. For a variety of reasons, most web browsers used to access the World Wide Web are not usable by most people with mental retardation. Although individuals with mental retardation may not use the Internet for all of the purposes listed previously, the types of things that can be done using the Internet are growing and people with mental retardation could benefit.

In addition, computers and the Internet have considerable potential for both teaching and curriculum adaptation and augmentation. The use of the Internet as a means of presenting material provides a potentially powerful and relatively simple way to adapt and augment the curriculum. Most curricular materials are typically in print. One of the benefits of the Internet is the capacity to use graphic images in a variety of ways, from icons to hyperlinked pictures to streaming video. Unlike written materials, which become unchangeable once printed and distributed, web pages can be modified relatively easily. For example, with the use of advance organizers, one could fairly easily take narrative content from a textbook, put it into text and HTML format, and hyperlink key concepts or words in the text that, when selected, take students to another web page that defines the concept and provides other background information.

Converting traditional materials into digitized versions is sometimes difficult but not impossible. Educators need to be aware of issues pertaining to copyright and copyright infringement when adapting materials. A growing number of text or print materials are published with web- or computer-based materials to accompany them. If a material is not, there are ways to convert it into digital formats. The ***Educational Multimedia Fair Use Guidelines*** (Lehman, 1998) were developed by a coalition of copyright holders and educational institutions to provide educators, scholars, and students with guidelines on the fair use of intellectual property in digital technologies. These guidelines note clearly that "students may incorporate portions of lawfully acquired copyrighted works when producing their own educational multimedia projects for a specific course" and, likewise, that educators "may incorporate portions of lawfully acquired copyrighted works when producing their own educational multimedia projects for their own teaching tools in support of curriculum-based instructional activities at educational institutions." These uses are subject to certain conditions and restrictions and include conditions to ensure adequate citation and credit, but within those boundaries, curricular materials can be adapted for use for accessibility. (The *Educational Multimedia Fair Use Guidelines* can be found on-line at http://www.uspto.gov/web/offices/dcom/olia/confu/confurep.htm).

One of the barriers to computer use for people with mental retardation is the complexity of the software and operating systems available. The problem with software is the same as that with assistive technology devices, the general curriculum, and so forth: It hasn't been designed with principles of universal design in mind to ensure access by a wide array of people. Researchers at Ablelink Technologies have developed software that embodies the principles of universal design and is accessible to people with mental retardation. One example of this is WebTrek, a browser designed for use by people with mental retardation (see Figure 16.2). Davies and colleagues (2001) found that people with mental retardation were more effective at three tasks—*searching* for web sites, *saving* web sites to a favorites list, and *retrieving* saved sites from the favorites list—with the WebTrek browser than Microsoft's Internet Explorer. These authors suggested that the WebTrek browser was more usable because it used audio prompting, reduced screen clutter, was customizable, and used multiple means to minimize errors. These features represent, in essence, principles of universal design that would make browser use more accessible to all people. Similar principles have been applied by these researchers to other software products, including MoneyCoach, a budgeting/finance product (see Figure 16.3), and CompSkills, an accessible software program to teach basic computer skills (e.g., mouse use, keyboard use).

The design of software that embodies principles of universal design has considerable promise for providing access, and the following section identifies curricular mate-

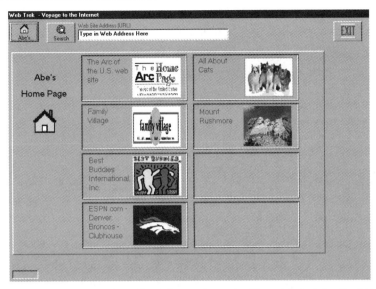

Figure 16.2. A screen from WebTrek, an accessible web browser for people with mental retardation. (Available: http:// www. ablelinktech.com/)

rials that are commercially available that employ such design principles. However, it is worth noting that the use of computers to access the Internet and to run software specifically designed for people with mental retardation represents only one aspect of the potential of computers to support access. A wide array of commercially available software products could be used to adapt or augment the curriculum and any number of emerging technologies (e.g., speech recognition technology) that would make computers themselves more accessible. As an example of the former, most word processing programs have a feature that takes narrative text and creates an outline form of the information. Teachers could use such features to adapt the curriculum and pro-

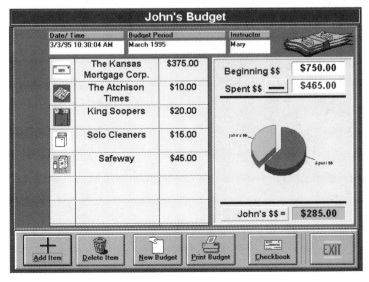

Figure 16.3. A screen from MoneyCoach, an accessible financial and budgeting software program. (Available: http:// www. ablelinktech.com/)

vide an advance organizer or could teach students to use the outlining features of the word processor to make their own outlines, a form of curriculum augmentation.

Universally Designed Curricular Materials

With the increased attention to enabling students with disabilities to gain access to the general curriculum, there is an emerging product base of curricular materials that are designed based on principles of universal design. CAST (1998–1999) has identified several such materials. The following paragraphs describe several such products to illustrate how universal design has an impact on accessibility.

Co-created by CAST and Scholastic Press, the WiggleWorks Scholastic Beginning Literacy program (Scholastic Press, 1995) provides a good example of a universally designed curriculum. WiggleWorks is an interactive print and CD-ROM product designed to promote literacy. The product offers multiple ways to change the presentation or representation of the information, including allowing teachers or students to change the size and color of text as well as the color of the text background. The product offers ways to change students' response to or interaction with the curriculum, allowing them to type text, record information, draw, or select words from a list. Students can then listen to their recording, hear their text read back through a text-to-speech feature, or expand or modify their drawing. WiggleWorks allows teachers to scaffold learning by limiting students to a specific program or task, thus eliminating other potentially confusing tasks. Also, teachers can record messages that provide customized or individualized instructions.

Another product developed by CAST is the *eReader* (CAST, 1998–1999), which adds spoken voice, visual highlighting, document navigation, or page navigation to any electronic text, independent of the source of that text. This device adapts the way curricular content (as digitized information) is represented or presented by enabling users to control reading speed, voice pitch, modulation, and volume and to use voice preferences built into the product. Students can use multiple means of interacting with the information through screen menus and buttons or keyboard commands.

CAST (1998–1999) also identified a number of products from more traditional commercial venues. For example, Edmark Corporation's Bailey's Book House products, a prereading program for use from kindergarten through second grade, incorporates numerous universal design features. Information is provided in multiple media, including text, images, sound, and animation, and students can select either open-ended exploratory learning or structured learning with explicit goals. One curricular exercise involves the creation of animated characters.

These products and materials represent only a sample of similar efforts that are emerging and ongoing. When teachers are aware of the potential benefits to students with mental retardation of technology-based materials and the use of technology to adapt and augment the curriculum, they can make purchasing decisions with these issues in mind.

SUMMARY

Assistive technology and advances in technology have considerable potential to benefit people with mental retardation. First, however, there is a need to overcome historic barriers that have limited the degree to which people with mental retardation gain access to such technology. The IDEA Amendments of 1997 put the onus on schools to identify students' assistive technology needs instead of just identifying students who might need assistive technology. Despite the previous mandate for IEP teams to ensure that assistive technology devices and services be made available to children with disabilities if required as a part of the special education or related services program, many students who could have benefited from assistive technology did not have access to such devices. The 1997 IDEA requirements for schools to determine the assistive technology needs of each student should help to bridge this gap.

It is likely that progress will continue to be made in using technology to adapt the curriculum, as illustrated by the materials developed by CAST. This application of universal design principles to materials and curriculum design is a necessary component of attaining access for students with mental retardation. Computer-based and software applications are becoming more and more important to the general curriculum, and we must ensure that operating systems and hardware are designed to be cognitively accessible and that software developers keep the strategies identified by Davies and colleagues (2001) in mind as they develop packages.

ADDITIONAL READINGS

Assistive Technology

Buhler, C., & Knops, H. (1999). *Assistive technology on the threshold of the new millennium*. Burke, VA: IOS Press.

Flippo, K.F., Inge, K.J., & Barcus, J.M. (Eds.). (1995). *Assistive technology: A resource for school, work, and community*. Baltimore: Paul H. Brookes Publishing Co.

Scherer, M., & Galvin, J. (1996). *Evaluating, selecting and using appropriate assistive technology*. Gaithersburg, MD: Aspen Publishers.

Universal Design

Bowe, F.G. (2000). *Universal design in education: Teaching nontraditional students*. Westport, CT: Bergin & Garvey.

Orkwis, R., & McLane, K. (1998, Fall). *A curriculum every student can use: Design principles for student access* (ERIC/OSEP Topical Brief). Reston, VA: Council for Exceptional Children.

17

Achieving Access to and Progress in the General Curriculum

Making Curriculum Decisions and Designing Educational Supports

FANNING THE FLAMES OF CHANGE:
LIGHTING A FIRE UNDER PEOPLE WITHOUT
BURNING YOUR BRIDGES

The premise of this book is that by addressing the mandates for access to the general curriculum in the IDEA Amendments of 1997 (PL 105-17), educators working with students with mental retardation can improve practice and enhance the educational and learning experiences of these students. We began with a discussion of the changing perceptions and understanding of the term *mental retardation* and how they might affect education, discussed curriculum design and planning, and explained the meaning of the federal mandates for access to the general curriculum. Chapter 3 introduces a model to ensure that students with mental retardation gain access to and progress in the general curriculum, depicted in Figure 17.1, and suggested five components that would be necessary to achieve this outcome:

1. The implementation of a planning process ensuring that a student's education program is designed based on the general curriculum, taking into account unique student learning needs (e.g., curriculum decision making) and involves key stakeholders as meaningful partners.

2. Universally designed curricular materials and high-quality instructional methods and strategies that challenge all students should be implemented on a whole-school or schoolwide basis.

3. Instructional decision-making activities should focus at the lesson, unit, and classroom level in order to ensure that students can progress in the curriculum.

4. Additional curricular content and instructional strategies should be designed and implemented to ensure progress for students with learning needs not met by whole school efforts.

5. Student and program evaluation processes that focus on personal outcomes should be implemented.

In this chapter, we revisit this model and these components as a way of summarizing the educational process for students with mental retardation and providing a step-by-step examination of efforts to provide high-quality educational experiences for students with mental retardation that ensure access to and progress in the general curriculum. These efforts start with districtwide curriculum design and planning, schoolwide interventions that focus on access for all students, and building and classroom-level curriculum and instruction decisions. Once these elements are in place, the focus turns to personalizing the education program, with individualized education program (IEP) decision making that focuses on curriculum adaptations and augmentations and the design of "special education" supports, including specialized instruction in alternative curriculum areas.

REMOVING STEREOTYPES AND CHANGING EXPECTATIONS

The first and most fundamental step in ensuring success in education for students with mental retardation is to ensure that general and special educators approach these students with high expectations for success. Feldman, Saletsky, Sullivan, and Theiss noted that "one of the best supported findings in recent years demonstrates that the expectations that teachers hold about student performance are related to subsequent student outcomes" (1983, p. 27). Moreover, students' expectations for their own performance

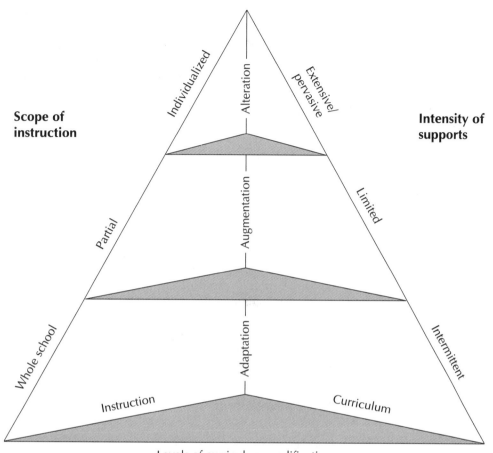

Scope of instruction

Intensity of supports

Levels of curriculum modifications

Figure 17.1. Model for gaining access to the general curriculum.

are strongly correlated with teachers' expectations for them (Wigfield & Harold, 1992). That is the reason for a strong emphasis on access to the general curriculum for students with disabilities: to raise performance outcomes by raising expectations of both teachers and students.

What do many educators expect of and from students with mental retardation? That question is not easy to answer from a data-based perspective due to the lack of such research. We do know, however, that teachers form expectations for student learning and progress according to diagnoses, *independent* of other information about student capacity, and that students who are diagnosed as having mental retardation are associated with the lowest expectations (Rolison & Medway, 1985). This is not news to most educators who work with students with mental retardation. Agran, Alper, and Wehmeyer (in press) surveyed teachers working with students with mental retardation and developmental disabilities about their beliefs and concerns about the IDEA access mandates and found that 68% agreed or agreed strongly when asked whether ensuring students' access to the general curriculum would help increase educational expectations for students with limited, extensive, or pervasive support needs.

Why is this? Certainly the low expectations associated with the mental retardation diagnosis are due, probably in large part, to the fact that students with mental retardation are among the lowest performing students in the school and are, by definition, performing below grade–age norms. To hold high expectations for students with mental retardation does not mean that one should expect an 18-year-old student with limited or extensive support needs to pass grade-normed tests in trigonometry or calculus. By advocating for high expectations and access to a challenging curriculum, we are not suggesting that educators ignore students' functional limitations. Students with mental retardation have unique learning needs that, almost by default, require curriculum modifications and alterations, primarily as a function of the students' age and level of support needs.

Stating that students with mental retardation should be held to high expectations suggests that educators not make assumptions about student capacity based on stereotypes formed by their understanding of the diagnosis. Historically, educational diagnoses have emphasized deficits—labeling students as educable, trainable, or profoundly deficient, which created intense stigmas. When using a deficits model, it is almost inevitable that expectations for student achievement and progress will be lowered, often with good intentions. As a result, some students are provided educational experiences that match their diagnosis and not their personalized needs.

Barriers due to diagnoses and low expectations can only be removed when the focus shifts from the student as the problem to consideration of the interaction between a student's functional limitations and the environment in which he or she lives, learns, or works. The curriculum and the classroom (whether school- or community-based) are the social contexts in which students with mental retardation learn. The first step in achieving progress in the general curriculum, then, is to examine those contexts.

Curriculum Design and Planning

The 1997 amendments to IDEA stressed aligning special education services and supports with the national focus on standards-based reform efforts so that students with disabilities might be held to high expectations, have access to a challenging curriculum, and be included in the accountability systems being established for all students. Changing expectations begins with changing how we think about disability. The next step in ensuring that students with mental retardation are held to high expectations and have access to a challenging curriculum focuses on designing and planning curriculum. Curriculum planners and designers should develop curriculum standards, benchmarks, and objectives with principles of universal design in mind—that is, with the intent that all students can have access to and progress in the curriculum. Orkwis and McLane defined *universal design for learning* as "the design of instructional materials and activities that allows the learning goals to be achievable by individuals with wide differences in their abilities to see, hear, speak, move, read, write, understand English, attend, organize, engage, and remember" (1998, p. 9). The use of open-ended instead of close-ended curriculum targets (e.g., standards, benchmarks) is one way to achieve such access. These terms describe the amount of specificity and direction provided by curriculum targets. Close-ended standards, benchmarks, or goals and objectives are specific and narrowly defined, whereas open-ended curriculum targets are more broadly written. Close-ended curriculum targets are often grade- or age-normed and leave little room for teachers to apply classroom-level decision making for universal access and differentiated instruction. Open-ended designs allow for greater flexibility as to what, when, and how topics are addressed in the classroom (Stainback, Stainback, Stefanich, & Alper, 1996) and facilitate school professionals' abilities and opportunities to respond to and support diverse individual student needs within whole-group instruction (Bingham, 1995).

Another component of universally designed curriculum involves how students are expected to respond to the standards. If such indicators are close-ended (e.g., student will submit a five-page written report), they limit the degree to which students with mental retardation can respond in an acceptable manner. If, however, the response opportunities are left open ended, allowing for multiple ways of responding, there is greater probability that all students will be able to demonstrate progress. The goal of curriculum planning and design is illustrated by Pugach and Warger, who observed that

> Different students will learn the curriculum to different degrees. They will do so in different ways and use their learning for different purposes. Not everyone (so the saying goes) is going to become a rocket scientist, so why design all curriculum around the needs of budding rocketeers? The challenge for educators is to facilitate a learning environment that teaches students fundamental learning-how-to-learn skills and encourages thinking, social, and communication skills, so that students can tackle new content in ways that better their current or future lives. (1996, p. 228)

Schoolwide Interventions: Benefits for All Students

Schools attempt to implement interventions that benefit all students and that decrease the need for individualized special education services and supports. These schoolwide efforts affect several areas and efforts, beginning with ensuring that building-level adoptions and adaptations of state or local standards retain (or add) the open-ended curriculum targets and benchmarks discussed in reference to curriculum design.

Second, building personnel should ensure that all students have access to high-quality instruction that is challenging and tailored to their unique needs and that curriculum adaptations are used to ensure access for as many students as possible. Chapter 8 discusses the wide array of building-level and classroom-level curriculum and instructional decisions that can ensure high-quality learning experiences for all students. Building- and classroom-level curriculum decisions should embody principles of universal design and materials used across the school should incorporate universal design features. Teachers should differentiate instruction through unit and lesson design strategies that use task analysis, cognitive taxonomies, and learning taxonomies to personalize instruction and should have support to learn and implement a wide array of instructional methods that reflect the content being taught and the needs of the learner. The use of technology is not, however, the only means of adapting the curriculum that needs to be considered. Curriculum adaptation refers to *any* effort to modify the *presentation* of the curriculum or to modify the student's *engagement* with the curriculum to enhance access and progress. A wide array of teaching devices and strategies enable such adaptation. Teachers can use advance organizers to present key themes, to present big ideas, or to provide students with an outline of the content of the lesson or can use scaffolding (i.e., temporary support for learning that is gradually reduced) to ensure student progress. It is evident that some learning strategies are not directly applicable to students with mental retardation. Kavale and Forness (1998) conducted a mega-analysis of meta-analyses of instructional strategies used with students receiving special education services, and among the strategies that did not have beneficial effects for students with mental retardation were imagery and verbal rehearsal. However, there are an equivalent number of strategies that have promise but have not been evaluated with students with mental retardation.

In addition, approaching behavioral and discipline issues with positive behavioral support requires schoolwide procedures that emphasize rewarding students for positive behavior and focus on identifying and changing those environmental circumstances that lead to problem behaviors. Such emphasis is complimented by procedures to promote student self-determination and by the creation of learning communities in which all children are valued and supported.

INDIVIDUALIZED EDUCATIONAL EXPERIENCES FOR ALL STUDENTS

These schoolwide supports form a necessary component in ensuring access for students with mental retardation. However, there are students who, despite these whole-school interventions, need more intensive supports. Some of these students may have a disability; others may not. At this level, it is important to consider small-group or partial-school interventions that provide more individualized learning experiences. Among these are curriculum augmentations such as those discussed in Chapter 4. Again, *curriculum augmentation* refers to the process of augmenting or expanding the curriculum in such a manner as to teach students skills or strategies that enable them to more effectively interact with and progress in the general curriculum. Many augmentations refer to teaching students cognitive strategies that enable them to more successfully navigate the curriculum, including study skills, note-taking strategies, or paragraph-writing strategies. Students might also be taught self-regulation or self-management skills that enable them to solve problems and engage in self-directed learning and how to apply such strategies to efforts in the curriculum. Such partial-school efforts may be ongoing or may be one-time efforts related to behavior or academic progress (e.g., targeted instruction to all sixth-grade students at the start of their first year in middle school on how to follow school rules related to walking from class to class in the hall, a session for targeted students on specific study skills).

PERSONALIZED EDUCATIONAL EXPERIENCES FOR STUDENTS WITH MENTAL RETARDATION

When schools implement schoolwide and partial-school curriculum decisions and educational supports, there is a reduced need to provide more intensive supports. However, a segment of the school population, including many students with mental retardation, may need more extensive and pervasive support strategies to ensure that the students receive an appropriate educational program. This individualized process begins with the IEP planning and decision-making process. This planning process should be person-centered, focused on the visions and dreams of the student and his or her family, held multiple times per year, and student-directed, enabling young people to begin to exert meaningful control over their lives. The IEP team should consider the use of assistive technology to accommodate for a student's limitations, negating the need for subsequent curriculum adaptations or augmentations. If schools have designed the curriculum in ways that are consistent with universal design principles, implemented schoolwide interventions, used building- and classroom-level curriculum and instructional decision-making processes to differentiate instruction, and included partial-school interventions to target specific social or environmental contexts, the IEP team may be ready to identify the alternative portion of the student's formal education program. It is likely, however, that in many schools, not all of these efforts have been implemented. It then becomes the responsibility of the IEP team, in tandem with the classroom teacher and other key personnel, to use the process described in Chapter 4 and depicted in Figure 17.2.

The IEP team is not intended to make every curriculum and instructional decision but instead to lay a framework on which teachers can build with campus- and classroom-level curricular and instructional decisions. As such, teachers working with students with mental retardation should implement building- and classroom-level processes to further personalize the student's educational program and to ensure greater success and progress. IEP teams are also charged with making decisions about a wide array of educational supports, including involvement in statewide assessments and test accommodations, and should do so with a focus on providing developmentally and chronologically age-appropriate experiences. As students with mental retardation age, an increased proportion of their learning experiences should occur within the community, and it is the IEP team's responsibility, in tandem with the teacher and other professionals, to ensure community-referenced planning that leads to community-based instruction. Such instruction should not be in conflict with or antithetical to inclusion because all schools, particularly high schools, need to focus on community-based learning and personal outcomes.

Only at this stage should IEP teams and teachers consider which alternative curricular content areas and instructional experiences are needed to complete the student's appropriate education program. Up to this point, that content has been referenced to the general curriculum. Many functional skills are evident in most state or local standards. For example, most states have standards that address healthy sexuality and development, and the needs of students with mental retardation related to sexuality and the development of social relationships can, likely, be met within the context of the general curriculum. Similarly, it is evident that state and local standards contain multiple references to component elements of self-determined behavior, such as problem solving, decision making, or goal setting, and the importance of promoting self-determination for students with mental retardation can be met by addressing similar issues for all students. In many (though not all) states, the standards include experiences that can be incorporated into traditional functional curricular components, such as transition-related skills, personal and self-care skills, and social skills.

When state and local standards are written as open-ended, there is room for students with mental retardation to show progress without necessarily meeting grade- or age-normed reference points. Areas of academic content form the most obvious cases in which close-ended standards and benchmarks make showing progress in the curriculum difficult, if not impossible, for students with mental retardation. When, however, such standards and benchmarks are open ended, students can be provided instruction that enables them to continue to progress and that is functional. We do not prescribe how much of a student's appropriate educational program should be derived from the general curriculum versus an alternative curriculum. We contend, however, that IEP teams and teachers must start with the general curriculum. When they do so, it is likely that all students will benefit from and be able to have access to some component of the general curriculum and that the use of alternative curricular content will be minimized.

Finally, the evaluation of a student's education program moves from being focused on student impairments to emphasizing personal outcomes (i.e., outcomes that are personally relevant to the student) and moves from being conducted within an empowerment evaluation framework in which the emphasis is on examining the efficacy of the

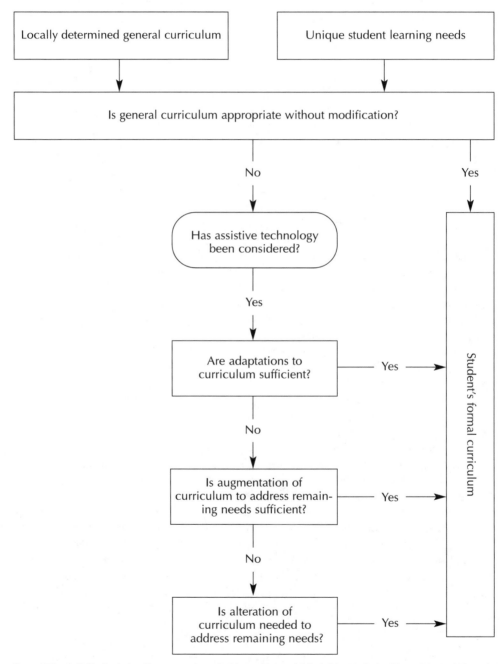

Figure 17.2. Individualized education program team decision-making model for helping students with mental retardation gain access to the general curriculum.

interventions and the social context, not strictly on student characteristics and impairments.

FUTURE DIRECTIONS: IMPLEMENTING AND SURVIVING CHANGE

The American novelist James Baldwin once remarked that most of us are about as eager to be changed as we were to be born and go through our changes in a similar state of shock. In describing the process of achieving access to and promoting progress in the general curriculum, we are not naive to the complexities that accompany such change. Implementing changes to ensure that high-quality educational supports for students with mental retardation is a complex process. The demands placed on schools with regard to responding to public and governmental demands to implement reforms in schools, including standards-based reforms, often appear unrelenting and overwhelming. Schools themselves are held to expectations by various stakeholders, from parents to communities to politicians. With each change, complex issues emerge that challenge professionals to examine and often modify their roles, functions, and practices. One can certainly understand how it may be confusing for many professionals to organize and manage schools or to proceed with changes that adequately support students who represent only a small portion of the total student population—such as students with mental retardation—in light of such constantly evolving, complex, systemic changes.

Multiple factors moderate the ability of professionals to deal with such changes and to utilize research in recommended practices, including 1) knowledge and learning, 2) attitudes and beliefs, and 3) contextual variables (Malouf & Schiller, 1995). Factors such as isolation, ambiguity of educational goals, heavy workloads, excessive regulations, lack of collegiality, and limited resources influence professionals' initiative and their ability to change their actions. Without in-depth discussions and responses that acknowledge the interplay of proposed changes on the purpose and conduct of schooling, responses to change are often isolated, piecemeal, or nonexistent (Noddings, 1995). After experiencing repeated cycles of the failure of the system to adequately implement recommended changes, educators are often left feeling cynical, skeptical, and disillusioned (Apple & Beane, 1995; Lortie, 1975).

It is virtually impossible to initiate change with actions that are purposeful and effective without a systematic framework by which to sort, analyze, evaluate, and critically reflect on issues important to the change process. Sands, Kozleski, and French (2000) described a process that enables professionals to respond to change within a framework that considers multiple vantage points. Implementing changes such as those discussed in this text requires the consideration of each of these vantage points.

The first vantage point is the *philosophical vantage point*, which addresses the underlying values or beliefs of a particular perspective. This philosophical vantage point serves as the basis for setting policy, organizing supports, and implementing practices. Equally important is the fact that the philosophical vantage point that accompanies the suggested changes will replace an existing vantage point. Achieving change requires that stakeholders affected by the change support the philosophical vantage point. The philosophical vantage point that is forwarded by this text emphasizes the importance of students with mental retardation receiving their education with same-age, typically developing peers and the importance of self-determination throughout the educational process. It embodies an emphasis not only on individualization but personalization and the belief that if students with mental retardation are taught using a wider array of teaching strategies and are exposed to a curriculum that is broadly conceptualized and includes various levels of curriculum modifications, they will progress. These beliefs are predicated on a conceptualization of mental retardation that is not focused on impairments but on ability and on the social and environmental contexts in which students learn. These beliefs challenge the beliefs held by many educators. Yet, if the changes recommended in the text are to be realized, it is important that processes are in place to provide professionals and family members with the opportunity to learn more about these perspectives, how they influence education, and why they are important.

A second perspective is the *governmental and policy vantage point.* Sarason (1996) noted that schools are, fundamentally, political entities, and the politics of schools, the distribution of power and authority, are influenced by governmental and policy issues. The changes proposed are, fundamentally, driven by governmental and policy issues. School reform efforts certainly have a political side to them. The role of policy is evident in several pieces of legislation: 1) the U.S. Department of Education's emphasis on funding a school reform model and 2) the guidelines for access to the general curriculum in the 1997 amendments to IDEA. Although federal and state policy can and does drive change in schools, it is important to recognize that unless other vantage points are considered and included, creating meaningful, systemic change by policy directive alone will likely not succeed. Sands and Wehmeyer noted as such, stating that "the presence of policy and legislation offering protections does not ensure either compliance or positive outcomes" (1996, p. 338). Of concern is whether the spirit of the legislation and policy is carried out on the organizational and professional levels (subsequent vantage points). The spirit of the access to the general curriculum mandate is that students with disabilities should be provided access to a challenging curriculum, exposed to high-quality instructional experiences, and provided with needed supports and accommodations that lead to higher expectations and educational progress.

The third vantage point is the *organizational vantage point.* This vantage point considers whether the goals of an organization's services, supports, structures, and assignment of personnel roles and responsibilities are consistent with the philosophy, meet policy and regulatory requirements, and are effective in achieving stated goals. The knowledge base at this level is gathered by program demonstration and evaluation, and consequent organizational change, restructuring, and design occur as a function of that information. Chapter 6 discusses an empowerment evaluation framework for engaging in such program evaluation activities that emphasize self-determination and focus on personal outcomes that have meaning and value to the student, his or her family, and other key stakeholders in the educational process. Chapters 7, 8, and 9 review the building-, classroom-, and instructional-level activities related to creating a learning community, making curriculum and instructional decisions, and providing instruction in inclusive settings. Furthermore, Chapter 14 discusses organizational issues pertaining to community-based instruction for students with mental retardation. These organizational factors are critical to the successful implementation of change. Professionals in education need to examine resource allocation and personnel use and use the broad array of strategies and methods identified to successfully include students with disabilities in general education settings. Perhaps most important, however, educators working with students with mental retardation must gain a voice in school reform efforts in their schools and districts to ensure that organizational factors emerging from these reform efforts take into account the needs of students with mental retardation.

The final vantage point is the *professional/procedural vantage point,* which examines the effectiveness of the organization's strategies, tools, and procedures for achieving organizational, policy, and societal goals and values. Model demonstration activities, research, and program evaluation efforts provide the answers to these questions. This text has introduced a wide array of such professional/procedural issues. Some of these have not had wide application in the education of students with mental retardation but have been successful with other students. Others have been developed specifically for students with mental retardation. We have not dealt extensively with areas tied to more traditional special education services and supports, primarily because the field has a wide knowledge base about those processes. We have not elaborated on what is traditionally referred to as a *functional curriculum* or the methods that have been used to teach students with mental retardation within this context for the simple reason that those processes and applications are well-documented in other sources and because teachers working with students with mental retardation already have a working knowledge of such procedures. This text assumes that the reader has a foundational knowledge of mental retardation, the ways in which that construct has been defined, and the prevalent teaching methods used. At the professional/procedural level, we need to broaden our knowledge and capacity to intervene with students with mental retardation using a wider array of instructional methods and strategies and then implement those strategies that prove to be effective in enabling students to gain access to and progress in the general curriculum.

These four vantage points—philosophical, governmental/policy, organizational, and professional/procedural—are useful in classifying the multiple variables that can support or impede our ability to respond to the types of complex changes that the access mandates present to the field. As schools and education professionals examine the issues pertaining to the access requirements, it is important that they consider each of these vantage points.

SUMMARY

The access mandates in the IDEA Amendments of 1997 present both a challenge and an opportunity for educators focused on the education of students with mental retardation. The challenge is to examine the demands of the school reform movement toward accountability and high standards in the context of what is best for students with mental retardation. This examination must include a self-evaluation of the educational programs of students with mental retardation and their efficacy or lack thereof. The opportunity presented is to raise expectations for students with mental retardation and to move the discussion beyond just where a student receives his or her educational program to include discussions of what is in that educational program and how it is implemented.

This opportunity and challenge is best represented, perhaps, in this passage from the IDEA Amendments of 1997:

> Disability is a natural part of the human experience and in no way diminishes the right of individuals to participate in or contribute to society. Improving educational results for children with disabilities is an essential element of our national policy of ensuring equality of opportunity, full participation, independent living, and economic self-sufficiency for individuals with disabilities. (Findings from Congress section, Part A [General Provisions], Sec. 601 [1])

This acknowledgment reflects the shifting views of disability discussed in Chapter 1. This section continues, noting that historically, the educational needs of students with disabilities were not met, students with disabilities were excluded from the public school system, and when students were in the public school system, curriculum and instruction did not meeting their learning needs. The findings from Congress acknowledge that much about this scenario has changed since the enactment of what is now called IDEA but then state that the implementation of IDEA has been impeded by low expectations and an insufficient focus on applying replicable research on proven methods of teaching and learning for children with disabilities. Section 601 of IDEA concludes by stating, starting in paragraph (5), that

> Over 20 years of research and experience has demonstrated that the education of children with disabilities can be made more effective by
>
> (A)   having high expectations for such children and ensuring their access in the general curriculum to the maximum extent possible;
>
> (B)   strengthening the role of parents and ensuring that families of such children have meaningful opportunities to participate in the education of their children at school and at home;
>
> (C)   coordinating this Act with other local, educational service agency, State, and Federal school improvement efforts in order to ensure that such children benefit from such efforts and that special education can become a service for such children rather than a place where they are sent;
>
> (D)   providing appropriate special education and related services and aids and supports in the general classroom to such children, whenever appropriate;
>
> (E)   supporting high-quality, intensive professional development for all personnel who work with such children in order to ensure that they have the skills and knowledge necessary to enable them
>
> > (i)   to meet developmental goals and, to the maximum extent possible, those challenging expectations that have been established for all children; and
> >
> > (ii)   to be prepared to lead productive, independent, adult lives, to the maximum extent possible;
>
> (F)   providing incentives for whole-school approaches and pre-referral intervention to reduce the need to label children as disabled in order to address their learning needs; and
>
> (G)   focusing resources on teaching and learning while reducing paperwork and requirements that do not assist in improving educational results.

The challenge and opportunity before us is to ensure that students with mental retardation are not left behind as special education pursues these goals and objectives.

ADDITIONAL READINGS

Individuals with Disabilities Education Act (IDEA) Amendments of 1997. (Available: http://www.ideapractices.org/law/IDEAMAIN.HTM.)

Kavale, K.A., & Forness, S.R. (1998). *Efficacy of special education and related services.* Washington, DC: American Association on Mental Retardation.

References

Adelman, H.S., & Taylor, L. (1997). Addressing barriers to learning: Beyond school-linked services and full-service schools. *American Journal of Orthopsychiatry, 67*(3), 408–419.

Agran, M. (1997). *Student-directed learning: Teaching self-determination skills.* Pacific Grove, CA: Brooks/Cole.

Agran, M., Alper, S., & Wehmeyer, M.L. (in press). Access to the general curriculum for students with mental retardation: What it means to teachers. *Education and Training: Mental Retardation and Developmental Disabilities.*

Agran, M., Fodor-Davis, J., & Moore, S. (1986). The effects of self-instructional training on job-task sequencing: Suggesting a problem-solving strategy. *Education and Training in Mental Retardation, 21,* 273–281.

Agran, M., & Moore, S.C. (1994). *How to teach self-instruction of job skills.* Washington, DC: American Association on Mental Retardation.

Agran, M., Salzberg, C.L., & Stowitschek, J.J. (1987). An analysis of the effects of a social skills training program using self-instructions on the acquisition and generalization of two social behaviors in a work setting. *Journal of The Association for Persons with Severe Handicaps, 12,* 131–139.

Agran, M., Snow, K., & Swaner, J. (1999). A survey of secondary level teachers' opinions on community-based instruction and inclusive education. *Journal of The Association for Persons with Severe Handicaps, 24,* 58–62.

American Association on Mental Retardation (AAMR). (1992). *Mental retardation: Definition, classification, and systems of supports* (9th ed.). Washington, DC: Author.

American Psychiatric Association (APA). (2000). *Diagnostic and statistical manual of mental disorders* (4th ed., text rev.). Washington, DC: Author.

Americans with Disabilities Act (ADA) of 1990, PL 101-336, 42 U.S.C. §§ 12101 *et seq.*

Angyal, A. (1941). *Foundations for a science of personality.* Cambridge, MA: Harvard University Press.

Apple, M.W., & Beane, J.A. (1995). The case for democratic schools. In M.W. Apple & J. Beane (Eds.), *Democratic schools* (pp. 1–25). Alexandria, VA: Association for Supervision and Curriculum Development.

Arc, The (1995). *The ADA and mental retardation: A question and answer fact sheet.* Arlington, TX: Author.

Arc, The. (1996). *Sexuality: Position statement #9.* Silver Spring, MD: Author. (Available: http://www.thearc.org/posits/sex.html)

Arc, The. (1999). *The Individualized Education Program and students with mental retardation: A Q&A factsheet.* Silver Spring, MD: Author.

Armstrong, D.G. (1989). *Developing and documenting curriculum.* Needham Heights, MA: Allyn & Bacon.

Armstrong, T. (1994). *Multiple intelligences in the classroom.* Alexandria, VA: Association for Supervision and Curriculum Development.

Association for Supervision and Curriculum Development (ASCD). (1999). *Curriculum mapping: Charting the course for content.* Alexandria, VA: Author.

Ausubel, D.P. (1960). The use of advance organizers in the learning and retention of meaningful verbal material. *Journal of Educational Psychology, 51,* 267–272.

Ausubel, D.P. (1963). *The psychology of meaningful verbal learning: An introduction to school learning.* New York: Grune & Stratton.

Bailey J., (1997, November). *Meeting high expectations* [Speech]. http://www.ed.gov/offices/OSERS/IDEA/speech_3.html

Ballenger, C. (1992). Because you like us: The language of control. *Harvard Educational Review, 62,* 199–208.

Bambara, L., & Cole, C. (1997). Permanent antecedent prompts. In M. Agran (Ed.), *Student directed learning: Teaching self-determination skills* (pp. 111–143). Pacific Grove, CA: Brooks/Cole.

Bandura, A.B. (1986). *Social foundations of thought and action: A social-cognitive theory.* Upper Saddle River, NJ: Prentice Hall.

Bandura, A.B. (1989). Human agency in social cognitive theory. *American Psychologist, 44,* 1175–1184.

Bandura, A.B. (1991). Human agency: The rhetoric and the reality. *American Psychologist, 46,* 157–162.

Bandura, A.B. (1997). *Self-efficacy: The exercise of control.* New York: W.H. Freeman and Co.

Bandura, A.B., & Wood, R. (1989). Effect of preceived controllability and performance standards on self-regulation of complex decision-making. *Journal of Personality and Social Psychology, 56,* 805–814.

Banks, J.A., & McGee-Banks, C.A. (2001). *Handbook of research on multicultural education.* San Francisco: Jossey-Bass.

Baron, J., & Brown, R.V. (1991). Introduction. In J. Baron & R.V. Brown (Eds.), *Teaching decision making to adolescents* (pp. 7–18). Mahwah, NJ: Lawrence Erlbaum Associates.

Bawrens, J., Hourcade, J., & Friend, M. (1987). Cooperative teaching: A model for general and special education integration. *Remedial and Special Education, 10,* 17–22.

Beck, J., Broers, J., Hogue, E., Shipstead, J., & Knowlton, H.E. (1994). Strategies for functional community-based instruction and inclusion of children with mental retardation. *Teaching Exceptional Children, 26*(2), 44–48.

Belmont, J., & Mitchell, D. (1987). The general strategies hypothesis as applied to cognitive theory in mental retardation. *Intelligence, 11,* 91–105.

Benson, L., & Harkavy, I. (1996). School and community in the global society: A Neo Deweyian theory of community problem-solving schools and cosmopolitan neighborly communities in a Neo-Deweyian "manifesto" to dynamically connect school and community. *Universities and Community Schools, 5*(1–2), 11–69.

Beyth-Marom, R., Fischhoff, B., Jacobs Quadrel, M., & Furby, L. (1991). Teaching decision-making to adolescents: A critical review. In J. Baron & R.V. Brown (Eds.), *Teaching decision making to adolescents* (pp. 19–59). Mahwah, NJ: Lawrence Erlbaum Associates.

Biehler, R.F., & Snowman, J. (1993). *Psychology applied to teaching* (7th ed.). Boston: Houghton Mifflin.

Bingham, A.A. (1995). *Exploring the multi-age classroom.* York, ME: Stenhouse.

Bishop, K.D., Jubala, K.A., Stainback, W., & Stainback, S. (1996). Facilitating friendships. In S. Stainback & W. Stainback (Eds.), *Inclusion: A guide for educators* (pp. 155–169). Baltimore: Paul H. Brookes Publishing Co.

Blatt, B. (1987). *The conquest of mental retardation.* Austin, TX: PRO-ED.

Blatt, B., & Kaplan, F. (1966). *Christmas in Purgatory.* Needham Heights, MA: Allyn & Bacon.

Bloom, B.S., Englehart, M.B., Furst, E.J., Hill, W.H., & Krathwohl, D.R. (Eds.). (1956). *Taxonomy of educational objectives: The classification of educational goals. Handbook I: Cognitive domain.* New York: McKay.

Bloom, B.S., Madaus, G.F., & Hastings, J.T. (1981). *Evaluation to improve learning.* New York: McGraw-Hill.

Board of Education v. Rowley, 458 U.S. 176, 102 S. Ct. 3034, 73 L. Ed., 2d 690 (1982).

Borkowski, J.G., & Cavanaugh, J.C. (1979). Maintenance and generalization of skills and strategies by the retarded. In N.R. Ellis (Ed.), *Handbook of mental deficiency: Psychological theory and research* (2nd ed., pp. 569–618). Mahwah, NJ: Lawrence Erlbaum Associates.

Borkowski, J.G., & Day, J.D. (1987). *Cognition in special children: Comparative approaches to retardation, learning, disabilities, and giftedness.* Norwood, NJ: Ablex Publishing.

Borkowski, J.G., Weyhing, R., & Turner, L. (1986). Attributional retraining and the teaching of strategies. *Exceptional Children, 53,* 130–137.

Braddock, D. (1998). Mental retardation and developmental disabilities: Historical and contemporary perspectives. In D. Braddock, R.. Hemp, S. Parish, & J. Westrich (Eds.), *The state of the states in developmental disabilities* (5th ed., pp. 3–23). Washington, DC: American Association on Mental Retardation.

Brown, A.L., & Campione, J.C. (1986). Psychological theory and the study of learning disabilities. *American Psychologist, 14,* 1059–1068.

Brown, A.L., & Campione, J.C. (1998). Designing a community of young learners: Theoretical and practical lessons. In N.M. Lambert & B.L. McCombs (Eds.), *How students learn: Reforming schools through learner-centered education* (pp. 153–186). Washington DC: American Psychological Association.

Brown, F., Appel, C., Corsi, L., & Wenig, B. (1993). Choice diversity for people with severe disabilities. *Education and Training in Mental Retardation, 28,* 318–326.

Brown, L., Branston, M.B., Hamre-Nietupski, S., Pumpian, I., Certo, N., & Gruenewald, L. (1979). A strategy for developing chronological age-appropriate and functional curricular content for severely handicapped adolescents and young adults. *Journal of Special Education, 13,* 81–90.

Brown, L., Nietupski, J., & Hamre-Nietupski, S. (1976). Criterion of ultimate functioning. In M.A. Thomas (Ed.), *Hey, don't forget about me!* (pp. 2–13). Reston, VA: Council for Exceptional Children.

Brown, L., Schwarz, P., Udvari-Solner, A., Kampschroer, E.F., Johnson, F., Jorgensen, J., & Gruenewald, L. (1991). How much time should students with severe intellectual disabilities spend in regular education classrooms and elsewhere? *Journal of The Association for Persons with Severe Handicaps, 16,* 39–47.

Brown, L., Shiraga, B., Rogan, P., York, J., Zanella Albright, K., McCarthy, E., & Loomis, R. (1985). The "why question" in educational programs for students who are severely intellectually disabled. In L. Brown, B. Shiraga, J. York, A. Udvari-Solner, K. Zanella Albright, P. Rogan, E. McCarthy, & R. Loomis (Eds.), *Educational programs for students with severe intellectual disabilities* (Vol. 15, pp. 17–42). Madison, WI: Madison Metropolitan School District.

Brownell, K.D., Colletti, G., Ersner-Hershfield, R., Hershfield, S.M., & Wilson, G.T. (1977). Self-control in school children: Stringency and leniency in self-determined and externally imposed performance standards. *Behavior Therapy, 8,* 442–455.

Bulgren, J., & Lenz, K. (1996). Strategic instruction in the content areas. In D.D. Deshler, E.S. Ellis, & B.K. Lenz (Eds.), *Teaching adolescents with learning disabilities: Strategies and methods* (2nd ed., pp. 409–473). Denver, CO: Love Publishing.

Bulgren, J.A., Schumaker, J.B., & Deshler, D.D. (1988). Effectiveness of a concept teaching routine in enhancing the performance of LD students in secondary-level mainstream classes. *Learning Disability Quarterly, 11,* 3–17.

Burns, B.J., & Goldman, S.K. (Eds.). (1999). *Systems of care: Promising practices in children's mental health.* Washington, DC: Center for Effective Collaboration and Practice, American Institutes for Research.

California Department of Education. (1998). *Health education challenge standards for student success.* Sacramento, CA: Author.

Carnine, D.W., Silbert, J., & Kameenui, E.J. (1990). *Direct instruction reading* (2nd ed.). Columbus, OH: Merrill.

Carr, E.G., Horner, R.H., Turnbull, A.P., Marquis, J.G., McLaughlin, D.M., McAtee, M.L., Smith, C.E., Ryan, K.A., Ruef, M.B., & Doolabh, A. (1999). *Positive behavior support for people with developmental disabilities: A research synthesis.* Washington, DC: American Association on Mental Retardation.

Carr, R.W. (1979). Goal attainment scaling as a useful tool for evaluating progress in special education. *Exceptional Children, 46,* 88–95.

Center for Applied Special Technology (CAST). (1998–1999). *The National Center on Accessing the General Curriculum* [On-line]. (Available: http://www.cast.org/initiatives /national_center.html)

Center on Human Policy. (2000). *The community imperative.* Syracuse, NY: Author.

Chadsey-Rusch, J., Rusch, F., & O'Reilly, M.F. (1991). Transition from school to integrated communities. *Remedial and Special Education, 12,* 23–33.

Chang, M.K. (1986). *Advance organizer strategy for educable mentally retarded and regular children.* (ERIC Document Reproduction Service No. EC 182 322)

Chiron, R., & Gerken, K. (1983). The effects of a self-monitoring technique on the locus of control orientation of educable mentally retarded children. *School Psychology Review, 3,* 87–92.

Clark, H.B., Lee, B., Prange, M.E., & McDonald, B.A. (1996). Children lost within the childcare system: Can wraparound service strategies improve placement outcomes? *Journal of Child and Family Studies, 5,* 39–54.

Cochran-Smith, M. (1995). Color blindness and basket making are not the answers: Confronting dilemmas of race, culture, and language diversity in teacher education. *American Educational Research Journal, 32,* 493–522.

Colvin, G.T., & Sugai, G.M. (1988). Proactive strageies for managing social behavior problems: An instructional approach. *Education and Treatment of Children, 11,* 341–348.

Colvin, G., Sugai, G., Good, R.H., & Lee, Y. (1996). Using active supervision and precorrection to improve transition behaviors in an elementary school. *School Psychology Quarterly, 12,* 344–363.

Comer, J.P. (1988). Educating poor minority children. *Scientific American, 259*(5), 42–48.

Committee on Appropriate Test Use. (1999). *High stakes: Testing for tracking, promotion, and graduation.* Washington, DC: National Academy Press.

Committee on Goals 2000 and the Inclusion of Students with Disabilities. (1997). *Educating one and all: Students with disabilities and standards-based reform.* Washington, DC: National Academy Press.

Cook, L.K., & Friend, M. (1995). Co-teaching: Guidelines for creating effective practices. *Focus on Exceptional Children, 28,* 1–16.

Cook, L.K., & Mayer, R.E. (1988). Teaching readers about the structure of scientific text. *Journal of Educational Psychology, 80,* 448–456.

Council on Quality and Leadership in Supports for People with Disabilities. (1997). *Personal outcomes measures.* Towson, MD: Author.

Cross, T., Cooke, N.L., Wood, W.M., & Test, D.W. (2000). Comparison of the effects of MAPS and ChoiceMaker on student self-determination skills. *Education and Training in Mental Retardation and Developmental Disabilities, 34,* 499–510.

Cutler, B.C. (1993). *You, your child, and special education: A guide to making the system work.* Baltimore: Paul H. Brookes Publishing Co.

Damon, W. (1986). *Social and personality development.* New York: W.W. Norton & Company.

Dattilo, J. (1987). Computerized assessment of leisure preferences: A replication. *Education and Training in Mental Retardation, 22,* 128–133.

Dattilo, J., Guerin, N., Cory, L., & Williams, R. (2001). Effects of computerized leisure education on self-determination of youth with disabilities. *Journal of Special Education Technology, 16,* 5–17.

Davies, D.K., & Stock, S.E. (1994). *PictureCoach and PocketCoach: An integrated multi-media training system for teaching and maintaining vocational skills for adults with developmental disabilities* (Phase I SBIR Final Report). Unpublished manuscript.

Davies, D.K., & Stock, S.E. (1995, March). *MoneyCoach: A functional multimedia computer program for maximizing independence in financial management for adults with developmental disabilities.* Paper presented at the 1995 California State University–Northridge (CSUN) Technology and Persons with Disabilities Conference, Los Angeles.

Davies, D.K., & Stock, S.E. (1997a, May). *Assistive technology and adults with development disabilities.* Paper presented at the Mission Possible Conference, Denver.

Davies, D.K., & Stock, S.E. (1997b). *PictureCoach and PocketCoach: An integrated multimedia training system for skill development for individuals with mental retardation* (Phase II SBIR Final Report). Unpublished manuscript.

Davies, D.K., Stock, S.E., & Wehmeyer, M.L. (2001). Enhancing independent Internet access for individuals with mental retardation through the use of a specialized web browser: A pilot study. *Education and Training in Mental Retardation and Developmental Disabilities, 36,* 107–113

Deci, E.L. (1992). The relation of interest to the motivation of behavior: A self-determination theory perspective. In K.A. Renninger, S. Hidi, & A. Krapp (Eds.), *The role of interest in learning and development* (pp. 43–70). Mahwah, NJ: Lawrence Erlbaum Associates.

Deci, E.L., & Chandler, C.L. (1986). The importance of motivation for the future of the LD field. *Journal of Learning Disabilities, 19,* 587–594.

Deci, E.L., & Ryan, R. (1985). *Intrinsic motivation and self-determination in human behavior.* New York: Kluwer Academic/Plenum.

Delattre, E. (1997, January). Psittacism and dead language: Not caring enough about the truth to seek words that capture it. *Education Week, 22,* 36.

Delpit, L. (1995). *Other people's children: Cultural conflict in the classroom.* New York: The New Press.

Delquadri, J., Greenwood, C.R., Whorton, D., Carta, J.J., & Hall, R.V. (1986). Class wide peer tutoring. *Exceptional Children, 52,* 535–542.

Deshler, D.D., Ellis, E.S., & Lenz, B.K. (Eds.). (1996). *Teaching adolescents with learning disabilities: Strategies and methods* (2nd ed., pp. 9–60). Denver, CO: Love Publishing.

Dever, R. (1989). A taxonomy of community living skills. *Exceptional Children, 55,* 395–404.

Dever, R.B., & Knapczyk, D.R. (1997). *Teaching persons with mental retardation: A model for curriculum development and teaching.* Madison, WI: Brown & Benchmark Publishers.

Doll, B., Sands, D.J., Wehmeyer, M.L., & Palmer, S. (1996). Promoting the development and acquisition of self-determined behavior. In D.J. Sands & M.L. Wehmeyer (Eds.), *Self-determination across the life span: Independence and choice for people with disabilities* (pp. 65–90). Baltimore: Paul H. Brookes Publishing Co.

Doll, R.C. (1996). *Curriculum improvement: Decision making and process* (9th ed.). Needham Heights, MA: Allyn & Bacon.

Dusek, J.B. (1996). *Adolescent development and behavior* (3rd ed.). Upper Saddle River, NJ: Prentice Hall.

Eber, L., Nelson, C.M., & Miles, P. (1997). School-based wraparound for students with emotional and behavioral challenges. *Exceptional Children, 63*(4), 539–555.

Edmark Corporation. (n.d.). *Bailey's book house* [Computer software]. Redmond, WA: Author.

Education for All Handicapped Children Act of 1975, PL 94-142, 20 U.S.C. §§ 1400 *et seq.*

Education for the Handicapped Act Amendments of 1986, PL 98-199, 20 U.S.C. §§ 1400 *et seq.*

Eisenhart, M., & Graue, M.E. (1993). Constructing cultural difference and educational achievement in schools. In E. Jacobs & C. Jordan (Eds.), *Minority education: Anthropological perspectives* (pp. 78–96). Norwood, NJ: Ablex Publishing Corporation.

Ellis, E.S., & Lenz, B.K. (1996). Perspectives on instruction in learning strategies. In D.D. Deshler, E.S. Ellis, & B.K. Lenz (Eds.), *Teaching adolescents with learning disabilities: Strategies and methods* (2nd ed., pp. 9–60). Denver, CO: Love Publishing.

Everson, J.M. (1995). *Transition services for youths who are deaf-blind: A "best practices" guide for educators.* Sands Point, NY: Helen Keller National Center, Technical Assistance Center.

Everson, J.M. (1996). Using person-centered planning concepts to school-to-adult life transition planning. *Journal of Vocational Rehabilitation, 6*(1), 7–15.

Falvey, M.A., & Grenot-Scheyer, M. (1995). Instructional strategies. In M.A. Falvey (Ed.), *Inclusive and heterogeneous schooling: Assessment, curriculum, and instruction* (pp. 131–158). Baltimore: Paul H. Brookes Publishing Co.

Federal Register (1999, March 12). Washington, DC: U.S. Government Printing Office.

Feeling smug? Try this final exam for eighth graders in 1895. (2001). *Ad Astra, 1, 29.*

Feldman, R.S., Saletsky, R.D., Sullivan, J., & Theiss, A. (1983). Student locus of control and response to expectations about self and teacher. *Journal of Educational Psychology, 75,* 27–32.

Ferguson, D., Kozleski, E., & Smith, A. (2000). *Inclusive and transformed schools: A framework for fundamental change.* Denver, CO: National Institute for Urban School Improvement.

Fetterman, D.M. (1996). Empowerment evaluation: An introduction to theory and practice. In D.M. Fetterman, S.J. Kaftarian, & A. Wandersman (Eds.), *Empowerment evaluation: Knowledge and tools for self-assessment and accountability* (pp. 3–46). Thousand Oaks, CA: Sage Publications.

Field, S., Martin, J.E., Miller, R., Ward, M., & Wehmeyer, M.L. (1998). *A practical guide to teaching self-determination.* Reston, VA: Council for Exceptional Children.

Filbin, J. (1994). *Identifying learner outcomes within curricular activities: A performance-based model.* Denver: Colorado Department of Education.

Flannery, K.B., Newton, J.S., Horner, R.H., Slovic, R., Blumberg, R., & Ard, W.R. (2000). The impact of person centered planning on the content and organization of individual supports. *Career Development for Exceptional Individuals, 23,* 123–137.

Flaxman, E., & Inger, M. (1991). Parents and schooling in the 1990's. *The ERIC Review, 1*(3), 2–6.

Flippo, K.F., Inge, K.J., & Barcus, J.M. (Eds.). (1995). *Assistive technology: A resource for school, work, and community.* Baltimore: Paul H. Brookes Publishing Co.

Ford, A., Schnorr, R., Meyer, L., Davern, L., Black, J., & Dempsey, P. (1989). *Syracuse community-referenced curriculum guide for students with moderate and severe disabilities.* Baltimore: Paul H. Brookes Publishing Co.

Freire, P. (2000). *Pedagogy of the oppressed.* New York Continuum Publishing Group.

Friend, M., & Bauwens, J. (1988). Managing resistance: An essential consulting skill for learning disabilities teachers. *Journal of Learning Disabilities, 21,* 556–561.

Fryxell, D., & Kennedy, C.H. (1995). Placement along the continuum of services and its impact on students' social relationships. *Journal of The Association for Persons with Severe Handicaps, 20,* 259–269.

Gardner, H. (Ed.). (1983). *Multiple intelligences: The theory in practice.* New York: HarperCollins.

Gardner, H. (1991). *The unschooled mind: How children think and how schools should teach.* New York: HarperCollins.

Gardner, H., & Blythe, T. (1993). A school of the future. In H. Gardner (Ed.), *Multiple intelligences: The theory in practice* (pp 68–80). New York: Harper Collins.

Gelb, S.A. (1997). The problem of typological thinking in mental retardation. *Mental Retardation, 35,* 448–457.

Government Printing Office (1999). *Twenty-first annual report to Congress in the implementation of the Individuals with Disabilities Education Act.* Washington, DC: Author.

Gersten, R., Woodward, J., & Carnine, D.W. (1987). Direct instruction research: The third decade. *Remedial and Special Education, 8,* 48–56.

Gersten, R., Woodward, J., & Darch, C. (1986). Direct instruction: A research approach to curriculum design and teaching. *Exceptional Children, 53,* 17–31.

Giangreco, M.F., Cloninger, C.J., & Iverson, V.S. (1998). *Choosing outcomes and accommodations for children (COACH): A guide to educational planning for students with disabilities* (2nd ed.). Baltimore: Paul H. Brookes Publishing Co.

Goals 2000: Educate America Act of 1994, PL 103-227, 20 U.S.C. §§ 5801 *et seq.*

Goldstein, A.P. (1988). *The prepare curriculum: Teaching prosocial competencies.* Champaign, IL: Research Press.

Good, T.L., & Brophy, J.E. (1994). *Looking in classrooms* (6th ed.). New York: HarperCollins.

Gould, S.J. (1981). *Mismeasure of man.* New York: W.W. Norton & Company.

Graham, S., & Harris, K.R. (1989). Improving learning disabled students' skills at composing essays: Self-instructional strategy training. *Exceptional Children, 56,* 214–231.

Greenspan, S. (1997). Dead manual walking: Why the 1992 AAMR definition needs redoing. *Education and Training in Mental Retardation and Developmental Disabilities, 32,* 179–190.

Grenot-Scheyer, M. (1994). The nature of interactions between students with severe disabilities and nondisabled friends and acquaintances. *Journal of The Association for Persons with Severe Handicaps, 19,* 253–262.

Grossman, H. (1995). *Classroom behavior management in a diverse society.* Mountain View, CA: Mayfield Publishing Co.

Haberman, M. (1994). Gentle teaching in a violent society. *Educational Horizons,* 131–135.

Hagner, D., Helm, D.T., & Butterworth, J. (1996). This is your meeting: A qualitative study of person-centered planning. *Mental Retardation , 34,* 159–171.

Hanley-Maxwell, C., Phelps, L.A., Braden, J., & Warren, V. (1998). Schools of authentic and inclusive learning. *Research Institute on Secondary Education Reform Brief, 1,* 1–10.

Haring, N.G., & De Vault, G. (1996). Family issues and family support: Discussion. In L.K. Koegel, R.L. Koegel, & G. Dunlap (Eds.), *Positive behavioral support: Including people with difficult behavior in the community* (pp. 116–120). Baltimore: Paul H. Brookes Publishing Co.

Haring, N.G., Liberty, K.A., & White, O.R. (1980). Rules for data-based strategy decisions in instructional programs: Current research and instructional implications. In W. Sailor, B. Wilcox, & L. Brown (Eds.), *Methods of instruction for severely handicapped students* (pp. 159–192). Baltimore: Paul H. Brookes Publishing Co.

Harris, K.R., & Graham, S. (1996). Memo to constructivists: Skills count, too. *Educational Leadership, 53,* 26–210.

Hass, G., & Parkay, F.W. (1993). *Curriculum planning: A new approach* (6th ed.). Needham Heights, MA: Allyn & Bacon.

Heath, S.B. (1983). *Ways with words: Language, life, and work in communities and classrooms.* New York: Cambridge University Press.

Hodapp, R.M., Burack, J.A., & Zigler, E. (Eds.). (1990). *Issues in the developmental approach to mental retardation.* New York: Cambridge University Press.

Hodgkinson, H. (1997). *Demographic future of Kansas: Complexities in the heartland.* Washington, DC: Center for Demographic Policy.

Hollingsworth, S. (1994). *Teacher research and urban literacy education.* New York: Teachers College Press.

Hollins, E.R. (1996). *Culture in school learning.* Mahwah, NJ: Lawrence Erlbaum Associates.

Holzberg, C.S. (1994). Technology in special education. *Technology and Learning, 14*(8), 18–22.

Holzberg, C.S. (1995). Technology in special education. *Technology and Learning, 15*(6), 18–23.

Horner, R.H. (2000). Positive behavior supports. In M.L. Wehmeyer & J.R. Patton (Eds.), *Mental retardation in the 21st century* (pp. 181–196). Austin, TX: PRO-ED.

Horner, R.H., Albin, R.W., Sprague, J.R., & Todd, A.W. (2000). Positive behavior support. In M.E. Snell & F. Brown (Eds.), *Instruction of students with severe disabilities* (5th ed., pp. 207–244). Upper Saddle River, NJ: Prentice Hall.

Hughes, C.A., & Petersen, D.L. (1989). Utilizing a self-instructional training package to increase on-task behavior and work performance. *Education and Training in Mental Retardation, 24,* 114–120.

Hughes, C.A., & Rusch, F.R. (1989). Teaching supported employees with mental retardation to solve problems. *Journal of Applied Behavior Analysis, 22,* 365–372.

Hutinger, P.L. (1994). Integrated program activities for young children. In L.J. Johnson, R.J. Gallagher, & M.J. LaMontagne (Eds.), *Meeting early intervention challenges: Issues from birth to three* (pp. 59–94). Baltimore: Paul H. Brookes Publishing Co.

Hyde, A., & Bizar, M. (1989). *Thinking in context: Teaching cognitive processes across the elementary school curriculum.* White Plains, NY: Longman Publishing Group.

Iacono, T.A., & Miller, J.F. (1989). Can microcomputers be used to teach communication skills to students with mental retardation? *Education and Training in Mental Retardation, 24,* 32–44.

The inclusive school. (December 1994/January 1995). *Educational Leadership, 52.*

Individuals with Disabilities Education Act (IDEA) Amendments of 1997, PL 105-17, 20 U.S.C. §§ 1400 *et seq.*

Individuals with Disabilities Education Act (IDEA) of 1990, PL 101-476, 20 U.S.C. §§ 1400 *et seq.*

Inge, K.J., & Shepherd, J. (1995). Assistive technology applications and strategies for school system personnel. In K.F. Flippo, K.J. Inge, & J.M. Barcus (Eds.), *Assistive technology: A resource for school, work, and community* (pp. 133–166). Baltimore: Paul H. Brookes Publishing Co.

Jacobs, R., Samowitz, P., Levy, J.M., & Levy, P.H. (1989). Developing an AIDS prevention education program for persons with developmental disabilities. *Mental Retardation, 27,* 233–238.

Jacobson, J.W., & Mulick, J.A. (1992). A new definition of mentally retarded or a new definition of practice. *Psychology in Mental Retardation and Developmental Disabilities, 18*(2), 9–14.

Jacobson, J.W., & Mulick, J.A. (1996). *Manual of diagnosis and professional practice in mental retardation.* Washington, DC: American Psychological Association.

Jefferson County Public Schools. (1995). *Exit outcomes and proficiencies.* Golden, CO: Author.

Johnson, D.W., & Johnson, R.T. (1991). *Cooperation and competition: Theory and research.* Edina, MN: Interaction Books.

Joint Committee on Teacher Planning for Students with Disabilities. (1995). *Planning for academic diversity in America's classrooms: Windows on reality, research, change, and practice.* Lawrence: University of Kansas, Center for Research on Learning.

Jorgensen, C.M. (1992). Natural supports in inclusive schools: Curricular and teaching strategies. In J. Nisbet (Ed.), *Natural supports in school, at work, and in the community for people with severe disabilities* (pp. 179–216). Baltimore: Paul H. Brookes Publishing Co.

Jorgensen, C.M. (1997). Curriculum and its impact on inclusion and the achievement of students with disabilities. *Policy Research Issue Brief, 2*(2), 1–14.

Joyce, B., & Weil, M. (1980). *Models of teaching* (2nd ed.). Upper Saddle River, NJ: Prentice Hall.

Joyce, B., Weil, M., & Showers, B. (1992). *Models of teaching* (4th ed.). Upper Saddle River, NJ: Prentice Hall.

Kagan, S.L., Goffin, S.G., Golub, S.A., & Pritchard, E. (1995). *Toward systemic reform: Service integration for young children and their families.* Falls Church, VA: National Center for Service Integration.

Kameenui, E.J., & Simmons, D.C. (1990). *Designing instructional strategies: The prevention of academic learning problems.* Columbus, OH: Merrill.

Kapadia, S., & Fantuzzo, J.W. (1988). Training children with developmental disabilities and severe behavior problems to use self-management procedures to sustain attention to preacademic/acdemic tasks. *Education and Training in Mental Retardation, 23,* 59–69.

Kastner, T.A., Nathanson, R., Marchetti, A., & Pincus, S. (1989). HIV infection and developmental services for adults. *Mental Retardation, 27,* 229–232.

Katims, D. (2000). Literacy instruction for people with mental retardation: Historical highlights and contemporary analysis. *Education and Training in Mental Retardation and Developmental Disabilities, 35,* 3–15.

Kaufman, A.S. (1994). *Intelligent testing with the WISC-III.* New York: John Wiley & Sons.

Kavale, K.A., & Forness, S.R. (1998). *Efficacy of special education and related services.* Washington, DC: American Association on Mental Retardation.

Kendrick, M. (1994). Public and personal leadership challenges. In V.J. Bradley, J.W. Ashbaugh, & B.C. Blaney (Eds.), *Creating individual supports for people with developmental disabilities: A mandate for change at many levels* (pp. 361–372). Baltimore: Paul H. Brookes Publishing Co.

Keyes, G.K., (1994). The time on computer program. *Teaching Exceptional Children, 27,* 20–23.

King-Sears, M.E. (1999). Teacher and researcher co-design self-management content for inclusive settings: Research, training, intervention, and generalization effects on student performance. *Education and Training in Mental Retardation and Developmental Disabilities, 34*(2), 134–156.

Kingsley, J., & Levitz, M. (1994). *Count us in: Growing up with Down syndrome.* San Diego, CA: Harcourt Brace & Company.

Kniep, W., & Martin-Kniep, G.O. (1995). Designing schools and curriculums for the 21st century. In J. Beane (Ed.), *Toward a coherent curriculum: The 1995 ASCD yearbook* (pp. 87–100). Alexandria, VA: Association for Supervision and Curriculum Development.

Knowlton, E. (1998). Considerations in the design of personalized curricular supports for students with developmental disabilities. *Education and Training in Mental Retardation and Developmental Disabilities, 33,* 95–107.

Knowlton, H.E. (2000). *Access to educational, employment, and community environments by students in their late teens.* Unpublished data, University of Kansas, Lawrence.

Kohler, F.W., Ezell, H.K., & Paluselli, M. (1999). Promoting changes in teachers' conduct of student pair activities: An examination of reciprocal peer coaching. *Journal of Special Education, 33,* 154–165.

Kohler, F.W., & Strain, P.S. (1999). Maximizing peer-mediated resources in integrated preschool classrooms. *Topics in Early Childhood Special Education, 19,* 92–102.

Kounin, J. (1970). *Discipline and group management in classrooms.* New York: Holt, Rhinehart and Winston.

Kovalik, S. (1993). *Integrated thematic instruction: The model* (2nd ed.). Oak Creek, AZ: Books for Educators.

Kozol, J. (1992). *Savage inequalities: Children in America's schools.* New York: HarperCollins.

Kucer, S.B., Silva, C., & Delgado-Larocco, E.L. (1995). *Curricular conversations: Themes in multilingual and monolingual classrooms.* York, ME: Stenhouse.

Ladson-Billings, G. (1994). *The dreamkeepers: Successful teachers of African-American children.* San Francisco: Jossey-Bass.

Lagomarcino, T.R., & Rusch, F.R. (1989). Utilizing self-management procedures to teach independent performance. *Education and Training in Mental Retardation, 24,* 297–305.

Lakin, K.C., Hayden, M.F., & Abery, B.H. (1994). An overview of the community living concept. In M.F. Hayden & B.H. Abery (Eds.), *Challenges for a service system in transition: Ensuring quality community experiences for persons with developmental disabilities* (pp. 3–22). Baltimore: Paul H. Brookes Publishing Co.

Langone, J. (1990). *Teaching students with mild and moderate learning problems.* Needham Heights, MA: Allyn & Bacon.

Lave, J., & Wenger, E. (1991). *Situated learning: Legitimate peripheral participation.* New York: Cambridge University Press.

Lawson, H., & Briar-Lawson, K. (1997). *Connecting the dots: Progress toward the integration of school reform, school-linked services, parent involvement and community schools.* Unpublished manuscript, Miami University, The Danforth Foundation and the Institute for Educational Renewal, Oxford, OH.

Lederer, J.M. (2000). Reciprocal teaching of social studies in inclusive elementary classrooms. *Journal of Learning Disabilities, 33,* 91–106.

Lehman, B.A. (1998). *The conference on fair use: Final report to the commissioner on the conclusion of the conference on fair use.* Washington, DC: U.S. Trademark and Patent Office (Available http://www.uspto.gov/web/offices/dcom/olia/confu/confurep.htm).

Lenz, B.K., Alley, G.R., & Schumaker, J.B. (1987). Activating the inactive learner: Advance organizers in the secondary content classroom. *Learning Disability Quarterly, 10*(1), 53–67.

Lenz, B.K., Bulgren, J.A., Schumaker, J.B., Deshler, D.D., & Boudah, D.J. (1994). *The content enhancement series: The unit organizer routine.* Lawrence, KS: Edge Enterprises.

Lenz, B.K., Ellis, E.S., & Scanlon, D. (1996). *Teaching learning strategies to adolescents and adults with learning disabilities.* Austin, TX: PRO-ED.

Lenz, B.K., Marrs, R.W., Schumaker, J.B., & Deshler, D.D. (1993). *The content enhancement series: The lesson organizer routine.* Lawrence, KS: Edge Enterprises.

Lewis, T.J., & Sugai, G. (1999). Effective behavior support: A systems approach to proactive school-wide management. *Focus on Exceptional Children, 31*(6), 1–24.

Lewis, T.J., Sugai, G., & Colvin, G. (1998). Reducing problem behavior through a school-wide system of effective behavioral support: Investigation of a school-wide social skills training program and contextual interventions. *School Psychology Review, 27,* 446–459.

Liston, D.P., & Zeichner, K.M. (1996). *Culture and teaching.* Mahwah, NJ: Lawrence Erlbaum Associates.

Longwill, A.W., & Kleinert, H.L. (1999). The unexpected benefits of high school peer tutoring. *Teaching Exceptional Children, 30,* 60–65.

Lortie, D. (1975). *Schoolteacher: A sociological study.* Chicago: University of Chicago Press.

Lovett, D.L., & Haring, K.A. (1989). The effects of self-management training on the daily living of adults with mental retardation. *Education and Training in Mental Retardation, 24,* 306–307.

Lovitt, T.C. (1995). *Tactics for teaching* (2nd ed.). Upper Saddle River, NJ: Prentice Hall.

Luckasson, R., Coulter, D.L., Polloway, E.A., Reiss, S., Schalock, R.L., Snell, M.E., Spitalnik, D.M., & Stark, J.A. (1992). *Mental retardation: Definition, classification, and systems of supports* (9th ed.). Washington, DC: American Association on Mental Retardation.

Luckasson, R., & Spitalnik, D.M. (1994). Political and programmatic shifts of the 1992 AAMR definition of mental retardation. In V. Bradley, J.W. Ashbaugh, & B.C. Blaney (Eds.), *Creating individual supports for people with developmental disabilities: A mandate for change at many levels* (pp. 81–96). Baltimore: Paul H. Brookes Publishing Co.

Lunsky, Y., & Konstantareas, M. (1998). The attitudes of individuals with autism and mental retardation towards sexuality. *Education and Training in Mental Retardation and Developmental Disabilities, 33,* 24–33.

Lyman, F.T., & McTighe, J. (1988). Cueing thinking in the classroom: The promise of theory embedded tools. *Educational Leadership, 45,* 18–24.

MacDuff, G.S., Krantz, P., & McClannahan, L.E. (1993). Teaching children with autism to use photographic activity schedules: Maintenance and generalization of complex response chains. *Journal of Applied Behavior Analysis, 26,* 89–97.

Mace, F.C., Shapiro, E.S., West, B.J., Campbell, C., & Altman, J. (1986). The role of reinforcement in reactive self-monitoring. *Applied Research in Mental Retardation, 7,* 315–327.

MacMillan, D.L., Gresham, F.M., & Siperstein, G.N. (1993). Conceptual and psychometric concerns about the 1992 AAMR definition of mental retardation. *American Journal on Mental Retardation, 98,* 325–335.

Maheady, L., Sacca, K.M., & Harper, G.F. (1988). Classwide peer tutoring with mildly handicapped high school students. *Exceptional Children, 1,* S2–S10.

Malone, L.D., & Mastropieri, M.A. (1992). Reading comprehension instruction: Summarization and self-monitoring training for students with learning disabilities. *Exceptional Children, 58,* 270–279.

Malouf, D.B., & Schiller, E.P. (1995). Practice and research in special education. *Exceptional Children, 61,* 414–424.

Martin, J.E., Burger, D.L., Elias-Burger, S., & Mithaug, D.E. (1988). Applications of self-control strategies to facilitate independence in vocational and instructional settings. In N. Bray (Ed.), *International review of research in mental retardation* (pp. 155–193). San Diego: Academic Press.

Martin, J.E., & Marshall, L.H. (1996). ChoiceMaker: Infusing self-determination instruction into the IEP and transition process. In D.J. Sands & M.L. Wehmeyer (Eds.), *Self-determination across the life span: Independence and choice for people with disabilities* (pp. 211–232). Baltimore: Paul H. Brookes Publishing Co.

Martin, J.E., Marshall, L.H., Maxson, L., & Jerman, P. (1993). *Self-directed IEP: Teacher's manual.* Colorado Springs: University of Colorado at Colorado Springs, Center for Educational Research.

Martin, J.R. (1992). *The schoolhome: Rethinking schools for changing families.* Cambridge, MA: Harvard University Press.

Marzano, R.J., Pickering, D.J., & Pollock, J.E. (2001). *Classroom instruction that works: Research-based strategies for increasing student achievement.* Alexandria, VA: Association for Supervision and Curriculum Development.

May, D.C., & Kundert, D.K. (1996). Are special educators prepared to meet the sex education needs of their students? A progress report. *The Journal of Special Education, 29,* 433–441.

McCabe, M.P. (1993). Sex education programs for people with mental retardation. *Mental Retardation , 31,* 377–387.

McCabe, M.P., & Cummins, R.A. (1996). The sexual knowledge, experience, feelings and needs of people with mild intellectual disability. *Education and Training in Mental Retardation and Developmental Disabilities, 31,* 13–21.

McCarl, J.J., Svobodny, L., & Beare, P.L. (1991). Self-recording in a classroom for students with mild to moderate mental handicaps: Effects on productivity and on-task behavior. *Education and Training in Mental Retardation, 26,* 79–88.

McFadden, D.L., & Burke, E.P. (1991). Developmental disabilities and the new paradigm: Directions for the 1990's. *Mental Retardation, 29,* iii–vi.

Miner, C.A., & Bates, P.E. (1997). The effect of person centered planning activities on the IEP/transition planning process. *Education and Training in Mental Retardation and Developmental Disabilities, 32,* 105–112.

Mithaug, D. (1993). *Self-regulation theory: How optimal adjustment maximizes gain.* Westport, CT: Praeger.

Mithaug, D. (1998). Your right, my obligation? *Journal of The Association for Persons with Severe Handicaps, 23,* 41–43.

Mithaug, D.E., Martin, J.E., & Agran, M. (1987). Adaptability instruction: The goal of transitional programming. *Exceptional Children, 53,* 500–505.

Mithaug, D.E., Martin, J.E., Agran, M., & Rusch, F.R. (1988). *Why special education graduates fail: How to teach them to succeed.* Colorado Springs, CO: Ascent.

Mithaug, D.E., Wehmeyer, M.L., Agran, M., Martin, J.E., & Palmer, S. (1998). The self-determined learning model of instruction: Engaging students to solve their learning problems. In M.L. Wehmeyer & D.J. Sands (Eds.), *Making it happen: Student involvement in educational planning, decision-making, and instruction* (pp. 299–328). Baltimore: Paul H. Brookes Publishing Co.

Monda-Amaya, L.E., & Pearson, P.D. (1996). Toward a responsible pedagogy for teaching and literacy. In M. Pugach & C. Warger (Eds.), *Curriculum trends, special education, and reform: Refocusing the conversation* (pp. 143–168). New York: Teachers College Press.

Moon, M.S., Hart, D., Komissar, C., & Friedlander, R. (1995). Making sports and recreation activities accessible: Assistive technology and other accommodation strategies. In K.F. Flippo, K.J. Inge, & J.M. Barcus (Eds.), *Assistive technology: A resource for school, work, and community* (pp. 223–244). Baltimore: Paul H. Brookes Publishing Co.

Moore, S.C., Agran, M., & Fodor-Davis, J. (1989). Using self-management strategies to increase the production rates of workers with severe handicaps. *Education and Training in Mental Retardation, 24,* 324–332.

Morrison, G.S. (1993). *Contemporary curriculum K–9.* Needham Heights, MA: Allyn & Bacon.

Mortweet, S.L., Utley, C.A., Walker, D. Dawson, H.L., Delquadri, J.C., Reddy, S.S., Greenwood, C.R., Hamilton, S., & Ledford, D. (1999). Classwide peer tutoring: Teaching students with mild mental retardation in inclusive classrooms. *Exceptional Children, 65,* 524–536.

Mulhern, T.J. (1975). Survey of reported sexual behavior and policies characterizing residential facilities for retarded citizens. *American Journal of Mental Deficiency, 79,* 670–673.

National Association for the Education of Young Children (NAEYC). (1997). *Position statement on developmentally appropriate practice in early childhood programs serving children from birth through 8.* Washington, DC: Author.

National Information Center for Children and Youth with Disabilities. (1993). Including special education in the school community. *News Digest, 2*(2), 1–7.

Nebraska Department of Education. (1995). *Family and consumer sciences education: Curriculum development.* Lincoln, NE: Author.

Newmann, F.M., & Wehlage, G.G. (1995). *Successful school restructuring.* Madison, WI: Wisconsin Center for Education Research.

Nikolay, P., Grady, S., & Stefonek, T. (1997). *Wisconsin's model academic standards for health education.* Madison: Wisconsin Department of Public Instruction.

Nirje, B. (1969). The normalization principle and its human management implications. In R.B. Kugel and W. Wolfensberger (Eds.), *Changing residential patterns for the mentally retarded* (pp. 227–254). Washington, DC: President's Committee on Mental Retardation.

Nirje, B. (1972). The right to self-determination. In W. Wolfensberger, (Ed.), *Normalization: The principle of normalization* (pp. 176–198). Toronto: National Institute on Mental Retardation.

Nisbet, J. (Ed.). (1992). *Natural supports in school, at work, and in the community for people with severe disabilities.* Baltimore: Paul H. Brookes Publishing Co.

Noddings, N. (1995, January). A morally defensible mission for schools in the 21st century. *Phi Delta Kappan,* 365–368.

O'Brien, J., & Lovett, H. (1993). *Finding a way toward everyday lives: The contribution of person-centered planning.* Harrisburg: Pennsylvania Office of Mental Retardation.

Odom, S.L., McConnell, S.R, & McEvoy, M.A. (1992). Peer related social competence and its significance for young children with disabilities. In S.L. Odom, S.R. McConnell, & M.A. McEvoy (Eds.), *Social competence of young children with disabilities* (pp. 3–36). Baltimore: Paul H. Brookes Publishing Co.

Office of Special Education Programs (OSEP). (1999). *21st Annual Report to Congress on the Implementation of the Individuals with Disabilities Education Act.* Washington, DC: Author.

Office of Special Education and Rehabilitation Services (OSERS). (2000). *A guide to the individualized education program.* Washington, DC: Author.

Oregon Developmental Disabilities Council Family Support Initiative. (1989). *A study of the status of families in Oregon where one or both parents are considered intellectually impaired.* Salem, OR: Author.

Orkwis, R., & McLane, K. (1998, Fall). *A curriculum every student can use: Design principles for student access* (ERIC/OSEP Topical Brief). Reston, VA: Council for Exceptional Children.

Ornstein, A.C., & Hunkins, F.P. (1988). *Curriculum: Foundations, principles, and issues.* Upper Saddle River, NJ: Prentice Hall.

Owens, T.R. (1988). Conducting a goal-based evaluation. In T.R. Wermuth (Ed.), *Evaluation technical assistance: Dissemination series* (pp. 138–145). Champaign: Secondary Transition Intervention Effectiveness Institute, University of Illinois at Urbana-Champaign.

Palincsar, A.S. (1986). Metacognitive strategy instruction. *Exceptional Children, 53,* 118–124.

Palincsar, A.S., David, Y.M., Winn, J.A., & Stevens, D.D. (1991). Examining the contexts of strategy instruction. *Remedial and Special Education, 12,* 43–53.

Paris, S., & Newman, R.S. (1990). Developmental aspects of self-regulated learning. *Educational Psychologist, 25,* 28–42.

Pauley, C.A. (1998). The view from the student's side of the table. In M. Wehmeyer & D.J. Sands (Eds.), *Making it happen: Student involvement in education planning, decision making, and instruction* (pp. 123–128). Baltimore: Paul H. Brookes Publishing Co.

Peleg, Z.R., & Moore, R.F. (1982). Effects of the advance organizer with oral and written presentation on recall and inference of EMR adolescents. *American Journal of Mental Deficiency, 86,* 621–626.

Perez, J. (1991). What is whole language? *First Teacher, 12,* 5.

Perske, R. (1972). The dignity of risk. In W. Wolfensberger (Ed.), *Normalization: The principle of normalization* (pp. 199–221). Toronto: National Institute on Mental Retardation.

Peterson, R. (1992). *Life in a crowded place: Making a learning community.* Portsmouth, NH: Heinemann.

Polloway, E.A., Patton, J.R., Epstein, M.H., & Smith, T.E.C. (1989). Comprehensive curriculum for students with mild handicaps. *Focus on Exceptional Children, 21*(8), 1–12.

Polloway, E.A., Smith, J.D., Chamberlain, J., Denning, C.B., & Smith, T.E.C. (1999). Levels of deficits or supports in the classification of mental retardation: Implementation practices. *Education and Training in Mental Retardation and Developmental Disabilities, 34,* 200–206.

Powell, R., McLaughlin, H.J., Savage, T., & Zehm, S. (2001). *Classroom management: Prespectives on the social curriculum.* Columbus, OH: Merrill-Prentice Hall.

Pressley, M., El-Dinary, P.B., Gaskins, I., Schuder, T., Bergman, J., Almasi, L., & Brown, R. (1992). Beyond direct explanation: Transactional instruction of reading comprehension strategies. *Elementary School Journal, 92,* 511–554.

Pugach, M.C., & Warger, C.L. (1996a). Challenges for the special education-curriculum reform partnership. In M.C. Pugach & C.L. Warger (Eds.), *Curriculum trends, special education, and reform: Refocusing the conversation* (pp. 227–252). New York: Teachers College Press.

Pugach, M.C., & Warger, C.L. (1996b). Treating curriculum as a target for reform: Can special and general education learn from each other? In M.C. Pugach & C.L. Warger (Eds.), *Curriculum trends, special education, and reform: Refocusing the conversation* (pp. 1–22). New York: Teachers College Press.

Ramey, S.L., Dossett, E., & Echols, K. (1996). The social ecology of mental retardation. In J.W. Jacobson & J.A. Mulick (Eds.), *Manual of diagnosis and professional practice in mental retardation* (pp. 55–65). Washington, DC: American Psychological Association.

Realon, R.E., Favell, J.E., & Dayvault, K.A. (1988). Evaluating the use of adapted leisure materials on the engagement of persons who are profoundly, multiply handicapped. *Education and Training in Mental Retardation, 23,* 228–237.

Realon, R.E., Favell, J.E., & Phillips, J.F. (1989). Adapted leisure materials versus standard leisure materials: Evaluating several aspects of programming for persons who are profoundly handicapped. *Education and Training in Mental Retardation, 24,* 168–177.

Rehabilitation Act Amendments of 1992, PL 102-569, 29 U.S.C. §§ 701 *et seq.*

Rehabilitation Act of 1973, PL 93-112, 29 U.S.C. §§ 701 *et seq.*

Reis, E.M. (1986). Advance organizers and listening comprehension in retarded and nonretarded individuals. *Education and Training of the Mentally Retarded, 21,* 245–251.

Reiss, S. (1994). Issues in defining mental retardation. *American Journal on Mental Retardation, 99,* 1–7.

Rivera, D.P., & Smith, D.D. (1997). *Teaching students with learning and behavior problems* (3rd ed.). Needham Heights, MA: Allyn & Bacon.

Roehler, L.R., & Cantlon, D.J. (1997). Scaffolding: A powerful tool in social constructivist classrooms. In K. Hogan & M. Pressley (Eds.), *Scaffolding student learning: Instructional approaches and issues* (pp. 6–42). Cambridge, MA: Brookline Books.

Rolison, M.A., & Medway, F.J. (1985). Teachers' expectations and attributions for student achievement: Effects of label, performance pattern, and special education intervention. *American Educational Research Journal, 22,* 561–573.

Rosenshine, B., & Meister, C. (1992). The use of scaffolds for teaching higher-level cognitive strategies. *Educational Leadership, 49,* 26–33.

Rosenthal-Malek, A., & Bloom, A. (1998). Beyond acquisition: Teaching generalization for students with developmental disabilities. In A. Hilton & R. Ringlaben (Eds.), *Best and promising practices in developmental disabilities* (pp. 139–155). Austin, TX: PRO-ED.

Rowe, M.B. (1986). Wait time: Slowing down may be a way of speeding up! *The Journal of Teacher Education, 31*(1), 43–50.

Rusch, F.R., McKee, M., Chadsey-Rusch, J., & Renzaglia, A. (1988). Teaching a student with severe handicaps to self-instruct: A brief report. *Education and Training in Mental Retardation, 23,* 51–58.

Ryndak, D.L., & Alper, S. (1996). *Curriculum content for students with moderate and severe disabilities in inclusive settings.* Needham Heights, MA: Allyn & Bacon.

Sage, D.D. (1996). Administrative strategies for achieving inclusive schooling. In S. Stainback & W. Stainback (Eds.), *Inclusion: A guide for educators* (pp. 105–116). Baltimore: Paul H. Brookes Publishing Co.

Sailor, W. (1991). Community school. In L.H. Meyer, C.A. Peck, & L. Brown (Eds.), *Critical issues in the lives of people with severe disabilities* (pp. 379–385). Baltimore: Paul H. Brookes Publishing Co.

Sailor, W. (2002). Devolution, school/community/family partnerships, and inclusive education. In W. Sailor (Ed.), *Whole-school success and inclusive education: Building partnerships for learning, achievement, and accountability.* New York: Teachers College Press.

Salend, S.J., Ellis, L.L., & Reynolds, C.J. (1989). Using self-instruction to teach vocational skills to individuals who are severely retarded. *Education and Training in Mental Retardation, 24,* 248–254.

Sands, D.J., Kozleski, E., & French, N. (2000). *Inclusive education for the twenty-first century.* Belmont, CA: Wadsworth/West.

Sands, D.J., Spencer, K., Gliner, J., & Swaim, R. (1999). Structural equation modeling of student involvement in transition-related actions: The path of least resistance. *Focus on Autism and Other Developmental Disabilities, 14,* 17–27.

Sands, D.J., & Wehmeyer, M.L. (1996a). Future directions in self-determination: Articulating values and policies, reorganizing organizational structures, and implementing professional practices. In D.J. Sands & M.L. Wehmeyer (Eds.), *Self-determination across the life span: Independence and choice for people with disabilities* (pp. 331–344). Baltimore: Paul H. Brookes Publishing Co.

Sands, D.J., & Wehmeyer, M.L. (Eds.). (1996b). *Self-determination across the life span: Independence and choice for people with disabilities.* Baltimore: Paul H. Brookes Publishing Co.

Sapon-Shevin, M. (December 2000/January 2001). Schools fit for all. *Educational Leadership, 58,* 34–39.

Sarason, S. (1985). *Psychology and mental retardation: Perspectives in change.* Austin, TX: PRO-ED.

Sarason, S.B. (1990). *The predictable failure of educational reform: Can we change course before it's too late?* San Francisco: Jossey-Bass.

Sarason, S.B. (1996). *The predictable failure of educational reform.* San Francisco: Jossey-Bass.

Schalock, R.L. (1996). Reconsidering the conceptualization and measurement of quality of life. In R.L. Schalock (Ed.), *Quality of life: Vol. I. Conceptualization and measurement* (pp. 123–139). Washington, DC: American Association on Mental Retardation.

Schalock, R. (2001). Definitional issues. In D. Croser, P. Baker, & R. Schalock (Eds.), *Embarking on a new century.* Washington, DC: American Association on Mental Retardation.

Schapps, E., & Solomon, E. (1990). Schools and classrooms as caring communities. *Educational Leadership, 47,* 38-42.

Scheerenberger, R.C. (1987). *A history of mental retardation: A quarter century of promise.* Baltimore: Paul H. Brookes Publishing Co.

Scholastic Press. (1995). *WiggleWorks Scholastic Beginning Literacy program.* New York: Author.

Schorr, L.B. (1997). *Common purpose: Strengthening families and neighborhoods to rebuild America.* New York: Anchor Books.

Schumaker, J.B., Deshler, D.D., & McKnight, P. (1989). *Teaching routines to enhance the mainstream performance of adolescents with learning disabilities.* Final report submitted to U.S. Department of Education, Special Education Services.

Schunk, D.H. (1981). Modeling and attributional effects on children's achievement: A self-efficacy analysis. *Journal of Educational Psychology, 73,* 93–105.

Schunk, D.H. (1994). Self-regulation of self-efficacy and attributions in academic settings. In D.H. Schunk & B.J. Zimmerman (Eds.), *Self-regulation of learning and performance: Issues and educational applications* (pp. 75–99). Mahwah, NJ: Lawrence Erlbaum Associates.

Schunk, D.H. (1996). Goal and self-evaluative influences during children's cognitive skill learning. *American Educational Research Journal, 33,* 359-382.

Schunk, D.H., & Cox, P.D. (1986). Strategy training and attributional feedback with learning disabled students. *Journal of Educational Psychology, 78,* 2001–2010.

Schunk, D.H., & Swartz, C.W. (1993). Writing strategy instruction with gifted students: Effects of goals and feedback on self-efficacy and skills. *Roeper Review, 15,* 225–230.

Schunk, D.H., & Zimmerman, B.J. (Eds.). (1994). *Self-regulation of learning and performance: Issues and educational applications.* Mahwah, NJ: Lawrence Erlbaum Associates.

Schunk, D.H., & Zimmerman, B.J. (1998). *Self-regulated learning: From teaching to self-reflective practice.* New York: The Guilford Press.

Schwartz, A.A., Jacobson, J.W., & Holburn, S. (2000). Defining person-centeredness: Results of two consensus methods. *Education and Training in Mental Retardation and Developmental Disabilities, 35,* 235–258.

Schwier, K.M. (1994). *Couples with intellectual disabilities talk about living and loving.* Rockville, MD: Woodbine House.

Scotti, J.R., Speaks, L.V., Masia, C.L., Boggess, J.T., & Drabman, R.S. (1996). The educational effects of providing AIDS-risk information to persons with developmental disabilities: An exploratory study. *Education and Training in Mental Retardation and Developmental Disabilities, 31,* 115–122.

Sienkiewicz-Mercer, R., & Kaplan, S.B. (1989). *I raise my eyes to say yes: A memoir.* Boston: Houghton Mifflin.

Silver, H.F., Strong, R.W., & Perini, M.J. (2000). *So each may learn: Integrating learning styles and multiple intelligences.* Alexandria, VA: Association for Supervision and Curriculum Development.

Sinclair, M.F., & Christenson, S.L. (1992). Home–school collaboration: A building block of empowerment. *IMPACT Feature Issue on Family Empowerment, 5*(2), 12–13.

Singer, G.H.S., & Powers, L.E. (1993). Contributing to resilience in families: An overview. In G.H.S. Singer & L.E. Powers (Eds.), *Families, disability, and empowerment: Active coping skills and strategies for family interventions* (pp. 1–25). Baltimore: Paul H. Brookes Publishing Co.

Sizer, T.R. (1992). *Horace's school: Redesigning the American high school.* Boston: Houghton Mifflin.

Smith, B.J., & McKenna, P. (1994). Early intervention public policy: Past, present, and future. In L.J. Johnson, R.J. Gallagher, & M.J. LaMontagne (Eds), *Meeting early intervention challenges: Issues from birth to three* (pp. 251–264). Baltimore: Paul H. Brookes Publishing Co.

Smith, J.D. (1999). Social constructions of mental retardation: Impersonal histories and hope for personal futures. In M.L. Wehmeyer & J. Patton (Eds.), *Mental retardation in the 21st century* (pp. 379–393). Austin, TX: PRO-ED.

Snell, M.E. (Ed.). (1994). *Instruction of students with severe disabilities* (4th ed.). New York: Merrill.

Snell, M.E., & Janney, R. (2000). *Social relationships and peer support*. Baltimore: Paul H. Brookes Publishing Co.

Sonnenschein, P. (1981). Parents and professionals: An uneasy relationship. *Teaching Exceptional Children, 14,* 62–65.

Sowers, J., Verdi, M., Bourbeau, P., & Sheehan, M. (1985). Teaching job independence and flexibility to mentally retarded students through the use of a self-control package. *Journal of Applied Behavior Analysis, 18,* 81–85.

Spring, J. (2000). *The intersection of cultures: Multicultural education in the United States and the global economy*. Boston: McGraw-Hill.

Stainback, S., & Stainback, W. (1992). *Curriculum considerations in inclusive classrooms: Facilitating learning for all students*. Baltimore: Paul H. Brookes Publishing Co.

Stainback, S., Stainback, W., & Jackson, H.J. (1992). Toward inclusive classrooms. In S. Stainback, & W. Stainback (Eds.), *Curriculum considerations in inclusive classrooms: Facilitating learning for all students* (pp. 3–17). Baltimore: Paul H. Brookes Publishing Co.

Stainback, W., & Stainback, S. (1990). Facilitating peer support and friendships. In W. Stainback & S. Stainback (Eds.), *Support networks for inclusive schooling: Interdependent integrated education* (pp. 51–63). Baltimore: Paul H. Brookes Publishing Co.

Stainback, W., Stainback, S., Stefanich, G., & Alper, S. (1996). Learning in inclusive classrooms: What about the curriculum? In S. Stainback & W. Stainback (Eds.), *Inclusion: A guide for educators* (pp. 209–219). Baltimore: Paul H. Brookes Publishing Co.

Stancliffe, R.J. (1997). Community living-unit size, staff presence, and residents' choice-making. *Mental Retardation, 35,* 1–9.

Stancliffe, R.J., & Abery, B.H. (1997). Longitudinal study of deinstitutionalization and the exercise of choice. *Mental Retardation, 35,* 159–169.

Stancliffe, R.J., Abery, B.H., & Smith, J. (2000). Personal control and the ecology of community living settings: Beyond living-unit size and type. *Mental Retardation, 105,* 431–454.

Stancliffe, R., & Wehmeyer, M.L. (1995). Variability in the availability of choice to adults with mental retardation. *Journal of Vocational Rehabilitation, 5,* 319–328.

Sternberg, R.J. (1994). *Thinking and problem solving: Handbook of perception and cognition*. New York: Academic Press.

Stock, S.E., Davies, D.K., & Secor, R. (1996). *WorkSight: A multimedia based job matching system for individuals with developmental disabilities to enhance self-determination and success in career selection* (SBIR Phase I Final Report). Unpublished manuscript.

Strully, J.L., & Strully, C.F. (1989). Friendship as an educational goal. In S. Stainback, W. Stainback, & M. Forest (Eds.), *Educating all students in the mainstream of regular education* (pp. 59–70). Baltimore: Paul H. Brookes Publishing Co.

Sugai, G., & Horner, R.H. (1994). Including students with severe behavior problems in general education settings: Assumptions, challenges, and solutions. In J. Marr, G. Sugai, & G. Tindal (Eds.), *The Oregon Conference monograph 6* (pp. 102–120). Eugene: University of Oregon.

Sugai, G., Horner, R.H., Dunlap, G., Lewis, Nelson, C., Scott, T., Liaupsin, C., Ruef, M., Sailor, W., Turnbull, A., Turnbull, H., Wickham, D., & Wilcox, B. (1999). *Applying positive behavior support and functional behavioral assessment in schools*. Washington DC: Office of Special Education Programs (OSEP) Center on Positive Behavioral Intervention and Support.

Sugai, G., Sprague, J.R., Horner, R.H., & Walker, H.M. (2000). Preventing school violence: The use of office discipline referrals to assess and monitor school-wide discipline interventions. *Journal of Emotional and Behavioral Disorders, 8,* 94–101.

Swanson, H.L. (1991). Introduction: Issues in the assessment of learning disabilities. In H.L. Swanson (Ed.), *Handbook on the assessment of learning disabilities: Theory, research, and practice* (pp. 1–20). Austin, TX: PRO-ED.

Sykes, G., & Plastrik, P. (1993). *Standards setting as educational reform*. Washington, DC: American Association of Colleges for Teacher Education. (ERIC Clearinghouse on Teacher Education, Trends and Issues Paper, No. 8).

Tashie, C., Jorgensen, C., Shapiro-Barnard, S., Martin, J., & Schuh, M. (1996). High school inclusion. *TASH Newsletter, 22*(9), 19–22.

Technology-Related Assistance for Individuals with Disabilities Act of 1988 (Tech Act), PL 100-407, 29 U.S.C. §§ 2201 *et seq. U.S. Statutes at Large, 102,* 1044–1065.

Testimony of Richard Riley, Secretary, U.S. Department of Education: Hearings Before the Committee on Economic and Educational Opportunities Subcommittee on Early Childhood, Youth and Families, House of Representatives, 104th Congress. (1995). Available: http://www.ed.gov/ Speeches/06-1995/idea-1.html.

Texas Education Agency. (1996). *Texas essential knowledge and skills.* Austin, TX: Author.

Thorin, E.J., & Irvin, L.K. (1992). Family stress associated with transition to adulthood of young people with severe disabilities. *Journal of The Association for Persons with Severe Handicaps, 17,* 31–39.

Todd, A.W., Horner, R.H., Sugai, G., & Sprague, J.R. (1999). Effective behavior support: Strengthening school-wide systems through a team-based approach. *Effective School Practices, 17*(4), 23–37.

Tomlinson, C.A. (1995). *How to differentiate instruction in mixed-ability classrooms.* Alexandria, VA: Association for Supervision and Curriculum Development.

Tomlinson, C.A. (1999). *The differentiated classroom: Responding to the needs of all learners.* Alexandria, VA: Association for Supervision and Curriculum Development.

Tossebro, J. (1995). Impact of size revisited: Relation of number of residents to self-determination and deprivatization. *American Journal on Mental Retardation, 100,* 59–67.

Trace Center. (1995). *The principles of universal design.* Madison, WI: Author.

Trammel, D.L., Schloss, P.J., & Alper, S. (1994). Using self-recording, evaluation and graphing to increase completion of homework assignments. *Journal of Learning Disabilities, 27,* 75–81.

Turnbull, A.P., & Turnbull, H.R. (1978). *Parents speak out: Views from the other side of the two-way mirror.* Columbus, OH: Charles E. Merrill.

Turnbull, A.P., & Turnbull, H.R. (1996). Self-determination within a culturally responsive family systems perspective: Balancing the family mobile. In L.E., Powers, G.H.S. Singer, & J.A. Sowers (Eds.), *On the road to autonomy: Promoting self-competence in children and youth with disabilities* (pp. 195–220). Baltimore: Paul H. Brookes Publishing Co.

Turnbull, A.P., & Turnbull, H.R. (2001). *Families, professionals, and exceptionality: A special partnership collaborating for empowerment* (4th ed.). Upper Saddle River, NJ: Prentice Hall.

Turnbull, H.R. (1986). *Free appropriate public education* (2nd ed.). Denver, CO: Love Publishing.

Turnbull, H.R., & Turnbull, A.P. (2000). *Free appropriate public education: The law and children with disabilities* (6th ed.). Denver, CO: Love Publishing.

Udvari-Solner, A. (1995). A process for adapting curriculum in inclusive classrooms. In R.A. Villa & J. Thousand (Eds.), *Creating an inclusive school* (pp. 110–124). Alexandria, VA: Association for Supervision and Curriculum Development.

Udvari-Solner, A., & Thousand, J.S. (1995). Promising practices that foster inclusive education. In R.A. Villa & J.S. Thousand (Eds.), *Creating an inclusive school* (pp. 87–109). Alexandria, VA: Association for Supervision and Curriculum Development.

Urdang, L. (Ed.). (1984). *The Random House college dictionary.* New York: Random House.

Utley, C.A., Mortweet, S.L., & Greenwood, C.R. (1997). Peer-mediated instruction and interventions. *Focus on Exceptional Children, 29,* 1–23.

VanDenBerg, J., & Grealish, E.M. (1998). *The wraparound process.* Pittsburgh, PA: The Community Partnerships Group.

Vandercook, T., York, J., & Forest, M. (1989). The McGill Action Planning System (MAPS): A strategy for building the vision. *Journal of The Association for Persons with Severe Handicaps, 14,* 205–215.

Villa, R.A., Van der Klift, E., Udis, J., Thousand, J.S., Nevin, A.I., Kunc, N., & Chapple, J.W. (1995). Questions, concerns, beliefs, and practical advice about inclusive education. In R.A. Villa & J.S. Thousand (Eds.), *Creating an inclusive school* (pp. 136–161). Alexandria, VA: Association for Supervision and Curriculum Development.

Vockell, E., & Milhail, T. (1993). Instructional principles behind computerized instruction for students with exceptionalities. *Teaching Exceptional Children, 25,* 38–43.

Vygotsky, L. (1978). *Mind in society: The development of higher psychological processes.* Cambridge, MA: Harvard University Press.

Wacker, D.P., & Berg, W.K. (1993). Effects of picture prompts on the acquisition of complex vocational tasks by mentally retarded adolescents. *Journal of Applied Behavior Analysis, 16,* 417–443.

Walcott, D.D. (1997). Education in human sexuality for young people with moderate and severe mental retardation. *Teaching Exceptional Children, 29*(6), 72–74.

Ward, M.J., & Kohler, P.D. (1996). Promoting self-determination for individuals with disabilities: Content and process. In L.E. Powers, G.H.S. Singer, & J.-A. Sowers (Eds.), *On the road to autonomy: Promoting self-competence in children and youth with disabilities* (pp. 275–290). Baltimore: Paul H. Brookes Publishing Co.

Warger, C.L., & Pugach, M. (1993). A curriculum focus for collaboration. *LD Forum, 18,* 26–30.

Warren, J.S., Edmonson, H.M., Turnbull, A.P., Sailor, W., Wickham, D., & Griggs, P. (2000). *School-wide application of positive behavioral supports: Implementation and preliminary evaluation of PBS in an urban middle school.* Unpublished manuscript, University of Kansas.

Watson, D.L., & Tharp, R.G. (1993). *Self-directed behavior: Self-modification for personal adjustment.* Pacific Grove, CA: Brooks/Cole.

Weatherford, R. (1991). *The implications of determinism.* London: Routledge.

Weaver, R., & Cotrell, H. (1986). Using interactive images in the lecture hall. *Educational Horizons, 64*(4), 180–185.

Wehman, P. (1981). *Competitive employment: New horizons for severely disabled individuals.* Baltimore: Paul H. Brookes Publishing Co.

Wehmeyer, M.L. (1996a). Self-determination as an educational outcome: Why is it important to children, youth, and adults with disabilities? In D.J. Sands & M.L. Wehmeyer (Eds.), *Self-determination across the life span: Independence and choice for people with disabilities* (pp. 17–36). Baltimore: Paul H. Brookes Publishing Co.

Wehmeyer, M.L. (1996b). A self-report measure of self-determination for adolescents with cognitive disabilities. *Education and Training in Mental Retardation and Developmental Disabilities, 31,* 282–293.

Wehmeyer, M.L. (1998a). A national survey of the use of assistive technology by adults with mental retardation. *Mental Retardation, 36,* 44–51.

Wehmeyer, M.L. (1998b). Self-determination and individuals with significant disabilities: Examining meanings and misinterpretations. *Journal of The Association for Persons with Severe Handicaps, 23,* 5–16.

Wehmeyer, M.L. (1999). Assistive technology and students with mental retardation: Utilization and barriers. *Journal of Special Education Technology, 14,* 50–60.

Wehmeyer, M.L. (2001). Self-determination and mental retardation. In L.M. Glidden (Ed.), *International review of research in mental retardation* (Vol. 24, pp. 1–48). Mahwah, NJ: Lawrence Erlbaum Associates.

Wehmeyer, M.L., Agran, M., & Hughes, C. (1998). *Teaching self-determination to students with disabilities: Basic skills for successful transition.* Baltimore: Paul H. Brookes Publishing Co.

Wehmeyer, M.L., Agran, M., & Hughes, C. (2000). A national survey of teachers' promotion of self-determination and student-directed learning. *Journal of Special Education, 34,* 58–68.

Wehmeyer, M.L., & Bolding, N. (1999). Self-determination across living and working environments: A matched-samples study of adults with mental retardation. *Mental Retardation, 37,* 353–363.

Wehmeyer, M.L., & Bolding, N. (2001). Enhanced self-determination of individuals with intellectual disability as an outcome of moving to community-based work or living environments. *Journal of Intellectual Disability Research, 45,* 1–13.

Wehmeyer, M.L., Bolding, N., Yeager, D., & Davis, A. (2001). *Quality 18–21 services for students with mental retardation.* Unpublished manuscript, University of Kansas.

Wehmeyer, M.L., Kelchner, K., & Richards, S. (1995). Individual and environmental factors related to the self-determination of adults with mental retardation. *Journal of Vocational Rehabilitation, 5,* 291–305.

Wehmeyer, M.L., Kelchner, K., & Richards. S. (1996). Essential characteristics of self-determined behaviors of adults with mental retardation and developmental disabilities. *American Journal on Mental Retardation, 100,* 632–642.

Wehmeyer, M.L., & Metzler, C.A. (1995). How self-determined are people with mental retardation? The National Consumer Survey. *Mental Retardation, 33,* 111–119.

Wehmeyer, M.L., Palmer, S.B., Agran, M., Mithaug, D.E., & Martin, J. (2000). Teaching students to become causal agents in their lives: The self-determining learning model of instruction. *Exceptional Children, 66,* 439–453.

Wehmeyer, M.L., & Patton, J. (2000). *Mental retardation in the 21st century.* Austin, TX: PRO-ED.

Wehmeyer, M.L., & Sands, D.J. (Eds.). (1998). *Making it happen: Student involvement in education planning, decision making, and instruction.* Baltimore: Paul H. Brookes Publishing Co.

Wehmeyer, M.L., Sands, D.J., Doll, B., & Palmer, S.B. (1997). The development of self-determination and implications for educational interventions with students with disabilities. *International Journal of Disability, Development, and Education, 44,* 212–225.

Wehmeyer, M.L., & Schwartz, M. (1997). Self-determination and positive adult outcomes: A follow-up study of youth with mental retardation or learning disabilities. *Exceptional Children, 63,* 245–255.

Wehmeyer, M.L., & Schwartz, M. (1998). The relationship between self-determination, quality of life, and life satisfaction for adults with mental retardation. *Education and Training in Mental Retardation and Developmental Disabilities, 33,* 3–12.

Wehmeyer, M.L., & Ward, M.J. (1995). The spirit of the IDEA mandate: Student involvement in transition planning. *Journal of the Association for Vocational Special Needs Education, 17,* 108–111.

Wehmeyer, M.L., Wickham, D., & Sailor, W. (2000). *A whole school model of positive behavior interventions and supports and access to the general curriculum.* Unpublished grant proposal, University of Kansas.

Weinstein, C., & Mignano, A., Jr. (1993). *Elementary classroom mangement: Lessons from research and practice.* New York: McGraw-Hill.

Whipple, H.D. (1927). *Making citizens of the mentally limited: A curriculum for the special class.* Bloomington, IN: Public School Publishing Company.

Whitehouse, M.A., & McCabe, M.P. (1997). Sex education programs for people with intellectual disability: How effective are they? *Education and Training in Mental Retardation and Developmental Disabilities, 32,* 229–240.

Whitman, T.L. (1990). Self-regulation and mental retardation. *American Journal on Mental Retardation, 94,* 347–362.

Wigfield, A., & Harold, R.D. (1992). Teacher beliefs and children's achievement self-perceptions: A developmental perspective. In D.H. Schunk & J.L. Meece (Eds.), *Student perceptions in the classroom* (pp. 95–121). Mahwah, NJ: Lawrence Erlbaum Associates.

Wiggins, G., & McTighe, J. (1998). *Understanding by design.* Alexandria, VA: Association for Supervision and Curriculum Development.

Williams, R.R. (1989). Creating a new world of opportunity: Expanding choice and self-determination in lives of Americans with severe disability by 1992 and beyond. In R. Perske (Ed.), *Proceedings from the National Conference on Self-Determination* (pp. 16–17). Minneapolis, MN: Institute on Community Integration.

Wolery, M., Bailey, D.B., & Sugai, G. (1988). *Effective teaching: Principles and procedures of applied behavior analysis with exceptional children.* Needham Heights, MA: Allyn & Bacon.

Wolfe, P., & Harriot, W. (1997). Functional academics. In P. Wehman & J. Kregel (Eds.), *Functional curriculum for elementary, middle, and secondary age students with special needs* (pp. 69–103). Austin, TX: PRO-ED.

Wolfensberger, W. (1972). *Normalization: The principle of normalization.* Toronto: National Institute on Mental Retardation.

Wolman, B.B. (1973). *Dictionary of behavioral science.* New York: Van Nostrand Reinhold.

Wong, B.Y.L. (1991). Assessment of meta-cognitive research in learning disabilities: Theory, research, and practice. In H.L. Swanson (Ed.), *Handbook on the assessment of learning disabilities: Theory, research, and practice* (pp. 265–284). Austin, TX: PRO-ED.

Wood, D.J., Bruner, J.S., & Ross, G. (1976). The role of tutoring in problem solving. *Journal of Child Psychology and Psychiatry, 17*(2), 89–100.

Wood, M.M., & Long, N.J. (1991). *Life space intervention: Talking with children and youth in crisis.* Austin, TX: PRO-ED.

Wyatt v. Stickney, 325 F. Supp. 781 (M.D. Ala. 1971), 344 F. Supp. 373 (M.D. Ala 1972).

Yin, R.K., & Schiller, E.P. (1990). Managing evaluations. In T.R. Wermuth (Ed.), *Evaluation technical assistance: Dissemination series* (pp 160–172). Champaign: Secondary Transition Intervention Effectiveness Institute, University of Illinois at Urbana-Champaign.

Zemelman, S., Daniels, H., & Hyde, A. (1993). *Best practice: New standards for teaching and learning in America's schools.* Portsmouth, NH: Heinemann.

Zimmerman, B.J. (1986). Development of self-regulated learning: Which are the key subprocesses? *Contemporary Educational Psychology, 16,* 307–313.

Zimmerman, B.J. (1994). Dimensions of academic self-regulation: A conceptual framework for education. In D.H. Schunk & B.J. Zimmerman, (Eds.), *Self-regulation of learning and performance: Issues and educational applications* (pp. 3–21). Mahwah, NJ: Lawerence Erlbaum Associates.

Index

Page references followed by *f* or *t* indicate figures or tables, respectively.